ONLINE GAME PIONEERS
AT WORK

Morgan Ramsay

Foreword by Richard Bartle

Online Game Pioneers at Work

ISBN-13 (pbk): 978-1-4302-4185-0

ISBN-13 (electronic): 978-1-4302-4186-7

Managing Director: Welmoed Spahr
Acquisitions Editor: Michelle Lowman
Editorial Board: Steve Anglin, Mark Beckner, Gary Cornell, Louise Corrigan, James DeWolf, Jonathan Gennick, Robert Hutchinson, Michelle Lowman, James Markham, Susan McDermott, Matthew Moodie, Jeffrey Pepper, Douglas Pundick, Ben Renow-Clarke, Gwenan Spearing, Matt Wade, Steve Weiss
Compositor: SPi Global
Indexer: SPi Global

Distributed to the book trade worldwide by Springer Science+Business Media New York, 233 Spring Street, 6th Floor, New York, NY 10013. Phone 1-800-SPRINGER, fax (201) 348-4505, e-mail orders-ny@springer-sbm.com, or visit www.springeronline.com. Apress Media, LLC is a California LLC and the sole member (owner) is Springer Science + Business Media Finance Inc (SSBM Finance Inc). SSBM Finance Inc is a Delaware corporation

For information on translations, please e-mail rights@apress.com, or visit www.apress.com.

Apress and friends of ED books may be purchased in bulk for academic, corporate, or promotional use. eBook versions and licenses are also available for most titles. For more information, reference our Special Bulk Sales–eBook Licensing web page at www.apress.com/bulk-sales.

Any source code or other supplementary materials referenced by the author in this text is available to readers at www.apress.com. For detailed information about how to locate your book's source code, go to www.apress.com/source-code/.

For Dad and Mom, who survived breast cancer;
my sister Leilani and brother-to-be Ryan;
and my best friend Brendan Johnson (1984-2013).

Contents

About the Author

Morgan Ramsay, bestselling author of *Gamers at Work: Stories Behind the Games People Play* and *Online Game Pioneers at Work*, has interviewed nearly 50 leaders in entertainment, technology, and sports, including EA founder Trip Hawkins, Gaikai CEO David Perry, and former NFL punter Chris Kluwe.

As the Founder, President & CEO at Entertainment Media Council, the association for business leaders in the video game industry, Mr. Ramsay works with entrepreneurs, C-level executives, and senior managers to advance interactive entertainment by addressing the toughest challenges facing the global business community.

Previously, Mr. Ramsay was the Managing Director at Heretic where, for seven years, he provided strategic communication expertise to various clients, from small businesses to the Fortune Global 500, including working with the White House to recognize United States Navy veterans on behalf of the President of the United States of America.

Visit theramsayinterviews.com for a complete list of his interviews, and direct all business inquiries to morgan@theramsayinterviews.com.

Foreword

Accidents happen:

You play online games; you make online friends.

By chance, some of these friends make games, or have friends who make games, or have friends of friends who make games; or who don't make games, but want to make games.

They need someone with your talent; you start working with or for them, making games.

One of your games becomes a hit. You make more games. By chance, some of these are hits too.

A larger company is looking to buy a company with the profile of the one you're working for, so they do. You're more financially secure, but you feel strangely less satisfied.

Other people you know in the industry feel the same way. You have complementary skills. You leave your job to set up a new company together.

One of the many, many investors you pitch to likes your ideas. You get funding. You start making games.

By chance, one of your games is a hit. History repeats itself. By chance, more games are hits. By chance, a larger company wants a piece of your company. They buy it. You're now wealthy, respected and in demand. You've proven yourself. Now, you can do pretty well whatever you want in the games industry. So, you do: you give the public great games.

All by chance.

This same story, give or take a few fanciful details, is repeated throughout this book. Why, then, would you want to read it over and over? It's the Brownian motion theory of success: right place, right time, right luck, could happen to anyone. The truth, of course, is that if you look at those "fanciful details", you'll realize that chance barely has a speaking part in this drama.

All the people interviewed in this book are passionate about games. You think you're passionate? They're passionate. They're also highly creative in what they do, whether that's making games or enabling other people to make games.

You think you're creative? They're creative. They want to say things through games which they can't say by working for someone else. They're passionate enough that they're willing to put their career on the line to start a company from scratch just so they can create what they want to – what they have to – create.

Is there risk involved? Well yes. The risk is that they're even worse at developing games than they think they are; worse at running companies than they think they are. They know they have too much to learn, they know that the road ahead isn't so much full of potholes as of gaping chasms, but they're passionate enough to set out anyway.

Some people have the passion, but not the creativity. They fall into chasms and they're never going to get out. Other people, like me, have the creativity, but not the passion. They hit a pothole, don't like the jolt, and spend the rest of the journey trying to avoid every single obstacle in their path and never getting anywhere. Other people have both the passion and the creativity: sure, they may take a wrong turn and drive off a cliff, but they patch themselves up, drag themselves into another vehicle, and soon they're back taking a wiser route to the same destination. Eventually, they make it there.

Those are the people you're reading about in this book.

Morgan has assembled an astounding collection of online game founders for this series of interviews. Given the demands on their time and their degree of success, you might expect them to be divas who speak nothing but anodyne platitudes for eight minutes then they flounce off – but they're not like that at all. Every one of them is honest, open and generous with their time. They tell things just the way they are, without any spin, and with insights freely flowing.

That's either a feature of successful game developers or a testament to Morgan's interviewing skills. I suspect it's a combination of both.

One thing is for sure, though: it's no accident.

—Richard Bartle
Co-creator of MUDs

Acknowledgments

Online Game Pioneers at Work continued my work from *Gamers at Work: Stories Behind the Games People Play*, subsequently and almost interminably without rest between them. I would be remiss to not again acknowledge everyone who had been instrumental to that first book. Yet, something feels off about copying the acknowledgments of another book verbatim.

Instead, I will thank just a few people whose specific contributions were essential: Adam Kahn, Alena Smychkina, Annie Luther, Greta Melinchuk, Linda Åström, Molly Mulloy, and Tiina Oikarainen. I will also thank Lisa Revelli and Tomoyuki Akiyama, for their assistance with DeNA founder Tomoko Namba, whose interview does not appear in this book.

I would also extend my gratitude to my good friend, Zachary Jacques of ZJ Transcription Services, whose hard work we balanced with many hours playing online games. Dear Zack, it's just no fun winning all the time!

Introduction

On October 14, 2008, Richard Garriott de Cayeux became the first video game developer to travel into space, a journey made possible by a true spirit of adventure and a fortune earned as a role-playing game pioneer and entrepreneur. Richard's fascinating story, from teen game developer to astronaut, is just one of the 15 diverse, detailed, and enlightening interviews with 16 industry leaders in *Online Game Pioneers at Work*.

Like Garriott, video games have come a long way over the last 40 years. From the lab to the arcade, and from the arcade to the home, the video game market continues to expand. There are not only new platforms and genres, but new and exciting ways to discover, buy, and play video games. There are, effectively, whole new worlds to explore.

The Internet has made a significant contribution to the advancement of the video game as an entertainment medium and as a business, connecting a diverse number of players around the world and frequently at scales beyond anything we would have ever imagined.

Indeed, many of the creative and business leaders in this collection of interviews have at times commented on the pace at which the online game will displace other forms of interactive entertainment. Online games are everywhere. They're on mobile phones, tablets, and virtual reality headsets. They're digitally distributed, streamed in real time, and played in web browsers. They're free-to-play, buy-to-play, and subscriber-only. They're social, casual, and massively multiplayer; they're sandboxes, theme parks, and virtual worlds. They're esports, played by amateur and professional cyberathletes, covered by ESPN, and watched by audiences rivaling those for other sports and competitions.

More than just an entertainment product category, online games have produced wide-ranging social benefits, too. Online games connect disparate groups of people within safe, virtual spaces, enabling players to communicate, cooperate, and learn together more effectively without the physical and social boundaries that hold us back in the real world. While some developers of serious games construct virtual environments where we can practice vital workplace and emergency response skills, others create online experiences from which we come away better informed.

In *Gamers at Work: Stories Behind the Games People Play*, published in 2012, I spoke with 18 founders of successful console and PC video game companies about their stories and what we could learn from them. I wanted to learn about the challenges of entrepreneurship, and specifically, how those who had gone before managed to come out alive and on top.

With *Online Game Pioneers at Work*, I continue that good work through interviews with 16 founders of successful online game companies, but with an eye toward the shift to the online future of video games. In this collection, you will enjoy some of the deepest treatments of the business of video games, as well as some of the most exhaustive and illuminating interviews with working founders of major entertainment companies.

I hope the questions I've asked have revealed insights into online games that you will find informative, uplifting, and never less than entertaining.

—Morgan Ramsay
Founder, President & CEO
Entertainment Media Council

David Perry

Cofounder, Gaikai

After a two-year stint at Virgin Games designing and programming video games such as *Disney's Aladdin*, *Cool Spot* for 7UP, and *Global Gladiators* for McDonald's, **David Perry** founded Shiny Entertainment in 1993.

Shiny Entertainment developed a number of hit games, including *MDK*, *Sacrifice, Messiah, Enter the Matrix*, and *Wild 9*, but the studio was best known for *Earthworm Jim*. *Earthworm Jim* quickly emerged as a global franchise replete with a TV series produced by Universal Cartoon Studios, a Marvel comic book series, and fast food promotions with the Carls Jr. and Del Taco restaurants. Over the years, Shiny Entertainment has changed hands many times, passing from Interplay to Atari to Foundation 9 and finally to Amazon.

In 2009, Perry cofounded Gaikai, a technology enterprise that built the fastest proximity network in the world, enabling gamers to play major video games with only a web browser. Three years later in July, Gaikai set a Guinness World Record as "the world's most widespread cloud gaming network," and Sony Computer Entertainment acquired Gaikai for a staggering $380 million. Today, at Sony, Gaikai's streaming technology powers several key features of the PlayStation 3 and the PlayStation 4.

Ramsay: Before you founded Shiny, you worked at Virgin?

Perry: Yeah, I grew up in the UK and ended up at Virgin Games in Irvine, California. They had asked me to come out and make a McDonald's game for them. I ended up making that game, which was called *Global Gladiators* and won

Game of the Year awards. Virgin Games became very interested in trying to see what else we could do. I decided to stay and we ended up making another "advertising" style game called *Cool Spot* for 7UP.

Cool Spot was based on the red dot from the 7UP logo. Sega published that game and then came back to Virgin with the rights to *Aladdin*. We made *Disney's Aladdin* for the Sega Genesis and that, despite an insane timeline, turned out to sell well. So, this little team had generated an awful lot of money for Virgin and Sega. We thought, "Hmm, maybe it's time to actually think about doing something different here."

At that time, I was offered a job to go work at the Sega Technical Institute. I was very tempted by that, but I ended up also getting an offer from Playmates Toys, the people who made the toys for the *Teenage Mutant Ninja Turtles*. They made a lot of money from the *Turtles* and were interested in getting into video games, so they asked if I would join to help them do that. I told them, "Well, no, why don't I start a game company and then you fund it? If you fund it, I'll give you the first three games." They agreed, and we ended up with a publisher that was funded and new to video games. They didn't have strong, preconceived expectations. Playmates really left it up to us to see what we showed up with and they put in a lot of effort to help us find licenses.

If you think about it, they were all licensed, so Playmates expected that we'd just make something licensed. We were off talking to all of the studios—Universal, Sony, and others—trying to find rights for a new game. We were getting very serious about *Knight Rider*. Remember David Hasselhoff's TV show and the talking car? We were looking at different properties, but we couldn't find the perfect fit. We finally agreed that we would make our own title. That turned out to be *Earthworm Jim*.

Ramsay: Starting a company is arguably more challenging than taking a job. Why didn't you just go work for them?

Perry: I was interested in having a team and doing our own projects. I was less interested in just being an interactive management guy in charge of other people's properties, making games I wasn't so interested in.

Ramsay: Did you have any experience as an entrepreneur?

Perry: Yeah. When I lived in the United Kingdom, I first started at a company called Mikro-Gen. It was a real job, so you had other programmers there and managers. I learned quite a lot there but I was very tempted to see if I could go it alone. I did go it alone and started developing games myself. I put together a team and we made a game called "Beyond the Ice Palace" for five different platforms. I realized that it's hard when you're relying on other people.

When you're just one person, you can get stuff done but when you've got five people, you're responsible for the output of all of them. It was hard, I was naive. I found that to be not so fun. I only did it one time and then I went back to working for somebody else. So, I flipped back to something in between, which seemed like a safe happy zone, where you've got some structure around you, but on the other hand, you get to really build and do whatever you really want to do. I like that.

Ramsay: Was starting Shiny Entertainment within your comfort zone?

Perry: I don't know what it is about me, but I tend not to think too much before I act. If I sat and thought about it, I might have been able to talk myself out of it. I'd have found all these reasons to not move forward. I call it "pointing at the hurdles." You see all these hurdles and you just sit there and point at them: this is a problem, that's a problem, and this is a problem. If you don't do that and just start moving forward, usually you find yourself on the other side, wondering what happened. You don't even see the hurdles as you're just going through this whole process. Whatever it takes, it's just the next step, the next step, the next step, and then, finally, you're at the end of the track. You've built a company and you've had to do whatever was necessary. If you needed to raise money, you just did. If you needed to meet certain people in Hollywood, you just did. You found a way. That's what I like. No matter the stuff we've done, and the people we've worked with, I don't know if you could necessarily plan it.

Ramsay: Did you have a business plan?

Perry: No, we did not have a real business plan but we had worked out what it would cost for the team to make a game. We were surprisingly accurate. We had this running joke about how accurate that actually turned out to be because we had made our best effort at working out all of the costs and it actually worked out. It wasn't a business plan though, in the sense of having fully worked out our marketing strategy and everything else. There were other people taking care of those pieces for us. We didn't have a plan that you would use to raise money or something like that. It was a little lighter. In fact, we didn't need a formal plan. That really wasn't necessary for the publisher we were with.

Our plan was simple: this is how much it will cost to get the game done. They just wanted to have that game, so they weren't really worrying about how much money we were making. They were more worried about what they were going to do on their end and if it made sense for them. It wasn't as hard to raise money then as it probably is today. But if you find someone who wants the product, you'd probably still have the same situation today. You've just got to find someone who wants it and has their own plans for the software. There is a lot less friction then and it's not like you're trying to twist anyone's arm.

Ramsay: Instead of a plan, you had a clear vision of where you wanted to take your company?

Perry: We had a general idea about how we would do an animated game with the team we had. The team was very, very good at 2D pencil drawn animation. We had done multiple games in a row that scored very high in graphics, so we'd gotten to a point where that was expected of us. We had to deliver something that was graphically very good. Luckily, we had enough talent to deliver. *Earthworm Jim* received multiple Game of the Year awards. But it wasn't like we were just focusing on making role-playing games, simulations, or something else. It was very clear that we were going to make some kind of action-oriented animated platform game. The team had a funky style of humor as well, which permeated the final experience.

Ramsay: Was there a point where Shiny Entertainment was just you?

Perry: I was "technically" the original founder but a bunch of people joined me from Virgin. There were a few new people who joined shortly thereafter. It wasn't like I was sitting in an office with nobody and then slowly trying to recruit people one after another. There was a group of guys who wanted to work together right away.

As the founder, I was responsible for the company; however, I really should have sought advice. Let's just say there was a lot of learning by making mistakes. The rule I follow now is just to not repeat mistakes.

Ramsay: What kind of commitment did you make?

Perry: Payroll was my biggest concern, so we had to deliver. If I had sat back and thought about it all upfront, I might have not moved forward. The trick is to be able to pivot when something isn't working. You've got to be able to pivot and deal with it in real time. If something's taking too long, costing too much, or you didn't get the people you wanted, it's up to you to find a way to solve that problem in real time.

Ramsay: Did you have a family at that time?

Perry: I did, but no children. It's funny. It's another sort of meta theme of the video-game business. The video-game business takes up just about all of your life. The wives and girlfriends were always coming to the office because, at that time, there was no real external life. It's just work, work, work, work. There's a movie called *Indie Game: The Movie.* Have you seen that yet? You should check that out. It's a really good way to see behind the scenes of people making games. You could see how much fun it is. You can also see how much spare time they look like they have. It just becomes a way of life.

Ramsay: Who were some of the people who came over from Virgin?

Perry: There were super talented people like Nick Bruty, Mike Dietz, Nick Jones, Steve Crow, Ed Schofield, Andy Astor, Tom Tanaka, etc. It was a small group. I think we hit around nine. Doug TenNapel was a new hire. He wasn't from the original team, but he came up with the Earthworm Jim character, which was exactly what we needed at the time. If you look at the credits of *Earthworm Jim*, you'll see all the people who helped make it.

Ramsay: Had you worked with these people before?

Perry: Not all of them. I worked with Nick Bruty for many years. I worked with Mike Dietz at Virgin. I worked with Nick Jones before in the UK. We had an artist called Steve Crow who was also British. The group was reasonably closely knit. We definitely weren't like a bunch of strangers.

Ramsay: Did you have to really convince anyone to join you?

Perry: There was one guy who I was trying to get: Christian Larsen. I was very frustrated that I couldn't convince him to join. He was a key person I really wanted and didn't get. He was the fish that got away. He did the graphics for the *Jungle Book* video game for Disney and his graphical ability at the time was just remarkable. He had started a company with somebody else and had to see that through. I still wish he had joined us.

Ramsay: When you brought on the first nine people, you hadn't done any real planning but you knew why you wanted those people.

Perry: Yeah, you just believe in the people. I think the industry is still that way. Gaikai was formed the same way. You find talent, you bet on the talent, and the talent sets out to make something good. It's just a case of working out what that is. With really great people, you can make something fresh. The real challenge is not the idea; it's finding the talent to make it. Once you find them, hold on tight; you'll get some really good stuff. That's what happens.

Ramsay: Some game developers want to start a business to make games, so they operate with the expectation that their first game is just one of many to come. Others build teams for that first game and that's all they care about until they're forced to care about something else. The difference is subtle but it's there. Which were you?

Perry: Yeah, I agree. The company was not relevant. It was not about the company at all. The company was a function to make games. There was no one who aspired to build a business. They were all about just making games and getting the next game done and hoping people like it. We very much had a focus on the next game and "this new hook is going to be cool!"

Ramsay: That latter approach doesn't usually work out well for many developers, but apparently, that approach worked for you.

Perry: It did. It worked out well. The one thing that happened with Shiny that got funky was the team was very 2D-based and the industry was going 3D. At the time, I was concerned about that.

It's funny. Someone pointed that out to me recently. That was the one time in my career where I actually sat and thought about things. I actually sat and thought, "Well, this is really concerning and..." Blah, blah, blah. I ended up agreeing to sell the company to Interplay. It's just funny because the press quoted me recently saying that selling to Interplay was the biggest mistake I had ever made.

So, the team actually had very good 3D chops but they just hadn't done that before. They investigated 3D, they did an amazing job, and they made *MDK*, which was very respected for its time. And so we didn't just come out with a 3D game; we came out with a leading 3D game. I was kicking myself.

I did that another time. I did that with the rights to *The Matrix*. When they first offered me the rights, I turned them down. I kicked myself pretty hard after that. You can't always win, right? You make some dumb decisions along the way. Turning down *The Matrix* and selling Shiny were two of my worst decisions along the way.

Ramsay: How do you know what you need to get the game done?

Perry: You need good level design. You need good art. You need good audio. We outsourced the audio to Tommy Tallarico. Ultimately, you just need to know that you've got strong people responsible for every piece. You need to be confident that the game is going to look good, sound good, and play good. That's your starting point.

Ramsay: What was your first game? Earthworm Jim, right?

Perry: The first game we did was *Earthworm Jim*. I programmed that on the Sega Genesis. The last game I programmed was *Earthworm Jim 2* before I drifted over into the dark side—management.

Ramsay: How did the concept for *Earthworm Jim* come about?

Perry: My animation director said that he would like to hire a guy, Doug TenNapel, so we decided to give him a test to see if he was good. For his test, he had to design a character and animate it. The character he came in with was *Earthworm Jim*. If you can imagine, we're looking at all these different properties and thinking about what to do, and then this guy shows up with a funky worm in a suit. I loved it! I can't remember exactly how we went about it, but the team just went, "This is great! We could make a game based on this!" And off we went. It was just a completely different path based on seeing something that inspired us.

Ramsay: This is how you determined where to spend your money?

Perry: Are you inspired? Are you excited? Do you have a lot of ideas? I think that's generally the way game design goes. If the room is filled with crickets and no one's got any ideas, it's probably not really working out—whatever the theme you've chosen. But if the room is filled with ideas and people are excited about it, then you're probably onto something. You can just feel it in the room whether you're onto something.

Ramsay: With Doug TenNaple's art test, you had your inspiration. What else did you need?

Perry: We had Playmates Interactive, the toy company that was going to become a game publisher. That was great because that's what we needed. We needed somebody that would just take whatever we built and sell it, and so that's what they did.

Ramsay: You've said that you're not the type to think through things, but were you ever concerned about Playmates' experience with games?

Perry: No, that was to our advantage because, if you were to talk to any of the video-game publishers and say you wanted TV commercials, most of them would be like "oh, we don't do that," but with the toy company, no one ever questioned whether there would be a TV commercial. For them, that's just how you do this, right? You do TV. We had a TV commercial without having to ask for it, as part of the package of what they do. Pretty cool. That was a big deal. I think that was the first dedicated TV commercial we ever had.

Ramsay: Earthworm Jim also had a TV series, right?

Perry: Playmates is a toy company, so they really wanted to make toys, too. The problem is that to make toys at that time, you really wanted to have a television show to market the toys. We went to Universal and we were trying to get Universal to make the TV show. That was pretty fun. One day, I had to go to Universal at 9 AM. I had a meeting to pitch *Earthworm Jim* to the top executives there. I go in this room and there are all these executives. And then the Chairman comes in. Everyone's cowering before him. He starts arguing with some poor executive in front of me, and I'm thinking, "Oh, my God. This is so intense."

If you can imagine, I'm just sitting there waiting for this argument to end and then he looks to me and goes "okay, start." And I'm going to be talking about an earthworm in a cybernetic suit. I'm like "well, there's this earthworm..." and off I go. I start pitching *Earthworm Jim* to them and he stops me in the middle of the whole thing. He says "stop" and I'm like "okay." And he goes "pigs" and I go "what?" He says, "This is confidential. There have been dog movies. There have been cat movies. But there has never been a pig movie. We need to do something with pigs. Write that down." And people are writing that down. It was so funny because I think that may be the moment when they decided to do *Babe*.

He decided in that meeting to move forward. Before Universal agreed to make the TV series, there was one more step. The TV guys needed to want toys to be made and the toy guys needed to want the TV series to be made because the TV series would advertise the toys while the toys would advertise the TV series. It's a circular Catch-22 thing. So, I invited the head of the TV show group and the head of toys to dinner. We all looked each other in the eye and I said, "I'll make the game if you make the toys and if you make the TV show." We agreed at dinner to do that. That's the way to get a deal done. It's hard. Those are deals where I've heard many times that people say "I can't get this without that" and you get stuck. I think the trick is just to get everyone to dinner and all agree simultaneously. So, then, we had a TV show, we had a toy line, and we had a video game.

The video game was very, very high profile. We had lots and lots of magazine covers. The fact that it was everywhere led us to get lots of other licenses. Marvel actually signed the comic book rights, Warner Kids Network did a deal to air the TV show, and then we licensed everything you could imagine, from underpants to bedspreads to Halloween masks.

If you think about it, for a new startup to have all of this activity going on, I think that was very, very, very new for its time. A small developer licensing out wasn't something that you really saw happening back in those days. Once we got into the stride, we realized that this was important. With our next game, *MDK*, I think we ended up getting in around 50 to 60 deals for practically every joystick, pair of 3D glasses, video card, and even the iMac. If you bought an iMac, *MDK* came preinstalled, so we were making money off each iMac. It was really the Wild West when you realized that there were other ways to sell video games other than just retail.

Ramsay: If you were to start another game company, would you go to another toy company? Or any company friendly to merchandising?

Perry: I probably would. I would go nontraditional. I would try to find an interesting angle or someone that's interested in games and I'd be their route to games. I'd look for someone who has been thinking about it or watching the space and then do a deal with them. Yep, that's exactly the way to go.

Ramsay: What was your very first challenge on the business side?

Perry: Business challenge? Good question. I think the biggest business challenge was when I made a gross mistake. Remember, I was programming and then I went to the dark side of management. I realized as a manager that if I could get more games running, then we'd make more money as a company.

The theory was that if you make one game at a time, you'll make X dollars. But if you make four games at a time, you'll make four times X dollars, right? That's fatal mistake number one. What you're really doing is simultaneously diluting your focus and talent. And you're expecting to make more money from that?

It doesn't quite work that way. So, basically, your head explodes because you're now trying to do four things at once and the team gets all spread apart. It just doesn't work. We did make *Sacrifice*, *Messiah*, *RC Stunt Copter*, and *Wild Nine* that way though.

Ramsay: How many people did you have then?

Perry: Oh, wow, that's a good question. I would imagine probably about 60 or something like that. The place was packed.

Ramsay: Did you have a single team working on four games?

Perry: We had four separate teams making four different products.

Ramsay: Was that a problem?

Perry: I think it comes down to that first thing I said about talent. If you find good talent, the game gets more potent. I just like the idea that if you have the best people who you could recruit, you should have the best working on a single title. I just think that's the best way to do things. I mean, maybe it works for some people, but I find that splitting your attention is very hard to manage.

Ramsay: How did you discover that?

Perry: There was one key problem. I was at a position in my career where I could make whatever I wanted. That was bad. That means you wake up one morning and you say "I like RC Stunt Copter so I'm going to make a game based on that" and we would just go and do that. That's not really very cool. On the other hand, whenever we went and made licensed properties, we would make a lot of money back, usually. There was a bit of an ebb and flow. You do something that you find creatively interesting and then you do something to pay bills. You basically say, "Look, I'm sorry, you didn't make very much from that one, but now I'll do something big that will make money and you'll be fine." And that's kind of what we did.

Ramsay: But you were very successful at that time. Wasn't that the goal?

Perry: No, we were actually just trying to make a difference. We were very dedicated to pushing forward technology for video games. We had done that to some extent with pencil drawn 2D art, but now we needed to do that in 3D. We invested very heavily into moving technology forward and I was starting to place bets on where I thought things would go in the future.

And so the tech that you saw coming out of our team was pretty cutting edge. There's a technology called 3D tessellation. Instead of having a 3D model that you would build and predefine, we would actually generate the model from a description. It's a bit hard to explain. You know the way that TrueType fonts work? You can scale them to any size. They don't store the letter "A" in every size. They store a mathematical description of the letter, so that it can be generated at the size of a building and it will be perfect.

We did that with 3D for game models, so you could actually regenerate the character in real time and have polygons move around. We would actually tell the engine which parts of the body mattered and which parts didn't, so it could steal polygons from the small of your back. But if it stole your nose, that would be bad. Your nose would disappear and it would look weird, right? You had to kind of say, "Nose is very important. Hips are important. Don't make the hips suddenly disappear." But the game would actually be generating everything on the fly.

I loved that the technology we were making would scale forward. If new hardware came out, the game would use more polygons automatically. There were just lots of technology ideas that we were investigating. We were enjoying that and getting a lot of attention from Intel, 3D video card companies, and others because they were very interested in showing off very cool technical demonstrations of what their hardware could do.

There was a famous day that I gave a speech with Peter Molyneux at E3. In the same pitch, he demonstrated *Black and White* and I demonstrated *Sacrifice*. As a perfect example of what I'm talking about, Intel decided to give me a piece of hardware that I had never seen before. It was a liquid-cooled, secret research PC that they just showed up with and put it on to the desk right before the talk started. That's a perfect example of where the game would modify itself to use the power of that machine. I was able to show the game looking really cool. Letting people see what the tech was going to look like in the future was pretty cool.

Ramsay: To what extent were you focusing on technology?

Perry: At the time, there was a big focus on technology and it was far too much. I was bringing in people who, quite frankly, didn't even care about video games. They just cared about 3D graphics. That was a mistake. Our culture started to break. We had people who were just hardcore game guys and then we had guys who thought games were just for kids. "Everything would have been fine if it wasn't for those meddling kids," as they say in *Scooby-Doo*. Coming out the other side, we realized that the game guys were critically important if you want to make fun games.

Ramsay: You were president of Shiny Entertainment from day one. Did you ever feel like you needed to take a step back?

Perry: Not really. I was very engaged with what we were doing. No, I didn't feel any need to step back at all. When Interplay bought the company, I put some energy toward Interplay so that I could understand their business more but my real focus was on Shiny. It never really changed. Even going to Atari, I was supposed to spend more time with Atari, but just like Interplay, I found myself focused on Shiny.

Ramsay: Tell me about the lead up to the sale.

Perry: After *The Matrix* came out, the movie was a monster hit so the directors reached out to us again. They asked, "Would you like to talk about *The Matrix Reloaded?*" Now, at that point, it was the hottest license in the game business so I was very excited about it. They had visited and seen our shop and what we did. We had a good relationship.

Other game companies were trying very hard to get the rights from Warner Bros. Because we were working with the directors, we had a very strong chance of actually getting the rights and we ended up getting them. But Interplay, financially, wasn't really ready to make big epic games with movie footage, television advertising, and everything else. The best move that Interplay could make was, after the deal was done, to sell the company. That's what we agreed to do.

Well, the question then was "would someone want to buy us?" It turned out to be very easy to get a buyer. With such a hot property, we were perfectly positioned—we were at the right place at the right time. Atari was very bullish and I was very impressed at how they had a very clear plan. They wanted to get a big property and get behind it. That's what they did. So, they gave us whatever we needed to make sure that the game got done.

To be honest, we had taken on a little too much with the property. We had to make a PlayStation 2 engine, a Game Cube engine, and a PC engine to make the game even possible. To make engines and games at the same time is actually kind of hard, so the team had really bitten off an awful lot. And then, of course, we were trying to innovate and do new things that had never been seen before. That created a lot of production work, like how to get movie footage made and how to tell the story. This was the first video game where the directors had really written parallel story lines between the movie and the game, and then they shot the movie footage for both. It was a very new idea at the time. To actually deliver that, and to know that you had a date that the movie was going to launch and there was no option to slip, it was something that, as you know, a lot of game companies struggle with. It's hard to do. It was an intense time—a very intense time.

Ramsay: What was selling the company like for you as the founder?

Perry: Well, it was great. It was financially very nice for me. I was in very, very good financial shape. And I was inspired because *The Matrix* was important and we had to build a team.

And we even had crazy stuff happen in the last three months of the project. Our landlord leased out the building out from under us with no apologies. He basically said, "I see your team's growing so much. I assumed that you weren't going to extend your lease, so I've leased it to somebody else." What? It was a nightmare. We went through a lot of crazy stuff.

Gamers would never know that this kind of nonsense happens in the background. At Atari, I was very interested in a new idea for a game. It was called *Plague* and I started designing this game. I was very inspired and excited to do it because it had new ideas that you hadn't seen before. The budget was 19 million dollars and Atari said, "We can't afford 19 million. Can you do it for less?" I got the budget down to 17 million, but going down two million dollars was really hurting the experience in my mind.

That made me realize that I'm not so sure if I want to stay and do this now. I wasn't sure if the game would turn out the way I expected. I wanted to do something really shockingly good. At that time, I was talking to the *Earthworm Jim* team about reforming and the team agreed. I started that whole process and then Atari said, "Look, we can't afford to start anything new so we can't do that." That just made my mind up. I was done, so I was like, "Okay, I'm done now. I'll see you later. Bye, bye."

Ramsay: How did you feel about first losing control of your company and then having to leave it behind?

Perry: Well, I expected that I was going to help them sell the company. I knew that if they were in financial trouble, they'd have an asset called Shiny Entertainment, which can generate money. Shiny shouldn't have been costing them money. Shiny should have been making them money. I believed very strongly that I could sell the company again, so I proposed that to them. But Atari wasn't interested; they believed that they could do that themselves. I was more than happy to let them, but I thought I would help facilitate a sale externally and that's what I did.

I went out and started to talk to investors and people who would buy the company. I ended up pairing them up with the people who actually bought it. It took a different course than I expected. I had some investors reach out who were interested in not buying Shiny but buying Atari. And so we actually went back to Atari with a proposal to buy the whole company and Atari wouldn't even consider it. It wasn't an option. That scuttled the whole thing.

As far as Shiny goes, I did make the first introduction to get someone to buy it, but it took about 10 months before Atari actually agreed to sell it to them. There was a long lull and in that lull, I just got on with my life.

Ramsay: You just got on with your life. What do you mean?

Perry: I can't quite remember the timeline but I got involved in a bunch of different projects that I found interesting. I was consulting on *The Simpsons*. I was working with Acclaim as a consultant on free-to-play. I was funding my own projects like Game Investors and Game Industry Map. And I was going to the conferences, hosting lunches, and just having a good time.

It started to get very interesting at Acclaim because we were learning about China and Korea. I was flying down there with the CEO, and in the end, Acclaim offered me a job as Chief Creative Officer. I ended up taking that job and eased back on all of this other stuff. I focused more on free-to-play and bringing Asian games to the West.

Facebook was taking off at the time so we were doing a whole bunch of research on Facebook, trying to understand virility and game sharing. We were also discovering issues with digital distribution, the cost of acquiring players, and how important that would be to the future of the business. And so we were investing in new technologies to try to make games easier to play without having to download them.

We were working on interesting server-displacement technology that would allow you to play games on a server but see the output in Flash. If you wanted to edit a level, you would edit the level with web tools, which would actually modify it on our servers and then the game experience, like sprite coordinates and things like that, would be sent to Flash. At the end of the day, while we had games running from the cloud, they still looked like Flash games; they didn't look magical.

There were a lot of other companies that realized the cost of players was too high, so they started making Flash games, too, like Zynga and many others. There was a lot of movement toward trying to make games more accessible. I was very interested in how to make games incredibly accessible and the number one way to do that was to play the whole damn thing from the cloud.

I went to DICE in 2009 and I gave a speech about this and a whole bunch of other stuff. Some engineers from the Netherlands contacted me and said that they had been working on this technology; they already had it working. They sent me a link and I was able to play *World of Warcraft* and games like *Spore* all the way from the Netherlands in my web browser. I went, "Oh my God. This is the Holy Grail! This is what we've been searching for." So, I left Acclaim. I joined them and became a cofounder of Gaikai.

At GDC 2009, we demonstrated the technology to press and investors, and, at the same show, OnLive was launched. From that day forward, it was clear that we weren't alone in this space. It was us, OnLive, G-Cluster, PlayCast, and whoever else came along. "Cloud gaming" was something that really got going. We put a lot of energy into evangelizing it and trying to get people excited about it. A year later at E3 in 2010, you really saw the momentum and we really started to demonstrate the potential. We signed with Electronic Arts. We were able to put very big games onto the web so that people could start to play from the cloud properly.

I was just at the Cloud Gaming Conference and today there are lots of companies. There's actually a conference for cloud gaming and there are companies talking about all of the different things you can use this kind of technology for. It's not something that I think is going to go away. I think it's going to be a piece of the future of the business.

Our story seems to end with Sony buying us, but what they actually did is start our next chapter. What do you do when you have a company like Sony behind you? What do you do with that?

It's a very fun brainstorming exercise to think of the potential things you can do when you're dealing with a company that makes phones, televisions, and consoles. They've got so much content and thousands of games. And the games are standardized to a controller. When you put a PC game on a TV, the game still needs a keyboard and a mouse. That's a problem. But now we had a library of console games that used a joypad controller. What can you do with all that? We were enjoying thinking of the possibilities.

Ramsay: How'd you get involved with Gaikai as a cofounder?

Perry: I can't remember exactly how that discussion went, but basically, "Why don't we start a new company together?" It's very hard to raise money when you're a company from the Netherlands. It's much easier when you're an American company. I was kind of the gateway to getting an American company started with "boots on the ground," as they say, and I was able to go meet with the various companies here very easily.

Ramsay: Who were the other cofounders? How far along was the company by the time you were involved?

Perry: There were two others: Rui Pereira and Andrew Gault. They had a tech demo. They could demonstrate that the technology was working, but there wasn't a global network of servers. It wasn't commercially ready. The technology was hard for me to experience it properly because, if you can imagine, every time I pressed a key, that key press was going all the way to the Netherlands, rendering, and then coming all the way back. There was such an enormous delay. As I was playing a game, I just had to imagine what it would be like if the servers were in Los Angeles, for example.

Ramsay: When you joined Gaikai, what was the first thing that you did?

Perry: The first thing was to try to get datacenter space. We reached out to all of the top-tier datacenter networks, and we convinced a company called Savvis to work with us and give us access to their data centers.

When you're a startup, you don't want to spend a lot of money, so Savvis was very happy to work with us on the pricing, etc. We were able to get our servers into five or six datacenters really quickly. This was great because when we're talking to a company in New York, for example, I could send them a link and they could have a good experience in New York.

Ramsay: You went after the datacenters before you started talking to people about money?

Perry: We were talking to people about money as well but we started by trying to raise money in Europe. Raising money in Europe turned out to be very difficult. We kept refining our pitch until we finally nailed it. Offers started coming in from American investors. We just found that, in general, American investors seemed more aggressive and willing to invest.

Ramsay: Why is raising money in Europe difficult?

Perry: It was probably our pitch. You know, "Hmm, I should have said this" or "I forgot to mention that" or you listen to the questions you get back and you're like "I thought that was clear?" Now you've got to fix your pitch. After awhile, you can tell that your questions are answered and they understand what you're saying. At some point, you start to feel like somebody might actually say yes. It's actually good to get out there and practice. We got our first investment in December 2009.

Ramsay: I read that you joined Gaikai in 2008.

Perry: Technically, in 2008, I was just thinking about the concept while the engineers were working on it in the Netherlands. I officially joined after my DICE speech which was January 2009.

Ramsay: And by the end of the year, Gaikai was funded. You know, you're a game developer and you joined a technology company.

Perry: I know, it's funny, isn't it? It's funny but that's really what this is all about. The game industry is becoming more technical. In the old days, you made games, you stuck them in a cartridge, and you just sold the cartridge and you'd have no idea whether people liked it or whether they were getting frustrated. We just didn't know.

But the more that servers became involved, the more we were able to collect data and say, "Wow, people are getting stuck on level 7 in room 4." We can now fix that and issue an update. This is where the world's going! It's becoming more and more connected. Developers are directly connecting with gamers. We'll end up making better games because of it.

It's inevitable. We'll have more and more discussions about datacenters, the cloud, metrics, and studying the data and trying to learn about what motivates gamers, what they like, and what they don't like. And we'll be able to use that information to try to make the best software possible. It's a different world. The world is evolving so quickly. It's amazing.

Ramsay: Making the switch from working from one perspective to working from another can be difficult. How easily did you transition from working in development and publishing to working at Gaikai?

Perry: It's different for me because I'm into learning about things. That's what I do. I'm not that interested in just being into one thing. I used to be an engineer but I also used to do design. I used to do audio. I used to do art.

I got into licensing. I got into publishing executive positions. I just keep learning as I went and then, suddenly, I'm building servers on my dining room table. I found that fascinating: getting those servers up and running, data centers, and learning about all of this stuff.

Now, I'm at Sony and I'm learning how they operate at that size of a company, learning how they make consoles and looking forward to the future and all that. It's very fascinating for me. While I'm in the tech space, now I'm squarely back in the game business but in yet again a new position. That's very interesting. As long as I keep learning, I'm interested.

Ramsay: How many employees did Gaikai have initially?

Perry: Initially, in the U.S., there was just me, and then the guys from Europe came over. We added a third guy, so we ended up with three from Europe. I started to build a team here: hiring more engineers, more executives, and everybody else. We basically built the team over time starting from 2010. But, you know, I was literally sitting in an empty office waiting for the other guys to arrive from Europe and we quickly scaled up from there. In a short amount of time, we were up to around 30 people.

Ramsay: Was your approach to recruiting similar to your approach at Shiny, at least in terms of how you identified your needs?

Perry: The DNA of Gaikai is all networking, video compression, video decompression, and lots of technology people. We have to lean very heavily toward very technical engineers. It's not a game company, so we don't have animators and traditional artists. It's not the same sort of structure as a normal company, so we don't have motion capture and a lot of physics programmers and all that. We're very engineering-driven, specifically by engineers who can innovate.

Ramsay: What did you learn about building a team for a technology company that could double as lessons for game development?

Perry: I think the big change when you're building a company these days, whether you're making games or tech, usually you're trying to make the highest quality software in the most efficient amount of time using an efficient amount of people. How the company is managed will define who lives and dies going forward because the cost of games just keeps going up. There are great books out there now to help people think about ways to get to the point quickly. Instead of building a massive sprawling game and then finding out that no one wants to play it, you can quickly get data to prove that people like your game before you spend a whole bunch of money.

Someone once said at a conference, "Just make the landing page for your game and put a 'play now' button on it. If you can't get anyone to click that button, 'Thank God that you didn't make that game.'" If you click the button, the website will say "sorry, the game's not available yet," but all you're doing is tracking to see if you can get anyone to click and whether anyone cares. It was a funny idea but it actually makes sense.

Can you imagine if you built a big game, stuck it there, and no one wanted to play it? Trying to work out what you've got as quickly as possible is a concept that's consistent across technology and games. Just get to the point. What is the core of the game? Why do people care? How long do they play it for? What level of fun are they having? Find that core and build around it. What a lot of people do instead is they spec it all out and then they build something without really knowing for certain that the core is awesome. The data can help you figure that out really quickly and maybe open up your mind to a whole new idea for the game. You might find that you designed a game to do one thing but something else is more fun.

Ramsay: How quickly did the business model for Gaikai come into focus?

Perry: We were actually forced to think about. We did an awful lot of analysis of all the possible business models that we thought gamers would like. But if I sell you a game in the cloud, I have to be certain that you will have servers available to you wherever you go 24/7.

So, we decided to focus on demos. We would invite you to play the demo: "Hey, would you like to check out this new game that just shipped?" And that meant we could balance the load on our servers. We could keep our servers running at a high capacity while not having to buy lots of them. That was the theory. Instead of building out the service and then sitting there, praying and hoping people will come, we go the other way. We'd build out the service, invite people to play, and the more sites we get onto, the more people we can invite to play. That became the strategy. How many sites can we get onto? How many digital TVs? Everywhere we were, we'd grow our audience and we'd build our network like that.

Ramsay: Why did Gaikai focus on selling to enterprises? OnLive was going directly after consumers.

Perry: We were trying to avoid competing against anybody from the start. When a publisher offered to invest in us, we said no. When a retailer offered us money, we said no. We were trying very hard to be Switzerland. We weren't taking sides with anybody. We wanted everyone to see Gaikai as valuable to them and none of them to see us a competitor. To be clear, if I start to sell games directly to gamers, I become a retailer and I'm in competition with other retailers. If I start building micro-consoles, I become a direct competitor to console companies. I didn't want to do that.

Ramsay: A publisher offered to invest in you? How were publishers reacting to Gaikai when you talked to them?

Perry: Once we started demonstrating, the initial reaction was: "We'll give this a try. Let's see what happens." After that, we improved the calls to the service, so the quality of the experience just got better and better, so they put us on more and more pages.

And then we found that each time we got a game in a certain genre, other people in that genre would reach out to us. So, when we put a MMO up, we'd get lots of companies with MMOs contacting us. We'd put out a shooter and then the other shooter companies would call.

Nobody wanted to be the company that wasn't represented. If you think about it, you don't want to go to a retailer's website where you can't play games. That was where we found ourselves: if one company was doing it, then their competitors wanted to do it, too. We were able to help that along, so generally, the service marketed itself to some extent.

Ramsay: I remember sitting in the Gaikai booth at the E3 Expo, watching you show the technology to Jay Wilbur at Epic Games. He seemed to be quite impressed. Was his reaction typical?

Perry: Well, the thing is that a lot of engineers were on record saying that cloud gaming was impossible. That was really good because it meant that expectations were very low. When they came into the room and they saw something that wasn't what they expected, they were easily quite surprised. We were seeing tweets from people saying, "What is this? Voodoo? What is going on here? How is this possible?"

It's just amazing how a lot of the things that you experience on the Internet aren't optimized for speed. We have this general feeling of malaise on the Internet. It's like the Internet's quick, but it's not that quick, and yet it is actually really quick. There's just a lot of stuff that isn't optimized for speed.

When you take the time to optimize for speed, it's quite remarkable what it's capable of. We used to get people in all the time who'd say, "Look, this is impossible. It will never work. I can't even play a YouTube video on this computer. It stutters." And then we would run our demo and it would run really well and they would be like, "Okay, how can you do that and Google can't"? The answer would be "because there's a server in your city and we're delivering a direct connection to you fully optimized. They're serving millions of people from centralized locations and you're not the highest priority to them; and, in that situation, your experience doesn't match the real capabilities of the Internet."

Ramsay: There was a time in 2012 when I felt like every week Gaikai was announcing a new deal with Walmart, Samsung, or some other major corporation. Yet, while big contracts capture headlines, I wonder if you were also working with smaller companies?

Perry: Yes, we were. We had an internal goal to get to 100 million monthly users who we could get games in front of and we were trying to get there as quickly as we could, so we were signing a lot of small companies and web-sites. We would put games on every site that we signed and then we would add that traffic to our reach list. We had a whole team of people going out and just signing a lot of gaming sites and publisher sites, trying to get as many eyeballs as we possibly could. Once you get past 100 million, you start to get to the point where you can really move the needle for people. That was a lot of work.

Ramsay: What do you mean by "move the needle for people"?

Perry: What I mean by that is you could give us your game and then we could press a button and have your game appear that day in front of the traf-fic to tons and tons of different sites. Your game would then have immediate reach across all of those sites. We could even do big sites like YouTube and Facebook. Say you had your own Facebook Page. We could put your *actual* products right onto your Page. That was pretty cool.

Ramsay: When you joined Gaikai, you were very excited about your pros-pects and then everything just ballooned upward from there. Were you ever worried about anything?

Perry: Yeah, the worrying thing was that there was a lot of competition. There were a lot of people competing for the same clients, customers, and gamers. And part of the worry was from trying to keep an eye on what everyone else was up to and making sure that we were aware of what was going on. There was a certain level of paranoia. I remember Bill Gates talked about that in a book once. You *have* to be kind of paranoid about what else is going on. I think you have to be constantly watching and paying attention. That's what we were doing because we were trying to get the best games as quickly as possible.

Ramsay: What led to the acquisition of Gaikai by Sony Computer Entertainment?

Perry: We had signed Samsung and LG, so we were very excited about our position there. We had signed the number one and number two television companies in the world and they had committed to using our cloud as their gaming cloud. We were pretty excited about the potential. Then it seemed like the perfect time for someone to come in and buy us because, if they didn't, we would have ended up running those services ourselves.

Ramsay: Did you put the word out that you were looking to sell?

Perry: We never did put the word out that we were going to sell. That was kind of funny. It was a sort of a mishmash of random events that caused that to happen. We never actually said to someone, "Oh, we want to go sell the com-pany." That entire problem started when someone asked me, "What will you be doing in five years?" I said, "I think someone will have bought the company by then." And that caused a whole lot of chaos, right, because "oh, Gaikai's for sale." No, that's not what I said, but you know how that goes sometimes.

Ramsay: Reports suggested that you put out a figure of $500M.

Perry: I didn't put a figure out there. Someone picked that out of the air.

Ramsay: That's interesting. I remember thinking that initial price was part of your strategy to drive up bids.

Perry: Nope, not at all. It's times like that where you're trying to lay low and get your deal done. You don't want a whole bunch of press. We were reading that press going, "Oh my God." You never know what the press the next day will say.

Ramsay: Did that unwanted press lead Sony to make an offer?

Perry: We had already been talking to Sony at that point.

Ramsay: Was Sony your only suitor?

Perry: I think there were a lot of companies that would like cloud gaming, so there were plenty of people who we had talked to over time who were interested in the company. But we just hadn't met that perfect partner yet, where they had everything we were looking for.

Ramsay: Sometimes founders are very attached to their companies. When you sold Shiny, you just wanted to get out. What about Gaikai?

Perry: This deal is a major level up for us because it allows us to think much bigger now. We're thinking much bigger than we were before.

Ramsay: Now that you're part of Sony, how has your role changed?

Perry: It hasn't changed at all. I'm still the CEO at Gaikai. It just has a new tagline. It's a Sony Computer Entertainment company.

Ramsay: Gaikai isn't on the path to being absorbed?

Perry: No. They have a history of doing this. Naughty Dog is a great example.

Ramsay: When you look back on your journey from Ireland to Gaikai, what are your thoughts?

Perry: Let's call this Year 30 in the business. I think the trick that I've found is the whole industry stays incredibly fun as long as you keep moving with it. It's very easy to get off the train. The train is moving very fast but if you stay on it, it stays very interesting because the industry evolves every single year so dramatically. It's quite stunning and I think it's actually accelerating with mobile, VR, the cloud, and everything else.

So, I'm very much trying to stay at the innovative end of the game industry and not just stay stuck in "I used to make games and then I left and I went to do something else." I'm staying in and I'm very much enjoying trying to predict what's next, which is very hard to do. It's very hard to guess what's next. There are so many opportunities but it's fun.

I'm the guy who was on stage arguing with the retailers to prepare distribution for the future and it's that kind of stuff that I get very passionate about. I don't have the same restrictions, or at least I didn't, on me that normal employees have, so I was able to speak my mind. I very much enjoyed evangelizing things, concepts, and companies while, at the same time, trying to think forward. One of the best things that happens is when you're asked to give speeches about the future of the business; that forces you to sit down and think. Where *is* the industry going? That helps make your decisions. It's a healthy cycle to get into. I highly recommend it.

Emily Greer

Cofounder, Kongregate

The brother-sister duo Jim and **Emily Greer** cofounded Kongregate in 2006 as an online portal, platform, and community for sharing and playing primarily Flash video games in a variety of genres.

By 2010, Kongregate was supporting more than 8,500 developers across 30,000 games when GameStop, the largest video game retailer in the world, acquired the company to bolster its move into digital distribution.

In February 2014, Emily Greer became CEO, where she remains. Jim Greer stepped down to focus on CounterPAC, a super political action committee that "seeks to bring sanity and transparency to money in politics."

Kongregate, now a leading web and mobile game publisher, supports more than 20,000 developers across 80,000 games. With more than 18 million monthly unique visitors and three billion plays, many top-rated games are only available at Kongregate and are played by millions of players.

Ramsay: You cofounded Kongregate with your brother Jim. Who had the idea to start this company?

Greer: Jim actually had the idea for Kongregate. He was working at Pogo and really loved the community. Jim had the idea of building that type of community, focused on profiles and achievements. I had a different background. I wasn't in games at all, but I thought it was a good idea. It would be more fun than what I was doing. What did I have to lose? I volunteered to be his cofounder and that was six years ago.

Ramsay: What was your background?

Greer: I started in book publishing out of college, but I didn't like making subjective decisions about what other people will like. I stumbled into direct marketing, which was very numbers-based and analytical. I was doing mostly catalogs, e-commerce, and retail marketing. I was working with big Excel spreadsheets, database queries, and things like that. I was working on merchandising, too.

Ramsay: Did both of you leave your jobs?

Greer: He had already left EA when I volunteered. I think he gave notice, but EA didn't want him to stick around during that period; he was out the door immediately. But my company wanted me to stay on as long as possible because my boss had recently left. I agreed to stay on until the end of June, and we started working on Kongregate in May 2006. But we were working more than full-time on Kongregate almost immediately.

As we were quitting our jobs, we knew exactly what we were going to do. I think that was one of our advantages. We were in our 30s and had savings. Once we decided to do it, there wasn't any point in continuing to work elsewhere to bring in income. If we didn't get any traction in a year or so, we would have reconsidered, but by then, we had received funding.

Ramsay: Did you have any experience with startups?

Greer: I did not. Jim had a small five-person game studio in Austin. They published a real-time strategy game through Activision six or seven years earlier. He learned a lot from that. But a Bay Area idea of a startup? I didn't have any experience with that. I didn't really know what I was getting into.

I had some experience with web development. We would start building a website and see where we could go from there. But I really had no idea. Jim had more of a sense of what we were going to do. We were going to get a demo going, get that far, and then try to raise venture capital money. He was more familiar with the process, so he led the way.

We talked to everybody we knew who had gone through a startup, started a company, or been in that world. We asked them out for coffee, got their advice, and got introduced to more people who could help us. That was tremendously useful. We got a lot of advice, good and bad, but much more good. We started talking to venture capitalists who, once we could demo the site, gave us term sheets.

Ramsay: Did you bring on anyone as advisors?

Greer: We didn't sign anybody up as formal advisors, but there were people we talked to regularly. When we closed our angel round right around the end of October, seven or eight different Silicon Valley investors became very much our advisors. We would reach out to them throughout the whole process, especially when we were raising a venture round with Greylock. Once we signed with Greylock, our board became very important to us. Having a board meeting every month was a really good exercise in how to get external feedback on what we were doing.

Ramsay: Was pursuing venture capital your first approach to raising capital?

Greer: Jim and I put in some of our own money. Our father also put in some money. We knew together that was an amount we could run the company on, including hiring a few people for a six- to nine-month period. But we always saw that as a first step to getting us venture money. We considered only two real options: bootstrapping with money from friends and family, and venture capital. If raising venture capital hadn't worked out, I think we would have probably continued on with friends and family. We focused on venture though, and that worked out.

Ramsay: When you take money from friends and family, you risk putting money between you and your relationships with them. You took money from your father. Did you have a formal arrangement with him?

Greer: We had discussions, but we didn't sign anything. When we took our initial angel round, his loan was converted into stock at the same rate as the money we took in the angel round. The arrangement was formalized then. But we were using the money in advance of that agreement. We might have told him that when we get funding, he'll be treated like a regular investor. I think he accepted investing in our company as something he should do. He believes that if you're going to lend money to friends and family, do it if you think it's the right thing to do, but don't expect to get it back.

Ramsay: Taking money from friends and family can be stressful. Was taking that loan from your father the most stressful part of starting Kongregate?

Greer: No, to me, any financial jeopardy is the most stressful part. For example, have you heard of the game World of Goo? Ron Carmel and Kyle Gabler, the two founders of 2D Boy who made World of Goo, were our good friends. They were leaving to start their studio at the same time, so we rented an office together, which was actually an apartment. Kyle lived in the back. The living room was our shared office, halfway between my apartment and Jim's. Our half of the rent was something we took on, but in the grand scheme of things, that was one of the small things.

We then hired a contract programming shop to help us get started on our demo and a web design firm to get started on the look. We spent money on those two things, and we eventually hired our first employee. When you start hiring employees, that's a big, definite risk. You're making a promise to pay them and continue making payroll. People's lives and their ability to pay rent depend on you. That's a huge responsibility.

Ramsay: Before you volunteered to be Jim's cofounder, did you have any reservations about starting this company?

Greer: I did, actually. It's a funny story. His now-wife-then-girlfriend asked him to tell me about the idea and get my approval before he quit his job. She trusted me. Jim is an inventive type of guy, and I'm more conservative and practical. She thought that if I thought Kongregate was okay to do, it was probably okay. Over the years, Jim had many ideas for startups he discussed with me. I always listened with an open mind, but with some skepticism. As he was talking me through the business, I thought he was making sense. I gave my thumbs-up and, two weeks later, that's when I volunteered to be his cofounder.

I knew there could be risks though, but I wasn't thinking about the risks. Whatever we'd encounter, we'd figure out. I thought the worst that could happen was we'd have wasted some money, learned a lot, and we'd go back to the kinds of jobs we had before. I was confident we could find those jobs again. That's what I was thinking. I didn't know enough about the video game industry. If I had known more, I'd have been more skeptical.

Kongregate today is fundamentally the same as when we launched. I think that to have something so fully formed that it doesn't change substantially through the creative process is unusual. Jim was taking a lot of inspiration from Pogo though, which he'd worked on directly and understood, so we weren't starting from total scratch. We were starting with a model of how one thing worked, and then expanding that model into a totally different type of platform that was open so anybody could upload their games.

Ramsay: Were you worried about EA?

Greer: We were definitely very worried about the copyright issues with freely uploaded games. We knew that was a big problem at YouTube and other video sharing sites. We spent a lot of time thinking about the issues, the DMCA Safe Harbor Provisions, and things like that. We were worried, but in large part, our fears never came to pass.

Ramsay: What about raising venture capital? You had never done that.

Greer: Sometimes in the venture market, people are very excited to invest in different industries. We were going into a good time for games. Raising money was easier than people should really expect. We were definitely lucky, but we still put in quite a lot of effort.

We learned a lot from pitching to so many people. Each time you pitch, you get feedback, and you see how people react to what you're saying. You can take what you've learned to the next pitch, present more strongly, and anticipate questions they're likely to ask. As we went through the process, we really honed our presentation. Jim's pitch was really strong while I tended to specific questions. By the time we were closing our funding round, we were really comfortable, and we really knew how to paint a picture of what we were trying to do and why it was important.

I'd also say that having something really tangible to show them, so that they could see how it was working and that we could get something done, was crucial. Those things were very important. The process was endless—and slow, slow, slow, and then really dramatic. "Hurry up! Make a decision." Once they got the sense that there's any kind of competition, everything changes very radically. That was interesting.

Ramsay: Not unlike Wall Street, the venture capital industry is often associated with a notorious gender gap. What did you think?

Greer: As a woman, it's always interesting to go into a male-dominated situation like the venture world, and the venture world is a little more extreme than others. Most VCs aren't consciously sexist. Many have pretty successful wives, but they're investing in the individual as much as the idea. They're looking for people who look like people who have been successful in the past. As there have been fewer successful women entrepreneurs, it's a little bit harder. And if you don't have an engineering background, that's way harder. Sometimes the dynamics of being the only woman in the room are a little strange, but we got funding and it was all fine.

Ramsay: How are the dynamics strange?

Greer: If you walk into the average venture capital firm, there are a few very pretty, young receptionists and assistants. They're the last women you'll see. It's a dynamic where women are in one part and men are in the other. That's a little strange. I didn't experience anything so overt that you could easily talk about in a courtroom and go "aha, that's sexism" but there was a lot of subtle stuff that stacked up. Many firms and individuals were fine, but some treated me and Jim very differently, occasionally acting as if I was not in the room. It was very obvious that the firms were funding Jim, not me. But, as I said, we got funded, and I was able to prove my value.

Ramsay: Was Kongregate in development when you signed your first round?

Greer: We were going into our closed invite-only alpha test right about the time we were getting term sheets. I think that sped up the process. Once something is coming up closer to launch, that becomes a forcing function for venture capital. People are afraid that if it launches and it's successful, they'll have lost a chance at a lower price.

Ramsay: What was the first thing you did after you were funded?

Greer: Hired more people. Jim and I were able to hire somebody who we thought highly of and who we worked with at a previous company, and I hired a designer who I brought with me and he brought an engineer. We were building something that was changing every day and that was getting more fun every day. A small team of just ten people can get a lot done and have a lot of fun. That period of intensively building the website was amongst the most fun we had before we launched publicly.

Ramsay: Was the hiring process strictly transactional? Or did anyone need to be convinced to join your startup?

Greer: Our contractors knew exactly what they were getting into; they didn't need much convincing. But I did spend some time on hiring my designer away from the catalog business. I had to convince her we were a stable business, that we had something real. Most of the people we hired were pretty excited to join a small company making games. We hired web programmers, and most web programmers are gamers, so they'd rather build a website around games than around financial software.

Ramsay: When you were pitching Kongregate to VCs, did you find yourself tempering your vision to address their feedback?

Greer: Not really. The feedback we got was more about how we were going to get games and how we were going to get customers. They didn't have answers, but they were asking questions, and we were asking ourselves those same questions. We thought public relations and viral hooks would bring in players. We had a very concrete plan for how to get games and game developers. Our first hire was a game scout. He would look for existing games across the web, find developers, and make the decision to bring their games over to Kongregate easy.

YouTube was just taking off, growing through embeddable videos, so they also asked a lot of questions about how we could do embeddable games. We said we would work on it once we got the basic product done, but we had our doubts. As experiences, games are more immersive than videos. That was what we mostly pushed back on, and we just kept building.

Once you have momentum, more people are willing to sign onto what you're doing, but once we had funding and a board, there was pressure to go in different directions. Would we bring everything to Facebook? What would we do in mobile? How would we extend the platform?

Ramsay: Their primary concerns were reach and return?

Greer: Yeah, like how would we get the initial traction to bring players in? We thought that if we have free games, the players will come, so we concentrated on getting games and game developers. That was basically right. It didn't work out exactly how we thought it would, in terms of how the games would spread, and what the different sources of traffic would be. Search, for example, turned out to be way more important. That wasn't something we were really thinking about for games.

Ramsay: I assume you had a business plan?

Greer: We did. I planned out all of our costs and the types of employees we would hire. I don't think our plan ended up matching reality. We were always hiring to need. On the other hand, in a startup, half of your employees are going to be engineers! I didn't know that. The line item for engineering hires was the most important one and we matched that. All of our other costs were planned out. I still have that spreadsheet around. It's amusing to look back and see what I got right and what I got wrong, although nearly everything I was thinking about didn't turn out to be reality. Thinking through what we were going to need and what things were going to cost are very valuable, but it's barely a treasure map.

Ramsay: How did you determine whether you needed to hire someone?

Greer: In general, our philosophy has been to hire carefully, conservatively, and when we're in need. For a 10- to 20-person startup, the salary of any one individual is a significant part of the budget, so the performance of any one person is crucial to the company's growth. Dead weight endangers the jobs of everybody who works there. And the hardest thing a startup owner has to do is lay people off, so we do whatever we can to be certain about a candidate before we bring them on full-time. I think we have occasionally been too conservative though. We've muddled through things when we should have invested.

Ramsay: When you look back on your planning spreadsheet, you can see what you got right and what you got wrong. What did you get right?

Greer: Weirdly, I got the amount we would need to spend right. What we spent it on was not right, but the approximate time, amounts, when we would have to buy servers, and the total amounts of payroll and payroll taxes were roughly correct.

The traffic forecast was way off. I radically underestimated how many unique visitors we would get, and I radically overestimated the number of visits and page views we would get from any single visitor. In the long term, the curve looked less like a hockey stick and more linear than I expected.

My idea about where we were going was correct, but it took about twice as long as I expected to get there. In some cases, that was partly because engineering always takes longer than you think. I'd forecast us launching something and we'd start growing immediately, but what really happened was that we'd launch things and nothing much would happen for a few months. We'd figure it out, kick it into gear, and we'd have a real business.

So, basic direction? Good. Timing? Not so great.

Ramsay: Why does engineering always take longer than you expect?

Greer: You have these big projects in your mind, so you think that when you launch a feature, it's finished. But you always have to go back. You learn the feature works differently and has different bugs.

Frankly, early on, we had a lot of scaling issues. We built things quickly. We used Ruby on Rails, which was especially notorious for being very easy to write code with, but not necessarily scalable code. Features that worked just fine when 100 people were using the site would break as soon as we had 20,000, or 100,000, or a million people. The servers would crash. The database would get overloaded. The site would slow down to a painful crawl. Users would see errors frequently. Things like that.

We spent a fair amount of time on rewriting things that had already been launched because they weren't scalable. Once we understood the problem, I think it took us 18 months to get through the vast majority of our scaling problems, and to get the right person in charge of fixing them. I'm not going to say we never had problems with scaling after then, but they never became daily critical problems again.

Ramsay: A year and a half to solve scalability? How long did getting Kongregate ready to launch take?

Greer: The first code was written within six weeks. We were thinking the whole site would take several months. I thought we needed at least three or four months to have something workable, and I think we were roughly in that time period. We didn't set a goal and say, "We're going to launch on this date." We thought, "Okay, these are the features we think we're going to need. Let's see how long it takes us." We were just trying to move quickly and see what we could do.

Ramsay: How was development organized?

Greer: Agile. We were working on feature by feature and adding things up. We were figuring out how to do things, and how to use agile methods. We were learning as we were going. We changed our methodology quite a few times over the first 18 months. By the time we were two years in, we had our current methodology, but we're continuing to improve.

Ramsay: Were there any other technical challenges early on?

Greer: We spent a lot of time on figuring out the kind of chat server to use. We started with an off-the-shelf system and a prototype we ended up being pretty unhappy with. We ended up completely starting from scratch with a different open source system and a different engineer. We were using a system that wasn't customizable in the way we really needed it to be.

Cloud hosting was starting out, and we were one of the first major clients of Engine Yard. They were working out their kinks as we were working out our kinks. That caused a lot of problems. Essentially, we had two very fast-growing untested services on top of each other. We ended up moving on relatively early and getting our own dedicated stack. They went on to have a great business. If we had started with them a year later, it would have worked out better. Two new technologies together can be bad.

Ramsay: Had you thought of any other ways to deliver content?

Greer: No, we've stayed true to our original business plan: advertising for free users, virtual goods in free games for everybody else, and the potential for a subscription model. They took a little longer to come to fruition, but that's pretty much what happened.

The Flash game ecosystem had been pretty exploitative and not transparent. People were making games for fun; they just happened to make money accidentally. We came around right about the time Mochi Media started up. We were going to developers and saying, "You deserve a cut of the revenue from your games." That helped change the dynamic, especially once Flash game licensing started up. Sharing revenue with developers was very new, so that was our big innovation.

I think together we made a big difference. When we started, the average Flash game developer made a few hundred dollars, or a few thousand dollars, with really successful games. Now, five and six figures are common.

Ramsay: What was your plan for attracting game developers?

Greer: Our plan was to make uploading to Kongregate a really easy decision and to make everything nonexclusive. The very simple upload process would be no harder than putting a video on YouTube. And then we'd place a carrot, promising web share so that they would be guaranteed to get something in the long term and something fair.

Since we didn't have advertising revenue, or any revenue to share in the early days, we wanted an immediate carrot to get people in. We started having weekly and monthly contests for the best games. Anybody who had served up a pretty good game had an excellent chance at making several hundred dollars to up to $1,500 in contest prizes. We wanted to make the process frictionless with pretty much no work involved and only an upside.

I remember when we went into our closed alpha. We started off with a few games one of our programmers made in 24 hours in his spare time. Within the first week, we had 25 games. We were completely overjoyed! Within the first month, we had 100 games. Pretty soon, it became clear we would get lots of games. At first, people were uploading for the contest prizes, and then, eventually, people were uploading for exposure and ad revenue.

Ramsay: Sounds like you effectively used the closed alpha to seed the platform. Is that right?

Greer: Our plan was to get the basic functionality implemented: you can register an account, you can upload a game, you can play a game, you can rate a game, and you can earn points.

We wanted to get developers first because we needed content, but we also knew developers were influencers. If they liked the site, the word would spread to gamers. In the closed alpha stage, you had to request an invite, we would grant access, and you could register. I think we were in the closed alpha for a week. When we had about 20 games, Jim reached out to the press. We were featured on TechCrunch and a couple of other places. That quickly brought in several thousand invite requests.

We were adding new features every week. We were closing a round, too. Right around Christmas, we dropped the invite requirement, so you had to be registered to play. You still couldn't play as a guest yet, but you didn't need an invite to register.

In February, we dropped the registration requirement. Anybody could play games as guests. It was a little arbitrary when we did that. We started getting spikes of traffic to the games on our site, and the traffic continued rolling up from there. In March, we added the challenge system, where you could earn rewards, which we felt was really key. And then we made our official announcement, started talking to the press, and launched.

Ramsay: What types of games were on the site then?

Greer: Greg McClanahan, our director of games and achievements now, was our game scout. He just went through the different game websites on the Internet, found games he personally liked, researched the developers, and collected their information. Greg reached out to them, and the first ones he reached out to tended to be the first ones we got. The games varied, from action games to a lot of puzzle games to platformers. Now that I think about it, the genres were pretty wide even back then. They were mostly male-oriented games, but almost every genre was represented.

Ramsay: Had you prohibited any games? Were those rules in place?

Greer: We set the line at around PG-13. No nudity. No excessive violence. Nothing racist or hateful. I think the first takedown for content we did was a game called Dirty Girl, where you watched an attractive anime girl and gradually took off pieces of her clothing until you got her fully naked. That was our first content takedown. People still joke about Dirty Girl.

Ramsay: Would you say that the role of game scout served a business development function?

Greer: Yes, although it wasn't business development in the traditional "take people out to lunch and sign a deal" sense, especially in the Flash game world. Back then, the business was very, very amateurish. It didn't work that way, so we didn't think of him as business development. He didn't think of himself as business development.

Greg is one of the shyest people I have ever known, but he's a really good writer and very friendly in the world of the Internet. He didn't even own a phone because he didn't like to talk to people on the phone. Greg would write up an e-mail, explaining Kongregate and why it was good and why they should put their games up. He customized the e-mail to whatever game he had played just to prove that he really was who he said he was. He really knew their games and really wanted them on Kongregate. He searched their sites and the Web for their e-mail addresses or AOL Instant Messenger (AIM) screen names. And he would just send them e-mails, or hit them up on AIM, and convince them to upload their games.

Ramsay: How long did Greg act as your game scout?

Greer: He worked on that side for only a short time. Kongregate had enough traffic, enough people liking the contest prizes, and enough developers all talking to each other online that we quickly started getting games regardless of whether we went after them.

For the first year, I was watching Newgrounds, a great original games site. They have a daily e-mail about the top content and a weekly top games list. I was watching those lists to see what games we didn't get, and initially, we weren't getting any of it. Within six months, we were getting three quarters. By the end of the year, anything that Newgrounds got, we also got. So, the game scout job disappeared.

But instead of losing all of those relationships he built up with game developers, he started using them to get games earlier, and to get developers using our API so that we could put achievements in them. Greg eventually negotiated sponsorships for unreleased games. Still, we would never put business development in his title.

Ramsay: After all, you'd have to pay him more!

Greer: We pay him plenty! The work he did makes him one of the most important contributors to Kongregate's success. Greg deserves a ton of credit and as much money as we can give him.

Ramsay: I'm sure he'll be happy to hear that. We've talked about how you attracted developers. How did you attract players?

Greer: We worked on making the site a more fun, more interesting, and more individual place than other sites. There isn't now, and there wasn't then, a lack of places to play free games online. What we tried to do was have a cleaner site with fewer ads, no pop-ups, and none of the things that were really aggressive and annoying. We wanted a better place where you could play games. If you went to another site and you didn't have an account, you might have been able to play a game, but there'd be no lasting record of your plays. We wanted a place where everything you did had meaning, where you were building up your Kongregate profile, earning points, leveling up, and collecting achievements in a social atmosphere where people could see and interact with you.

If we had all of the games, and if I did a good job with filtering what was on the homepage and telling you what to play, Kongregate would be a sticky place. We were never viral in the sense people talk about now though. Individual games went viral, but we didn't. We just kept bringing in new traffic and keeping the old traffic, like in Katamari Damacy, where if you just keep what you roll up, you'll keep getting bigger.

Ramsay: Of course, that is one way to grow slowly, too.

Greer: You can grow pretty fast. I guess I'd describe it not as slowly but as steadily. You can get a million players in a few days, but if you don't retain them, what does it matter two months on? I don't think we got a million in the early days, but we got new players and we kept them. We had three million unique visitors within our first year. That was certainly not slow. It just wasn't the viral "hockey stick"-type of growth that people think of. It was just, you know, going up 10% or 20% every month. That adds up.

Ramsay: Did you provide developers with ways to share their games and promote them?

Greer: We did, but that never did all that much. Games started to get a lot of traffic by getting picked up on blog sites, Digg, Reddit, and things like that where individuals would promote them. We put in a lot of tools for individual users to e-mail, IM, and share games; and we put in a way for developers to let people know about their games. Those things drove some traffic, but it was dwarfed by what we got from game sites linking to them.

We had really clean URL structures that had the names of the games, and we quickly got links from external sites to those games. We were planning for search, and we were doing things that were good for search, but that wasn't really our strategy. And it turned out that people didn't search for "zombie games;" they searched for "Boxhead." They didn't search for "tower defense games;" they searched for "Desktop Tower Defense." We ranked high in search engines for games we had, and that drove a lot of traffic. Each game we added then added to our traffic, and so we kept growing and growing and growing.

Ramsay: Other than relying on fans to find games they want, how did you help players discover new games?

Greer: There are a lot of people who go to free game sites and they want to play the new games. They get a mix of games, from horrible mouse avoiders with terrible art to some really good games. A lot of people came to Kongregate because we were consistently getting all of the new games, and using our users' ratings to decide what to feature on the homepage. On any given day, there was new content, and if you just played what was on the homepage, you were going to have a reliably good experience. I think people liked that.

Ramsay: Was launch day full of anticipation?

Greer: Yeah. It was! We already had a pretty big traffic spike before then, larger than when a well-known developer released a preview. I don't know if you've ever played the Fancy Pants Adventures games, but the preview of Fancy Pants Adventure World 2 on our site got on the front page of Digg. We got a pretty big spike of traffic from that. We were steeling ourselves for that level of traffic again; it was pretty close. The announcement got picked up at a bunch of places. I mostly just remember worrying about the servers. I was constantly checking to see how the site was running and how many people were online.

The bigger day was actually the next day. The announcement went out on Thursday, and we got picked up. On Friday, we got an e-mail in the morning from Fox News asking if we wanted to be on the Fox Report with Shepard Smith that afternoon. Jim needed to be ready to be interviewed live at noon downtown in a TV studio. That was pretty exciting.

I remember going from our office where we didn't have a TV and walking back to my apartment with our one employee to go watch Jim do his interview. That was just completely fun! It's also funny because they used a fake backdrop of the Painted Ladies in Alamo Square in that TV studio. That happened to be the view from my apartment. So, I was looking at Jim being interviewed in front of that background, and I could see that same background through my apartment window.

But that interview completely, completely destroyed the site. We were frantic. I mean it wasn't even that the site was slow or broken; you just couldn't get to the server. It went from being really exciting to really stressful. We were frantically trying to figure out what was crashing and what we could do. That's what I remember mostly: the excitement of being on live TV and then just desperately trying to fix the site so all these people could see the site we just released.

Ramsay: Did Jim have any prior media training?

Greer: I think that was the first time Jim was on TV. He had done some public speaking, been on panels, and things like that. He's a natural. We had been presenting our company to different people so much for the previous nine months that talking about Kongregate had become very, very natural. Pitching 50 or 70 VCs and making Kongregate sound sexy, exciting, simple, and understandable in less than a minute was not that different.

Ramsay: How well did the changes you made to Kongregate hold up after the first day?

Greer: It was a gradual process. We would fix one problem and be fine at that level of traffic, but then we were constantly growing and every new level of traffic uncovered a different problem. We were in some level of pain for at least another nine months. It was never as dire again as that total blackout post being on national TV, but it was a constant stress and worry. It took a solid year of essential changes, hiring additional people, and getting the right person in charge that fixed it. We had already been through a lot of the worst.

We had our own dedicated servers; that was important. And we got one engineer who was really good at scaling stuff. He got things fixed pretty well in the six weeks from when he started, and we were consistently keeping up with our rate of growth. The event that took us down in the first year would not even be a noticeable blip in our traffic now. We get that kind of traffic in a minute, so it'd take a really big event to shake things up.

Ramsay: How much traffic were you looking at on the day of the TV interview?

Greer: I don't think we had more than 100,000 visits. We have many millions of visits per day now. It's funny to think about how devastating less than 100,000 visits was then.

Ramsay: How successful was the launch? You had all that traffic, you were on Fox News, and you solved a variety of problems, but how sticky was Kongregate?

Greer: The launch was definitely successful, but it was not the most successful day we had in the next six months. That day was just another sign this was going to work.

Ramsay: When I say "launch day," I should probably say "launch months"?

Greer: Yes, I would say. It was a rolling process. It's funny. For our fifth anniversary, we wanted to do something, but nobody could agree on what date made sense to call our fifth year anniversary. Is it the day we started the closed alpha? Is it the day we did PR? That was a little arbitrary; a lot of people had already discovered the site. We decided to use the day we announced our achievement system, one of the most fundamental and popular elements of the site—and one of our biggest differentiators. But we still can't pick a date for the start of Kongregate. It was a gradual rolling unveiling. We'd like to have an official date we could hang our hat on. It would probably have helped our PR a little bit had we concentrated on those details. But I wouldn't change the way we started.

Ramsay: Which grew faster during those six months: the number of developers uploading content to Kongregate or new users?

Greer: In terms of gross numbers, definitely users. Right now, Kongregate has between 15,000 and 20,000 developers, 55,000 games, and 15 million users. In the early days, developers were overrepresented. We always had a very small minority, but the number of games was growing at a fast rate. We actually got to a critical mass of games before we got to a critical mass of users, but then those games were bringing in the users.

Ramsay: The launch was a sign that Kongregate was going to work out. Did you think otherwise before that you point?

Greer: When we started Kongregate, I didn't think we were going to fail, but I knew that was the more likely outcome. I was giving the company a year, and thinking this was an adventure. When we closed that first round, I was starting to really feel that Kongregate was going to be something. By the time we launched, and we were getting games, and we were getting in a lot of users, Kongregate became very real to me. This wasn't a year-long adventure in trying to build something. We had built something, so the question became "how big is this going to be?" Kongregate would be a long-term commitment. We had a business.

Ramsay: Were you able to answer that question?

Greer: I wanted Kongregate to grow. I think I knew pretty early on the site was going to be a success with users and developers. Almost a year before we started, we had one game that started adding digits to our revenue. We could look at that game and say, "This is why this one was successful. Let's look for more like this." We had something to work with, and that's when I started to have hope.

In 2008, when we started selling advertising directly to advertisers, and we got the first few bigger checks, I began to have confidence that the ad business was going to work. We were also launching a monetization model with virtual goods we had planned from the beginning. It was, initially, pretty much a failure. We had negligible revenue from virtual goods for months. At the end of 2009, it was still not smooth sailing, but I did feel like we were going to start making a profit based on the growth patterns and how much our expenses turned out to be. I was certain.

Ramsay: What did you learn from the initial failure of the virtual goods business?

Greer: That it's really hard to make a good multiplayer game, and that it's really hard to make a good virtual goods game that makes people want to spend money. We knew that virtual goods could be big. They'd been big in Asia. There hadn't been a lot of success stories yet in Western markets. There were a few doing well like Maple Story.

We started off thinking, "We've got all of these Flash developers. We're going to help them jump up to the next level of making games with virtual goods, and help fund them to make multiplayer games that use them." We funded probably six games—only half of them ever launched, and most of those took twice as long and cost twice as much. We learned pretty quickly that just because something is multiplayer doesn't mean that that's enough to make people hand over money.

We also learned that it's really hard for somebody who has been making small, single-player Flash games to jump up and make a big game. It's almost a different skill set. You have to deal with not just a client but the server, too, and you need to be thinking about what you're going to charge from the beginning. I don't know if we learned what the answers were, but we learned some of the assumptions we made were wrong and everything would be harder than we thought.

What worked were the games that came over to Kongregate which had been designed from the start to be MMOs on their own sites. We were able to learn from so many different games that came onto Kongregate. We were able to look at them and say, "Okay, this what they have in common, and this is what's important." Many years later, we'd go back to developers, give them advice on monetization, and suggest changes to their games. We were in a position to help developers make games that monetize, but we had to learn how to do that first.

Ramsay: Was Kongregate intended to be a publisher, and not just a distributor?

Greer: We planned that pretty much from the start. We hired somebody to be a game producer after we got our round from Greylock in the fall of 2007. It took us about 18 months to two years to totally fail at it.

Ramsay: Publishing is something you don't do anymore?

Greer: Actually, we're getting back into it a little bit. Having learned so much over the last few years though, we're not starting with concepts. That was part of the problem before: we were funding concepts. We're starting much later in the process, and we're making smaller bets. We're putting in more expertise instead of just straight up giving them money.

For instance, we were working with a studio that had a half-finished game. We were funding the final three months of work. It was a game we could play, and we could already tell that the game had a basis for fun. Now, we're giving them a lot of advice on polish and on how to monetize. We feel like we're in a position where we can make sensible choices, and we can recognize what kind of team can make a game that will be a success.

Ramsay: Speaking of success, why did you sell Kongregate to GameStop? The company was doing well, and at first glance, Kongregate doesn't appear to be a good fit for the largest retailer of video games.

Greer: We were just breaking even, actually, and we had to make a decision between growing more and investing in various businesses, like mobile. We were looking to either raise an additional round of funding or consider an acquisition because that made sense then.

We had been fielding acquisition interests for awhile, but we hesitated to agree to any. When GameStop expressed interest, we didn't think much of it. GameStop was a little unexpected. As we got to know them and they got to know us, it made more and more sense. We really appreciated that they believed in Kongregate, the direction we were taking it, and they wanted us to continue to do that in San Francisco.

You look around the Bay Area and you see a lot of acquisitions, where the companies were absorbed into larger companies and you never hear from them again. Google is notorious for this; they invest in the engineering and product teams, but then they throw away the products. That was not the exit we wanted. And once you take funding, you're accepting that at some point, you need to give your investors an exit. We were doing well, but it was clear we weren't going to be an IPO candidate any time soon.

So, what if we sold? We were considering our options, but we were also very much asking, "What would happen to the company and the employees after we sold?" While we were going through the negotiations with GameStop, we came to the conclusion that GameStop was going to be one of the best possible homes for Kongregate as a company. We decided to go ahead and take the deal.

Ramsay: What were your concerns about selling Kongregate?

Greer: It was giving up my baby. That was my biggest concern: losing control of something we'd spent so much time on and invested so much money in. I knew what GameStop and others were telling us. What was being a part of another company going to mean for us on a day-to-day basis? Was what they were telling us correct? Who would I be working with? That has a very big impact on your day. We were also worrying about whether we were selling ourselves short. Were we thinking about selling too early? Those were our biggest concerns.

Ramsay: How did you know when you were ready to sell?

Greer: I don't know if we ever knew we were ready. We were just in a process and the process had a lot of momentum. You jumped on the train or you didn't. I didn't feel terribly ready. I felt pretty nervous about it. I'd made objective lists in my mind that this was going to be a good thing. I could see that, but I still didn't feel ready. And it all happened very fast. I didn't get very much sleep during the process. As part of our due diligence, I had to find every contract we ever signed in the last four years, every financial statement, because we were trying to disclose every potential risk to the company. There was just a tremendous amount of work and worry.

Ramsay: Why did GameStop want to buy Kongregate? Do you know? Retailers don't often look to buy companies like yours.

Greer: How the digital transition would affect GameStop was a big concern for them. They are very familiar with the state of Blockbuster, another Dallas company that was tremendously successful but which was essentially killed by the transition from retail to digital. GameStop is thoughtful about these things, and they were planning for digital in their main business. They were looking to bring in new blood, new companies, and invest in digital. I think they wanted to bring in knowledge of digital distribution. I think that was very much what they had in mind with Kongregate.

GameStop had an investment bank and was working with a guy named Rusty Rueff, who Jim knew from EA, who was introducing them to a lot of companies, including us. They looked at a lot of companies, and they felt we were a good starting point for their digital strategy. That's how they came to make the decision and make the offer.

On the one hand, we're very different, but at our core, we are fairly analogous in that we're both distributors of core games to core gamers. We do it online. They do it in stores. To be frank, I had a background in retail, so it was somewhat comforting to be bought by a retailer. It's a business I understand. For Jim, it was more uncomfortable though.

Ramsay: Well, now, GameStop, a retailer, became a publisher through Kongregate. That's very interesting.

Greer: Ultimately, but at a very, very small scale relative to a company like Activision.

Ramsay: When the deal was struck, what was that moment like?

Greer: It was very overwhelming. I hadn't been on vacation in almost two years, and we had been in negotiations, so when we thought we had hit an impasse, I went to Italy. In the morning of the first day I was in Italy, we got the offer we ended up accepting. The deal took over my vacation. I spent a lot of my vacation on 10:00 PM conference calls with lawyers and investment bankers. I think it is normal in the closing process for there to be one emergency almost every day for a month.

But the moment when that two-inch thick pile of paperwork was in front of us, and we were really doing it, that was both anticlimactic and emotional, if that's possible. We sold Kongregate in 10 minutes in a lawyer's office, and we didn't own it anymore.

It was also strange because it was still very much under wraps. We weren't even able to tell our employees yet, and we couldn't talk to anybody else. I had stayed up all night, gathering signatures from our investors and teaching our father in Italy how to use a scanner via Skype screen share. I was very short on sleep, excited, and a little bit sad altogether.

And then I went and played softball, and got a concussion that night. I was underneath a fly ball, kind of spaced out, and caught it with my face instead of my glove. So, my general advice is "don't play sports after you sell your company! Give it at least 24 hours."

Ramsay: How hard were those 10 minutes in the lawyer's office?

Greer: That was the hardest thing and still one of the harder things. A few years in, GameStop has been a good home for Kongregate. We've doubled our revenue two years in a row, but I still miss being able to decide things. There are still many things I can decide quickly with Jim, but there are things, especially concerning HR and accounting that can't be done that way anymore, and I miss it. But I try to remind myself of all the nights I didn't sleep because I was worrying about the company.

Doug Whatley

Cofounder, BreakAway Games

When Disney bought ABC in 1996, the $19 billion acquisition included OverTime Sports, the studio responsible for bringing ABC Monday Night Football and college football to video games. Only two years later, OverTime Sports was shuttered as Disney sought to exit the video game business.

On that day, former OverTime Sports executive producer **Doug Whatley** and his father-in-law, corporate training executive Joe Biglin, cofounded BreakAway Games, bringing along nine of Whatley's colleagues. At the time, Whatley's goal was to build a small, independent studio focused on sports games. In the intervening years, BreakAway abandoned entertainment.

Working with government agencies, from the United States Department of Education to the Intelligence Community, and major corporations and universities, BreakAway has become a leading developer of serious games that help people learn skills that save lives, successfully respond to natural disasters and terrorist attacks, and lead social change.

Ramsay: I understand you've been in the industry awhile.

Whatley: Here's a quick background. I did some shareware games on my own long, long ago in the early and middle 1980s. And that got me a job working at what became America Online, which was Quantum Computer Corporation back then. I came in to do games, and worked with them on a few initial pilot projects. It just so happened that they had to do a PC version of their online service, and I knew how to program a PC, so I ended up as the lead on America Online software.

I took a job at MicroProse in 1989 and moved up to Baltimore. I worked at MicroProse for seven or eight years, and I ended up as the producer of the sports division. MicroProse did a joint venture with ABC Sports, and I moved over to head up all of the technology for the joint venture. Halfway through the joint venture, ABC Sports bought out MicroProse's part, so one day, we were suddenly working for ABC instead of MicroProse.

A year after that, Disney bought ABC, so I was then suddenly working for Disney. We did that for about a year. In one of the many reorganizations that Disney does, they decided they weren't going to do any more games, and they closed the game studios they had acquired, including us. I took the whole development team from that joint venture, which was then called OverTime Sports, and started BreakAway.

Ramsay: What was your position at MicroProse?

Whatley: I came in as a programmer and ended up in design. Eventually, I became a producer and managed one of the divisions there. When I first started, I worked on a game called Darklands, which was about the only role-playing game that MicroProse ever did. It was actually a very cool game. I worked on Gunship 2000, too. Civilization was being done right then, so I did a little work on that. I then started doing the sports games. We did Ultimate Football, and I also helped manage the UK sports games, including a soccer game and a Formula 1 racing game. I was on the team that did Pacific Air War, but half of us were doing sports games and half of us were doing World War II flight simulators.

Ramsay: When I interviewed MicroProse cofounder Wild Bill Stealey, he talked more about the military games than the others.

Whatley: Right. Him being a pilot, he was very focused on the flight simulators, especially the military sims.

Ramsay: I take it you had a chance to work with Sid Meier?

Whatley: Yeah, that was pretty cool. I got lucky in that when I took the job there, I shared an office with another programmer and we were directly across the hall from Sid's office. We were always trying to horn our way in on everything going on in there.

Ramsay: Was he "The Sid Meier" then?

Whatley: Not really. He was known within the game community, but within MicroProse, he was everything. That was why he got to do what he wanted to do. He was just so respected within MicroProse that they allowed him to eventually put his name on the games.

Ramsay: Wild Bill said that Civilization was Avalon Hill's IP and he—

Whatley: —had to fight them off! Yeah, that is true. Avalon Hill had a game called Civilization that was a board game. MicroProse's Civilization was not that board game ported to the computer, but they both had the same sweep of history and were based on that.

At MicroProse, we hired a bunch of Avalon Hill designers for that very reason. Railroad Tycoon itself came out of the train board games that were around. The train board games were really fun and popular board games, but they were more like big puzzles. You won by figuring out how to best lay out your track compared to everyone else.

What Sid did with that idea though was to put it on the computer and simulate the management side. You had this whole sim where you were making money, figuring out where the raw materials are located, and figuring out how to get them to the market. He just added another layer on top of what the board games did.

The original idea for Civilization came out of the same thinking as in the board game, but over that whole design, he and Bruce Shelley completely re-envisioned it so that it really wasn't the board game. But they did have to fend of Avalon Hill with the lawsuit.

Avalon Hill is located here in Baltimore. We ran in the same community. We knew each other. Everybody at MicroProse played board games, so we knew those guys pretty well. It was funny because the designers at Avalon Hill could care less about the computer game. They thought it was cool, but the owners saw an opportunity to get some money out of somebody.

Ramsay: When did you start developing sports games?

Whatley: Right around that time. I always wanted to do sports games. One of the people we hired was Ed Fletcher, who I still work with today. He was one of the founders of Bethesda Softworks

Ramsay: I thought that name sounded familiar.

Whatley: Yeah, he had developed all of their early games, including Wayne Gretzky Hockey. He loved sports. Both of us are really big football fans. From the earliest days, we were conspiring to get MicroProse to make a football game. As it happened, right when Cal Ripken was breaking records and passing Lou Gehrig in continuous games, and at the height of his popularity, Cal Ripken's agent came to MicroProse to license his name for a baseball game. That was interesting enough for MicroProse to decide they wanted some sports games. We started down that road while they negotiated that license, and then he signed with somebody else.

The baseball game fell through, but that got the ball rolling internally. We took Ed's knowledge of what he had done for the hockey game and built a football engine using that. At that time, MicroProse was really having its biggest problems, and that was right before Spectrum HoloByte came in and bought us. After Darklands and Gunship 2000 shipped, I didn't really have a specific project I was working on. When the sports stuff got going, they just said, "Look, keep working on this football game. We're not going to publish it, but we don't have anything else for you to do."

So, it was just me and one other guy working on this football game. This went on for about nine months. We were tinkering around, being sports geeks, and building a really detailed sports sim rather than trying to finish a game since they had told us it wouldn't be published.

And then, right out of the blue, someone showed up and had the license to use the names of NFL players and coaches. They were looking for somebody to take this license and use it, so MicroProse just decided, "This is a good enough license. We'll ship your game."

Well, this was July and football season started, of course, in August or September, so they said, "Okay, that game you're working on? We're shipping it in a month. Get it cleaned up and let's go." The game was, honestly, not really that much fun. It was a hardcore sim that was something the public wouldn't really want to deal with. We tried to clean the game up and we shipped. It went out as NFL Coaches Club. It actually did pretty well. Not great, but far better than they expected.

Over that time period, Spectrum HoloByte came in and bought MicroProse. They couldn't figure out what to do, so we made the second version. But I think the Coaches Club disbanded, so we didn't have the Coaches Club license. The game would just be called Ultimate Football. Some of the people at ABC Sports really liked it, so they negotiated a deal for us to do a Monday Night Football game for them. That's what led to the joint venture between ABC Sports and MicroProse.

We did another year of Ultimate Football before that deal got done, then two years of Monday Night Football, and then an ABC Sports college football game. I spent six years on football games.

Ramsay: Was Ed working with you?

Whatley: No, Ed was still at MicroProse. Our team was divided in half. I made the football games and he did the Pacific Air War flight sim games. And then when they did the joint venture and spun us off, they just took my half of the team; he stayed with MicroProse and I moved. We were in the same building though. When I ended up working for Disney, we were still in the same offices, but he was still there at MicroProse. He left MicroProse and went for maybe two years up to EA in Vancouver and managed their NBA franchise.

Ed came back to Baltimore and founded what's now Day 1 Studios. It was started up by Hasbro, Tony Parks, and that whole group, but he sold off his part of it and came to work for me here at BreakAway. So, we've worked together for the better part of three decades now.

Ramsay: ABC not hiring Ed doesn't make sense to me. He and Christopher Weaver were responsible for Gridiron, which Chris described to me as "the most realistic physics simulation of football."

Whatley: Yeah. I don't know if I'd quite say that. At the time, it certainly was a great game, but it was back in the days where we played with just X's and O's on the screen. And I made all of those early football games with Ed telling me how he had done Gridiron and Wayne Gretzky Hockey. They actually used the same physics concepts.

Ramsay: Describing Gridiron as "the most realistic physics simulation of football" doesn't make the game sound very fun to me.

Whatley: Actually, it was a hell of a lot of fun! Gridiron was a physics simulation in the sense that on a 2D plane, each of your players had mass and weight. If your guy ran a certain way and into someone else, he would block them, as a simulation of billiard balls would on a table. That was far more realistic than the fake canned plays that Madden did back then. Gridiron was simple enough though to just be a lot of fun.

Ramsay: When did you start up BreakAway Games?

Whatley: So, at the time, Disney was looking to expand its game business and they were buying up studios. I would go around and help them evaluate different ones. In the meantime, we kept doing the sports games, helping with all of that, and we made the Indy Racing game while they built their Indy track at Disney World in Florida. They were thinking that sports would be the next big part of their entertainment empire.

We fit perfectly in Disney's strategy at first, but the sports stuff didn't work out so well and neither did the games. So, they came in one day and said, "Okay, you're being laid off in nine months." We had a long window to shut that place down. Normally, when this happens in the video game business, you'd show up in the morning to the locks having been changed.

The nine months ended in January 1998. On the day I closed the doors to the OverTime Sports studio for them, I filed the paperwork for BreakAway Games. We had plenty of time to plan what we were doing.

Ramsay: What was everyone doing for those nine months?

Whatley: We ramped down and let some people go earlier, but over those nine months, we shipped a college football game, a racing game, and I think we put out some expansion packs for those. We just looked out over the next nine months, figured out what we could do, and delivered games. In a weird way, it kind of really made everyone conscientious of what we were doing. Knowing we were going to start a new business, we wanted the stuff that was being shipped out there to be as good as it could be.

Ramsay: When did you start thinking about starting up your company?

Whatley: Well, I had never thought about it until that time and it just seemed like, "Well, what else are we going to do?" There really weren't any game companies around here. MicroProse had fallen on really hard times. Firaxis was around, but I think they were the only other one. There wasn't a lot to do unless we all moved. It just made sense.

The football game we did was made Sports Game of the Year by a couple of magazines, so we thought we had a perfect opportunity. Almost as soon as we knew we were shutting down, we came up with the idea of starting another company and began talking to people we knew in the industry, trying to line up some contracts. I don't remember the exact details, but we pretty much had it worked out. Bill Stealey had left and gone down to North Carolina where he started Interactive Magic. He had taken a lot of the management and people from MicroProse, so we knew all of them, and almost immediately, we had a contract to do a football game.

We started right up, working on that title. We didn't get very far. We probably worked on it for three or four months, and then Interactive Magic just collapsed, ran out of money, and shut down all of their projects. And then Bill got an investor in down there and they got some more money. But they didn't want to do any sports games, so they signed us to do a new contract for a military game based on the Army Rangers. We worked on that for another nine months until Interactive Magic once again went out of business. Neither game shipped nor got anywhere near to shipping, but it gave us work for our first year.

We were looking for new projects. Having designed some board games myself, I had some ties with the board game community, and I had a contact who was a senior guy at Booz Allen Hamilton who wanted to do some games for the military. He hired us to take some board games he had designed for the military and turn them into computer games. For the first three or four years, that was what BreakAway did—until we started working with Sierra's Impressions studio. They brought us in because of the MicroProse background. They wanted us to do Civil War Generals 3. We started the project, but in one of their reorganizations, they decided that a higher priority was for us to make a follow-up to Pharaoh. We made an expansion pack called Cleopatra: Queen of the Nile. If you just look at what was expected from a game versus how it actually sold or was received, that's probably the most successful game we've ever done. It's amazing how much e-mail we still get every day about Cleopatra.

But that got us into working with Sierra on those real-time strategy history-based city builder games. We worked with them on the Greek themed one and we built Emperor: Rise of the Middle Kingdom. We worked with them on redoing Pharaoh. The Impressions studio was busy with other stuff, so we pretty much took over that line until Sierra died.

Along the way, EA shut down the Jane's flight sim studio located here and I hired all of the people from there. We already had a lot of experience with flight sims, so we started working for Microsoft. Originally, we did a bunch of the artwork for Flight Simulator and Train Simulator, and then we got a contract with them to do Scuba Sim for them. We worked on that for a year and a half and then that whole studio was disbanded. Our partners there moved to a new group within Microsoft that was going to do kids games, so we actually built a city-building community sim. It was very much like The Sims, but more cartoony and targeted at younger kids. But, of course, once again that studio was disbanded. They actually gave us the rights to that game, called Cooligans, and we went out trying to sell it, but as a small publisher, we couldn't get any traction.

With all that experience in real-time strategy, we were brought in by EA as their go-to third-party group for the genre. We worked with them on The Lord of the Rings: Battle for Middle-Earth, the sequel, and the expansion for the sequel. We also made an expansion pack for Command & Conquer 3 and worked on several other games in that series. At the same time, we were working with Firaxis on all of the expansions for Civilization 3.

That led up to about five years ago when it was getting obvious that the entertainment games business was just too volatile. Zynga popped up and things like that were happening. We were so successful with serious games and games for training that we just decided that was a more stable, better business to be in, and we abandoned the entertainment business. We still do little things here and there, but really, we've focused on serious games and probably 80% of what we do now is healthcare training virtual environments and training games for schools. We're doing a biology curriculum that all takes place in a game, and we're working with the Educational Testing Service that does the SATs on games that replace tests. Kids can just get online and play a game, and the game then tells the teacher what level they're at in math, science, and so on.

Ramsay: Were the Booz Allen games part of your entertainment business?

Whatley: The Booz Allen games were our first serious games. They were more like turn-based strategy though with huge environments. We were taking data for all of Asia, turning it into the map, and mapping thousands of units in combat, fighting in that environment. It was actually used by the Army to run a lot of their big war games when they studied new concepts.

Ramsay: After so many years of developing entertainment properties, what did you think of fully dedicating your company to serious games?

Whatley: It made perfect sense. At MicroProse, we talked a lot with the military about using games for training. When we were working with ABC Sports, we talked with NFL teams about using our games for training and analysis. The idea that people would use games for real purposes was always floating around.

All of us were doing games then because this was the place where the most innovation was happening. Everyone was a really good programmer, artist, whatever, and we needed that creative outlet. The video game business really let us push the envelope, and we started thinking, "Wow, wouldn't it be cool if you could use games to replace textbooks? Wow, wouldn't it be cool if businesses used games for training?"

It was then really cool to actually step in with the military, get our clearances, and go build classified scenarios and study what would happen. While BreakAway was obviously started to be a business, we were excited by the opportunity. How can we go find places that don't yet realize the power of games? Can we convince them to use games to change the world? We were quite idealistic. That was what inspired BreakAway.

Ramsay: You weren't the sole founder?

Whatley: My other cofounder was my father-in-law, Joe Biglin, and he had nothing to do with the game industry; he was in corporate training. He had been saying to me for a long time, "I'd love to use these games in corporate training." And so that was all part of where we saw it going.

Ramsay: You started the company with a subject matter expert?

Whatley: Right. Exactly.

Ramsay: Did you have any experience with starting businesses?

Whatley: No. No, I knew nothing about it. It's shocking how naïve I was.

Ramsay: What about your father-in-law?

Whatley: He came out of business and had a MBA. He had a lot of the accounting training and capabilities that could really help. I'd have never survived without him knowing a lot of that stuff, but he certainly had no idea entrepreneurially what it was like to start a business. Luckily, he was able to fall back on his accounting and MBA knowledge to figure out how we should do the paperwork and get things rolling.

Ramsay: What did you think you'd have to do to get things rolling?

Whatley: What I thought we had to do was demonstrate to one of the game publishers that we had a good enough development team to create games for them. That's a big part of anything in the video game industry: convincing them you've got the team that can execute on a vision. In terms of making a business successful, that actually had little to do with it.

We wrote up a business plan when we first got started and planned things out through five years. When years later I found that business plan and looked at it, the numbers matched exactly where we were in the fifth year. We had about the same number of people, we had about the same amount of revenue we had projected, and everything matched the numbers, but when you looked at the plan for what we were going to do, there was absolutely nothing we had done that was the same.

Ramsay: Nothing at all? What was different?

Whatley: Well, we started thinking that with the strength we had in doing sports games, we were going to start off doing sports games. In the first year, we'll do this football game. In the second year, we'll do a basketball game. In the third year, we'll do a baseball game. We'll grow this way because each of those sports games is done annually. By the fifth year, we'd be doing historical real-time strategy games, and we'd be creating simulations for the Army. The skill sets and the people we needed for sports and serious games were completely different, and we had historians and experts on the military working for us as opposed to anyone in sports.

Ramsay: You planned to focus on developing sports games despite the fact that your cofounder had experience with corporate training?

Whatley: I didn't say we were smart about it. That's my point exactly. We had a sense of what games could do, but we didn't honestly believe people would pay us to do it. We thought people would pay us to do sports games, so the business plan was based on what we thought people would pay us for. We had a dream that we'd be doing these other things; the sports games didn't get funded, but the dream actually did.

One reason we never got more of the sports contracts was that companies like EA signed exclusive licenses with the NFL, so nobody else could do those games. There were barriers like that thrown up along what we thought would be the easiest path to success.

When we started talking to people in the military, we found that while we thought we had such a radical idea of using games for training, they had already figured that out. The people in the military were already seeing their kids playing games and going, "Hey, why don't we use these for training?" It wasn't such a hard sell for us to get in there and do the thing that we thought would be next to impossible.

Ramsay: When did you start building your team?

Whatley: We had about five people who came from the ABC Sports team. What ended up happening was that five-person team worked on the game contracts we had, I did all the programming for the military, and I would just pull in the artists when I needed some art. My father-in-law was out doing business development, going to conferences and trade shows and figuring out places that might be interested in using games.

Ramsay: You had a small team. Was everyone being paid?

Whatley: No, but it wasn't too bad in the first year. We had the contract to do the football game for Interactive Magic that paid the team for awhile, and then there was the Army Ranger game which paid them for awhile. So, they were working on those products that never actually shipped, but they were getting paid. There were gaps when we had to find something else and that was when we were backfilling with the military work. I was also able to do most of the programming for the military for the first two years.

Ramsay: Were you bootstrapping? Did you and Joe put in some of your own money to get going?

Whatley: We were bootstrapping. We put in a few hundred thousand dollars each.

Ramsay: That's a pretty good amount of starting capital.

Whatley: It is. I was lucky because I was at America Online.

Ramsay: You came out well from AOL then?

Whatley: Yeah, I mean, for working there for a couple of years and doing programming, I had no idea. When I left, they weren't public yet, and I left with a few hundred shares of stock I just assumed would never be worth anything. When they actually went public, they multiplied the number of shares into way more than that very quickly. I didn't get rich, but I had a nice nest egg that bought me a house and gave me money to bootstrap my own company.

Ramsay: And you decided to use the rest on developing sports games?

Whatley: Yeah, I didn't say I was smart.

Ramsay: When you said that you worked on sports games for six years, I caught a hint of exasperation.

Whatley: Well, actually, it was great. I love tinkering around building sports games or just building games, so it was great fun, but the stress of every year having to ship a football game did get to me after awhile.

Ramsay: What about the culture around sports games?

Whatley: That actually is a lot of fun. Working for ABC Sports and doing Monday Night Football have to be the best perks in the world. We used to get to go to every Monday Night game. I went to several Super Bowls and met all kinds of celebrities and sports figures. Great perks.

In the video game industry, people tend to gravitate toward games they like, so we drew people in who were really big sports fans, who were into simulating sports and building that experience in a game. We had a great group of people who were really into football. We had had some really good times. That whole time period was a lot of fun.

Ramsay: Other than a few hundred thousand dollars, what else did you give up to start this company? Did you have a family?

Whatley: At that time, I just had a wife, and she was in the video game business, too. We met at MicroProse. She worked at a few different companies, including Bethesda Softworks and Empire Interactive, where she was head of marketing for a year and a half. She worked with John Smedley when they had a co-marketing deal with Sony. She was working out of Bethesda Softworks and I was getting BreakAway started with her dad. My wife wasn't as much into games as I was, but she came out of the business. She knew what we were getting into, but it can be hard on the family and everything.

Ramsay: Do you have any regrets about the way you started?

Whatley: Yeah, although most of them are more about business than about the creative side. I wasn't much of a businessman. A lot of the bureaucratic details, rules, and the decisions you make about how you set up the company were… well, we were very lackadaisical. I was very lackadaisical about a lot of that. It always ended up becoming a problem for some reason or another. You need to pay attention to the business. If you don't and you actually survive for awhile, that'll come back to get you.

Ramsay: Can you describe a problem that arose out of your lethargy?

Whatley: Well, when we started, we were deciding on the parameters for hiring people. We made the decision that everyone would start with two weeks of vacation, and for every two years of employment, you'd get another week of vacation. That was how we put it in the employee plan.

Well, we've now been around over 17 years and a couple of our people are still here. It's unrealistic for an employee to have 12 weeks of vacation. Even if you want to reward them, there are other ways. It was a mistake to not think ahead about how that rule would play out for long-term employees.

Along the way, we had to redo that, and when you have to change something like that, you have to go to your most valued people and say, "Look, we made a mistake and we've got to take away a couple of weeks of vacation from you and figure out a way to reward you in a different way."

What was supposed to be a reward for our best employees ended up becoming a problem. Just as a practical matter, you can't run a business and give everyone that much vacation time in the long run. That's just one thing I'm sure someone who had more experience would have caught when we made our plan.

Ramsay: How involved was your cofounder with the business side?

Whatley: Very. I was much more focused on programming and doing game design. For the first five years or so, he really ran the office, the business, did the books, and everything else to keep the business growing.

Ramsay: Did he eventually leave?

Whatley: Yeah, he is running his own business that he started separately now. At the time, it came down to him wanting to go after the corporate market, and make serious games for corporate training. He thought that was a really great use for games. But we weren't ready. We didn't have the revenue to just go try to take over a new market. So, he went off to do what he wanted to do and started his own business, but we agreed that if he landed a deal where he needed programmers and artists, we'd step in and do the work.

Ramsay: When you talked to Joe initially about him starting this company with you, did you have to convince him?

Whatley: Not really. He was excited about what games could do. We probably didn't talk enough about what that meant upfront. I didn't have to convince him to do it, but I also don't think we discussed enough what our expectations were.

Ramsay: Did you discuss clearly dividing up your responsibilities?

Whatley: I wouldn't say there was a discussion that led to clear division of responsibilities. I said, "I'm going to do the development and you're going to do the business side. Let's go." But the first contract that came along was an entertainment contract. He had never actively done a contract with a game company, and although I'm a development person, I had been involved in negotiating contracts with entertainment game publishers. I ended up doing the contract. So, right from the beginning, we had subverted the division of labor. I did a lot of the business development because I came out of the video game industry. I had all of the contacts with game publishers. But I couldn't really do business development for corporate training, so he had to do that instead of me. We ended up taking tasks based on who was better positioned, and that just led to more and more confusion.

Ramsay: Your expectations for this company were based on having been part of companies before. How did the reality match up?

Whatley: I think the reality generally matched up. We got an initial contract to do a sports game. We weren't sure what the publisher was going to do, but we knew they were having trouble, so we used temporary office space for three or six months. We just moved in there and started working, never even thinking about what it means to actually have an office or whether we looked professional.

We had such a developer's mindset that it was like, "Okay, we've got a contract. Let's start programming. This place will let us put our chairs in and start working, so let's do it. Let's go." In retrospect, we could have done a lot better if we had put out a more professional image, if we had a website, if we had coherent e-mail addresses, and if we just appeared to be more stable. When you're a developer, you just think that all clients will care about is whether you're a good developer. You don't think you need to show that you're professional.

Ramsay: You've done all sorts of different contracts for entertainment and serious games. Do you develop any original properties?

Whatley: Yes, we have, and we would have liked to have done more, but we never had the security, the bankroll, or the willingness to take the risk and put a lot of effort in. If you're going to spend your own money to create what it takes to land a bigger deal, that's a big risk. And that's part of the reason we're still around. We haven't taken those risks.

Ramsay: Are you content with the client-agency model?

Whatley: I wouldn't say we're content, but I don't believe that creating your own IP from scratch and convincing someone to publish it will work. What would work would be a more collaborative relationship with a publisher, where together you create IP that you can own and turn into a real product line.

Ramsay: When did your serious games business take off?

Whatley: Our government work started as early as 1998 and that business grew and grew over the next six years. But that was more government contracting than serious games. In late 2003, we were actively pitching game development to government agencies and organizations in other industries. We were consciously trying to use games to solve specific problems. That's when I think we were really doing serious games.

We were still doing mostly military work, but we were also working with the Department of Justice and the Department of Homeland Security. We made our first healthcare games for the government. That business jumped us into the commercial and education spaces by 2007.

Ramsay: Do you remember your first serious games pitch?

Whatley: We were approached by the Department of Justice. I don't even know how we got in touch with them, but they came to us and set up a meeting with some of their people. I went in and pitched them on using real-time strategy to teach. After 9/11, one of the biggest problems people identified was interagency communication and crisis response, so the DOJ created the National Incident Management System (NIMS) Protocol. They tried to standardize it across the country. We had heard about this. The DOJ were trying to convince fire, police, and county governments and everything else across the country to adopt the NIMS standard.

So, I pitched them on using a real-time strategy game where the players would be firemen, policemen, or the mayor all playing a real-time strategy game together. I convinced a couple of people from the local fire and police, and some people from the DOJ, to just meet us at a restaurant. We sat around, had appetizers, and I pitched this idea to them and they actually liked it. I think it was probably a year later that one of them actually found some funding to allow us to create that first game.

Ramsay: I expected to hear that your first pitches didn't go well.

Whatley: There were some that didn't. But I think more of them succeeded than failed. In the past, everyone would say that what they do is really serious and not a game, so they weren't going to do something frivolous—even after you explained that games have been used for centuries to practice very serious things like war.

But that's the natural response from most people looking at change. We often found a champion within an organization who really understood what we were saying about games. They'd get all passionate and pitch it, but they'd come up against the same roadblocks. We'd have organizations ready to adopt our proposal, and then somebody would just kill the deal because they just didn't understand why anyone was doing anything with games.

Originally, our company's name was BreakAway Games. We actually had to go back and legally change that to just BreakAway Limited. We still have a break-awaygames.com website, but we also have a breakawayltd.com website. Ten years ago, a lot of government computers actually had filters that would block websites when the word "game" came up.

Ramsay: I can't imagine an agency like the Department of Justice calling anyone up and saying, "Hey, we want to do a video game." What do you think motivated their interest in video games?

Whatley: Generally, somebody in the organization who is into games themselves understands how they can be used, or they saw their kids using games and thought they could use games, too. They usually convinced their organization to study the idea. I doubt we'd have ever closed a deal with any of those groups if we didn't have an internal champion. We didn't always know who our champion was, but there's always somebody.

Ramsay: How many of your clients came to you?

Whatley: I'm guessing three quarters of our clients approached us. We do a good job of getting our name out there. When people decide to make a game, they call us. We're at least in the position that we'll get the first call.

Ramsay: Do you try to provide ways to help people champion your expertise within those organizations?

Whatley: We make ourselves very easy to get a hold of, but we also work closely with researchers, write and present white papers at conferences, help support the scientific validity of using games for training, and show that there have been very serious uses of games.

For example, Incident Commander, the game we made for the DOJ, was shipped to 100,000 municipalities and organizations. The DOJ just sent copies to every county police and fire department with a letter saying, "You might use this to better understand how to use the NIMS Protocol."

We set up a website where people who were playing could share their stories and ask us questions. A paramedic had played the game and was sent to assist with the response to Hurricane Katrina. He was sent down to Baton Rouge, Louisiana, into the disaster area as part of a group that had to set up a temporary 800-bed hospital. The hospitals in the area had been wiped out. He later wrote a letter to the DOJ. It was very detailed. He said that, if he hadn't played our game, he would never have known how to start from scratch, to set up a hospital, and to keep that hospital working.

Obviously, we took that letter, contacted him, got more details, and made that story as widely available as we could to show people that games can actually save lives, make things better, and be really effective.

Ramsay: Could you explain how doing business with the government is different from the typical developer-publisher relationship?

Whatley: The first difference is the bureaucracy of contracting and the rule system. The Federal Acquisition Regulations (FAR) rule everything. In a regular entertainment deal with a publisher, everyone wants to get the game on the store shelves. If somebody screws up the paperwork, the publisher will say "Oh, well. We'll figure that out and get it cleaned up, but let's keep moving." That doesn't ever happen with the government. The bureaucracy rules. Every "T" must be crossed. Every "I" must be dotted.

Doing business with the government is very hard, and learning how to work that environment has taken us a lot of time. Understanding contracting is one of the biggest reasons for our success when we compete with other game companies for the same business. Our experience with the bureaucracy gives us a big advantage.

The second difference is that, in the commercial environment, you can ask people who buy your game in the store, "What features do you want? What do you like about it? What do you not like about it?" You can get a sense what the market wants. When you're working with the government, there's a reason they've come to you. There's a problem they're solving, there's

they have, and there are regulations they have to follow. But just what needs to be done in the game isn't always clear. It's a lot harder to know what you have to do to be a success when you're working with the government.

Ramsay: There's a bidding process for winning government contracts. Do you always bid on the contracts you get?

Whatley: Almost always. We have to do that. For some of the smaller projects, you can get a contract without it being put out for bid, but for anything sizeable, the regulations force agencies to put out requests for proposals (RFP), so you have to learn to play that game.

Ramsay: How do you find contracts?

Whatley: If you go to FedBizOpps and just search for "game", there are two things you'll find. First, you'll get confused by the national parks looking for game wardens, and then the second thing is that the military hires a lot of people like referees for kids' soccer games. But if you ignore those two things, you will find quite a few contracts listed.

You can search places like FedBizOpps, but to succeed, you need to spend the time doing business development, going to the users, and getting to know what they need. That's true for the government just like any industry.

Ramsay: With a term like *request for proposal*, I would assume that when an organization comes to you about a contract, they're interested in you placing a bid. They're not actually offering you a contract yet?

Whatley: Correct. Usually, the government and large organizations are required to get multiple bids on any project. The RFP isn't an offer of a contract. You still have to compete and win the contract. There are multiple steps to the process. We'll get a call and someone will say, "We think a game would help us do something." We'll tell them our opinion about the best way to do it, what type of product needs to be done, and then at some point, we'll get a message saying, "Okay, that thing we were talking about? Next month, it'll show up as an RFP coming out of some agency." For military business, there are different Program Executive Offices (PEO) which put out RFPs and manage contracts.

Once a job gets to that level and into that bureaucracy, the people who want it done are no longer involved. The contracting group takes over. But you'll now know to be looking for something, and when the RFP comes out, you'll respond, hopefully, in the best way possible.

Ramsay: How's the competition for these contracts?

Whatley: Pretty heated, actually. You have to know what you're doing. You need to know what the customer wants to win any significant number of them. All the business development we do is to better understand how to respond to RFPs because there's a good amount of competition.

Ramsay: For most people, government contracting is confusing. Can you demystify the process?

Whatley: No!

Ramsay: No? Well, what happens after you make a bid?

Whatley: What I always tell people about government contracting is that the process is divided up to try to ensure that no one defrauds the government. That's probably their ultimate concern: they don't ever want to get snookered on a bad contract or something. There are all kinds of rules about that, and because of that, they separate everything out.

So, you'll work with people who have a problem, who have a need, who want a product. You'll figure out what they need and plan everything out. And then they'll hand off the job to the contracting people who will write up an RFP, post it, evaluate the proposals, and then decide who wins. And not only do those contracting people not know anything about you, but they don't know anything about the people with the problem. All they do is contracts. Whether you win the contract boils down to how closely your proposal matches the RFP, and you hope the RFP matches what the ultimate client actually needs.

There are really two sides to contracting: one side is getting to know the clients, learning about their problem, gaining their trust, and all of those things you do with normal business development; and the other side is realizing that the paperwork has to be perfect. No matter how well you do business development, if you don't do the response well, you're not going to be awarded that contract. I wouldn't say there's a lot of mystery to it, but it involves a lot of work and time.

Ramsay: When you're first approached before there's an RFP, are you effectively consulting on a project?

Whatley: Yeah.

Ramsay: So, you could end up in a situation where you spend a lot of money on consulting and end up not getting the contract?

Whatley: Correct.

Ramsay: Has that ever happened to you?

Whatley: Yes. Yes, absolutely. More than once.

Ramsay: How big of a hit do you take?

Whatley: A couple of times, we've taken really big hits. For really big government contracts, there will be a couple of years when they're out there talking to people, getting everything in place, putting out the RFP, giving everyone six months to respond, and then picking a winner. For the winner to receive an award notification, that's on average in the four to five months range, so the whole process can be a two- or three-year cycle. The contracts that are awarded are, at base, one-year contracts, but they can put option years on them, so they will often be four-, five-, or six-year contracts. Landing one of those can set your business up for a long time. When you work for a couple of years to get one of those, and then it doesn't happen, it is quite devastating.

Ramsay: How many contracts are you typically bidding on at any one time?

Whatley: In terms of fairly sizeable ones, three to five. There are times when there are smaller contracts like Small Business Innovation Research (SBIR) programs that come out. At times, we can end up doing seven or eight in a very short period, but they're generally smaller responses.

Ramsay: Sounds like enough work to sustain a game developer?

Whatley: Yeah, there's definitely enough. There's enough for quite a few companies; not just us.

Ramsay: It's surprising because this isn't a world you really hear about, unless you go to the serious games conferences.

Whatley: Right. There's a lot out there. There's defense, Homeland Security, the whole Intelligence Community, the Department of Education, the Department of Labor—and all of them have their own needs and they're doing some level of requisition. Across the government, there are quite a number of RFPs posted every year.

Ramsay: What does the government call video games now?

Whatley: These days, they sometimes call them games, but more often than not, they'll call them simulations. Simulation is a more acceptable term.

Ramsay: I know the simulation contracts sometimes involve hardware. Do you bid on only the software contracts?

Whatley: Yeah, although if a war college wants to build a new sim center, create a new training sim, and build a curriculum around it, it's not unusual for us to put together a team with a prime defense contractor who can manage a big project, a hardware manufacturer to build the machines and equipment, and a university or a training group to create the curriculum. We wouldn't do the hardware, but we'd be on the team.

Ramsay: What role do you typically play on that team?

Whatley: It varies. Sometimes the team just needs a game developer to sit in and advise. If game development is a minimal part of the proposal, then they just tell us, "Okay, you guys sit here, so we can show the client we have a game company on board," and I go sit in the back of the room to wave the flag. If the proposal is very focused on the game, they'll put us front and center, and my job will be to use my game credentials to convince the client that the team can actually deliver on a fun, real game.

Ramsay: At BreakAway, what's your role? I know you're the head honcho, but do you work on the creative side as well?

Whatley: I no longer work day to day on any one project usually. I will drop in and check on things occasionally just to help out, but I do business development, meet with the clients and learn their problems, and then I can design the game conceptually. I can map out technically how it will work. In a way, I'm the chief technology officer and chief game design officer. That is necessary to write up the proposals and pitch concepts to clients, but once we get a contract and get to work, we have great developers and designers who take over from there.

Ramsay: Speaking as the chief game design officer, are serious games fun?

Whatley: Occasionally, they are not fun in a classic game sense. They are always fun in a way to achieve their goal, or, at least they are engaging. For example, we did a game called A Force More Powerful, which is used around the world to teach how to organize nonviolent resistance movements. The game is very engaging. Once you get into the game, you're in the middle of trying to overthrow a regime. You have to manage your whole movement, the personalities of other people you are working with, play politician, and deal with the press. It's like playing Civilization. You can just get sucked in by everything you're doing and it's a lot of fun. But it takes hours to get to know all of the information as you get into the scenario, and that isn't classic game fun.

Ramsay: How do you measure whether a game has achieved its purpose?

Whatley: The clients will do studies and, many times, they'll tell us to bring in 50 people, test them, and have them play the game, test them again, and find out whether they learned something. Most projects start by defining the learning objectives; success is determined by that metric. After many studies the client will publish a paper validating that the game achieved its purpose.

Ramsay: In my opinion, the defining characteristic of a game is interactivity. If the player can't do something and receive feedback, there's no game. Do you build any feedback loops into your games to determine whether players are learning what they need to learn?

Whatley: I have a couple of quick answers to that. We use AI to identify whether players are not doing the right things and we can pop up a dialog box that says, "Hey, you're forgetting something. You're a doctor and your patient is dying here. You never checked his airway to see if he's choking on something." That's what the education people call "scaffolding." That is most definitely a feedback loop.

When we're trying to teach people, scaffolding is very important so we can teach them things along the way. It's not unlike a help system in a regular game. The first time you sit down to play Halo, the game says "hey, point your gun over here" and "the A button does this." You learn the whole system along the way and we do the same thing, except we're teaching them about their real job or subject in school.

The after-action review is also very important, especially in team building games where everyone plays through something and then it stops and says, "Okay, here's what you all did, here's what you did right, and here's what you could have done." We spent a lot of time on those as well. That is a larger feedback loop that can be used within an educational setting.

Many training games require very detailed feedback loops. The game visuals and the user interface are core to the success of a product. If the patient doesn't exhibit the symptoms a doctor would look for to successfully diagnose a condition, the game isn't any good for training or assessment, so the visual and auditory feedback loops are of primary importance.

The user interface is also important because we need to keep the user engaged and immersed, but we also need to provide the necessary feedback that a person would have in the real world. The training needs to transfer to real-world skills and not just teach them how to play a game.

Ramsay: How are your serious games used?

Whatley: Many games are used to teach people, but they're also used for analysis and idea generation. For example, we might create a sandbox military simulation so that someone can test how a situation might change if a UAV could fly twice as high and twice as fast. They can play around with those ideas very easily. They might find out that a UAV that can fly twice as high and twice as fast doesn't actually help, so why should they spend billions of dollars on developing faster UAVs when that technology doesn't change the battle space? I made all that up, but that's how our games might allow people to play around with ideas.

We also use serious games to assess people and their skills. These days, you can often play a game instead of taking a test, and we will actually be better able to assess your level or whether you're learning than paper tests.

Ramsay: Are you familiar with the work of Ian Bogost?

Whatley: Absolutely.

Ramsay: Ian says that he develops serious games as communication media instead of as tools. The purpose of their games is not to simulate action or test decisions; the purpose of their games is learning. How are your serious games different from his serious games?

Whatley: You can think of his as Tetris and ours as Civilization. The reason I make that comparison is he wants you to play for five, ten, or 15 minutes and get a message or experience a new viewpoint. Our games are almost never quick sound bite things. You have to immerse yourself in them and look at big concepts. We don't have a message we're trying to communicate. We have a system we want you to understand. You can tinker and see how your actions within the system change things. Ian's games might have you consider a different perspective on the impact of a free market economy, whereas we would create a game that simulated that economy. There's great value in what each of us do.

Ramsay: What other types of serious games are there?

Whatley: There are simpler training games, like Reader Rabbit or something that's just going to drill you on vocabulary or math skills. Throughout that whole spectrum, from rote facts to big concepts, there are different types of games that help you learn and train more efficiently.

Ramsay: How much is networking part of the games you develop?

Whatley: Now, all of them are online. The cloud is a big part of the main deployment mechanism. But many of our games are sandbox simulations of large systems that are impacted in many ways by multiplayer more than anything else. In hospitals, fire, police, and the military, responding to a crisis is all about people coordinating their actions to get the best response.

Online is hugely important for us being able to do something that has never been done. In the past, to have a town practice responding to a tornado, you pretty much had to shut down the town. All of the hospitals and personnel, every fire and policeman, every public and every fire and policeman, and every public works person had to take the day, not do their real job, and pretend they were responding to some incident.

Anyone who is not working a shift can practice responding to a tornado like it's their real job, but in a distributed multiplayer environment, we can now provide a venue for large groups and organizations to practice skills and procedures in a way that wasn't practical in the past. Multiplayer is changing the way a lot of organizations do training.

Ramsay: Do you operate your multiplayer games on your servers?

Whatley: Sometimes. Sometimes we put them out in the cloud, like Amazon EC2 or Microsoft Azure. There is often a good reason to put these things out in the cloud because, for security reasons, we can't put them on client servers. We like to operate these games somewhere where clients can get to them and have control of them without having to go through the process of installing and securing a server. But if setting up and maintaining a server helps the client, we'll provide that for them.

Ramsay: Is hosting a separate business for you?

Whatley: Not really. In the future, it could be, but it's not necessarily a long-term solution. If we're going to set up a server for someone, it's usually because we can do it faster. By the time they get their server up nine months later, they can transfer everything over. Hosting is not an ongoing business, but it's something we have to do to enable our clients to be able to get things working more efficiently.

Ramsay: When did your corporate training business take off?

Whatley: That really didn't take off until 2010. Some corporations had dabbled, but a few years ago, there was a real turning point. They quit showing up at conferences to check on things and started actually spending money.

Ramsay: Why were corporate clients slower to adopt serious games?

Whatley: As you'd expect, the corporate world is focused on the bottom line. If a company sees a product that can improve their bottom line, they'll buy it. They're not really into doing the research to figure out what would work. A big company will pay any amount for a product that'll make them money, speed them up, or make them more efficient, but they're not funding research to come up with new technologies to do that. The corporate world wants to be able to pop in, buy something, and implement it next month. Those of us who were creating serious games just weren't ready with products for them to do that, and government and healthcare organizations needed five-year projects just to see if something works.

Ramsay: How weren't you ready?

Whatley: Five years ago, if I had a client who wanted to teach addition to their employees, I'd have said, "I can create a game that teaches addition to your employees, but you have to fund the development of the whole game." Today, if they show up, I can say, "I have a game that teaches addition. How do you want the game customized for your employees?" We just didn't have the technology ready to be turnkey for many clients.

Their upfront investment is minimal because all we're doing is customizing the game to the specific content they want, not creating the software from scratch. They're perfectly happy to just pay for a license to use what we already have. What we have has already been used by other people, so they're confident we can quickly turn around a solution that'll work.

Ramsay: When you deliver a product to a government organization, does the government own that product?

Whatley: Not technically. You just can't charge the government again. There have been cases where when the government funds something, that product becomes public domain. These days, they try to encourage you to take ownership. There's what's called government purpose rights. For example, if the U.S. Army funds a training tool, the U.S. Army can now use that training tool for free forever. It's theirs and they get any updates we make to it. They will never be charged another penny, but we can sell that training tool to anyone outside the government. They want us to do that because they want us to continue maintaining the product.

Ramsay: Unless the product is classified.

Whatley: True.

Ramsay: Have you ever developed classified games?

Whatley: Yes, we have.

Ramsay: And that's as much as you can tell me?

Whatley: We have all of our security clearances and everything because we do that type of work all the time.

Ramsay: How much trouble was getting your employees cleared?

Whatley: It takes time. I wouldn't say it's a lot of trouble, but it takes a lot of time to get a lot of people through. We've probably got close to 30 employees who are cleared.

Ramsay: Out of how many employees?

Whatley: 45.

Ramsay: You're a pretty small studio then?

Whatley: Yeah. We're probably medium as they go. For a large chunk of our lifetime, we had between 100 and 120 employees, but entertainment games will have 75 people on a team. Serious games are smaller. Serious game teams are more in the 15- to 20-person range.

Ramsay: What's your team composition like?

Whatley: A third of the team is art, a third is programming, and a third is design. We do a lot of design. In that category, I include documentation and scenario creation because we have to learn so much about the subject matter. We're probably heavier than your standard game developer in design. And we're probably lighter in art because, although the quality of the art has to be as high, we don't need as much art content.

Ramsay: What do you mean by that?

Whatley: If you buy an entertainment game, you're going to want a hundred hours of entertainment. You'll want enough scenarios that are different, so you have to create artwork for a snow world, a desert world, a forest world, and for each of the different levels. When we're training the military how to work in Afghanistan, we just need Afghanistan, so we don't create as much artwork for each product as we otherwise would.

Ramsay: Your company is in a position where you get the first call when customers need your expertise. I imagine that you can pick and choose your projects. How do you select what you want to work on?

Whatley: There isn't a specific methodology. It really comes down to evaluating whether we have a chance to win a contract. Is the product something that will fit our plans for our technology roadmap? Or will the product match up to the types of technology we maintain?

If the RFP is so far outside the box of things we're good at, or if we don't think we have a good chance of succeeding, we won't put in the effort. We're also often working on multiple proposals at once and they take a lot of work, so we have to decide whether we can take on more work.

Ramsay: You don't have a driving interest in a particular type of project?

Whatley: We are interested in games. There are a lot of things like gamification that don't strictly involve building a game which we'll do occasionally, but we're not going to sign a contract to help a grocery store chain gamify their coupons. That's just not of interest to us. We like games where we can build a system you can engage with.

Ramsay: Serious games have genres, too. Is there a genre you like?

Whatley: Our strength is strategy, real-time and turn-based. We do strategy best and gravitate toward those projects. Any game where we have the whole hospital working, you're playing multiplayer, and you're managing a crisis is perfect for us because that's a real-time strategy game where we're using a hospital as a base. However, we also frequently do first-person games for healthcare, where you're moving around in a 3D environment and interacting with patients. That isn't as near-and-dear to what we like to do, but it's a strength of ours.

Ramsay: When I spoke with Wild Bill he said that for a game company to be successful, the company needs to be known for doing one thing really well. But you've been around for awhile and you're generalists.

Whatley: Well, I would point out to Bill that he was known initially for flight sims, but in the later years, Civilization, X-COM, and Railroad Tycoon made the MicroProse name. I can understand his point that, as a sales organization, building a business is easier when you're known for something, but MicroProse succeeded because they allowed their designers to work on what they were passionate about. That's how we are. We're all over the map, but we wanted to do work on each of the games we've made.

Ramsay: What are your thoughts about gamification?

Whatley: It's a fad. It can be useful, and it's not that there's never value to it, but gamification rarely has the depth of value of a real game. The reason why elements of gamification work in games is because you like the game and they are the icing on the cake, not because they are the game.

Ramsay: A client comes to you; they want gamification. What do you say?

Whatley: Why do you want that? What are you trying to achieve? We can discuss how gamification would or would not achieve that goal. In most cases, I'd argue that gamification will not achieve what they want; at least, gamification will not be long-term solution. Gamification absolutely works if the underlying system is actually fun and engaging. I can easily imagine that a lot of people are hugely into coupons, but you're not going to make doing taxes fun because you give a few badges away on a website. But there are all kinds of systems in the world that some types of people just like.

Ramsay: What can games be used for that they aren't being used for now?

Whatley: We've just finished working with a group on a game that treats depression. It's just a role-playing game, but the game teaches life skills for dealing with depression. Some of the fantasy storylines play into having a positive attitude and fighting against having a negative attitude. Using games this way has not really been thoroughly explored yet. It's very interesting to see how you can use immersion to treat behavioral issues.

We've also seen computer and board games used for crisis and family counseling. If you sit a family down in front of a counselor, they might not want to make themselves look bad, but if you get people competing in a game, they'll lower their guard and their real personalities will come out.

This works for teaching leadership, teamwork, communication, consensus building, and creative thinking. Games can teach those things far better than anything else we have right now. It's not like you can just take a game, have someone play it, and suddenly they're a leader, but games can be tailored to develop those skills. There's a really exciting future ahead of us, where games can be put to use in places we haven't thought of yet.

Ramsay: How is a game that teaches leadership and communication different from, for example, a competitive online role-playing game that involves guild leadership and raid team communication?

Whatley: I don't actually think there is a significant difference in the things you do. In World of Warcraft, a natural leader can start a guild, get people organized, and lead them on a raid and succeed. But that's using their natural leadership within the game environment. Games that teach are different in that they create opportunities for the player to test their own leadership skills, put them in the position where they have to take charge, and help them hone their leadership abilities. It's not that the gameplay is any different; it's that there is a hidden hand, guiding people to exercise the skills that they might not already be using.

Ramsay: In a virtual world, you have the option to start a guild but that's a choice you can make. In a serious game, that's a choice you have to make?

Whatley: In a serious game, it is a choice you are taught to make. The serious game succeeds if it can show you a new and hopefully better way.

Ramsay: There's an organization in San Diego called The Virtual Reality Medical Center. They use games to treat phobias and traumas.

Whatley: Yeah, they've done fear of spiders and all kinds of things. Yeah, I'm very aware of them and they've done some great work. But that's not the gameplay itself changing you; that's using the sights and sounds to help someone. That's all very valuable and I don't want to put a negative spin on what they're doing. I think as we begin to actually use the gameplay to bring out subtler skills and emotions, and help people refine those skills and emotions, we'll see really exciting uses that go beyond using exposure therapy to help patients practice coping.

Ramsay: How is what you're suggesting different from games that use exposure therapy? Are the differences mechanical, or superficial?

Whatley: They're usually not superficial. One of the age-old tricks or cheats of developing entertainment games is we simplify things that aren't fun. Civilization can make up its own definitions for democracy and communism, but a serious game can't unwind those things. They need to be as real as we can simulate, and we have to design a game that's engaging without simplifying the player's experience. Those differences can't be superficial. At the same time, the setting in which you use the game is important to achieving the purpose, and sometimes the same game mechanisms can be used in different ways to achieve different things.

Ramsay: What are the challenges of creating those games right now?

Whatley: Any game costs a lot of money and not everyone's willing to put up that amount of money for something they haven't seen concrete proof that it does what you say it can do. You need to find some real advocates who are willing to try something and do a prototype. But the actual implementation is a major chasm we all have to cross. The time and expense to get from nothing to something makes it hard to get started. That's going to be true for the next few years as all of us create these games and prove they do what we say they do. So, we need patience.

Ramsay: Why don't you go out now and develop a proof of concept?

Whatley: We're doing that. We've created games that teach and educate. We now have several of them in schools, testing that they teach what we said they teach. But that takes awhile because if you're teaching leadership, for instance, you need to not only create the product and then run some people through it, but then you need to see if their leadership is better.

Ramsay: Has your role changed over the years?

Whatley: As we've grown, I've done less technical work and I've become less involved with the minute-to-minute decisions of individual projects. But beyond that, my role hasn't significantly changed. To some extent though, I've matured in my ability to run a company enough to know the way I used to do things wasn't the way I should've been doing it. I've learned to manage people better and manage the business better.

Ramsay: What's the difference between founding a company and managing the company you started?

Whatley: As a founder, you are intimately linked with your organization, emotionally and in every other way. But you still have to manage your company. You definitely need the technical and creative people with the vision, but you need somebody who's sitting back and herding them in the right direction, as opposed to just creating something cool or building a neat product. Managing isn't just getting the product done; it's getting the right product done for the right market in the right time.

Ramsay: And yet you weren't much of a manager when you started?

Whatley: I was very much focused on the products and the quality of the products, and not on making the company successful in the earlier days. I'm now much more likely to go, "That's a really cool idea. I'd really love to have that program, but that's not what we should be doing." Part of our problem was there were times when I was so wrapped up in a project that the company didn't get managed. We would raise our heads up from the project only to find out we were in big trouble.

Ramsay: Would you say you've survived this long out of sheer persistence?

Whatley: Yes. I always say: "a good entrepreneur is someone who is too dumb to know when to quit."

Ramsay: BreakAway has grown over the years. As the cofounder and CEO, do you ever feel disconnected from the day-to-day?

Whatley: Frequently. At any given time, we're doing at least three or four projects and often a few more small ones. I will know pretty well what a couple of them are doing day-to-day, but you just can't focus on that many things at once. I very much enjoy when I get to spend time on, and dive into, a specific project.

Ramsay: Do you know every employee's name?

Whatley: I don't know many of them as well as I used to. I may know someone's name, but I may not know if they're married, have kids, or whatever. For the most part, I will get to know them. There are 15 or more people I have worked with for 20 years. Part of the reason we can have a flat organization is there are a lot of people who I can depend on because we have worked together so long.

Ramsay: As the company has grown, so too has the distance between you, the work, and the people. How has that distance impacted your role?

Whatley: I don't think my role is that different from when I was the producer of a major game project and had 20 people under me. I can't be friends with everybody the way I could on a smaller team. It just doesn't work to be that close to people. Sooner or later, that'll lead to problems.

Ramsay: How do you try to stay connected?

Whatley: I try to let everyone see what everyone else is doing. I make the teams give demos and project reports—as frequently as we can without imposing on them—to not just me but to all of management and the other teams. They know that, periodically, they'll have to show off, so they're motivated to put their best foot forward.

But we also always treat those discussions as opportunities to talk about what's going right, what's going wrong, what's needed, and what's not being provided. By keeping those conversations as frequent, as open, and as frank as possible, new employees can feel comfortable with speaking up when they're having trouble.

Ramsay: When you look back at everything you've done, have you missed any opportunities you shouldn't have?

Whatley: Oh, yes. There have been so many missed opportunities. We could have been where we are now ten years ago had I known then what I know now. There's no doubt about it. We all have learned a lot over time, but we'll just have to apply what we've learned going forward.

And sometimes the market's just not ready for you, even if you have a great idea. You can bang your head on the wall all you want, but people won't buy it until the situation is right.

Ramsay: Where do you want to take your company?

Whatley: It would be really cool if we created a product that really had an impact on the world. If we could create a product that was used globally, and depression in the world went down by 5%, or 10% less people died as a result of fewer medical errors, that would be awesome. That's where we're pushing forward. We think games can have that big of an impact.

Ramsay: How can you hope to get your corporate masters to buy into your altruistic goals?

Whatley: They will follow the return on investment. If we are reducing depression by some noticeable percentage, insurance companies will step up and want us to do that. If we're saving lives or making things work more efficiently, they will be the first to beat down our door. I don't worry about that. When you're making a real impact, they will pay whatever it takes to get you into their shop.

Ian Bogost

Cofounder, Persuasive Games

Ian Bogost and Gerard LaFond cofounded Persuasive Games in 2003 to create video games that persuade, instruct, and engage. That same year, the duo made their mark on history, creating *The Howard Dean for Iowa Game*—the first video game commissioned for a U.S. presidential campaign.

Bogost and Persuasive Games have continued to move the video game industry in new and exciting directions, pioneering games as editorial content for the New York Times and using video games to address critical issues, such as airport security, clean energy, and tort reform.

Dr. Bogost is the Ivan Allen College Distinguished Chair in Media Studies and Professor of Interactive Computing at the Georgia Institute of Technology. A satirist, sometimes critic, and ambiguous Twitter personality, Bogost appeared on The Colbert Report in 2007 to celebrate how video games can make a difference. He is the author of several books, including *Persuasive Games: The Expressive Power of Videogames*.

Since this interview was conducted in 2013, Bogost has continued to write and speak about games, media, and other subjects through, among other work, his role as a Contributing Editor at *The Atlantic*, the author of *How to Talk About Videogames*, and a editor of the *Platform Studies* series from MIT Press and the *Object Lessons* series from *The Atlantic* and Bloomsbury.

Ramsay: You've led a distinguished academic career. You're a professor, public speaker, and a prolific author. Why video games?

Bogost: Right. I have degrees in areas that seem to have nothing to do with making software or video games. I got my undergraduate degree in philosophy and comparative literature, and then a master's and Ph.D. in comparative literature.

Comparative literature is one of these fields that doesn't mean anything to anyone who doesn't know what it is already. It doesn't really matter what it is, other than to point out it's one of those areas where people mix stuff up. While I was in school, I was also working in industry, and I had other bizarre working experiences, from software development to financial services, and then design work, and print and digital publishing.

I teach now in a program where our students do this deliberately. At Georgia Tech, I teach computational media, which is half computer science and half liberal arts. That's awesome. When I was in school, you had to make a choice between being an engineer or a humanist.

I was always interested in bringing those worlds together, more than they already were. Games are good examples of computer media that naturally fits at the intersection point between computing and culture. In an interesting leap of faith, I finally quit my full-time job and committed to two things: finish my Ph.D., and create a game development studio, to see what paths those might open up. It was like a hedge. Either I can do game development professionally, or I can do higher education professionally. Of course, I ended up doing both.

Ramsay: How did you get started with the studio?

Bogost: I had worked together with my business partner and cofounder, Gerard LaFond, in technology consulting and development during the dot-com era. Gerard also has an interesting background. He was a philosophy student as an undergrad, and then got an MBA before becoming a general manager at CitySearch.

We worked together building software for e-business, consumer packaged goods, automotive, and entertainment at a boutique agency at the end of the first dot com era. Gerard ran business development, and I was running the technology group. We had done a lot of marketing, development, e-business work, and some games, like licensed add-ons for films. Probably the biggest was the online development work around the launch of the first *Spider-Man* movie for Sony. We worked on huge e-business projects for the Honda Motorcycle Division, and we made some games that were tie-ins for Hollywood films. We did a lot of work for Columbia TriStar in those days. Gerard was trying to bring in business. I was trying to make the promises we had to make things we could actually accomplish technically and within the resources that were available. This is how things work in that business, right? You try to find the friction point between what you need to say to get work and what you can drum up as a solution to the problem at hand.

We had a good working relationship. We seemed to be on the same page about doing something bigger, or at least more meaningful, than just solving other people's silly marketing problems. Since we both had worked extensively in advertising and marketing, very near the start of the studio, we thought if we built a base in advertising work, we could use that as a springboard from which to build the studio, and then move into other domains, like education and politics.

After we started in early 2003, the opportunity to create a game for the Howard Dean presidential campaign arose. It's hard to remember now, but that was the beginning of online grassroots political outreach. A lot of people were online, especially on broadband, for the first time. The idea of the blog was new. It was a different era. It was pre-YouTube, pre-Facebook, and pre-Twitter. And this was an interesting first public project. Everyone knew about Howard Dean. It was also the first time there had been an official US presidential candidate video game. That was an interesting way for the studio to come out of the gate. We built that game together with Gonzalo Frasca's studio, Powerful Robot, with next to nothing. In a very short time, we got the game out right at the end of the year.

Ramsay: Did either of you have experience with starting companies?

Bogost: I had not, at least not in a meaningful way. I had set up business entities that were working on smaller projects. Just before Persuasive Games got started, I got involved in an educational publishing venture. That's a company that still exists; it's just in a very niche publishing market. I knew what it meant to set up a company and how the basics of that work. I also had set up a previous company just for consulting work, but nothing that we thought might have a big future. I don't think Gerard had been involved in starting up new ventures. He had a lot of experience starting up new divisions and new offices within CitySearch as they were expanding rapidly though.

Ramsay: You invested some of your own money. How did you manage that risk? What did you expect would come of your investment?

Bogost: I just assumed the funds were sunk. I could take a modest amount of funds, and throw them away without feeling like the loss would be catastrophic. This was going to be an experience that might have an upside, but I wasn't banking my future on it. At the same time, once I quit my marketing job, something had to happen. Persuasive Games had to ramp up and provide something approaching a proper income, or I had to get a job in academia. If we had lost everything, that would have been okay. We hoped though that the business would turn into a viable entity that sustains itself.

Ramsay: You didn't put together a business plan?

Bogost: Not even remotely. I had done that before. I put together a business plan and sought funding for the publishing business. I even toyed with starting up a web business. Before the blog was a big deal, I had an early build of software that provided blog-like services for families. I had a half-developed product and tried to build a business plan for that. I poked around, seeking money. I just found the whole experience boring and soulless.

I didn't want to be in business that way. I didn't want to have a "startup," to have a "company," or to have a set of meetings with PowerPoint slides or whatever. We had a good sense of what we could accomplish by modeling our business around a combination of service work. When we had enough experience, we didn't feel like writing it down in greater detail would benefit anyone. Plus, we weren't looking for external funding, so we never had to prove our salt to anyone else. And I'm terrible at trying to make my ideas match other people's expectations.

Ramsay: Were you on the same page with Gerard about how to start up?

Bogost: Oh, we were both looking to make money and to do something interesting. Over and above anything else, we wanted to be on our own. And we were aware that we had to set our expectations at a level we could actually meet. Our time didn't cost us anything. There were opportunity costs, I guess. And we thought, "Well, we'll give this a shot." When we did the Howard Dean game, we got a large amount of attention right away—a lot of press.

But more than the money, which was small, we had cracked open something that might have a future in spreading the gospel of how games can be used. That's almost what the company has always been. We've made money doing this. We haven't gotten rich doing it, but we always had this secondary mission of just trying to do our part, showing how games can be used outside entertainment.

Ramsay: Were you working in academia yet then?

Bogost: I wasn't working in academia at the time. I had been working in tech still, making good money, but I was just sick of it. It was awful. For years and years, I had been working too much and on other people's stuff. It wasn't very gratifying.

Ramsay: What about a family?

Bogost: I was married. By then, I had a three-year-old, and my daughter was under one. I was almost never around though, and my son remembers that; he was old enough. But my daughter doesn't have any real memory of those days when I would be at work all the time. Now, almost a decade later, I'm just around all the time. Since I've been working at my own company, and in the very unusual circumstance of academic life, I do a lot of work, but I also have a lot of flexibility in my schedule. That was a big factor in trying to rebalance my family life.

Ramsay: When did you become a professor?

Bogost: About a year after starting Persuasive Games, I got the job at Georgia Tech. We were in Los Angeles before, and we moved the studio to Atlanta. I wasn't terribly fond of the idea of becoming a university professor. I imagined I would have to do what I had to do as a student, which was kind of lie, cheat, and steal to get away with studying and writing about the things I wanted to. I was very ambivalent about what was going to happen next, but I was also totally confident that if something went wrong, I would be able to get a good high-tech, games, or entertainment industry job and everything would be fine.

The studio predated my coming to the university. Luckily, because Georgia Tech is very encouraging of entrepreneurship and outside activities within the boundaries of our employment agreement, they were totally fine with me living in two worlds. And those worlds have definitely been incredibly, mutually beneficial. In some ways, any attention I get commercially benefits the university, and my credentials, the Ph.D., and affiliation with a major technical research institute lend credibility to the work we do at the studio.

Ramsay: Why did you take a job at Georgia Tech?

Bogost: The job presented itself. It was an opportunity that was unusual. I had told myself that I wasn't going to take a university position unless it was right, unless it was really a good opportunity. Professionally, the job would have to allow me to really work on the intersection of culture and computation, particularly in the context of games. Georgia Tech started these degrees in digital and computational media at all levels, so there was a chance to really do the work I hadn't been able to do as a student, and to be a part of building a program that I might have benefitted from if I had access earlier.

Ramsay: Beyond the Howard Dean game, what did you envision Persuasive Games doing? Did you imagine it'd just be you and Gerard against the world?

Bogost: We never talked much about growth in the early days because we were really trying to keep lean in order to fund projects. We were really trying to get something back out of the company, too, because we weren't spending other people's money. We really needed to see some income immediately, so we tried to remain very, very small and agile—and then we just became very fond of that. I think, partly, it's because Gerard and I are not the world's best managers, and we had been working remotely anyway. Even ten years ago, it was so easy to work from almost anywhere; that gave us the freedom to have family lives.

And we weren't after the self-gratification of having a logo on the wall, or the validation that comes with looking like a real business. We just wanted to work on cool things. And working on cool things turned out to be pretty easy at the time. We were able to be competitive and scrappy, and we got a lot of attention which brought more attention which brought more opportunities.

Ramsay: Did you hire out the engineering work?

Bogost: I can program. I do a lot of work on our games. We do hire out though because I don't want to work on the games all the time. We've done that partly by having a small number of employees during our boom years, and often by just bringing in people we work with on specific projects.

I think we would have never done our most interesting work had we tried to build a small- to medium-sized business quickly. We would have gotten wrapped up in our run rate, we would have had to go out and find ways of sustaining that rate, and then we would have definitely been responsible for those mouths we had to feed.

Ramsay: You know, Persuasive Games doesn't sound a typical studio.

Bogost: Is there a typical studio anymore? Our studio has always been a hybrid between a services organization doing game development on behalf of other companies, and a small, independent studio. The business really got off and running right when the services model and serious games were compromised by the financial collapse of 2008—just before the distribution channels we now take for granted had really arisen. Our timing was a little bad in that regard.

Before then, it wasn't really possible to make money on small-scale, downloadable or online games. We had a little ad revenue, but we didn't have the downloadable and mobile channels that are available now. So, the idea behind the studio from a business perspective was always to stay independent and bounce between a combination of services revenue and independent sales.

If you look at a company like Area/Code, which became Zynga New York, they were doing similar things: a lot of advertising or entertainment work-for-hire deals, and they were slowly developing a stable of their own games, too. They managed to hit that peak at the right time to be acquired, although that didn't necessarily work out the way they'd hoped in the long run.

Often, the services work we do never sees the light of day. Consulting is interesting because it gives you a chance to see a lot of different problems. It's also sometimes frustrating. Shipping games is much more appealing than just solving hypothetical problems, or telling people to not make games, which is what we spend a lot of our time doing.

Ramsay: Do you work with publishers or self-publish?

Bogost: For most of our work, we've either distributed it ourselves, or it's been published in a very particular context. For example: games meant to be distributed through after school programs or implemented in a corporate Internet training system. For our own original work, we've both self-published and worked with publishers.

Ramsay: Did the Howard Dean game fit with your vision?

Bogost: One thing that's interesting to me is that games can be used for lots of things in addition to entertainment. It stands to reason that the ways of developing, publishing, marketing, selling, and using those games are just as varied.

This is fairly obvious when you think about other media. If you worked on commercial and fine art photography, like taking portraits for magazines or photographing food for *Gourmet*, the processes and methods of working would be different from managing your portfolio for gallery installations and fine art sales.

With TV and movies, the moving image is a general purpose medium you can use for big blockbuster films you see at the cinema. But you can also use the moving image to make little instructional videos to post on YouTube, or that play when you get on the airplane to tell you how to buckle your seatbelt.

We're often working in modes of game development that are different from the commercial entertainment industry, so our relationship to the business of games is more complex. With that said, we occasionally work in the ordinary entertainment game space. In those cases, publishing has less to do with methods than with the compatibility of our games with the interests of the marketplace.

Ramsay: Did Howard Dean's campaign managers come to you?

Bogost: I got introduced to one of their campaign advisors around the late summer or early fall of 2003. We talked about doing the game, and they were immediately on board with the concept.

Ramsay: Has buy-in always come that easily?

Bogost: Oh, god no. That's always been the hardest thing when working with organizations that aren't familiar with games: getting them to buy into the value of games. I would say, generally speaking, the most common issue we've had has been comfort and commitment. The problem is not even the idea; a lot of folks are interested in making a game, even if they haven't done it before.

The problem comes when they realize what that actually means—that, no, we'll actually make a video game and they'll release that game and people will play it. At that point, it's often very startling to our clients that this is actually happening. Where we've had the most success is when someone high up in an organization has endorsed not games specifically, but the idea of experimentation and taking risks with new things.

And where we haven't had success, that alignment has been absent. The typical issues are very boring. It's not so much about people's misconceptions; it's more about their aversion to risk in their jobs. If you're a brand manager at a consumer goods company, or the editor of a newspaper, you have a lot of work to do. People like that just want to go home at the end of the day. They don't want to stick their neck out for something that might not be worthwhile.

For instance, we were working with the *New York Times* doing newsgames—games as journalism—back in 2007. Our editor was well-meaning, but they just didn't want to try this new stuff in a way that would allow us the freedom to experiment and figure out what it meant to make games about news issues, and to do them quickly. They were overworked, concerned, and no one was rewarding them for these experiments.

Ramsay: When you meet with prospective clients, do you try to figure out what they need first? Or do you instead start with the game you want to make, and then find someone who needs that game made?

Bogost: It's happened both ways. The way we run the business? More of the former. We have a lot of interests and enjoy working on a diverse set of problems. Occasionally, if we have the resources and the wherewithal, we'll make a game we want to do. But in other cases, one of the interesting things about the consulting model is that you get to see a lot of different problems that you wouldn't have encountered otherwise, and try to help organizations solve them, even if in a small way.

Ramsay: How do you go about developing a game around an issue?

Bogost: It's actually a pretty straightforward process for me. Think about what games are; they're systems you interact with. The games we make are about real-world systems. If we want to teach someone how to do a job or represent a political issue, we make a game that shows what it's like to be somebody working in a job, or one that characterizes the complex choices that arise when you allocate resources in a civic context. And through these games, you find there's not one way to do things.

We've done corporate learning games—games for employees to play as a way of either practicing or learning their jobs. We've done this for line workers in retail and food service, and general managers in hospitality. In those cases, one way to get a sense of how a real-world system works is just to go into the business and do the training. I did the new employee training at Cold Stone Creamery, for example, and we did the same with hoteliers. And we've had to do research on more abstract topics, like a pharmaceutical or chemical process, a set of civic or political issues, or a particular legislative proposal.

We have to either learn enough so that we feel like we have a good understanding of the model, or work with experts who know more than we do.

The first step is to learn about the system we're modeling, and then get an angle on that system. What are we trying to say about it? Are we trying to just depict how it works? Or are we trying to make an argument about it to say there's a solution we would like you to consider? Are we trying to advocate for a particular course of action? Should you take this next step in your political life? Or should you buy this product? That's the second step. What's the argument? We try as hard as we can to get our partners to tell us what they're trying to do, what problem they're trying to solve, and why they want to make a game.

Ramsay: With entertainment games, you measure success by sales. Since your games tend to be communication media, how do you measure their success?

Bogost: In most cases, our clients are interested in getting an idea across, altering a set of possible behaviors, promoting a product or service, or providing some version of what they do in a different way. Measuring the success of such initiatives usually involves the tools that you use to measure marketing of any kind: the number of visitors, or players, or the amount of plays, or the popularity of a game, particularly if you're giving it away. You can use these as stand-ins for sales.

When we develop corporate learning games, we look at whether we can get employees to play these games of their own volition without any reward. When they play those games because they're useful, we've been able to show that engagement is much higher and lasts longer. The employees talk about and engage with the material in a way you can't imagine with other training options.

Ramsay: Do your games tend to be naturally pedagogical?

Bogost: Some of our games are pedagogical. They're trying to get something across. Others are really quite exploratory. They may not look it on the surface, they may not sound like it, but they represent the operation of some system. They don't have a specific conclusion or action. Often our games really just show the dynamics of something—the conditions under which something operates.

We made a game a few years back about creating clean energy through wind farms, but we wanted to demonstrate the political issues involved. For example, one problem with wind energy is that out in the country where there's enough consistent wind conditions to put up a turbine farm, people just don't want them there. They don't want their view or pastoral hillside disrupted by these big, ugly turbines. So, it's not so much that we have an opinion that we're presenting—that we think it's right or wrong to pursue a particular energy strategy—but that we wanted to show that this dynamic is at work and worth considering.

Ramsay: When players say "that game sucks," they really mean the game wasn't fun, and not everyone enjoys the same games. With a corporate learning game, does the game have to be fun for the game to be successful or effective?

Bogost: No. It's a terrible idea for these games to try to compete for the entertainment time of their employees because then the game has to be interesting and it has to not suck, right? What that typically means in a business context is that the game must earnestly engage with whatever aspect of the business it deals with. That might mean explaining and characterizing some aspect of a job; providing helpful, useful practice so that an employee knows it better; setting up the context in which they're working; or enabling them to practice the skills associated with that work or what have you. That's different from being fun, right? It gives you a deeper knowledge about the job that you do.

And you might call that gratifying. It's actually really gratifying for employees, especially public-facing service employees who are working on the line in big organizations. It's very gratifying to understand why the hell they're doing the things they're doing. It makes their job feel less arbitrary and more meaningful. But it isn't necessarily fun. A job is a job. Treating the job seriously, not trying to trivialize it as an entertainment experience, gives it more value, not less.

Ramsay: I'm sure you've read Raph Koster's book, where he argues that fun is learning. Would you agree with his conception of fun?

Bogost: Raph and I talk about this a lot. He and I are closer than ever before in our conception of fun, but my problem with his idea is that it's too cognitive. His idea of fun is too much about this quasi-neuroscientific analysis of what fun means. For me, this practice of discovery, of learning something new or deeper about something, does seem to be intimately tied to what we call fun. And even in entertainment games, we find them fun not because they're distracting or amusing, but because they give us a system to explore. When we explore that system, we find gratification in finding new parts of it, or returning to familiar ones.

I'm skeptical that fun is a cognitive process. The idea that fun is learning puts too much of the work—or too much of the success of that work—on the player. This is where Raph and I disagree, I think. He's very much of the opinion there's this co-creative process of equal contribution from player and the game. Obviously, you need a player experience to have an emotional response to it, but to me, in large part, the fun in a game is in structuring it so that the play space it creates is compelling, rather than that the burden is placed on the player to feel a certain way and then just to measure the nuance or quantity of that feeling.

A subtle distinction, but I think it's one of the differences between Raph's thinking on fun and mine. For me, fun is where the action is whereas, for Raph, the player's experience is more prominent.

Ramsay: As communication media, your games have to engage players in a conversation, but a conversation takes at least two.

Bogost: Yeah. The danger in the games I make is they have to invite a player to experience a topic they might not otherwise have cared about at all. When you buy a *Grand Theft Auto* game, what are you getting? You take it home, you play it, and you have a set of responses to it, but you knew you were already interested. You had to pony up some money to get what you expected.

If I give you a game about wind energy, or your otherwise forgettable job, I can't rely on the idea that you're coming voluntarily to the game with open arms. My audience is always going to be a little suspicious. At the same time, players have to be open enough to the material such that I can meet them halfway.

Part of this idea of opening a conversation is just "hey, I'm going to prove to you that the thing that I made a game about is worth it, that it deserves having a game about it, that it's not silly or a gimmick or a joke to make a game about ice cream portion sizing or about the features of this new SUV." I think that can be done for anything. I don't think there's a set of topics for which it can't be done.

Ramsay: How do you build progress tracking and evaluation into your games?

Bogost: It's a lot of soft measurement, like whether a player has demonstrated an ability to synthesize the ideas inside the game into a little nugget of wisdom. And then it's up to them to act on that wisdom. That part you never get for free. The idea that you can put a piece of media of any kind in front of people and then, magically, their behavior changes? I just don't believe it. I don't think it's possible.

Ramsay: You're quite widely known as a vociferous critic of gamification. Why do you hate gamification so much?

Bogost: It's a lie. It's snake oil. It's a way of making the promise, the appeal, and the sexiness of games feel like games can be easily tamed and put to use in business without actually doing the work of putting games to use in business. It's a type of consulting pretending to use games as solutions. Gamification is just a perversion of behaviorist economics.

In relation to game design, gamification has little to nothing to do with it. In relation to business solutions, gamification isn't necessarily about solving any problems. All gamification developers care about is providing consultancy services to organizations that want to get in on the game of getting in on the game of games. The difference between making games and gamification is the difference between cooking and driving. They just have nothing to do with each other.

Ramsay: Quite a visceral reaction, but you're a professor. Taking an objective position, studying every dimension of the problem, why is gamification not a lie? Why is gamification not snake oil? Why doesn't gamification work?

Bogost: The argument I'm making about gamification is largely one that has to do with the rhetoric and presentation of the material. There are these management trends that come and go. When they come, there's always somebody there to capitalize on them, to oversell them, to build conferences around them. The argument I make about gamification has nothing to do with the output of the gamification business. The gamification business seeks to produce a commodity to be sold in the same fashion to everyone as a general solution, that works in all cases, at a low cost, with a high reward, and then to strip mine that interest until the trend burns out and the next trend comes along.

So, the idea that there are specific examples of incentive-based reward programs that have results, that can demonstrate results, has nothing to do with gamification. Gamification completely fails to acknowledge its predecessors in business intelligence and incentive programs, and just gives lip service to these things. But at the end of the day, gamification is really just sugar water; it's a gloss that you paint over the existing practices that you're already doing. Adding a little bit of slightly game-y incentive-based applications to them in order to make it appear as though you've ticked off the box of a video game strategy within your organization.

I'm very cynical about this because the values gamification represents as a way of engaging individuals with a business is just repellent to me. Gamification is like saying we can get people to accommodate our wishes when we take them hostage and threaten their lives. I don't think there's a reason to justify that behavior.

Ramsay: Hostage taking works, I guess. Does gamification?

Bogost: Well, gamification works, insofar as the purpose of gamification is to get organizations to buy gamification services. That's the point of gamification. It works pretty well at that. Whether it works in the business contexts it's deployed in is completely irrelevant to the gamification world. They need enough examples that seem to be reasonably coherent, such that they can point to them as case studies.

But the truth is that even the people who are buying these things, they don't really care if they work or not; they're buying them so that they can keep up with the corporate Joneses. Gamification has established itself as a trend you'd better be talking about when you're a brand manager, HR manager, or whatever.

When your boss asks you, "I've heard about gamification. Are we doing that?" You have to say, "Oh, yes. We've investigated that. In fact, I'm attending this conference..."

Ramsay: Supermarkets have been using loyalty programs for a long time. To me, gamification applies the loyalty program model to other problems.

Bogost: The loyalty programs in supermarkets aren't really loyalty programs. They're more like hostage situations. Basically, the supermarkets say, "Hey, I'll make you pay a worse price on our products unless you give me data associated with everything you buy." You use those cards, so that you can be tracked by supermarkets, who then build complex databases of purchase patterns.

Real loyalty programs provide a way for customers and businesses to talk about what they value and what they want in return for the value they provide. Real loyalty is bidirectional. You can't have real loyalty if it only moves from the customer to the organization. Gamification doesn't create real loyalty because it's just trying to trick or fool people into doing something they might not if they really understood what was happening.

That has been going on for a long time, and that is by no means exclusive to games or loyalty programs. We've debated endlessly about whether tricking people into doing things they might not do is a virtuous business practice. In the past, we admitted they're tricks; we didn't glorify them as entertainment experiences. We ought to admit now and again that gamification is that same kind of trick, where a business is just trying to dupe you out of your money and your dignity.

Ramsay: Moving on, your games don't have a specific conclusion or action, but how do you have a game that doesn't have an end?

Bogost: If we were dealing with workplace safety, customer service, the assembly of a particular menu item in a restaurant, or what have you, you want to understand how they work or practice to get better at them. So, the ending of one of our games is not so much a place and time when you're done. Instead, you've played through the missions or the levels or something, and you feel like, "Okay, I've got a sense of this system. I have a sense of how this works in the manner that it's been presented, and that's something I can return to in my mind later. That these are the dynamics that are at work in a particular situation."

Ramsay: Some would call that point where the player expresses their understanding "grokking the pattern." As a designer, how do you know when players have reached that point?

Bogost: One method of understanding that pattern is recognizing that it's incomplete. You see that it's just one piece of a larger puzzle, and it has to be reincorporated into a set of other practices, whether those are exercised through games or not. People sometimes think they want an answer, like "just tell me what to do, and I'll do the things right." But the thing that's right to do varies and part of what a game can offer is a sense of that variation: that any general rule has to be altered, mixed, or blended into other varied circumstances.

What we end up doing in life is taking little bits of knowledge and reassembling them in ways we've never seen before, or ways we've seen before that have slight variations and those variations end up mattering a great deal. So, part of grokking the system also involves being able to see the limits of the system you've grokked and the places where the system breaks down.

Ramsay: Do your games try to capture that point where players see where the system breaks down?

Bogost: I think they try to be honest. They don't try to over-portray the wisdom they are passing on, sometimes through humor or visual abstraction. In a corporate learning context, there's some really boring but serious matter-of-fact instruction and information dissemination that has to occur. The challenge that we face is to rise above the noise and give players something memorable. I think one of the reasons we use these sort of cartoon-like scenarios is to acknowledge that we're not capturing everything, that we're abstracting the real world.

Ramsay: Do your games test whether player have internalized that wisdom?

Bogost: I really don't think you can do this. I think what you can test in a game is whether a player has understood the game. A game can test whether the player is good at playing the game, but that's all it means. If you want to talk about the experience they had in the game outside of the game, then that has to take place outside of the game, right? You have to reflect and discuss. That's why I'm so obsessed with discourse analysis; of looking at the ways that people talk about the experience they had in a game in relation to what they know or what they thought they knew about the topic. That's where I look for synthetic evidence.

But there are a lot of folks who think, "I'll just plug this into my learning management system, and ask a series of quiz questions." You'll pass that module, and you'll be certified in whatever aspect of the training regimen you've been asked to be certified in. All that stuff reflects only the player's performance in the system. It doesn't have anything to do with their ability to put their new wisdom to use.

Ramsay: If the game can't provide that feedback, do you need someone in the room to pull them away?

Bogost: I think one problem with this work is that often the framework for that feedback isn't put into place. Some games we make are played in a very specific context. For example, there's a management retreat for general managers of hotels in a particular hotel chain. This is a real scenario we've done. It's facilitated by instructors, and there's a small number of participants who do a wide variety of activities, including play a game. They play the game, they discuss, and they play the game again, looking at it differently. And the game becomes an experience they can return to at home. But I think, by and large, this doesn't happen enough.

Ramsay: You've said that you run a small business.

Bogost: It's definitely a small business. I don't even know that there was a time in my life when I was comfortable using the word "entrepreneur" for what I do. I'm now totally, just completely, disgusted by that term. It has been so invaded by the startup world.

We provide a set of very custom solutions, and we also make our own games. We provide a very boutique service. It's the kind of company venture capitalists would derogatorily call a "lifestyle business"—a thing that can't possibly grow, doesn't want to, and is therefore corrupt because it's not trying to scale to a billion dollars as quickly as possible.

We have a small business. It's a small business that comprises a portion of our incomes as partners. We're doing what may not ever be work that can be done at a large scale. I'm not bothered by that. It's an interesting and challenging set of problems that has allowed me to see a variety of little corners of the world I wouldn't have been able to see otherwise, to make some weird and hopefully interesting games. And these are games that have had a modest impact in a variety of different contexts, that have been gratifying both to make and see played, and, in many cases, have been ungratifying to see made and not played.

A lot of our business is telling people to not make games, by the way. "Please don't make a game. It will do you no good." Sometimes we get paid to reach that conclusion, but I find that to be just as useful as a conclusion that results in me making a weird game.

Ramsay: Well, telling people to not make games doesn't sound like a very sustainable business model for someone who makes games.

Bogost: It is sustainable because it's not a lie. I think our reputation matters. We don't just make games because someone knocked on our door and said, "We're willing to spend some money." We want to make the games that ought to be made, not just any game that could be made. It's maddening and just completely demoralizing to me to work on something that shouldn't exist, or to work on something because there wasn't anything better to do. I just don't want to do that.

Ramsay: How small is a small business?

Bogost: How do you measure businesses these days? I think the ways we measure businesses are stupid. Do you measure businesses by revenue? Do you measure businesses by the number of employees? What do we measure businesses by? We are a company whose permanent staff is two and whose typical staff is about three to five. We bring in a small amount of revenue every year. It's a strange thing to have to justify, right? You'd never ask somebody the opposite question like, "How big is a 'big company'? 10,000 employees? 50,000 employees? That big?"

Ramsay: I think I would, actually! I know you're working a few jobs in addition to Persuasive Games. Would you be able to quit those jobs and make games full time?

Bogost: We could do it. I couldn't do it and maintain the same lifestyle I currently have though. It would be different. It would be possible to sustain a living on this work for sure. But I've also scaled it down partly because I don't have to rely on it year over year for my personal income. That looks like it's completely ridiculous, unsustainable, and not repeatable. I actually think this is a pretty common pattern for small businesses these days, where you've got a little thing and that little thing does a certain amount of work for you. Maybe it's not enough to sustain your whole family, but it's one corner of your life.

Ramsay: You don't aspire to "make money while you're sleeping"?

Bogost: In this particular business, if we were to do that work, it would be through original work rather than client work. A lot of the original work we did early on was a little bit early in mobile location-based games, news games, and weird political games. We had unfortunate timing in getting a lot of stuff to market when there weren't any distribution channels.

But even if you look at app store-style game development, it's hardly a sure thing. There are very few individuals or small businesses that sustain themselves on that work because you're charging 99 cents for a game. Well, either that, or you have one of those free-to-play monstrosities that tries to extract enormous amounts of money by virtue of advertising and network effects. Everybody wants to make money while they sleep, but that would be a different business for us.

Ramsay: How would you say you're different from indie developers?

Bogost: I think we share a lot in common with indie developers. We do independent development. We also do development for other people and organizations. Some indie developers do this, too. They'll do consulting or freelance work, and then they make their own games. In that respect, we have a lot in common. But one difference between us and the indie scene is that there is a lot of indies who are young, up-and-coming twentysomethings who have all the time in the world to just make their game. They can live on a shoestring budget and do their thing. I think that's awesome. I wish I could do that, but that's not what we're doing; we're at a different stage in our lives.

Ramsay: In much of your work outside the studio, you've become a captain of mockery.

Bogost: There's definitely a large percentage of my work that is satire. There has been some of that work at Persuasive Games, too. We did this weird game that was a mockery of Kinko's business practices. I like humor. I like satire and parody. It's a very serious business actually. There's a gravity to humor, particularly black humor. Satire has never been at a higher fever pitch. The fact that people think of Jon Stewart and Stephen Colbert as serious journalists when they're really comedians is because the news business is in such dire straits that their mockery feels more real than the reality. Satire is a very serious way to communicate ideas.

Ramsay: Isn't satire also a safe comedy?

Bogost: There's risk in satire. If you mock everything in the same way, then it becomes meaningless. It's precious. It can't be used all the time. I think in that respect, it's a little too easy to do send ups and mockery when in some cases a more serious approach to a real issue is recommended.

All that said, I think that there's plenty of room for more humor and more satire in games than we've seen. Humor is not as common in games as it is in other media. A lot of the games we think we love for their seriousness we actually love for their humor. We're talking today, the day before the release of *Grand Theft Auto V*. That's a good example of a series that's incredibly satirical and snide, but which also has this gravity that people mistake for seriousness.

Ramsay: You also use Twitter for satire as well.

Bogost: My Twitter persona is very ambiguous in that regard. I think a lot of people are not sure if I'm straight-faced. I love that format where anything might be either exactly what it says or just the opposite, which is the way I feel about the Internet in general.

Ramsay: When you were promoting your book *Persuasive Games: The Expressive Power of Videogames* in 2007, you appeared on The Colbert Report. How did appearing on that show affect your business?

Bogost: Obviously, any attention is attention that pays dividends. If somebody hears about my writing and they work for an organization that might want to make games, they start to look into who might make games for them and they'll find my name. That has some direct benefits. The indirect benefit is I really am interested in this stuff. I'm committed to the results, not just the money.

Potential clients often ask, "How much will it cost for you to consult for us?" I often answer "twenty bucks" or whatever the cost of my book is at the time. I'll say, "Just go buy the book. The book won't give you a personal solution to your specific problem, but all the approaches are in there. Have at it."

I think by giving these ideas to the world and simply inviting everyone into the conversation rather than thinking everything needs to be owned and tightly controlled, that every exchange has to be under NDA and I have to bill every hour of my time, well, all that stuff is a little weird to me.

Ramsay: The path to success for many people involves building up and out.

Bogost: We've had those thoughts. We've worked at larger companies in the past. We had large teams. We were part of those organizations. We had that experience. But we didn't have that sense that "oh, this is what a company is. I want to build a company that has this many people." If anything, we didn't want to deal with the difficulties of worrying about making payroll, keeping everybody afloat, and having enough business to sustain the company." But we've talked about it in the past. Mostly, we've talked about taking investment for various projects because, at that point, you've got to be all-in and ramp up fast. Certainly, one of the reasons why we've never done that is because we just didn't want to be forced to run the company according to somebody else's desires.

Ramsay: You're satisfied with just profitability?

Bogost: I don't know what it would mean to be satisfied with anything. I'm satisfied with some of the work we've done, and with some of the what I think are influential contributions to a variety of fields. That's where I find the satisfaction; it's not really in the business part. That's nice, but that's just gravy for me. Satisfaction to me is really the feeling of having accomplished something in the world that I'm interested in.

Ramsay: When I talk to founders of large enterprises, I always ask them about quality of life. For them, quality of life often comes down to free time. But you seem to fill up your time as much as possible.

Bogost: I have a lot of friends who are in that situation; they're running large companies in various industries. I think everybody's got their own ups and downs. I've got to do a lot of wrangling on my own. We don't have as much stuff that just takes care of itself.

I was hanging out as a game designer in residence at PopCap Games over the summer. They're a pretty big studio that's a part of a very large company. I had forgotten what it was like to have a kitchen in your office, where you just go in and there's food and drink there all the time. There are little things like that, or like having someone take care of accounting. Sometimes I wish I just didn't have to deal with every little detail. And then, of course, at Georgia Tech, I have a handful of students who work for me; it's like a small research organization.

I have to keep them fed, manage what they're doing, meet with them, and make sure that everything is going according to plan. That takes up time, too.

If anything, if I could imagine a different approach to living my life, it might involve somehow having the resource flexibility to just do exactly what I want to be working on at any moment with no demands from elsewhere. I'd like to think that if I were lucky enough at some point to have the material resources to not have to worry about work ever again that I wouldn't invest those resources in silly things like another company. I would try to use them to figure out what I can contribute when I'm not distracted by all the things I have to be distracted by to make a living.

Ramsay: Do you ever get tired of your many responsibilities?

Bogost: Everybody gets tired of their job. I have a pretty good situation. I try to remind myself that even when I get annoyed, it's a good set up. There's going to be nuisances everywhere. I'm fortunate to have the ability to remember how other situations work. One of the nice things about spending some time in a large company, like when I was at PopCap, is remembering what it's like to come into work every day. I don't want to come into work every day, actually. I want to have a lot of flexibility.

Ramsay: I was watching Conan O'Brien interview Harrison Ford a few months ago. At the end, he said, "You've reached a stage in your career where you can do whatever you want." Shaking his head, Ford lamented, "I wish that were true." It occurred to me that no matter how high you rise, you're always hustling.

Bogost: I think everybody's hustling, and hustling more than they once were. And even people who work salary jobs are hustling now, too, because you have no idea if you're going to get laid off next week. You have a suspicion that once this product is done, your team is going to be made redundant. On top of that, we all have these identities online now we have to hustle: "Here I am. I have to say something interesting today on the Internet or you will forget about me!" Even when we're not selling something explicitly, we're constantly hustling.

Ramsay: When you are selling something explicitly, you have to qualify to hustle. Book publishers won't sign you unless you have a platform, for example.

Bogost: Well, while you are building a platform, speaking, and engaging, they want you to have a website where you're talking about nonsense. It's something that everyone has to do. We don't do it enough because there is a cost to it. I think it's the flipside of this golden age of independence. There never really was independence; it was just a license to have other obligations.

Ramsay: To what extent does social media impact the time you have available to your business?

Bogost: Or available to anything else? The Internet has become a destructive compulsion for everybody. It's there to keep us busy while the Internet companies take over and destroy the universe! I feel both obligated to, and disgusted with, my relationship with these tools. You have to—it's an ecosystem now. When you do what I do, largely hocking ideas into the idea space, it's a place with a very short memory; you have to constantly return to it. But it's a place with a short memory partly because we've made it so by filling it with all of our chatter.

Ramsay: Sometimes people try to avoid social media by going cold turkey. What do you try to do to avoid being overburdened?

Bogost: The main thing I do is I have a work computer that's online but offline. It has the Internet, but it doesn't have all those accounts set up, like downloadable Twitter clients, instant messaging, and all that stuff. When I know I need, or want, to be disconnected, I'll just go there, and it's a physically different workspace. I wish there were more of those spaces. It used to be possible on airplanes to escape, but now you can get Internet access in the air, too. There's almost nowhere you can go without cell phone coverage anymore. All of those nooks and crannies are increasingly unavailable unless you fashion them yourself, so you have to fashion them yourself.

Ramsay: You're definitely not a fan of gamification, but isn't social media modeled on what gamification purports to be?

Bogost: Well, yeah, people like to count their chits, I guess. It'd be interesting to see what social media would be like if you just took all the numbers out. In fact, there was somebody who made a plugin or something for Facebook that removed the "this is how many friends you have, this is how many likes, and this is how many shares." It definitely gave Facebook a different tenor, when you didn't know how many followers you had, or how many times your last tweet was retweeted, favorited, or all this crap we count as if it mattered.

What if we could see something else? What else would we want to see? For me, the key is the way we've influenced people, or how much we've contributed to something bigger than ourselves. Those are things we could try to measure, if we weren't so busy measuring the number of times we clicked on stuff, which is basically what all those numbers end up meaning.

Ramsay: Is that drive to measure our social capital really our fault? Or are we enabled by Facebook, Inc., Twitter, Inc., and other companies?

Bogost: You have an onboard computer in your car that tells you your current fuel economy, and you try to maximize your moment-to-moment driving patterns. It's not exactly the same. It's certainly not limited to digital technology, but it certainly is an example of this feedback system that has been around for decades. We've been counting stuff for a long time.

I don't think you can point to Facebook or any specific example that started all this. The Internet has just amplified that, and allowed us to do it for everything, not just for a subset of our experiences. Maybe it should give us pause. Not so much that the measurement itself is a problem, but do we want to do it to everything? Do we want everything to have a little gauge on it?

Ramsay: Do your clients want more numbers to count?

Bogost: They often think they do. They often express that they do: "We want to increase our stickiness, or our page count; or we want to increase engagement." That's sort of nebulous: what does it even mean when people say that?

The number of people who click on something, or the amount of time they spent staring at your website, may or may not have anything to do with the growth of your business or there might be other values at work. But it's an easy way to pretend that it does, so we can build a collective delusion that we have a generally accepted and scientific way of measuring stuff.

Ramsay: Along with an increasing dependence on metrics, everything has to be social, in the cloud, or whatever happens to be popular at the moment.

Bogost: Well, everyone uses the same buzzwords as everybody else does. When you point it out to them, they're embarrassed. The best thing you can do to fight this stuff is ask, "Everybody's talking about this, but what does it really mean? What does it mean to you to be social?" And they realize they have no fucking idea what they're talking about. They're just spouting back the thing they heard at the last meeting, what they think their boss wants to hear, or the thing they think will allow them to keep going another day. And usually it does. That's the thing. Everyone's involved in this complex game of cat and mouse where if they all look the same, they can point to the guy next door and say, "We're doing the same thing as everyone else." If you stick your neck out, it's easier to be blamed.

Ramsay: Are there any games you want made?

Bogost: I have notebooks full of stuff I think I might want to do. But I don't find the creative process anymore to be one of trying to realize some fully formed vision. It's more of a matter of allowing a set of unformed ideas to realize themselves to a point, and then suggest a path that they follow. There are other kinds of games I would like to make, but in my current lifestyle, where I have a lot of different things going on, I have to be a little bit particular. At this stage, I'm interested in trying to make stuff I feel great about. But I do have to admit it would be nice for one of those games to also be massively commercially successful.

Ramsay: In terms of game design, have there been opportunities you missed?

Bogost: There are just tons of things I had early inclinations about that were right in retrospect but that I didn't pursue or I didn't pursue enough. In 2003, when we did some of these campaign games around the election of 2004, they had early social features that would later become standard in games. We didn't have the social networks yet, but we had these ways of connecting with people via instant messaging and other mechanisms to draw them into our game. They became resources then by virtue of the fact we had reached out to them. This fit well with the notion of social outreach in the political sphere.

In 2004, I wrote pretty extensively about asynchronous multiplayer gaming. This was back in the era of *World of Warcraft* and *EverQuest*. The MMO was the way that multiplayer gameplay was thought of. Asynchronous play became incredibly huge in Facebook and mobile games.

We made a game called *Jetset* about the TSA and air travel. We had this whole location-based play thing where you could play in different airports, and you could get these little souvenirs related to the location you were in. That idea of checking in was around long before check-ins became popular with Foursquare.

But in all of these cases, we were too early. Even with newsgames, we were too early. They were overly complex. It turned out that what people wanted was a much simpler and shittier version of the same idea.

Ramsay: Where do you see yourself going? How many jobs is enough?

Bogost: I feel like I've got one job really. I don't really feel like I have more than one job, and that one job is to think about the meaning and application of games and media more generally, in the era of computation. I do that in a lot of ways. It expresses itself in a number of forms. At my studio, there's a particular game design we do. I'm interested in other kinds of game design and how they work, and how organizations function. I'm interested in teaching and thinking about the game design process as a practice we can refine. I'm interested in looking at individual games other people make. I try to identify and describe how they work, how they work well, or how they don't work well. It's all just one thing to me. It's just that I enter that process through all sorts of doors, windows, air vents, and even holes that I drill through the wall.

Victor Kislyi

Founder, Wargaming

Drawing on his Soviet upbringing in Belarus and a summer job in the White Mountains of New Hampshire, **Victor Kislyi** founded Wargaming in 1998 to develop and publish military strategy video games.

While the company's earliest properties, DBA Online and the Massive Assault series, never measured up to Kislyi's aspirations, World of Tanks brought Wargaming to the forefront of the free-to-play MMO market.

World of Tanks continues to dominate as one of the most sophisticated online worlds to date. In 2014, World of Tanks set a Guinness World Record with 1.1 million players simultaneously connected to one server.

Wargaming's catalog now includes World of Tanks Blitz for mobile platforms, World of Tanks: Xbox 360 Edition, and the upcoming World of Warplanes.

At the time of this interview, Wargaming had grown from a founding team of five to more than 1,600 employees around the world. Today, Wargaming employs more than 3,500 people in 16 offices. Kislyi remains the CEO.

Ramsay: What was your life like before 1998?

Kislyi: The game making actually started before that in 1996, but it was literally done in the dorm room or bedroom. We were just a couple of enthusiastic high school friends trying to make some games. Before 1998, we were making very amateurish games that went nowhere. But we trained, and we realized how hard it was. In 1998, we started to develop our first commercial product.

Ramsay: How old were you when you started making games?

Kislyi: I was 20. Before that, I was just a student. I was studying physics at the Belarusian State University. You know, students: they do have a little bit of free time, and we were using that free time to make games.

Ramsay: What led you to start a business?

Kislyi: We all were a part of the Soviet Union before 1991, and even during the Soviet Union years, we got introduced to the Western computer games culture. My father purchased probably one of the first Sinclair copycats for me—a Sinclair ZX Spectrum computer made by some guy at home. Of course, it was a pirated Spectrum with pirated cassettes and everything. There were no official Atari or Nintendo anything here; only a few of people had access to those. I invited all of my friends to play those first games on the ZX Spectrum. In certain institutions, the ZX Spectrum was the first IBM-style computer used for engineering, calculations, and computer-aided design.

They were also the first for PC games, like Civilization. As boys, we were fascinated with building empires, fighting battles, or driving tanks in interactive environments on computers. Plus, during the Soviet Union days, boys were supposed to be, let's say, military inclined. Strategy and military games really impressed us. After reading about how successful they were in the West, like Doom II, Warcraft, and Civilization itself, we thought, "Hey, why don't we make something like this, sell a million of copies, and become rich?"

It was not so much about starting a business. We had realized you have to make a game first, which is true today as well, so we experimented with C++ programming, to try to create a game which had never been created before. That's how we started, and we just started to make a good strategy game.

Ramsay: What strategy game was that?

Kislyi: The first game in 1996 was, ironically, a mixture of Panzer General and Risk. Panzer General was not yet released, and we did not have Risk, the board game, in the Soviet Union. The idea was that we'd make a global domination game with, essentially, a huge fantasy-like world map. We had certain maps that represented our planet, and other maps were created for the sake of strategic beauty. You would have countries supplying resources, which are used to buy various kinds of troops, and those troops would move on hexes or squares to fight tactical battles, like in Panzer General. You would have a mixture of ground strategy, rules for political alliances, and tactical battles, too.

Around this time, my family moved to a new apartment given to us by the government; it was a nice and big four-room apartment. And the first thing I did was draw a map on the linoleum floor with a permanent ink marker. I used little pieces of paper to represent troops and dried watermelon seeds to represent cavalry, and with that set of rules, we were playing a board game. My parents were not very happy, so they had to buy a carpet to cover the mess.

Next, when we had access to computers and programming. Just a bunch of friends from the physics department, we just decided to make that game on the computer. You can understand the production values meant it went nowhere, apart from teaching us what making even a simple, ugly game means.

Against the computer though, you could crush the computer at any level, so it was not fun for us. We realized that the only way to play the game was against live opponents. The game would have to be player vs. player. We used play-by-email mechanics, although you did not have to actually attack and send in by e-mail. It was a server-based game. You'd play through a client, automatically racking up your sequence of movements that would then be sent through the e-mail server to your opponent. Your opponent would just have to click a "check for opponent" and they'd see the board change.

However, without marketing and without production values, this game had nothing apart from some nice ideas and a basic implementation. There were really just a few people playing this game, pretty much all friends.

Ramsay: Were computers readily available to you then?

Kislyi: I clearly remember that when I was 14, we already had Yamaha computers. The country realized that information technology would be the future, so computers started to appear in various places. Parents bought Sinclair or Tera computers for their kids, and institutions had Yamaha computers for basic programming and algorithmic lessons. Since the early 1990s, although we were a part of the Soviet Union, we had quite a lot of computers in our lives.

Ramsay: When did you get a desktop computer at home?

Kislyi: It was probably 1992. There were again the IBM PC rip-offs made locally using the Intel-style processors. I first had a black-and-white monitor, and then I got the first 16-color VGA monitor. We would put together computers from spare parts. We would go and buy cheap RAM, new video cards, Sound Blaster cards, and so the computers were evolving on our desks.

Ramsay: How did you turn the board game into a business?

Kislyi: Okay, we did not use the word business. The beauty of the game development industry is that, and we believed it then and still believe it now, it's about the games. We believed that if you create a game that's enjoyable, smart, and beautiful, the business would evolve and wrap around that game easily, smoothly, seamlessly, and naturally. After that, you would just put sales and accounting people around it. We were not thinking business.

Ramsay: How many of you believers were there?

Kislyi: In the beginning, we had five or six guys, including my brother. I hired— I say "hired" but they were paid like $25 per month—a bunch of other friends from the university. We were driven by enthusiasm until 2000. There was no money. We just had a little money from my father who viewed this as a little toy for his sons and their friends. It was more about enthusiasm. We had thought, "We'll make a game that will sell one million copies, and that will make our business." By 2000, we had no more than ten.

Ramsay: Can I assume you didn't have a business plan?

Kislyi: No, I remember describing the business plan to an old lady who was a friend of my parents, right? She could not understand why a bright guy like me with parents coming out of science—my father and my mother are scientists in chemistry and physics—wasn't going into science like them.

I remember a conversation with her when I said, "Listen, ma'am. You make a game, whatever the cost is, and let's assume a year or two of production. And then the game sells 100,000 copies around the world, and each copy is, let's say, $30. You would immediately make a couple of million. That's a good business."

That convinced her. She stopped teaching me life lessons. You don't need a business plan. You just have to make a game that sells a million copies.

Ramsay: You were 20. Why didn't you have more business experience?

Kislyi: After the breakup of the Soviet Union, most parents wanted their kids to be businessmen. There were a lot of accountants and MBAs, and places you could go to study economics, study for an MBA. Thank God my father said, "No, you are not going to be an accountant; you're not going to be an MBA businessman." I am thankful to him for that.

His idea for me was more of an academic science career. He did not let me go for an MBA, but I considered it important, so I purchased a bunch of books about management. I just read. That was my business education, and that was enough. Plus, my true MBA was Civilization.

Civilization is a game that needs to be given to everyone on this planet who wants to do something in life. You build your empire, but in essence, it's your business. You sit there for two weeks, playing a couple of hours per day, and you have to deal with an economy, politics, army, exploration, religion, and production. Civilization is probably the best MBA experience ever. I did not have any business experience before. I had just a couple of books and Civilization. I played the first one, and now, I'm playing Civilization V.

Ramsay: Where did your entrepreneurial spirit come from, if not from your parents?

Kislyi: During the last two years of the Soviet Union, the Iron Curtain dropped, and especially after the breakup of the Soviet Union, we were introduced to books and television programs, like BBC, some American programs, films, and literature. I think the American Dream penetrated our society, and a lot of young people became excited about capitalism and the free market.

In 1995, I went to America to stay in New Hampshire as part of a student exchange program. I was working in the White Mountains for three months in a typical summer job, but I saw how beautiful this country was, how entrepreneurial it was. I was breathing in the American spirit, which helped me a lot. We started making our first game after I returned from America in 1995 or 1996. It was all inspiration; it was all enthusiasm.

Ramsay: There were five of you working on the first game?

Kislyi: Yes, my brother, Eugene, and three college friends.

Ramsay: Did they stay with you throughout the company?

Kislyi: Unfortunately, one of them died about seven years ago, but yeah, the rest of the guys stayed.

Ramsay: Are they still with the company?

Kislyi: Yes, most of the people are, but, of course, right now we have a lot of people, and people come and go. The old guard has mostly stayed with one or two exceptions.

Ramsay: I don't want to say "lead founder" because you weren't starting a business. How about this? Were you the project leader?

Kislyi: I have to say I was always the mastermind behind the things we do.

Ramsay: How did you convince the others to go along with you?

Kislyi: Most of the people who joined during the enthusiastic phase were computer science graduates or students who knew a lot of programming. They did not want to go and do scientific or business programming. Everybody was playing games. All boys were playing strategy games, of course, so it was easy. I said, "Hey, come on, join and let's make the best strategy game of all time." They could not refuse; it was that easy.

Ramsay: When did your team evolve into a business?

Kislyi: We understood that we would be making games, as a business, for a long time before we would be successful. You don't know whether the first game will be a success, or the second game, or the third, and so on.

And so we very wisely started a so-called offshore programming department. In the 1990s, Belarus had become one of the world's centers for outsourcing, flourishing in 2000. There were companies here doing custom programming for Microsoft, Oracle, and other big companies in the West.

We started something like this on a smaller scale, working on small websites, ecommerce, and accounting software; there were no video games. We were doing commercial software as contractors. That was a small business, but a business that was generating good money for us, enough to sustain our game development team, which we grew from 10 to 20 people.

We had that business experience which maybe other enthusiastic, independent game developers didn't have. We had discipline about time to market, project management, all aspects of software development, and all hardships, too. But there was no one particular date when someone said, "Okay, now we have a business." We were still dedicated to making the best game of all time. It just naturally happened. The money flowed, and the business evolved.

When we launched our first game, called DBA Online—DBA stands for De Bellis Antiquitatis, which is Latin for "Of the Wars of Antiquity"—we rented a server and put together a billing system. We had to have a website to promote the game, and we had to do some public relations. When the first $10 hit our account, that was when we started to build a real video game business.

Ramsay: Where did you get the first ten dollars?

Kislyi: Well, DBA Online was your typical tabletop miniature game. We licensed the rule set of the most popular Asian tabletop war game, and we made a complete computerization with thousands of historical troops. You would have Romans, Greeks, Asians, Chaldeans, Mongols, and all those troops you've seen in the Total War series. Our one-month subscription fee was $10, which gave you unlimited play. We thought that was a good price, and we had a few hundred, then a few thousand, players paying that subscription fee.

Ramsay: How long was the typical match?

Kislyi: One turn would take you five minutes up to ten. However, if your opponent was in New Zealand, and then you take your turn from somewhere else, you'd have to wait until the next day for him to wake up. One match could take up to 40 minutes across two weeks. You were able to play dozens of matches at the same time, but obviously, this wasn't a mass market feature.

Ramsay: Where did you go after you had your first subscriptions?

Kislyi: Well, the good news for us was that we tapped into the already existing, very hardcore, but very united, war games community—you know, the typical beer-and-pretzel war gamers. We allowed them to play the exact same rule set with the exact same armies and sophistication, in terms of tactics and strategy, over the Internet anytime and anywhere.

When we ended up with thousands of players, we realized that being niche can pay off in certain circumstances, but we wanted to do something more mass market. That's how Massive Assault came into existence. We actually took the rules of our very old game we had made in 1996, we had a bunch of bright guys create a nice 3D engine, and we refurbished the very old game into sci-fi. There were robots, tanks, and helicopters; futuristic heavy weaponry; and different planets and landscapes. That hit a sweet spot when Panzer General died off and Heroes of Might and Magic 5 had not yet been released.

Believe it or not, Massive Assault scored 80% on Metacritic and Game Rankings, which was not a typical thing for an indie game. As GameSpy put it, "strategy gaming has never been so sweet!" We essentially made a classical hex-based, turn-based Panzer General, and we blended relatively sophisticated political and tactical rules with very beautiful 3D visuals. That's how Massive Assault took off nicely. Massive Assault made us a name in the mass market game industry.

Ramsay: With Massive Assault, you wanted to take the game in a mass-market direction, so why choose sci-fi instead of fantasy?

Kislyi: Good point. We already had one of the deepest historical simulation games with DBA Online, and we realized that having a military history base for the game adds a lot of constraints, like archers cannot shoot more than a hundred meters, right? We wanted the freedom to make "wow" weapons, like big, walking robots shooting rockets. Nobody could say that wasn't realistic because nobody has seen big, walking robots shooting rockets!

Massive Assault could have been fantasy, but there were already a lot of fantasy games, and we didn't want any historical constraints. We just wanted to make a generic game with tactical variety, a wide range of weapons, and varying movement speeds. With sci-fi, you can design your own rock, paper, and scissors, and let your imagination carry you as far as possible.

Ramsay: Were you self-publishing?

Kislyi: We self-published DBA Online, and that was a great, great experience. With Massive Assault, we ran around the world, made some phone calls, and found a publisher. Matrix Games was a very niche, very classical turn-based strategy publisher. They weren't very big, and not very powerful, but they put the game in America for us. GMX Media was our publisher for Europe, and Akella was our publisher for Russia. Big names like EA and Microsoft would not take on turn-based strategy games, so they passed on us. We had to go with smaller, presumably more dedicated publishers to get the game to retail.

Ramsay: Why didn't you publish Massive Assault, like DBA Online?

Kislyi: Massive Assault was more of a mass market, retail product with AI and a single-player campaign. When you self-publish online, how do you get players? You need marketing dollars, right? With DBA, it was easy because we did viral marketing amongst the existing armchair generals, and that was easy because they were already well-organized. But with Massive Assault, we didn't have the marketing dollars to promote the game. We did not have access to retail, and at least, in those days, that was the only way to reach the mass market.

Ramsay: How well did the game do at retail?

Kislyi: The truth is the retail version did not bring us millions of dollars. We hit all of the negative aspects of working with a publisher that you can imagine, so aside from the advance, we didn't see a single dollar from the US market. That was a bitter experience. We saw more royalties from our European publisher, who did a really good job in England, Germany, and France; they were sending us checks every quarter. And we received good advance payments from Russia, somewhere between $20,000 and $30,000.

All in all, Massive Assault sold only around dozens of thousands of copies over a few years. The people who purchased the boxed game played through the single-player campaign fairly quickly, but the most enjoyable part was the online, face-to-face battles. That's why we made a spinoff, and we had a provision in our contract that allowed us to do so. We spun off an online-only version called Massive Assault Network, and again we were self-publishing like in the old days. Well, we realized that was very expensive.

Ramsay: What can you say about your experience with Matrix Games?

Kislyi: Believe it or not, on the day when we were supposed to submit the gold master, there was a big blackout in New York. This was 2003. The whole tri-state area had no electricity. Matrix Games is based in Staten Island, so we could not call them, we couldn't get them on ICQ, and we couldn't e-mail them. So, we missed the gold master date due to the blackout.

And then we found out we were missing online play codes in a number of boxes. GameStop, EB Games, or one of the big retail chains received a shipment without the codes, and they were not very happy, so they returned those copies and we immediately lost one retail chain from our distribution network. Everything was against us, and then there was piracy. Matrix never recouped the advance, so we never saw a royalty check.

Ramsay: There was a sequel, right?

Kislyi: Yes, we did Massive Assault: Domination, which was published again by Akella in Russia, and DreamCatcher Interactive performed well in Europe and America. The first Massive Assault obviously gave us a lot of mass market knowledge, like how to do public relations, marketing, and community.

I think Domination made our name in the game developer realm. Not everyone purchased the box, not everyone played the game, but everybody was hearing about Massive Assault. I toured with the guys from DreamCatcher in America. In Europe, PC Gamer and all of the magazines were talking about the game in interviews, hands-on demos, and those things. Domination was again very well accepted by the media, and it made a big splash. It made us decent money, again. Not millions, but more than the first, and it allowed us to move forward.

Ramsay: Many independent game developers struggle with landing publishing deals, and there you were in Belarus, signed and working with multiple publishers simultaneously on your first games.

Kislyi: Well, since the days of the first Massive Assault, an essential part of our business strategy was going places to meet new people. I was flying around the Western world meeting with, of course, magazines for interviews, but I was also going to GDC, E3, and other conferences to meet with publishers. I had realized that in order to be successful, you have to know everyone. That was my goal, and at a certain point, I did know everyone! We fostered good relationships with publishers at conferences, visited their offices, and talked about the past, present, and future. Those connections wove together into business.

Ramsay: Before World of Tanks, how big of a company was Wargaming?

Kislyi: In 2006, we had probably more than 40 people, and everyone was on salaries. Until World of Tanks, we were very amateurish but enthusiastic. There was very little income personally, enough to buy food and rent a small room to live in. I was living with my parents before then, and then I had ten years of unparalleled enthusiasm, just working to build the team, our experience, connections, and expertise for the future.

Ramsay: In 2007, you acquired Arise. Was that your first acquisition?

Kislyi: Yes. Arise was the same size as us. We were both small, so we just said to them, "Hey, come over. Let's join forces and make big games together."

Ramsay: How was acquiring another company even possible for you then?

Kislyi: Remember we had a side business, a non-game business where we were doing custom software development? We were doing that from 2001 through 2007. We had an ad serving technology called AdRevolver, which we used for banners in Belarus and a little bit of Russia. Our market was not big.

In 2004, BlueLithium, an ad network in California, called us and—it's a long story—they wanted to use our technology solution. We met each other for the first time in London, and we sold the technology to them while continuing as a research and development center for them. By 2007, BlueLithium was quite a big company with a lot of revenue from advertising, and Yahoo acquired that company for $300 million. We got good money out of the deal. That was our finest hour, our lucky day, and we wisely did not start buying Ferraris and islands. Instead, we invested heavily in our video game future.

With that money, at Wargaming, were able to double our team with Arise, and we started building a new real-time strategy game called Order of War, which was published by Square Enix in 2009. We had also already been playing with MMO technology, which led us to World of Tanks.

Ramsay: Mergers are sometimes hard to handle. What did you learn from integrating Arise into Wargaming?

Kislyi: Arise was more of an outsourcing company, so my message to them was simple: start making your own game. That worked! There are always difficulties though. They had their own game designers, who thought our game designers were not as good as they were; that always happens. Mergers take time and patience. You can't order people to be friends forever; you just have to wait. They were reasonable, and we were reasonable, so we just had to be smart and polite. The merger took maybe a year. There was no other way.

Ramsay: In the meantime, you were still growing quite rapidly.

Kislyi: Yes, of course. We were 60 and the Arise team was 50. We continued to hire people who were new to both teams. After one year, there were more new people than old. That, humorously, helped with the merger. We brought in so many totally new people that the merger wasn't an issue anymore!

Ramsay: What impact did bringing Arise into the fold have on your company?

Kislyi: The Arise team reinforced each and every department we had. Their programmers became part of our programming department, the quality assurance guys became our quality assurance guys, and so on.

Arise was mostly an art outsourcing shop, so they were experts on 3D modeling and texturing, where we had less discipline. We didn't need too much of that for turn-based games, so their art department was much stronger than ours. And they had a serious process for art production that became ours. That reinforced our art department big time.

We also had the shared goal of needing to do an MMO of our own. Nobody had time to think, "Am I Arise? Or am I Wargaming?" That big goal was in front of everyone—this big MMO, which presumably would make us rich and famous, or all of us would fail together if we didn't make it.

Ramsay: Why develop an MMO? They're expensive. Risky.

Kislyi: Being a traditional single player shop for such a long time, we knew definitely each and every nuance of that business, right? You have to finance a project's development times two, three, and sometimes even four years; and then you have to sign up with a publisher who controls retail shelf space. There are so many negatives, from just dealing with publishers to piracy to shelf space, that we could see the single-player box product business dying off.

By 2008, as you can imagine, there aren't any stories left to tell in games. We've seen it all in Doom II, Warcraft, StarCraft, Mass Effect, and so on; everything has already been done. There's no freaking way you can come up with a new story people will like, and customers now expect perhaps 24 hours of campaign content in a single-player box game. It's tougher now.

There was no hope at all to make another successful single-player box product. So, what was the next thing you could do? You can publish an MMO yourself. You don't need a box. And then there was the subscription model. For us, 2008 was a year of nonstop analysis of everything online.

And we realized we would need online server technology, so we contacted BigWorld Technology, which is a company that makes an engine for MMOs. We negotiated a license for their technology, although we did not yet know exactly what our game would look like. We flew our guys from Sydney for a week in Minsk to teach our programmers their SDK. We found out that it takes six to eight months just to build out the core technology and tailor that technology to our needs. While the programmers were working, we were looking at World of Warcraft, and Korean, Chinese, and Russian free-to-play games.

The result was World of Tanks because, of course, it was a bright idea to make a world full of tanks! But a lot of things in World of Tanks, like the mechanics, are the result of deep, deep analyses of other games and the market.

Ramsay: At Wargaming, are you just the CEO? Or do you have a hand in development?

Kislyi: Of course, as a founding father, I was designing all of our old games, but I can say that one of my smartest decisions was to not design World of Tanks. I said to myself, "Victor, you can design a good turn-based single-player game, but you've never designed a free-to-play action MMO before." That was new to me.

As we say, I stepped over my pride and let three Russian designers do it. They relocated to Minsk. They were big military enthusiasts, particularly tanks, and specialists in free-to-play games, mostly browser-based games in Russia.

For training, for approximately the eight months after we started working with the online technology, we had made a traditional fantasy game where elves and orcs would shoot arrows and kill each other with swords. When we showed that game to them, they said, "Okay, we won't pull off fantasy because there are hundreds of fantasy games coming out every year. Hey, let's do the same thing but with tanks." I asked, "Are you sure?" They said "yes" and convinced me they could design a game around tank battles.

The concept is simple, but if you play World of Tanks, there are so many elements in the game that had to be designed well and balanced. That was beyond my capability. I would rather concentrate on the business, bringing in more people, securing resources, and thinking about future opportunities. So, I stepped aside and let other people design the game.

Ramsay: Do you play World of Tanks?

Kislyi: Of course, I play World of Tanks fanatically. I have now played more than 11,000 battles. From time to time, bright ideas come to mind, and I let the designers know, but I'm in the same position as any other employee. We can chip in ideas, but there's a professional game design process. Some ideas go into the game, some are modified, and some of them just don't.

Ramsay: For World of Tanks, why again return to self-publishing? You had said that self-publishing is expensive, and this time you didn't know the business.

Kislyi: Well, there weren't as many free-to-play publishers. There were some new free-to-play publishers, but they were not as big as Sony or Microsoft.

We visited everyone. We met and spoke with Sony Online Entertainment, there was Microsoft, and every big publisher we knew from our single-player years. It took us quite a bit of analysis to understand that the problem with those publishers remains the same developer-publisher relationship. You create a product, put it in a box, ship it, and put it on a shelf; you do one or two patches; and then you start another two- to three-year development cycle.

With an MMO, especially with free-to-play, success is fueled by very frequent updates. If you have a successful launch, it does not mean anything if players consume your content faster than you can produce it. They will need new maps, new tanks, new gameplay modes, and twists in the mechanics pretty much nonstop, and very, very frequently.

So, at the end of the day, consumer wants a particular experience. The consumer doesn't care where they purchased the game, or whether we made it ourselves, or whether we have a contract with a publisher; consumers want what they want. It was a wise decision to not give the game to a publisher.

Ramsay: What about China?

Kislyi: In China, you must have a publisher by law. In China, we have a good publisher and our game is definitely a frontrunner for them, so they treat World of Tanks as their main title and that's good for us.

Ramsay: Where was World of Tanks first published?

Kislyi: We live in Belarus; it's a small country of ten million, but we speak the Russian language, and we are a part of the former Soviet culture. For us, Russia is our big, home market we understand. We were already one of the biggest and most respected game companies in the former Soviet Union. Our single-player products had tremendous success in Russia, so we decided to first launch World of Tanks in Russia on our own and see how it went.

You need a special understanding of just how many people would be needed to publish one tank game in Russia. Five, 15, 20, and no more? Today, we have 500 people who do only community management, customer support, events, and esports. That's just for one game. None of the publishers we had met from the MMO segment had that many employees for one game.

And it appears that if your game's successful, your problems begin. You have to pretty much reinvent the bicycle, and I think we did that. Russia taught us a lot of lessons, and then we expanded to the West.

Ramsay: Would you agree with the statement that the free-to-play business model is hard to get right?

Kislyi: Yes, absolutely. Big, traditional publishers were afraid of the word, and the media in the West was like, "Free-to-play? We're not touching this. We're not writing about low-quality Asian stuff." And publishers had the same attitude, "We don't see Western people playing these cheap Asian games." And we said, "World of Tanks is made in Europe!" There was a huge wall, a lot of prejudice toward free-to-play, and you wouldn't believe how damaging that was for us. We put in a lot of effort to get big media outlets like PC Gamer, GameSpy, GameSpot, and IGN to start writing about free-to-play games.

Ramsay: Why do you think free-to-play faced such an uphill battle?

Kislyi: So, the Asian games traditionally sell battlefields for money, like you buy a big cool sword or a big cool diamond, and put it into your weapon and you become invincible or just dominate the battlefield. That works well in China, but definitely not in the West. How you design your monetization so that people can play for free is very important. There is no one magic formula for free-to-play games though. If the game is for kids, you need a different monetization scheme; they don't have their own money.

Ramsay: How successful have you been with free-to-play?

Kislyi: Free-to-play is now the only thing we have. We have nothing else to sell. We don't have any other businesses, so all of our success, which obviously is there, is due to free-to-play.

Ramsay: And now the model is standard. Subscriptions are practically gone, although some developers now offer optional subscription packages.

Kislyi: We proudly think we were successful in breaking the customer, media, and industry perceptions of free-to-play. We were not only promoting and advertising World of Tanks, our product, but also free-to-play as a model, so that other developers could benefit. Back in 2008, they thought nobody would pay and you'd go bankrupt, but now the model is everywhere.

Ramsay: Wargaming didn't start out to be a business, but now Wargaming is an international conglomerate. Just how big is your company?

Kislyi: Today, we're at 1600 employees. One or two months, we had 1,500 employees. We have offices in 15 different cities, and we cover pretty much the whole world. In video games, this is a big company.

Ramsay: When you spoke to your grandmother, you had dreamed of selling a million copies of a game. You've done that, and then some, to say the least.

Kislyi: The future was definitely much brighter than those calculations I gave to my grandmother many, many years ago. But we don't feel the journey is over. In this online world, things happen quickly. There are a lot of successful businesses using online, social, and mobile for not only games, and you can see that they rise up really, really fast. Our audience is pretty much seven billion people. We have at least half of that connected to the Internet and now more even on mobile. I think we're only just beginning. We are very ambitious. There are oceans, literally oceans, to be conquered, and we haven't done that yet.

Richard Garriott

Cofounder, Origin Systems

 **Richard Garriott** and his older brother Robert cofounded Origin Systems in 1983 to develop, publish, and market the *Ultima* series and other products. That series, along with *Akalabeth: World of Doom*, one of the first role-playing games (RPGs) for the PC in 1979, defined the genre for decades.

After the release of *Ultima VII: The Black Gate* in 1992, Origin Systems was acquired by Electronic Arts (EA). Only three years later, the studio began work on *Ultima Online (UO)*, the massively multiplayer online (MMO) RPG that would quickly popularize the genre.

Disappointed with the greenlight process within EA, Garriott retired in 2000. With producer Starr Long and his brother, he then founded Destination Games. Acquired by NCsoft in 2001, Destination Games released *Auto Assault, City of Heroes*, and other titles until finally launching *Tabula Rasa*, a sci-fi MMO, in 2007 to critical acclaim. Ultimately, the game failed to find a foothold in the highly competitive MMO market, and NCsoft sunsetted the game by 2009.

In 2008, Garriott traveled to the stars aboard a Russian spacecraft bound for the International Space Station. He became the sixth private citizen to fly in Earth's orbit, and the first second-generation American astronaut. His father, Owen, spent nearly 70 days in space during his NASA career. Upon returning to Earth, Garriott was informed that his position at NCsoft had been terminated.

Garriott joined Portalarium soon after, which was initially focused on social games. In 2010, the company launched a collection of casino-style games on Facebook. By 2013, however, Portalarium was looking to Garriott's roots, announcing *Shroud of the Avatar: Forsaken Virtues*, a single-player and multiplayer fantasy RPG inspired by the *Ultima* series. A successful Kickstarter campaign in 2014 has since led Portalarium to raising more than $6.4 million for that property, and today, Garriott continues in his role as creative director.

Ramsay: You've led an interesting life, enjoyed tremendous success in your career, and you've even been to space. We should talk about everything, but let's start where all good stories do: where it all started.

Garriott: I started Origin when I was pretty young. I was 19. Origin was founded officially in 1982. Prior to that, I was a student in high school and then a few years in college, but I was already publishing video games. I started writing my first video games in 1974, the same year I entered high school. I published my first commercial video game in 1979. After working with a couple of publishers, my brother Robert and I decided to form Origin in 1982.

Ramsay: What were the early days of the video game industry like?

Garriott: It's interesting. In the 1970s, calling it an industry was a bit of a stretch. There really weren't any national, much less global, distributors of video game software. In fact, in the very earliest years, there weren't even peripheral computers, which didn't really come into existence until 1977. There weren't really even standardized platforms, you might say.

Those earliest days were very much about hobbyist activities. An analogy might be people who build model trains, airplanes, or something. There was very little in the way of organization, especially toward doing business. Even sharing knowledge and the creative process were quite minimal.

On one hand, that sounds very primitive. On the other, that time was a lot of fun. There were few competitors and fewer rules. You had this great freedom to explore, a sense you were on the leading edge of something that was going to be a wave of the future, or at least really relevant and interesting.

Ramsay: Did you have a commercial interest in developing video games?

Garriott: No, not at all. In fact, it wasn't clear that there could be the opportunity for anything commercial. The motivation was to create something amazing with this new amazing tool: the computer. It was really an artistic endeavor, not a commercial one.

Ramsay: How did you get involved with developing video games anyway?

Garriott: In my freshman year of high school, one of the classes I was taking had a computer terminal, and no one in the school knew how to use it. No class made use of it, and I have no idea how and when it was acquired and put there. But I figured out at least how to turn it on and connect it; it was a teletype with an acoustic modem that you could dial up to an offsite computer. I believe it was a PDP-11, and I just began to tinker with it.

And, in that school, the faculty knew me very well as a person who would do very well with independent studies. I was a regular serious competitor in science fairs, so when I expressed interest in having access to this machine and teaching myself how to use it, the faculty very quickly agreed. For my four years of high school, they gave me my own class, no teacher, no curriculum, and they counted BASIC as my foreign language credit, so I never took a foreign language in high school. I spent those four years of high school, writing game after game after game, making them bigger and better throughout.

Ramsay: Why games? Why not simpler programs?

Garriott: Well, because *Dungeons & Dragons* was published in 1974, and I had also just read *The Lord of the Rings*. Those things struck me at the same time, so games became the amalgamation of my strongest interests.

Ramsay: The games you made were role-playing games even then?

Garriott: That's right. In fact, I used to call them DND1, DND2, DND3—up to DND28. The clear inspiration was *Dungeons & Dragons*. As I was finishing high school, the Apple II came out, and I wrote DND28b, which was a port of number 28 to the Apple which finally had graphics, and that became my first published game *Akalabeth*, which is sort of the prequel to the *Ultimas*.

Ramsay: When did you become interested in selling your game?

Garriott: I had a summer job working at a ComputerLand store, which is one of the early stores where people would go buy Apples, Commodore 64s, and a few others. And most people who bought these early computers were buying them ostensibly to balance their checkbook or do some word processing on. I was always in the back working on my game.

It was the owner of the ComputerLand store who saw the game I was working on and said, "Look, Richard, this game that you have here in the back is way better than any other piece of software we sell on the store wall here. You really should package that and sell it."

Since there was no industry at that time, packaging and selling the game meant I went next door to the print shop and made some instruction manuals, bought some Ziploc bags, hand copied disks in the store there, and began to sell them from that store wall. Within a week or two, I was selling a few in the store, and it was one of those first few that got pirated all across the country.

Akalabeth eventually made it to one of the first national distribution companies called California Pacific, who called me up and said, "Hey, we'd like to sell this in stores all the way across the country. How would you feel about that if we paid you five bucks a unit?"

"That sounds fine to me," I said, and so they sold about 30,000 copies of *Akalabeth*. If you do that math, that's $150,000 for my work as a high school senior—double or triple my father's salary as an astronaut.

Ramsay: And what did your father think?

Garriott: Well, this was right as I was going into college, so on the one hand, he was like, "All right, well, I guess you just paid for your college, and that's a good thing." So, I was leaning a lot less heavily on his pocketbook for sure, and that was one very good aspect of it.

You know, what's interesting is with *Akalabeth* and *Ultima I* and *Ultima II*—the first three games that I created—each one made dramatically more money than their predecessor. And so my whole family is watching that happen, and my family though, "Well, of course, Richard, this makes sense to pursue right now because it would be stupid not to. But it's going so well that it surely can't last. Surely this will come to an end. This windfall will end and you'll need to go back to school, finish your degree, and get a real job." But none of us were really thinking it was the beginning of an industry. We had no idea it was the beginning of something that would be permanently growing. And it never ended.

Ramsay: You mentioned packaging games in Ziploc bags?

Garriott: That's correct, yeah. Little 5x7 Ziploc bags and Xeroxed heavy card instructions. You had eleven sheets of paper cut into fourths and stapled together to hand bind the little instruction manuals and things of that nature. Now the ones I made and shipped myself are so rare that they sell for something on the order of $10,000 dollars each on eBay now.

Ramsay: Jason Rubin told me he got started pretty much the same way with Naughty Dog in the early 1980s, selling games out of Ziploc bags. I'm wondering now why nobody put more thought into packaging then.

Garriott: Let me give my take on that. Drug addiction was sadly common during the early days of the industry. My first publisher, California Pacific, went out of business because the principals were drug addicts and snorted all the money they were making instead of paying people like me who were making their games. So, after they went out of business, and after I got the name "Ultima" back, I kept it as my own personal trademark.

I was already working on *Ultima II*, so I then said, "Hey, I'm Richard Allen Garriott. I'm interested in a publisher who's interested in publishing my next game." Every publisher in America was interested. I already had a strong track record, but then I said, "I don't want my games in bags anymore." Most all of my competitors' games were doing things like *Apple-Oids*, the *Asteroids* knockoff that looks like an Apple, or a Millipede instead of Centipede, or some play on words. Most early Apple developers were developing knockoffs of simple arcade games. I was already making virtual worlds in my mind, so I didn't want my game in a big Ziploc bag. I wanted my game in a box. I wanted a cloth map of my game to describe the reality of the game world. I wanted the manuals to be written as if they were real magic tomes and things of that nature.

So, although lots of publishers were interested in publishing Ultima II, when I asked for all of that, everyone put their hands back down—except for Sierra, which was called On-Line Systems at the time.

Sierra Online was the only company that agreed to my outrageous demands for putting my game in a box. *Ultima II* is actually the first game in the entire industry that was not packaged in a Ziploc bag. So, I think I can lay some level of claim to advancing us from Ziploc bags to boxes. Another one is the use of the term "avatar" as your character; that is, you, the real person from Earth, projected into a virtual world. Another one I often get some credit for is the term "massively multiplayer online role-playing games," or MMORPGs.

Ramsay: When did starting the company come into the picture?

Garriott: Right after Sierra Online, but just like California Pacific owing me a bunch of money, Sierra Online also started having financial trouble and quit paying their authors, including me. And so when both of these companies were going down, each time, I called my brother Robert who had multiple business degrees, and I said, "Robert, can you help me try to collect from these dirt bags who quit paying me the money they owe me?"

In both cases, he tried, and in both cases, we failed to get any of the money that was owed to me from those publishers. But after doing it twice, Robert then turned to me and said, "Richard, why don't you and I go into business together? Because, at the very least, I know that when I receive a check for selling your games, I will give you your cut first. You can make a lot of people unhappy in tough times, but I know the one person you can't make unhappy is the person who's laying the golden eggs—the person who's making the game—because without him, you have absolutely no future." And I said, "Well, that's a better deal than I've had so far." That's what started Origin Systems in 1982.

Ramsay: What was your brother's background then?

Garriott: He's five years older than me. He has two bachelor's degrees from Rice University, one in engineering and one in economics. He then went to Stanford University and got his master's degree in engineering. And he went to Sloan Business School at MIT and got another master's degree in business. While going through this over-education path, he worked at Texas Instruments designing RAM chips; and then he worked in venture capital, studying investments in entertainment software companies. He was basically the perfect person for tackling this business with me.

Ramsay: Did you personally have any experience with starting businesses?

Garriott: Oh, no. Don't forget I started making games in my freshman year in high school. I was the game guy. He was the business guy.

Ramsay: What did you learn in that short while?

Garriott: In those earliest days, we were both young and brothers, so we had plenty of what I would call "good fights." By that I mean something that made us better in business and something that made Origin a particularly shining example of a good early company, compared to our competitors.

I'll give you an example. Let's assume that a publisher had a royalty agreement with an American developer to sell a game in the United States. So, let's then suppose that game was licensed to sell in Japan. A company in Japan would build, market, and distribute the game, and pay the publisher a licensing fee. Royalties in those days were very high compared to today, something like 30%.

What the publisher would do is they would say, "Okay, well, now we've just received a licensing fee, so we'll pay the developer that same 30% royalty." Robert proposed that "we should do the same," and I would go, "Well, wait a minute. That's not fair. The manufacturing and marketing expenses have already been removed. It would actually be fair to pay a 50% royalty because by that time that licensing fee came in, that money had no process associated with it."

And Robert would argue, "Well, Richard, I don't disagree with what you conceptually consider fair, but fair in business is based on what you negotiate and what the industry has as a standard. If we pay our authors higher than the industry standard, that means our company will make less than other companies in the industry, and our company will be less competitive, less profitable, and less capable of maneuvering and acquiring and doing all of the things we need to do as a business. You'd be hurting the business to have this 'sense of fairness' that no other company feels like they need to have."

We had that argument, and we'd have those arguments, but we'd find some middle ground usually. I was always the author's advocate though. I was always the person there going, "Wait a minute, I am an author for my company. I may be an owner of the company, but I also get paid royalties. That's how I pay myself." Other authors in our industry knew that when they came to Origin, they would have someone who was fighting in their corner to make sure the company operated openly, above board, and fair to the creators of products. I think that was an essential part of Origin in the early days.

Ramsay: Given the nature of these arguments, did you work with your brother to put together a business plan?

Garriott: We did put together something of a business plan, but we weren't taking any outside money. We built the company all on money I had earned from *Ultima*. I mean, a business plan is usually there to sell somebody something, to convince somebody, "Hey, give us a bunch of money, and here's how we'll spend that money to try to earn you some money back." In our case, we had the *Ultima* series and we knew it was successful. By the time we formed the company, I was almost finished with *Ultima III*, so we got off to a pretty good, fast, quick, and easy start because of that kick start we had.

Ramsay: What was your relationship with your brother like prior to going into business with him?

Garriott: Well, interesting. I have two older brothers and a younger sister, and my two older brothers were playmates, you might say, and my younger sister and I were playmates. So, although we were brothers, and we went on some family vacations and outings together, throughout junior high and high school, he and my older brother hung out together while my sister and I hung out together. We weren't distant or argumentative by any means, but we didn't have any cause to be nearly as close as we did once we got into business.

Ramsay: When did you hire your first employee?

Garriott: Our first employee—well, let's see, I remember our first few employees. First was Jeff Hillhouse from Sierra who, to this day, has followed us around from company to company. We still work very closely with Jeff.

Another was a most interesting character. He was a gentleman in our industry known as "Doctor Cat." We ran an advertisement in a magazine, and we didn't even have a logo yet, so one of the employees of the magazine made up this ad with a compass rose as the backdrop behind the word Origin, announcing the existence of our company. We basically said, "Hey, we're Origin. We're going to change the world and make some great games. If you want to make great games, too, come join us down here in Houston, Texas."

A week or two later, Doctor Cat showed up at our door. And when I say "showed up at our door," I mean he literally showed up at the family house. He knocked on the door and said, "Hi, I'm Doctor Cat. I read your ad, and I am here to work for you." And he had moved lock, stock and barrel down to Texas from way up north, and he became one of our first and one of our strongest employees for the first ten years or so of our existence as a game developer.

Ramsay: Why did you start hiring in the first place?

Garriott: We wanted to not just be the publisher of Ultima. We founded Origin the same year as Electronic Arts, and a number of other early companies were formed that year, plus or minus one year. A couple of those earliest companies, like California Pacific and Sierra, had done such a poor job, squandering their money and putting themselves out of business, that we said we can do better. So we immediately tried to become one of the first great game—not only developers —but publishers. Origin throughout its existence was always in the top ten. That's something we were very proud of.

Ramsay: Early on, was Origin just you and Robert?

Garriott: No, even on the day we formed the company, we had Jeff Hillhouse, for example. We hired Keith Zabalaoui, a guy who's still in the industry today, and he now makes war games, I think. He was my neighbor who had helped me on a couple of my earliest games, so we hired him to make some games as well. And Chuck Bueche. Chuckles had published some games through Sierra, too. He had lived in Friendswood, Texas, near me, so he came back and joined us at Origin. On day one, Origin started with half a dozen to a dozen staffers.

Ramsay: Was there anyone outside the company whose advice you relied on?

Garriott: We had one person on our board, Bill Richards, who was an independent businessman. He was a friend of my father, and he was the only person amongst us who had really been through building a business. And my parents were both investors on the board, and there was my brother and me, of course, but Bill Richards was the one outsider, the one experienced person. I still chat with him periodically today.

Ramsay: What was your business model then?

Garriott: Yes, very good question. The reason we chose the name Origin, which originally was Origin Systems, was because we weren't even sure about whether games would be the big growth area that we'd stick with or whether we would get into operating systems or maybe even hardware.

In fact, in those very earliest days, there was one plug in the back of an Apple II for putting in a game control device. The plug was actually capable of running two joysticks, but no one ever made one. And there were games out like Crazy Climber, Robotron, and others in a coin-op arcade that used two joysticks. And so we actually went and built a prototype of a dual joystick, and I still have all of the components at my home. We built out this prototype and almost went to manufacture this dual joystick from Origin, except that the cost of doing plastic injection molding and to get the dye made was about $10,000. Anyway, we picked the name Origin to give us the freedom to go into either entertainment software or business software or hardware.

Ramsay: What then was your next step for your game business?

Garriott: Well, we were doing lots of other games that weren't as big of a hit as *Ultima*. The first time we did something that was as big or bigger than Ultima was when we discovered Chris Roberts and the *Wing Commander* series.

That again was a good stroke of fate in that it was after I had already moved Origin here to Austin, Texas. We were already hiring all the artists we could find in Austin. In fact, there were basically no computer-skilled artists in the world, much less in Austin, so we had to train them to work with a computer. One was a guy named Denis Loubet, who went on to draw every Ultima cover except Ultima II, and when we hired him, Chris was already trying to work with Denis on some of his early games. So, we hired his artist away.

That's how we became known to each other. Chris was writing small games mostly in England, but his parents lived in Austin, so he was spending time in Austin as well. He was trying to work with Denis who we had hired, so he came walking in the door, saying, "Hey, what are you guys doing hiring my artists?"

And we said, "Hey, we make games," and he made games, so we brought him on board at Origin as a partner. He then began to work on the Wing Commander series, which, until Ultima Online, was our biggest seller.

Ramsay: When I interviewed John Romero last week, I learned that Origin had two locations: New Hampshire and Austin. Is that correct?

Garriott: That's true. Well, technically, we even had more than two locations. We formed the company in my parents' garage in Houston, where we operated for about a year, and then we moved out to real offices in Texas for about a year. Then we moved first to Massachusetts and then New Hampshire for about three years, and then we split the company and a bunch of us came back to Austin when my brother stayed in the northeast before we all got back together again in Austin. Kind of a complicated story, but yes, there was a period of time where the offices were fully in the northeast, and for the longest of that period, we were in Londonderry, New Hampshire.

Ramsay: Did you have multiple offices simultaneously?

Garriott: We did. The way that transpired was we formed the company in my parents' garage out of convenience. It was free, and it was sort of centrally located in a sense between me in Austin, where I had started school, and my brother, Robert, who was already living just outside of Boston where he and his wife had just finished school. So, my brother was commuting to Texas for three weeks out of the month. After a year or so of him commuting to Texas, we all agreed to go to the northeast for a few years because Marcy, his wife, was expecting a promotion within AT&T Bell Laboratories where she worked.

And we were all young, and where our computers went, our jobs went, so we all moved to the northeast and we stayed there for about three years. By the time three years had passed, the company had then grown to a scale that it became difficult to move back to Texas because we now had hired a bunch of people who worked locally in New Hampshire. But it was always the plan for those of us who were from Texas to move back. And so a bunch of us who were unhappy with the cold weather, among other things, decided to up and move back to Austin, so that's how we got started in Austin. The Austin office grew very rapidly, and eventually, the northeastern office really had no choice other than to join us back in Texas.

Ramsay: Did the distance between Austin and New Hampshire affect how you or the company worked?

Garriott: Well, development and publishing, especially back in those days, were fairly distinct. Nowadays, online game development and publishing are sort of intermingled from the beginning and definitely through the life of the product. Back in those days, you would develop a game and then you would be pretty much done with it, and you would then ship it onward to retail, and after that, the developers really couldn't do anything with it. So, it was easier to do at that time than it would be now.

Ramsay: And you always had a team around you, correct?

Garriott: Well, by that time, sure, but I did all the early *Ultimas* all by myself. Obviously, the prequels and *Akalabeth* I did completely by myself. I wrote *Ultima I* completely by myself, except one small subroutine, which a friend of mine, Ken Arnold, helped develop, but then I effectively made *Ultima II, III,* and *IV* on my own. It was only starting with *Ultima V* that I began to have a staff of people who worked with me. That's about the time of the shift to Texas.

Ramsay: Which was most important to your development strategy: demonstrating new technology, or creating original works?

Garriott: Definitely both, but if you look at the 28 DND games I wrote, some of them I would never finish. I would start writing one, but I was also teaching myself to program while writing these games. There were no classes, and there were no books to read. It was all self-taught. When I wrote *Akalabeth*, which is like Ultima 0; the game was written in BASIC. It was the first game I ever wrote on the Apple II. When I finished it, I went, "Wow, that game sold 30,000 units and I never even meant to sell it. It doesn't have a story, and there's no way to win it." I thought, "Wow, I could do a much better game if I just started over."

And so I began the first *Ultima*. The first *Ultima* was also written in BASIC, but it was written with an eye toward users, not just myself, so it's a much better game than *Akalabeth*. And then when I finished *Ultima I*, which sold almost twice what *Akalabeth* sold, I thought, "Wow, now that I've mastered writing a game at all, if I mastered assembly, I could write a much better game."

So, I wrote Ultima II in assembly language. When I finished that, I said, "Wow, that was my first game in assembly! That language is much more powerful than BASIC, but that first version is pretty clunky. Now that I actually understand assembly, I can do a much better one."

You get the idea that what was happening was just to creatively fulfill my need and desire to do something much better than its predecessor. Because of how much I had learned, I was creating game that really were better, functionally and measurably better in every way you could slice it.

The sales trend followed that improvement. Whereas if you look at a lot of my competitors in those days, once they shipped one that was successful, they would then go, "Wow, we made a bunch of money with that. Let's change the story and the monsters a bit, and we can release version two and make some more money off that same game engine." Those games tended to sell to a subset of the people that bought and enjoyed the first one, so their sales declined over time. My sales went up over time, but again, I was not motivated by trying to gain more sales. I was motivated by trying to make better art.

Ramsay: Between *Ultima I* in 1981 and *Wing Commander* in 1990, Origin developed a variety of games, like *Ogre* and *Space Rogue*. How many employees did you have?

Garriott: At our peak, just before being acquired by EA in 1992, we had 250 or so, and then right after we were acquired by EA, we grew to 400. But then after UO in 1997, a lot of us started drifting out.

Ramsay: Did your role in the company extend beyond Ultima?

Garriott: I was the Ultima guy more than anything else, but I did also work with and on other projects by all means. The majority of my work was in Ultimas though, and helping out on other games along the way. Robert was CEO and the business guy.

Ramsay: Did you explicitly split your responsibilities that way?

Garriott: Absolutely. Yes, absolutely. In fact, if you tried to ask Robert for his opinion on any game, you'd be in trouble. He was not a gamer. He was never a gamer. If you got his feedback, you would find it fairly useless. On the other hand, he was a brilliant business person, so Robert had 100% control of the finances, and he made sure that in lean times, we survived and never went out of business. Between the two of us, I could make sure we made some great games and made sure we made great deals. Origin did well because of it.

Ramsay: Had you always intended *Ultima* to be a franchise?

Garriott: It depends on what you mean by "intend." Again, if you go back to the beginning, there wasn't much intention behind any of it. It was all creating art that we enjoyed and felt compelled to create. The growth of this industry was so fast, it was hard just to keep up with—much less have a sense of "wow, this is going to be an empire unto itself."

Interestingly, if I look at the games I've been the happiest with and the games I've been the least happy with, there's an interesting correlation. I think my very favorite games that I've built are *Ultima IV, Ultima VII,* and *UO.* And in all three of those games, while I was building them, my teammates, my friends, my family, my marketing departments, and any distributors that we were working with did not believe they were going to be successes.

But there are always things I believed in devoutly. I was changing the rules the most. I was going away from things that everybody else had already been doing. I just knew in my heart of hearts that this is what I needed to do, and I wanted to do it without regard for whether it sold better or worse. Most people told me to quit and not do it. But in all three of those cases, those games became the bestselling Ultimas I've ever done and the ones that I persevered through.

On the other hand, a lot of the games I'm the least happy with, like *Ultima VIII* and *Tabula Rasa*, I think could have been very good. But the reason why they fall on my least favorite list is because I listened to that same feedback. When we were striking out to do something new and people had misgivings, those were the times I gave into those misgivings, I settled, and I regret it.

Ramsay: What kind of feedback did you get from the naysayers?

Garriott: The feedback was different for each one. In the case of *Ultima IV*, it was the first game in the industry that included ethical parables and virtuous tales, forcing the player to live by a code of ethics instead of just running around and killing everything all the time. My friends and family and coworkers thought by taking this moral high ground in a game, it would drive people away because people just like to kill and blow things up. Now, if you read about the *Ultimas* and *Ultima IV* in particular, that's the reason the whole series is remembered. That decision I made with *Ultima IV* is what took it from a good game to being a great number-one bestselling game.

Similarly, with *Ultima VII*, that was the first time we did a super highly detailed sandbox virtual world where anything that looked like it could or should operate the way you would expect did when you interacted with it. The world was not just an art backdrop for you to fight monsters and hunt treasure in, but everything in the world operated as you would expect. People thought I was wasting my time. It took an enormous amount of time to code for all those levels, but that's when people began to go, "Richard Garriott is the Tolkien of role-playing games; his reality crafting is superb."

With *Ultima Online*, the sales projections at EA were miniscule. We had a hard time even getting permission to make it; no one believed that an online game could or would sell. When it shipped, it was the fastest selling game in Origin and EA's history, and within two years, it had outsold every *Ultima* combined. *UO* was phenomenally successful, and the first successful MMORPG.

In the case of *Ultima VIII*, EA does a great job selling sports games on a yearly cycle, and it was the first game I published after being purchased by EA, and they said, "Look, Richard, with our sports games, we've proven that shipping before Christmas is much more important than shipping after Christmas with all the features you want. We insist that instead of finishing after Christmas, cut out a bunch of features and ship it for Christmas." I did. It was the wrong decision.

Ramsay: EA acquired Origin in 1992. Why did you sell to EA?

Garriott: To answer that question, I need to say why we would sell to anyone. My belief about business in general is that as any new industry grows, there's an upheaval, and this first upheaval was the coming into existence of computer games. Lots of different players were mini companies, dozens of startups, and dozens of publishers were all vying for the attention of consumers.

What happens over time is that the distribution channels begin to close to all but the largest players. Look at Walmart. For a period of time, Walmart was selling 20% to 30% of all the games that were sold in the game industry. But the Walmart buyer, the person who puts the games on the shelf at Walmart stores, doesn't have time to speak with 50 different distributors of software.

Not only do they not want to take the time to talk with 50 distributors, but when you get to the bottom of those 50, you get to small companies that only have one or two products a year. If Walmart were to buy one or two of those products, and they didn't sell, it couldn't do stock balancing. They couldn't return that non-selling game for another one from the same company that might sell better to balance their stock and get things on their shelves that would sell.

And so Walmart basically started saying, "You know, instead of talking to 50 distributors, we'll just talk to the top five. If you're not one of the top five, frankly, you're financially irrelevant to us, so we just won't carry your products." Origin was always in the top ten, but always right about number ten. As distribution into retail began to close up, it became obvious we could not remain independent much longer at the size we were as a publisher.

We went through a careful process of considering our options. We looked at joining forces with Brøderbund Software; we really loved the Brøderbund team. We looked at joining forces with two or three smaller companies, where combined, we would make it into the top ten. But putting together a multi-company merger is very complex. So, of course, the option we took was to join forces with EA, who had previously, frankly, been a nemesis of ours. We had even had some legal run-ins with EA. But the people with whom we had those arguments and legal entanglements were no longer part of EA and hadn't been for many years, so when we considered all of our options, EA seemed like the place that could help us move boldly into the future better than anybody else.

Ramsay: When you considered Brøderbund, did you speak with the Carlston brothers? Were they there at the time?

Garriott: Oh, yes, absolutely. Yeah, exactly. We knew them very well. The Carlston brothers, and we at Origin, and a couple of other companies were the founders of the Software Publishers Association. We were the developers of the very first ever rating system for games. We knew each other very well, and we had a very deep admiration and respect for them.

Ramsay: Why did you choose to not go with Brøderbund then?

Garriott: I honestly don't remember what didn't work out. I don't remember whether it was that combined, we still weren't big enough, or if there were some other financial reasons why that didn't seem like the best course. I honestly don't remember, but we did consider it very carefully. It would have been an option we would have looked at very favorably.

Ramsay: What were the considerations with regard to EA?

Garriott: I would say the biggest positive was that EA had done very well in a whole wide variety of areas and platforms, but not specifically on PC and not specifically in RPGs. It looked to us like an area where we could really plug a hole for EA, and therefore, we would get the proper level of mindshare and support within what was a much larger organization. We thought we'd have our own niche carved out. The other big factor was the power to move stock into retail outlets. EA remained much stronger than every other company then.

Ramsay: You mentioned *Ultima Online* a few times. How did that get going?

Garriott: Starr Long and I were the champions of *UO*. We saw the growth of the Internet coming and said, "This is the moment when online games are going to be possible and not only possible but compelling." So, we began to pitch EA about this idea of making an online game to coincide with the emergence of the Internet and what an online game could be.

And EA was going, "You guys are nuts. The biggest selling online game in history is one of these AOL dial-up bulletin board games. It has 10,000 or 15,000 total lifetime sales. We need to sell millions before it's even interesting, and since you can't show us any big successes, we won't fund your game."

We went back during three different cycles of pitches, and three for three, they said no. After the third attempt, I just went to Larry Probst, who was the president of the company at the time, and I said, "Larry, I have to do this game. I know you guys have said no, but you have to let me build the prototype. I insist that you at least give us a few hundred thousand dollars to prove to you the power of this thing that we believe in."

Begrudgingly, he said yes. We built a prototype and that prototype we put up online and said, "Hey if anybody wants to help beta test it, it'll cost you $5 just to get the discs sent to you." And then 50,000 people signed up within the first week or two. EA's lifetime sales projection for the game had been like 30,000 units, so the fact that the number of people who wanted to play in a tiny beta was so much bigger than they had ever anticipated for lifetime, they went, "Oh, we get it." And the rest is history.

Ramsay: The way Raph Koster tells the story is that the project was a skunk works that the rest of Origin knew nothing about.

Garriott: That's not exactly right. In the sense that a skunk works is off the books and off the record, that's true, but everyone in the company knew about the game. *UO* wasn't a secret, but it was sort of the bastard stepchild that, frankly, EA didn't want and no one cared about.

If any other project wanted to hire someone, they were not allowed to work with us on *UO*. The same thing was true with office space. We operated in a hallway during the demolition of a floor around us because every other project was more important and they got the nice office space.

Until that demo, this was the project that only existed because of my insistence. EA wanted to kill it. Origin didn't care about it. It was completely unfunded. It just existed by sheer force of will until the demo. And then as soon as we got the demo working and people realized the power of it, it became the most important thing happening in EA's world, and suddenly, not only were the purse strings loosened, but everyone in EA wanted a piece.

Ramsay: Until *UO*, had you receive the support you wanted?

Garriott: I would actually say that EA originally gave us all the support we could ever want. In fact, frankly, I think we made a mistake in accepting too much "opportunity".

The first real struggle Origin had after becoming part of EA was not EA's fault; it was completely Origin's fault. Since EA looked at us as the PC and RPG saviors, they really hoped we would grow, build more products, and build more capacity to dominate PC and RPGs. We happily took on that challenge.

However, in the 12 months that transpired immediately after EA's purchase of Origin, we doubled in size. When you double in size, it means you take your entire management team and split them in half. For our second tier project leaders, that was a great opportunity for them to get a chance to take the reins and run a product. The problem is that we didn't have twice as many people capable of managing the millions of dollars it takes to create a product successfully, from beginning to end.

So, although we started twice as many products as we ever had before, we didn't finish twice as many products. In fact, half or more of those products ended badly. It wasn't EA's fault though. But the result was the first big downturn at Origin. A lot of those projects that already spent a lot of money started failing and a lot of staff started leaving. EA understandably began to lose patience and faith in Origin, so things got much harder after that.

Ramsay: Since you were originally brought on as the RPG division, what happened to the rest of your other projects?

Garriott: The only other highly successful project we had was *Wing Commander*, which I would still put in the RPG genre, but it was still well outside of anything anybody at EA was doing.

Whereas *Wing Commander* and *Ultima* were definitely our biggest series, there was a product called *Crusader*, which was our next tier product that at least had done well after the sequel. We got three versions of *Crusader* out, and all of those I would classify as action RPGs. But those are really the products we had active, so everything really did fit in that category.

Ramsay: Was EA's evaluation of Origin's post-acquisition performance one of the reasons why they were not thrilled about *UO*?

Garriott: No, I don't think so. Here is the way EA ran their greenlight process. Every six months, they convene a group of executives from different parts of the company, but most critically in the mix is the sales and marketing department. If you want funding, you put together a pitch document that describes the game, gives sample art, describes the team you'll need, describes your target audience, and everything else you would think of to make sure that the investor—in this case, EA—would need to know.

The first place you send that pitch document to is sales. They look at the pitch, and they go find comparables that are thematically like it or play like it. They look at whether it's medieval, modern, or whatever it might be, and they then look at the team and go, "How will this team do compared to whoever's making the number one best game like that out there in the world today?" Based on that, they give you sales projections and they say, "We project we could sell a million copies" or whatever that might be. To get a game greenlit in the mid-1990s, the projection had to be in the millions. Two to six million copies might be realistic for the bestselling games on the PC back then.

It's important to note that prior to the pitch we made for *UO* formally to EA, we had been looking at an online game pitch for decades. Every time we looked prior to the Internet though, we would have been using dial-up bulletin board systems like AOL, and they charged by the hour. The total number of users in any game that ran on those systems then was measured in the ones of thousands, too, so we're talking about three orders of magnitude below the top selling games that do not require being online.

So, when we pitched *UO*, we pitched it because we saw the Internet coming. We said, "Now is the time where anyone and everyone will be able to play online, and playing online is far more compelling than playing alone. This is the time to strike and to create the MMO genre." And although we made that case we thought fairly eloquently, the projection from the sales department at EA was a lifetime grand total of about 30,000 units. And how they got there was pretty simple. They basically said the only successful MMO-like games had been BBS games that had only 5,000 to 10,000 users at most. In this mix, the game Meridian 59 had at least been discussed or thought about, but the sales prediction for that game was something like 15,000 units lifetime.

And so they thought, "Oh, Ultima will do twice as well as the highest selling thing we can possibly imagine, so we'll give him 30,000 units lifetime." But that's inconsequential. You can't make a modern game that sells only 30,000 units. That's how many copies of *Akalabeth* I sold. I was basically being told, "Forget it Richard, you can't make this game." In fact, that's what they actually told me.

But, as I mentioned earlier, Larry Probst gave us $250,000, and when we released the beta disc and 50,000 people paid $5 to get it, suddenly, we got a lot of attention, which became a new problem.

Ramsay: Why was that attention a problem?

Garriott: Frankly, the attention became a huge problem because suddenly everybody realized, "This is so important that we can't let this ragtag team screw it up; we need to go help them." While we were having trouble with a budget that was too small in the beginning, we had real trouble with a budget that was too large and too many managers on the backend.

UO was a very difficult game to develop. It was truly a labor of love, a great joy, and everybody knew we were doing something really big and important. *UO* was very exciting but also very difficult. Part of the difficulty was building a prototype on the cheap with few resources. The code also wasn't written for scalability, so as the game became more popular, going from the tiny single world to the giant multi-sharded global game with tens of millions of players over its history, we struggled just to support the team, the code base, and the users.

Ramsay: Can you give me some examples of the problems that arose from being the hot property within EA?

Garriott: Yeah, so if you were an aspiring EA executive, there's only one president of EA, and that job opens up only once every 10 or 20 years. If you're aspiring to that top job, you take a tour of duty around EA. Origin became the place where managers came in to "prove" they could make a difference.

And the problem with that is they universally come in going, "Whatever my predecessor did was wrong, so I want to dismantle whatever their strategy was, and, of course, my strategy is right, so now I'm going to make you adhere to it, and I'm going to hire people around me to help with my strategy."

At least up until they leave within a year, and then the whole cycle repeats. It became a burden for us to try to just stay the course shall we say, and not get caught up in the "here's the latest person's great advice, passionate belief, and authority" to come in to try to tell us how we should do our jobs.

If that happened only once, it would have been survivable. The problem is that you can't keep changing your way of going about business or you end up treading water and going nowhere. In our case, by this late date in our relationship with EA, it was very common to have at least one new general manager per year, often two, as people would come over here to try to make their mark and then move on, disappear, or get fired or whatever it was, as we were the stop off in their tour of duty.

Ramsay: You lost some autonomy and had to deal with the bureaucracy of a large enterprise. Would you consider that one of the negatives of selling?

Garriott: Oh, absolutely. In fact, I would say that was actually much worse than we had anticipated. In particular, this was I really think unfortunately the true cause of the ultimate downfall of Origin. Prior to EA, Origin had been a very author-oriented company and great company stewardship came out of it.

That showed in our product success rates and our turnover. We had virtually no employee turnover prior to EA. We occasionally had to fire people, and there were occasionally people who'd leave for a better job elsewhere. But we also had an opinion about product development.

If a product looked good enough for us to invest in at the beginning, and if when we got two-thirds of the way into it and it no longer looks like it's worth investing in, we had two choices as a company. We can either cut our losses, or go ahead and finish it. If we finish it, and it doesn't make money, we've wasted that last piece of money we've just put into it.

Our opinion was that if we go ahead and finish it, first of all, we might be surprised when it does better than we thought, or when it at least brings back some of that last piece of investment. But even if it doesn't, the team which has finished a game is now stronger for having finished that game, seeing the results and seeing how it did and seeing why it did better or worse in the marketplace. That team will now be better prepared for the next title.

If we kill the project, we might save that last third of money, but inevitably, that team will split up. We'll probably fire a few of them, and the few we don't fire will leave. They're not going to believe their program was cancelled because what they made sucked; they're going to think the company stabbed them in the back, didn't like them, or didn't give them the support they needed. The team won't learn anything, and we won't gain anything when they disband.

We were a very stable organization, but EA had a very different mentality. EA believed that you always dump have a bottom 10% of your staff, and then hire people at the 50th percentile. When you do that, you've just improved the total health of the organization because you've moved the average up a notch. While that technically might be true; it was pretty darn draconian by our standards.

Additionally, EA believed that if you're going to make sports games like baseball, one of the things to do is to start three baseball games, and eventually, when you see one of them doing more poorly than the other two, you kill off that one, and then finally, when you get close to the end, you pick the one that's doing the best. You back that one and sell it, and the money you wasted on the first two false starts is actually relatively insignificant.

Businesswise, there's nothing wrong with that other than the fact that those other two teams were probably third-party independent developers and now they're probably completely out of business without even being consciously aware of the fact that EA was playing them against each other.

So, where Origin had always been this very nurturing, supportive environment with a lifelong commitment from the employer to the employees, EA on the other hand would describe itself as a wolf pack. They would say, "Look, we are a wolf pack. We are here to dominate. We are here to make the best games, find the best way to make the best games, keep the people who can make those best games, and it's survival of the fittest inside and out." By the way, to build a big company, I'm not knocking that, I actually have a very healthy respect for that as a business. However, it just wasn't what we had built.

It's not what I personally enjoy. It's not what I personally want to thrive within. And it's not what I think I've rebuilt now at Portalarium. But it was where we found ourselves. The lack of support we got on future things with Origin really grew out of that kind of fundamental strategy difference that we found ourselves in once we were on the inside.

Ramsay: Going back to *UO*, how involved were you with the prototype?

Garriott: Well, I am Mr. Ultima, so to speak. If I had to give credit to the main people that made UO what it was, number one credit goes to Starr Long. He's actually the guy who built the team, held the team together, and had the clearest vision of why and how. He became the director and executive producer. Another person who gets great credit is Raph Koster. Raph was the lead designer and he comes from the dial-up bulletin board background. He was the person who, by far, brought the closest thing to historical skill in online games to the degree that it existed. Raph embodied it very, very well. And a lot of what *UO* became, he gets a great deal of credit for. Lastly, there's me because of my vision for what *Ultimas* can and should be.

Ultimas are games where virtues matter. *Ultimas* are games where the world around you is not just a set for you to wander through and think that it's beautiful; it's a place that is completely interactive. Every cup, every bowl, every chair, every light switch to the degree there was any, and every object can be interacted with in the way that you would expect and have the results that you would expect that object to have. And that purity of vision of what is an *Ultima* came from me. With Starr as the arbitrator, Raph with his history in MUDs, and me with the history of what is an *Ultima* game, and our ragtag team of highly motivated youngsters, we made the game.

Ramsay: Who were the others?

Garriott: I don't mean to discount any of the other team members. They all played their parts. I was just giving a special callout to Starr and Raph. There was also Rick Delashmit; he was one of the early coders.

Ramsay: Raph told me that Rick Delashmit coded 80% of the game.

Garriott: That's possible. Raph was closer to that than me, so I would believe Raph. That would probably be especially true of the original version of the game. Rick was a very fast coder, but what's interesting is that Rick represented the quintessential high-speed hacker. He's probably responsible for coding the entire prototype or pretty darn close to it. By the time the finished game shipped? Hard to know. There were a lot more people involved by then.

Ramsay: For the prototype, what were your goals?

Garriott: For the prototype, we wanted to make a multiplayer game that looked like *Ultima VI* that combined PvP, PvE, the Eight Virtues, and even some story fragments in a homogenous, continuous no-loading world. And so while that was a mouthful, it was still pretty simple structurally. Not that it was easy to pull off. I just mean the task was clear.

Ramsay: What about technically?

Garriott: Well, the technical goals shifted a fair bit. Originally, when EA had 30,000 lifetime sales projected, we thought they were terribly wrong, so we gave ourselves an expectation of 100,000 lifetime sales, and we built a world that could handle 100,000 subscribers.

When we had 50,000 people sign up almost immediately for the beta, we then knew we were substantially under the mark. That actually caused us a real problem, both technically as well as for me—the fiction and the spirit of the game had to undergo a transformation. It was very important that everyone playing was part of the same reality. We were going to put them all in the same physical world, but with millions of players, that was not possible.

It started as a big disappointment because I'm going like, "Ah, I'm going to have to build duplicate copies of the world, and if one friend is living in one reality and another friend is living in another reality, they will evolve in these two realities. One could be more hostile and one could be more friendly, and that's going to bother me that people aren't having the same experience. When they go to the city of Trinsic, they're not seeing the same Trinsic because there's two differently evolved versions of the city."

And so I created a piece of fiction where I called each server set "shards." The term "shard" really comes out of *Ultima I* and the destruction of Mondain's Gem of Immortality, where different copies of the reality were put into each shard. We actually scattered shards in the game originally so that people could go and find and try to unify the servers back into a single server in theory. But the shards were my fictional explanation as to why the world was broken up.

Ramsay: You couldn't unify the shards though.

Garriott: Yeah, exactly. We actually put a fair bit of work into it. The players would find these shards, and take the shards back to a magical chalice. There would be scribes who would talk about other instances and how unification is coming, getting people to go out and find these shards, bring them back, have a slowly growing gem, and eventually, even unify a couple of shards back into one at some point. Over time, that plan just fell by the wayside due to the incredibly large number of other critical problems we had to solve.

Ramsay: When did you start thinking about the business model for *UO*?

Garriott: Even early on, we knew there wasn't going to be a retail price. And this was before anybody had considered free-to-play or other ways to charge. We never considered hourly because we always thought that, even in the old dial-up days, it was way too painful and dissuaded people from playing. We always knew *UO* would have a retail component and a subscription fee. We just figured that was the only fair way to present it at the time.

The issue was what the retail price and the monthly fee would be. The retail price was already fairly standardized at the time. We went with approximately $50 or $60 dollars, and that was largely set because of the retail channel. You had to have a box, you had to have discs, and there were physical components to that cost. When you go to retail, that's just where you end up for paying for the physical process of getting it to people.

The bigger question was "what's the subscription fee going to be?" There were two different numbers. There was a number we need and a number we could probably convince people to give us. And so we went in at the low end of our need. *UO* started at $9.95 a month, but most every other MMO went with $15, if not $20 dollars a month. We probably left a bunch of money on the table. But it was still gazillions more dollars than anybody could have imagined prior to that. I think *UO* remains about the cheapest MMO you could ever play.

Ramsay: If someone had approached you back then and said, "Hey, let's sell costume items in the game," what would you have said?

Garriott: Hard to know. My first response might have been, "Well, that's ridiculous. Just let them pay gold in the game and be done with it." If somebody had brought up the subject of buying assets for a premium in real money, it would have been laughed out. What wouldn't have been laughed at—but we still wouldn't have figured it out—was how to make real-money player-to-player transactions relevant and then try to take our cut. Almost immediately after we launched, there were black market items sold everywhere independent of us. Had there been a 10% fee on that stuff, we'd have made a bunch of money.

But it was hard to imagine implementing that and not running afoul of everything from money laundering charges to legal issues when people lose items because they expect the transaction to be protected. There were tons of interesting discussions about other ways to monetize, and where money was flowing that we made nothing on and had no ability to control. All that said, we were still pretty content with the way things turned out.

Ramsay: What were some of the other monetization ideas?

Garriott: The only other real big one was something I still have a strong affinity for. It's probably best if I describe it metaphorically. In *UO*, we built theaters, but those theaters were basically just buildings that looked like theaters. There was no ticket price, and there was no way to keep people in the theater from jumping up on the stage. And even the people who tried to put on a good play in the theaters, frankly, had terrible puppeteering tools to emote and actually put on a play that was anything short of terrible. People still tried though.

But what if we were able to control the variables, eliminate the bad and simply took a cut of 10% from the performances? Of course, there are service issues with that approach. Or perhaps this could have been the model: let's suppose you're a director and you can rent the theater. Renting the theater meant that I could say who gets to come in through the back door and get on stage, and everybody else has to come in through the front door. Anybody who comes in through the front door has to pay real money to come in and sit down in my theater, but they cannot interfere with the performance. And as the director, I probably paid a real $10 to rent the theater.

Ramsay: You were thinking about live performances back when it was still in beta? When was the beta?

Garriott: Yes, we launched UO in 1997. We probably did the beta in 1995.

Ramsay: I read about a story that you had an entertaining experience during the beta. Tell me about the assassination of Lord British.

Garriott: That was at the very end of the beta. That was like, literally, the last five minutes of the beta. Would you like my recounting of that story?

Ramsay: Sure.

Garriott: So, as the final day approached, first of all, we knew we were going to have to do a player wipe because, during the beta, people found exploits where they duplicated tons of gold. People had found all kinds of ways to steal everything from other players, and the balance of the dataset was wildly off by the time we were done with the beta process. Since we were going to do a player wipe, we decided to have a big event for the finale and thank everyone who had been there in the beta. No one had been charged during the beta other than the $5 for the disc, and as soon as we launched for real, we were going to start charging people a subscription fee.

We decided to do this day-long event where Starr Long and I would go from town to town all over the whole world, seeing as many of the players as we could face-to-face. Then we'd do a broadcast where everyone in the whole world would hear what we had to say. And so we planned this long series of stops and we went from town to town, shaking hands with people, saying thank you, and so forth, and even the first parts of it were amazing.

The number of people who were online and in each of their favorite cities was just astounding for us to watch. I would hope that the people there also felt that it was special. So, they would do things in various towns. In some towns, it was just a free-for-all. In others, people were organized and they had lined up their groups like all of the fighters in one place and all of the magic users in another place, or arranged by color in columns, much like a militaristic revealing of the troops, you might say.

There were funny things that happened, too. In the city of Moonglow, a huge number of people all stood across from where we were going to stand to make our speech, and while we were there making our speeches, all of them took off every stitch of clothing they had, faced north, and away from us and bowed, which basically means they mooned us in Moonglow.

And then, finally, we meandered to the last stop and the last stop was Trinsic. On the outer wall of Trinsic, Starr Long and I stood amongst the final group we were speaking with. We were within minutes of the servers coming down. We had another programmer who literally had his finger on the button. At precisely on the hour, he was going to turn the whole thing off.

As Starr and I were there chatting, a person who at that moment was unknown to us cast a Fire Field spell up in the parapet where Starr and I were both standing, actually engulfing both Starr and me in flames. My first instinctive reaction was to step backwards out of the fire, so I stepped away. But when I stepped backwards, I couldn't see what's happening farther up the north edge of the screen, and I thought to myself, "Oh, I don't need to walk out of this fire. I'm Lord British. I'm immortal. It makes no difference." So, I stepped forward back into the fire, assuming it was harmless to me—and then fell over dead. All of a sudden, we realized the horror of this moment.

The reason why I died was because six months previous, the last time we did a wipe, I had forgotten to set the immortality flag on my character. For six months, we had never noticed because no one had ever tried to kill Lord British. I had never been involved in anything even remotely dangerous, and my stats were very high, so killing me was not trivial. I had just been merrily going about my life for six months thinking I was immortal, and I was not. And when you die, including me when I die, everyone becomes a ghost.

As a ghost, if you tried to talk to somebody, you just went, "Ooo." So, I was there just ooo'ing. No one else was in my office. Everyone else was spread out around the building. And we didn't bother to get on a phone conference because we could all chat in the game, but now not me.

So, now I'm cut off from the rest of the team, and the rest of the team is going, "Oh my god, Lord British is dead. What do we do about it?" And part of the staff was doing things like trying to resurrect me, and part of the QA was on conference with each other going, "Quick, somebody figure out how to get Richard resurrected."

The other part of the group that was there were there invisibly or visibly to watch the final moments of the game with a couple of thousand players. And, in these groups, they were going like, "Who did it? How can we figure out who killed Lord British?" Later, we went into the data logs and found out it was a person named Rainz, but at this moment, we had no way to tell who had created that Fire Field. So, immediately, the staff was going like, "Well, we've got to punish the person who did it. We've got to find a way to punish the person who killed Lord British." But they couldn't figure out who it was, so somewhere in that throng of chaos, someone came up with the idea: "if we can't figure out who killed Lord British, let's kill them all."

That idea was quickly adopted by the rest of staff immediately, just so right as I'm resurrected, the massacre had already begun. All of the invisible employees had turned themselves visible, and people started summoning demons and dragons. People started directly using kill spells to just kill one player right after the other. They were summoning lightning storms, and, basically, any manner of mayhem the employees could think of to unleash upon these people in the audience. And, of course, we, the employees, thought this was hilarious.

However, some of the people being massacred didn't think it was nearly as hilarious as we did. What was happening to them is that when they were being killed, their ghost was sent all the way back to a shrine miles away from the city. So, in these last two or three minutes, instead of getting to sit there in Trinsic and watch the beauty of the whole world collapse, they were getting cast out into the wilderness as ghost. And so they're all wandering through the woods trying to find their way back while this massacre is going on throughout the city of Trinsic when finally kaboom, the whole server came down.

Ramsay: That sounds like a blast.

Garriott: It was. It was hilarious. But it did anger some of the players I must confess, but oh well.

Ramsay: So, in addition to mass destruction, UO had user-generated content. There were live performances, but there was player housing, for example?

Garriott: Player housing is a good example, I think. Players could craft equipment as well. With most things, you could decorate them uniquely, but the framework was preset. The player-created part was the choice of where to put them. So, you could build a town out in the middle of the forest if you wanted, but the houses and equipment were largely standardized.

And although we made little theaters, players would be "acting" in theory. People could put on whatever play they wanted from scratch. We just didn't give them very good tools for expressing themselves. In my mind, a strong game of the future would include the ability to make paintings, make individual pieces of sculpture, have much better tools for acting, in theory give you the SimCity-level of architectural control, the ability to compose music and play it with your friends, and the list could go on and on.

To me, the development team is always going to be outnumbered and outrun by the player base, so as long as the majority of the content must be made by the development team, there's no way for any reasonably sized, reasonably funded team to keep up with the consumption rate of the populace of even a modestly successful game. Ultimately, what you're really looking for is giving people the ability to create content that other players would consume.

Ramsay: Second Life found some success with that.

Garriott: There are games like Second Life that were open metaverse games where all there was user-created content. The problem with games that have nothing but user-created content is that they became giant minefields of junk. The majority of content that the majority of players create is unfinished, much less any good. People will start something, leave it in disarray, and move over to another piece of land. Then, they'll build something else and leave it in disarray, even people who finished their creations.

If you pick 100 people at random to make a great painting, you'd get zero great paintings. If you picked 1,000 people, you might get one good painting. In the real world, the stick figures and finger paintings that most of us make never get plastered on billboards for everybody else in the world to see; they're quickly thrown in the trash. Only the highest-quality works make it into stores and print shops. That economic reality is critical to sorting the chaff from those rare high-quality contributions.

Ramsay: Is there a relationship between the quality of content and the amount of money it makes?

Garriott: There's a general tendency in that direction by all means, but I would say quality is a difficult word. The word quality can easily be interpreted based on the eye of the beholder. What becomes popular may not be strictly speaking quality-related; it may have other intangible reasons for why it became popular, like if it has a particularly important or strong or catchy message, for example.

In Second Life, the majority of content created by the majority of people is not interesting, so you have to find a way to navigate to find things that are interesting. But the other interesting thing that it taught me was that if you try to write a simulation of everything, you don't make the best simulation of anything in particular. So, you end up with all these games in Second Life which were sort of B-side versions of those same kinds of experiences if you played it in a standalone way. And so while it was profoundly cool, Second Life uncovered a wide variety of good and bad lessons for the future in my mind.

Ramsay: Speaking of simulation, you did try simulating everything with UO.

Garriott: There's a little difference: the guidance I gave my team was that if you put it in the game, it must work correctly, but don't put anything in the game that you're not going to bother to do correctly. And so what I mean by that is if we had put horses in the game, then they need to move around, you need to be able to ride them, and they need to do the things that people would expect of a horse. And if you don't have the time to simulate the horse correctly, then don't put the horse in the game.

An interesting contrast to *Ultima* is the *Lineage* games from Korea that were developed by my previous business partners. If you look at *Lineage*, a lot of people would look at it and go, "Hey, it looks a lot like *UO*." In fact, the NCsoft folks would tell you it was inspired by *UO*. The combat and commerce aspect of *Lineage* were done very well and the visuals for the game *Lineage*, if anything, were far better than *Ultima*. The game was developed at about the same time as *Ultima*, and so the world you would go around in was gorgeous.

However, they did one thing that I very much disagree with from the *Ultima* design philosophy that I espouse. And that is you could walk through a village, and see barrels and chests and fish in baskets and all of those details that made the experience of walking through the town far richer, but if you walked over to any of it, none of it would react to your interaction. There was no chest you could open, and there was no barrel you could open or break or move. The only things in the world that responded to your interaction were monsters to fight and NPCs to get conversations from. The rest of the world was really just the visual tapestry. That's a perfectly good way to make a game that is about fighting monsters and talking to people in a beautiful environment. As long as that's your goal, great; they did a perfect job and it's extremely popular in Asia.

For me, I like interacting with the world. I think the world itself is a great opportunity to make me feel and invest and suspend my disbelief about the world that we're in. But if you start down the path of saying, "I can pick up the plate and cups and bowls off the table move them," well, then you don't want to break that logic halfway. If I can pick up the plate and cup and bowl, but I can't pick up the flower vase and the bottle, how would I have known to expect that other than it just didn't move? That is where I think a lot of even adventure games of the past have fallen flat.

I'm a big believer that when you put the player in a situation, the player needs to have the information and the rules of the game; and the physics of the game need to be consistent and thorough enough to let the player figure out the solution to the problem. An example I used to always give was if you're in my office right now, and the door is locked from the other side and you can't get out, and nobody can help get you out, you might first look to see if there are hinge pins that you could knock out and pull the door off backward. If that doesn't work and you're in an office with acoustic ceiling tiles, you could move some of those tiles and hop over the wall. And if that doesn't work, and you're really stuck in here and the place is on fire and you've got to get out, you could probably bash through a Sheetrock wall, if you really, really had to.

Ramsay: How do you help players find that content then so they don't get frustrated or lost?

Garriott: Well, you have to introduce it to them slowly. The case study I did there was with the doors in Ultima. A lot of times in Ultima, we'd build a variety of door types. There were wooden doors, steel doors, magically sealed doors with a blue edge around them, and unlocked and locked versions of all of those. If you ever wanted to get through a door, first of all, if they're unlocked, just walk through. If they were locked, you could hopefully find a key. But let's suppose you couldn't find a key. Well, then I gave wooden doors hit points, so if you walked up to a wooden door with an axe, you could chop your way through it and eventually the door would break and you would get on through. But then I added steel doors, so that if you walked up to a steel door with your axe, you would end up breaking your axe prior to breaking the door, and so the door would resist your ability to get through with your normal weapons.

I made those doors such that if you could maneuver a cannon nearby, you could fire a cannon at the steel doors and knock those doors down, too. And then I said, well, there's actually some doors I really just don't even want people getting into, so I made the magically sealed door, which you could just basically never get into without special requirements.

So, you just introduce those pieces slowly, and you make sure that people are learning the mechanics. When you add a wooden door, you put an axe in the room and lock the door. Leave somebody in a room with a wooden door and an axe and stone walls, and it's not that long before somebody figures out, "Let me try to pick up that axe and whack on the door." And so now you've taught people that kind of activity is at least one they should try.

Ramsay: The beta started in 1995 and the game was released in 1997. That leaves around two years for development. Was the dev cycle really that rapid?

Garriott: Yeah. It was relative to both time and cost. Compared to the tens of millions in MMOs that have been spent since then, it was quite modest at maybe $2-5 million in total spending, front to back.

Ramsay: Why do today's MMOs take longer and cost more?

Garriott: I think the main reason is that games are just bigger. There's a lot more art, a lot more geography, and a lot more features. *UO* had the advantage of shipping early, so it could have a smaller amount of territories, smaller amount of content, and smaller amount of features, and then grew once it was live. That's more difficult to do now. You have to compete with the existing games, and reach a higher bar than they've already reached.

Ramsay: *UO* also had a 2D world.

Garriott: Yeah, I think that when you go from 2D to 3D, it's harder to compare world sizes because you can stretch a polygon to be whatever amount of meters you want. Another way to compare world size fairly might be how many hours or days does it take you to wander through the entire world. From that standpoint, *UO* may have been comparable to *World of Warcraft*. I'm not even sure which would be bigger, if you did that comparison. But developing a 2D world was probably a lot faster than a 3D world like *World of Warcraft*, so it's hard to compare exactly. The combination of the contained scope of UO and 2D graphics made development easier and faster than other 3D games.

Ramsay: Which do you prefer: smaller worlds where a lot of things are happening, or larger worlds where you can travel across vast, empty spaces?

Garriott: I think empty spaces are a waste of time. Not that you don't want a few of them here and there to give you a good vista, where you're crossing the hill and watching the sun rise or set alone from a hilltop. Sure, there are plenty of times where getting some alone time is a good thing, but too many games have erred on the side of too much empty space. Content is expensive to create and usually boring to traverse, so it has exactly the wrong metrics. It takes a lot of time to build and it doesn't keep people busy very long. I think content in games should be spread out only just enough to give you the proper crescendo and lull cycles that make good storytelling.

Ramsay: When gamers talk about their favorite MMOs, they usually come back to UO and they say that the content and the gameplay of UO had more depth and was more meaningful than more modern experiences.

Garriott: Yeah, I would agree. I think that's exactly true. If you think about most every MMO today, they're all in the *EverQuest* or *World of Warcraft* model, generally speaking; they're very combat focused. And, by the way, as great combat and roleplaying mechanics games, *EverQuest* and *World of Warcraft* are phenomenally great games; they do a lot of things amazingly well. But if what you're looking for is a virtual world to live in, then after a year, how many times can you be on the level grind where your goal is to level up, go into a new territory, fight some new monsters, get some new armor, and repeat?

I think both *EverQuest* and *World of Warcraft*, and probably many others, do the combat challenge and reward cycles actually far better than *UO*, because they have been focused on that and are very skilled at that. *UO* focused more on professions, so that you could live an entire life in the world and never engage in combat. In other games, you can craft things, but you are also a combatant. Everyone playing *World of Warcraft* is first and foremost a combatant who might also be able to craft things on the side.

In *UO*, you had all kinds of fully developed professions that had nothing to do with combat, and it was the interplay between those professions that made such great content. For example, to be able to make swords, he would need metal ingots. To get the metal ingots, there would have to be miners who would go to the caves. The miners going into the caves were in danger from not only monsters but other players, especially on the way back from the caves when they had gold and other precious metals. So, the miners would hire protection from other powerful players who would say, "Look, I'm a level 10 guy. I'm happy to take you to the caves and back."

As a miner, you'd hire those guys to escort you from the dungeon and back, and, of course, those adventurers would need better equipment to help defend those miners, which means they were going back to the blacksmith to buy the equipment. And that sort of interdependence between the players of different types throughout *UO* is one of the key aspects that made the game so special.

Ramsay: One of my earliest memories of UO was the packaging. The box had two flaps with a spread beneath. On that spread, there were photos of real people and mini-dossiers next to them. Each dossier would read like, "In the real world, John is a banker, but in *UO*, he's a wizard." How did you go about marketing a fantasy world where you didn't have to be a hero?

Garriott: In a single-player RPG, every player becomes the one hero who saves the entire world. If you have everybody in the same world together, you can't tell each person in the world they will become the one person who saves the whole world, so therefore you had to have an angle.

UO was also trying something new in the following way, too. I'm not giving UO credit for this, other than timing, but there was a big shift in the perception of who would, should, or could play video games. In the first 20 years of video games, they were played by somewhat wealthy teenage males almost exclusively.

There were few people who weren't teenagers, virtually no women, and the computers and the software were relatively expensive. *UO* came out right at the time of a big shift where, suddenly, it was okay to be a gamer. You saw this happening in popular culture, typified by *The Revenge of the Nerds*. At about the time of *UO*, the tattooed, surfing skateboarders became gamers and began to work at game companies.

Ramsay: After the beta, what did you learn?

Garriott: Well, during the beta, it became obvious that we had two opposing and exacerbating problems. One problem was that the codebase for *UO* was fragile; we had only planned for a much smaller game, and it was built with the ragtag team I had described before. The codebase was pretty hacked together, and only barely holding together.

The opposing problem was that it was very clear that *UO* was going to be dramatically more successful than we expected. Our expectations were going up and up and up each month. Those two problems meant we were in trouble and we knew it, so when we launched the game, we were just struggling mightily to keep the servers running and to keep players happy.

Ramsay: What happened to the other projects at Origin? Were resources moved from them to *UO*?

Garriott: Yes, but that's another interesting story: the difficulties of *Ultima IX*. It had been very difficult to get resources for *UO*, so I had talked to EA and said, "Look, it's really important that you don't scavenge resources and move them from one place to another. Otherwise, you'll collapse things of value. You need to more equally distribute these resources."

When I was pitching *UO*, EA said, "We don't want it. We want *Ultima IX*." Once *UO* was clearly going to be a hit, they reversed their stance and said, "We're no longer interested in *Ultima IX*. We want you to work on only *UO*." I just said, "Screw you." I said, "Look, *Ultima IX* is already well in progress; it's the end of the trilogy of trilogies that I've been working on for my whole career. You can't pull the plug midway through."

I finished *Ultima IX* but only because I insisted on finishing *Ultima IX*. The struggle for resources between *UO* and *Ultima IX* is likely what eventually drove me from EA. I wasn't a team player in their mind. I wouldn't just open and close projects at their whim. Instead, I would insist on finishing what we had started. I became a real thorn in the side of EA management.

Ramsay: Did that resource strain affect *Wing Commander* in any way?

Garriott: I don't think it affected them negatively. *Wing Commander* was doing very well during this period, so *Wing Commander*, I think, had no resource issues. *Ultima* and *Wing Commander* were the two biggest properties at Origin, followed by *Crusader*, followed by a bunch of much, much smaller stuff. The much smaller stuff generally took the hit, but in most cases, not inappropriately.

Ramsay: What was your position in the company then?

Garriott: As now, I was creative director. I shun management whenever possible. I think my greatest value is in leading game design.

Ramsay: You said there are innumerable examples of Origin being very poorly managed by the people EA sent over after *UO* launched. Can you name names?

Garriott: Yeah, well, I would hate to specify any one individual. I would actually more broadly state that without regard to the quality of any individual person, the problem was each person would come in, starting with Neil Young, and they would stay for no more or no less than one year, and then a new EA general manager would show up on our doorstep.

Ramsay: So, the problem was not actually the work that the managers did, but the fact that there was no continuity between the transitions?

Garriott: Yeah, I would say that was the number one issue. It's impossible to be successful without continuity. However, the fact of the matter is also that, for many of the people, frankly, I think their plans were bad. And, to be perfectly honest, I can't think of a single manager post-Robert who had a particularly good plan.

Ramsay: You were creative director, but you were also the cofounder. You have a great deal of authority, power, and influence in your companies. How do you balance your leadership role with your actual creative responsibilities?

Garriott: That's actually very difficult, but it was something we learned how to do back when Robert and I founded Origin. It's just having a clear division of responsibilities. As painful as it was, you have to decide which things are in your control and which things are not. You know, hypothetically, a single person could be both the creative director and chief executive in a company.

Right now, I'm filling that role for Portalarium, but that's because Portalarium is tiny. But once any company gains any size, you really have to decide which side you need to do, which side you are skilled to do, and then you have to entrust somebody else to do the other side. Fortunately, in pre-EA Origin, we had my brother Robert who was a phenomenally good business person, and whose number one goal with the company was to make sure that he retained enough money to make sure we could live through any tough times, and then make sure that he invested in the tools and products that would make money and not waste money anywhere else. And that was sort of his philosophy.

And it was my job and a lot of the other creators' job to make games that sold well. But then Robert ultimately had control of the purse strings. One of the more painful days for me was the day when *Wing Commander* started outselling *Ultima*. *Ultima* had always been the lead dog when money or resources or key personnel were needed. *Ultima* would always get first pick, and then all of a sudden, *Wing Commander*'s getting first pick. And, suddenly, I am one of the founders of the company no longer getting first dibs. That was a tricky, personal moment to go like, "Okay, well, I guess that's the way the rules work, and I agree with the rules, so I have to live with the results." Anyway, so I at least respected the decisions, tough or easy, during that period.

Ramsay: Outside of the EA structure, was Origin itself very flat?

Garriott: As a general rule, we were quite flat. We did have an executive level of people who were responsible for different disciplines, whether that was product development, marketing, sales, or general management, but beyond that, even our teams were very, very flat. Everyone always felt that they could chime in on almost any subject the company was involved in.

We actually had a very upfront policy that anybody who wanted to see the details of the financials or the details of contracts or anything else they were welcome to do so and comment on them or criticize them. And that was part in parcel. I think I've said before why I felt that Origin was a very author-oriented company. One of the big concerns that developers had about a lot of companies is that those companies might be in one way or another ripping them off. Either there's somebody making a ton of money who really doesn't deserve it, or the company's retaining a lot of profits instead of distributing to the employees. There are all kinds of ways employees can perceive, sometimes correctly, that they're being taken advantage of by a company.

Ramsay: Was that organizational structure compatible with EA?

Garriott: Not at all. In fact, if you ask Larry Probst, or John Riccitiello, both would tell you that they thought EA blew the opportunity they had with Origin. That's not to say, by the way, that Origin didn't also blow its opportunity it had with EA. But the incompatibility is neither company's fault; it was just a difference, and a difference that served EA well for many years. It just wasn't particularly conducive to the way Origin had been built.

As I said before, EA openly and internally described themselves as a wolf pack. They described their whole corporate culture as survival of the fittest. Their whole corporate culture was whoever can dominate this next sector will win and get accolades and huge amounts of wealth, and anybody who falls a step behind would be cut loose. That mentality can be extremely successful. That devotion to domination can work extremely well to make sure you really do have the best people on the most important problems possible.

Origin was built on a different premise. Origin was founded on creating art, in a sense, which is not necessarily the best business plan. I mean if you can create the best art, then usually enough money will follow so that you can live just to create art the next day, but that does not make you the number one dog in town. Origin and EA started at almost exactly the same time, within a year of each other, but if you look at EA's growth, it was much more rapid. I would say it was largely because of this aggressive attitude that EA had in business, whereas we were trying to make sure we just didn't go out of business while allowing ourselves to make the art we wanted to create.

Ramsay: Do you think that if Origin had more layers of management that the organization would have at least fit better within EA?

Garriott: No, I don't think it was a layers issue. I think it was a corporate presence and understanding of the politics issue. I was always surprised when I would go to California to hear people telling stories about how our products at Origin were being discussed in our absence and often unflatteringly. And it was sort of a wakeup call that if we're not here to defend ourselves and constantly make the case for why we should continue to exist, the other wolves of the wolf pack here in California will beat us to the food and empty the plates before we even know that dinner's served, if you know what I mean.

Ramsay: There were internal fights over what?

Garriott: Oh, as always: resources. EA was producing 100 to 200 titles every year, so that's one to four titles every week that were launching through EA. If you wanted an end cap in a store, if you wanted any marketing to happen for your game, and, frankly, if you wanted the money to make your game at all, you had to be fighting all the time for your share of the resource.

Ramsay: Robert actually left EA before UO launched. Why did he leave?

Garriott: Robert is an entrepreneur. He would be happy building companies, whether they were game companies or airlines or almost anything else. Once we were acquired, he became a middle manager in EA. His interest was really just never to be a manager, so he just lost interest in being an employee.

Ramsay: His decision to leave was his own then?

Garriott: Oh, yes, absolutely.

Ramsay: How'd you feel about your brother taking off and leaving you to the wolves?

Garriott: I was worried. I knew that my first two publishers went out of business because they were drug addicts, owing me and their other developers a lot of money. Robert was the first competent business person I had had the chance to work with, so I knew there was a risk that Origin wouldn't succeed if just anyone took up the mantle. But I was comforted by the fact we had a lot of our old guard management and a good group of products in development. In spite of the fact that we knew it was a big loss, we felt we had some continuity and a safety net with EA around.

Ramsay: Had you and Robert discussed him leaving?

Garriott: I think so. Origin was a very open place. Everybody knew everybody's motivations, I especially knew Robert's. His decision didn't come as a shock by any means. We knew what his main interests were.

Ramsay: You left EA in 2000. You used a specific phrase to describe this event. You said that you were "driven to end up being parted from Electronic Arts." That sounds like you were forced out.

Garriott: Yeah, I was basically forced out. The longer version of the story goes like this. When we finished *UO*, our advice to EA was we should now do Wing Commander Online. At that point, *Wing Commander* was an even bigger property than *Ultima*, we thought it would naturally become an MMO, and we had the team that just finished a *Wing Commander* game available. But EA said, "We think *Ultima* was a special case. It's a roleplaying game that has 20 years worth of fans, and you've been teasing *UO* for decades. We're not prepared to believe that Wing Commander should be an MMO right now. Instead, we want you to build Ultima Online 2."

Our immediate advice was "we should not immediately begin a sequel because *UO* has just started; and it's growing and changing constantly." If we started UO2 right now, we'd be chasing a moving target, continually adding features to *UO*. We really recommend starting with *Wing Commander*. Oh, and by the way, the whole team that's working on *UO* is still working on *UO*, so what we have available is a *Wing Commander* team, not an *Ultima* team." And they said, "Nope, we really want UO2." Again, they do everything based on sales projection meetings, where they greenlight games, and UO2 was greenlit. Wing Commander Online was not, so off we went to work on UO2.

Fast forward a few years and EA comes back to us and says, "Hey, it's obvious UO2's going to take a long time and cost a lot of money because you're chasing *UO*," and we said, "Yes, that's exactly what we told you." And they said, "Well, in that case, we're going to stop UO2." So, they killed UO2, and got rid of the entire *Ultima* team. During this same period, the Wing Commander team left to Sony Online Entertainment to make *Star Wars Galaxies*. So, that game was built largely in the image of Wing Commander Online. It shouldn't be that shocking or surprising how that turned out.

Finally, EA said, "Look, we're just not interested in MMOs anymore. We think MMOs are too big, too risky, and too expensive. What we want you at Origin to do and you specifically, Richard Garriott, is make tiny games for Pogo.com, which we just acquired. Instead of costing $10 million, these games will cost $100,000 and they're web-based." And I said, "That's the wrong charge to put me on, but you're my boss, so if you tell me to go pitch games like that, I will pitch games like that." So, I pitched four or five games through their process.

The problem with these pitches is, although I think a lot of them were really quite good, that even if one could get through the pitch process at EA, it costs between $50,000 and $100,000 to get to the greenlight process. And by the time you get to the greenlight process, they go, "No, we don't want that one." And then I'm going, "Well, you've now said no to ten games in a row. We've spent way more than it would have cost to finish a few of these. Instead of having us running around in circles, making pitches you turn down and spending money we could be making these games with, why don't you just let us finish some games?" It was that kind of argument that sowed the seeds of my departure. It became increasingly frustrating for both EA and me.

Ramsay: What was the day of your departure like?

Garriott: Oh, it was a tragic day. That was a very tearful day from my end. It was the end of the thing I had built for 15 years. It was horrible.

Ramsay: So horrible that you soon started another company?

Garriott: Well, I remained retired for a year, and for that year, I wasn't much in the mood to jump back in to start anything. Robert and I began to at least ruminate about the game business, how EA had bizarrely given up the MMO throne, and that no US company—with the possible exception of Sony—was really stepping up to take the MMO mantle.

We were thinking about starting a company specifically focused on MMO development. So, about nine months into that year, the two of us began to put money into a bank account to start Destination Games. We were talking to some our old recently retired allies and were literally just getting started when EA decided to shut down most of Origin. On almost the day that my one-year non-compete agreement expired, EA laid off about 200 people at Origin. That was basically all of product development, customer service, QA, and so on.

In our mind's eye, this was EA giving us back the company we had recently sold them for free. We called up as many of those people as we thought we could manage, which was maybe a third, and we said, "Hey, would you like to reform together with us as Destination Games? We've only got a couple million bucks in the bank, we can't afford to pay all of you starting today, but as a team again, as the core of Origin, we are far more valuable than we'd be individually."

And you know that was not hollow and lost on the others. We announced the existence of Destination Games, and we already had employees who had made Origin great. Within a few days of that announcement, we got a call from NCsoft. NCsoft had seen *UO*, and they were inspired by *UO* to create a game called *Lineage* in Korea. *Lineage* was already ten times bigger than any US MMO and was, in fact, bigger than *World of Warcraft*.

But none of us had ever heard of it, so we were like, "Wait a minute! How is it possible that there's a country on Earth where there's a game that's ten times bigger than any game we've ever heard of and we've never heard of it?" So, we quickly were doing the research to figure this out. It turned out that NCsoft had this ginormous success in Korea, where one out of ten people in the country were playing *Lineage*. I mean, the game was on Coca-Cola cans distributed out of the vending machines all over the country; and they had three TV channels devoted to games, and one was devoted to *Lineage* almost exclusively.

NCsoft had an office in the US for three years already, and they were trying to find developers to make games for either the US or Korea. They were trying to launch *Lineage* in the US, but they couldn't find any partners to help them launch it. And we said, "Wow." They looked at us and went, "You guys are the guys that created the game we patterned our game after, and EA just cut you all loose. We would love to talk to you about co-developing games for the US and Asian markets as well. Can you help us distribute *Lineage* in the US?"

We said, "For us, that's perfect. That gives our sales and marketing people something to do until we actually manage to ship some products that we start developing in the US." The match seemed perfect. Within a week or two, we had inked a deal, and so Destination Games as a company only existed for literally a few weeks before we became part of NCsoft.

Ramsay: And you were again inside another large bureaucracy?

Garriott: MMOs are expensive. We had no illusions that with the money my brother and I put in the bank that we'd be able to fund the development of an MMO. We always knew we were going to need partners who had deeper pockets. We just didn't know what the nature of that partnership would be.

In this case, it appeared we had a much friendlier ally. There were actually many, very good things about the relationship with NCsoft like there is in many companies. With NCsoft, we did things like build and acquired the studios that made *Guild Wars* and *City of Heroes*, as well as a game out of Colorado called *Auto Assault*, as well as the games we built internally.

Ramsay: What was your original plan for Destination Games?

Garriott: We knew we'd be making RPGs, and we knew the first of those would be medieval fantasy. We knew it would be a Lord British-style virtual world. There was a deeper question as to whether that would be medieval fantasy, or more sci-fi, or more contemporary. We were fairly flexible as to what the setting would be, but we fully committed to do another RPG to pick up where we left off.

Ramsay: Can you clear something up for me? What's the difference between Destination Games and NCsoft Austin?

Garriott: Destination Games was the development studio. NCsoft Austin was the publishing arm.

Ramsay: I see. How was everything organized? What did you take away from your experience at EA and bring to Destination Games?

Garriott: We set out to find the best studios, individuals, and small teams that were developing MMOs and tried to bring them into NCsoft. We felt that was the only way that even NCsoft would not be swallowed up by somebody like EA. That's why we found Cryptic Studios, who did *City of Heroes* and *City of Villains*. That's why we found ArenaNet, who did *Guild Wars* and *Guild Wars 2*. And we went after NetDevil in Colorado that did Auto Assault. That was a very purposeful strategy to which I was personally leveraged extensively. Instead of NCsoft calling, it was Richard Garriott calling from NCsoft, and people would now take the calls. I was used as the bait to draw people into conversations.

Robert and I would give them the sales pitch we did at Origin. We were saying, "Look, we are building here in the US a publishing empire that is very much like Origin. It's going to be very author-oriented, it's going to be very developer-friendly, it's going to be very open, you're going to see how all the numbers work, and no one's going to get cheated." That message still worked very well and allowed us to grow NCsoft in the US much more rapidly than we had ever grown Origin. Within maybe 18 months or so, we went from zero revenue to a couple hundred million dollars in revenue.

Ramsay: Did Destination perform better than Origin?

Garriott: I would say the total revenues were definitely stronger and faster than at Origin. That's a really interesting question. A successful MMO makes a lot more money than a successful solo player game, in spite of the fact that *Wing Commander* at its peak was probably selling high single digits of millions of copies. I'm not sure we sold that many individual copies of any MMO, but the total revenue of these MMOs was dramatically higher. The subscription business model was still proving very fruitful before the marketplace was flooded.

Ramsay: Destination was founded in 2000 and joined NCsoft in 2001. There was a whole year there that something was happening. What was happening?

Garriott: The answer is not much. Robert and I put a couple million dollars in the bank so we could begin to noodle on how to reenter the game industry. We secured the name of Destination Games, I think we might have built a tiny little website that just, you know, said, "Yep, this is the Garriott brothers. We exist." Probably nothing more.

Ramsay: Who contacted you from NCsoft?

Garriott: Let's see, I don't remember the gentleman's name, but it was the person who ran their LA office. But within 24 hours of the first phone call, Jake Song, the author of *Lineage*, and TJ Kim, the founder of NCsoft, flew from Korea to come meet us in Texas.

Ramsay: You got to talk to TJ?

Garriott: Oh, yeah, of course.

Ramsay: What was he like?

Garriott: TJ's a great guy. One of the things I like about doing business in Asia is it's very different than doing business in the US. In the US, people do business based on the numbers. You know, "Let me look at the bottom line, and if the bottom line looks good, then we'll make investments or whatever."

Asian business practices are more relationship-oriented. They spend more time on getting the measure of the person with whom you're trying to do business, and if that measure is good, your belief is that you can make something work. You move onto the numbers as a second step.

So, we had a very good initial meeting. It was very obvious that TJ and Jake were on a course similar to ours, discovering this new opportunity in online games and believing there was a great future for at least the next five or ten years.

Ramsay: *Lineage* launched a year after UO, correct?

Garriott: Yeah, I think that's right.

Ramsay: By the time you were working for NCsoft, did you have any responsibility for *Lineage* in the West?

Garriott: No, but I did help by all means; my help though consisted of things like playing *Lineage* and giving feedback to the development team about what features could be enhanced or changed to get traction in the US. It was very clear even from that point in time, and it's still true today, that MMOs that sell well in Asia are not necessarily at all the same games that sell well in the US. I was more of a senior advisor to the team, but never a producer or director.

Ramsay: Did you figure out why *Lineage* was doing so well in Asia?

Garriott: It's a complicated answer. It's multifaceted. One reason was the environment itself. Korea has had such a longstanding post-World War II argument with Japan that they've banned the import of all game machines like Atari, Sega, Nintendo. So, if you're a gamer in Korea, you play on PCs, period.

Second, Korea is a physically compact urban environment, and the government invested in putting broadband into everyone's home. If you're doing online games, you are guaranteed that every person in the country has broadband, so that makes online games particularly desirable. With no console games to compete with and everybody having broadband access from their PC, that's a fairly homogenous environment to ship a game into.

A good MMO on PC has a lot of opportunities in Korea that it wouldn't have in other countries. On the game itself, one of the things they did particularly brilliantly was they started small and grew with the audience. I would say it's a similar story to *Minecraft*. In the rest of the world where the original Lineage was shipped, you could run around on only a single island, you could play only the fighter class, there were only a few monsters to fight, and only low-level armor to be acquired. As people played it, NCsoft rushed to bring in new creatures, new armor, new stories, and new places to explore. Their audience started small, but their audience grew as the game expanded very well.

Ramsay: How did you advise the developers to gain traction in the US?

Garriott: Lineage was a very Korean or Asian-style game in the following ways. You could sit with your mouse, click on the ground and walk, click on monsters to fight them, and click on NPCs to get information, but not much else. There were no chests to interact with, there were no puzzles in the game, there was no arcade combat or first-person shooter stuff in the game. The things that it did very, very well were not the traditional list of things found in American-style RPGs. So, our advice was to make sure the core features—exploration, discovery, and alternate combat skillsets—were available within the game.

Ramsay: When you started Destination Games, you wanted to build an MMO. When did you get a chance to do that? Was that game *Tabula Rasa*?

Garriott: Before we even met NCsoft, I used to call that game "Project X." I'd been talking about Project X for five years, even during the development of *UO*. When I went independent, I really wanted to do a sci-fi game. And when we joined NCsoft, Jake—who had just written *Lineage*—and I were both saying, "Well, the last thing we want to do is compete with our currently still operating very successful medieval games, so let's go do something in science fiction."

But then, two years later when Jake left NCsoft, we had to do a major regrouping. One of the key people for whom we had chosen for the style and direction was no longer there, and it wasn't our style and direction; it was his style and direction. So, we had to restart the project again.

When you have to restart a project like that, it's difficult to get back on track. You've already spent a fair amount of time on developing something that you really can't sustain, and you really need to go back and retool, which is what we did. But it meant that we were always under pressure of being too far behind and over budget, although we were really starting again from scratch.

Ramsay: What does starting over entail?

Garriott: Well, for example, when we were working with Jake, we were trying to make a game that would sell in Korea. In fact, it was more important that it sold in Korea than in the US because Korea's a much bigger market than the US. But as soon as Jake left, we realized our ability to make a game for Korea has just been cut off. The rest of us didn't really understand the Korean market, so our probability of success went way down. We said, "Look, what we really need to do is make a game we would enjoy and believe would be successful in the US market." So, we basically abandoned a lot of the core style and design detail of what was *Tabula Rasa* with Jake to make the new *Tabula Rasa* that was really targeted for the US market. It really meant we started over.

Ramsay: What was different and difficult about starting over post-Jake-Song?

Garriott: The thing that's different about being "post-Jake" is that although the team knows they're starting over, the company doesn't start their schedule over or start their funding over. The company looks at it and says, "Look, we know you lost your main guy, and we know you're having to do some significant retooling, but we've already been into 'this project' for two years and $10 million, so I sure hope you're shipping next year."

Ramsay: What year did you begin the game that eventually launched?

Garriott: Somewhere around 2003.

Ramsay: Tabula Rasa was released in 2007, so that was four years that the game was in development. Was sci-fi too new to you and your team?

Garriott: I actually believe science fiction and fantasy are very closely related. I think you can tell the *Lord of the Rings* story in a *Star Wars* universe just like you could tell the *Star Wars* story in a *Lord of the Rings* universe. One of my attractions to science fiction is that in science fiction, it's rare that people use magic to solve the problems of the good guys or bad guys.

Using a sci-fi story, you have one or two scientific breakthroughs like light travel or whatever it might be, but otherwise, you live within the constraints of reality. One of my common problems with a lot of fantasy is when magic is constantly saving the day because it's magic, not because it fits any pseudoscience.

And so when I write fantasy, I try to create fantasy that feels more like science fiction. It has a rational logic to it that is used consistently, not just "magic." So, when I started on *Tabula Rasa* in a science fiction environment, it still felt very familiar to my process for creating a medieval fantasy world.

Ramsay: How do you begin to even create a universe?

Garriott: You have to go back and ask, "What's the point of the universe? What's the story you're trying to tell?" Because everything comes out of that. It usually begins with: "what is the message?" Is your message about virtues? Is your message about how the fabric of society has begun to crumble due to a lack of moral fiber, or because politicians became too powerful?"

You know, one of the parts I enjoy the most though is the development of things like the languages and the histories and the stuff that I think makes the world feel real, that makes the world feel like it has depth. I'd like to think I learned that from being a big fan of Tolkien's work.

Ramsay: What did you come up with for *Tabula Rasa*? What was the plot?

Garriott: To me, *Tabula Rasa* was a futuristic fantasy RPG where the Earth is overrun by an alien species that is slowly taking over star systems one by one, and the surviving humans help other species rise up.

Ramsay: You had a third of the core of Origin and then you joined NCsoft. What kind of team did you have on that game?

Garriott: A large one. This game was made in the heyday of large MMOs. If you look at the growth of game development, you could go back to a time when you could make a game by yourself. Starting with *Ultima V*, it took teams of up to, say, a dozen, and then with *UO*, you had teams of up to 200. With World of Warcraft, you get into the many hundreds. Tabula Rasa was hundreds.

This style of game development has become not uncommon in the MMO field, but it is terribly costly—terribly costly to the point where it's extraordinarily risky to make these games, and extraordinarily costly in years of career time for anyone who works on them. You will get only a handful in your entire career.

It means you've spent incredible amounts of money, and an incredible amount of your entire life's career on something that probably won't work. I am actually pessimistic about the traditional development of most MMOs just because there's so few that succeed while their costs remain so high.

Ramsay: How do you cut the costs of a game like *UO* or *Tabula Rasa*?

Garriott: One key ingredient is to know you can build with existing tools. Half the effort and money going into a game's development is rebuilding the tools to render and operate the environment in which you're going to play. A lot of games do that to make sure they look better than what has existed before.

If you decide you're going to compete on the bells and whistles of a game, then you're doomed to spending an extra one to three years upfront on nothing but the bells and whistles. If what you're doing is a first-person shooter, that's probably a good investment because that's pretty much the only way to judge the difference between first-person shooters. They're all basically "run around in a maze and shoot each other" games.

If you're doing a game that has more depth, like a role-playing game, you're going to spend a few years on top of all the bells and whistles. Then, I think you should, in most all cases, use an existing development environment like Unity. Try to be judged and compete on content, not on the bells and whistles.

Ramsay: What about MMO engines like BigWorld?

Garriott: Yeah, I know them. The BigWorld guys were super talented, super devoted to making it work and created some very, very impressive technology. The problem is they were making technology; they weren't building a game. My team has, down through the years, evaluated BigWorld two, if not three, times and opted not to. It wasn't because it wasn't good technology; it just wasn't ever doing exactly what you needed. It was sort of an engine to solve one very specific problem of MMOs, but it wasn't the way to build an *Ultima*.

And there's this gap that's been hard to bridge. You can get just a render pipeline, of which now there are some very good solutions. There's the Unreal and Quake engines, and there other phenomenally good 3D render pipelines. If you're going to do a first-person shooter or something that starts there, and just add some extra features, you can buy those engines off the shelf today. You could even do that ten years ago and make a really darn good game.

The problem is that if you're going to do a game that's deeper than that, it was hard to define what tools to use. There were things like BigWorld, there were a handful of other people trying to do reality engines that were usable, but most of them were underpowered or failed our metrics in some way.

There was a big gap that existed, and, frankly, I'm pleased, surprised, and relieved that this gap has finally been filled with Unity. The competitors to Unity are also worth examination. Unity is now not only a highly competitive 3D render pipeline, but they have built a wide variety of these other tools they need to make a complete game. They also have enough third-party people making plugins for anything and everything you could imagine.

There are tons of inventors now creating technology that people who are on a common platform like Unity can all share with each other, and dramatically cut the time it took and the money that it took to make AAA games. Having to rewrite other people's engines has been the death of many companies.

That is absolutely historically true in our industry. That being said, for us, with Unity, that has not been true. Unity so far has proven to be a shockingly elegant environment. I'm impressed yet again with how well thought out Unity is as a development environment—just how very well object-oriented it is at all levels from the top to the bottom. It really truly is easy to pull code, functions, and add art, music, trigger events, AI, and conversations. "Dropping content in and out of a Unity environment is trivial" might be overstated, but not by much.

Ramsay: How much time and money do you think Unity actually saves you?

Garriott: There's no question that it saved us many man years and many millions of dollars.

Ramsay: Getting back to *Tabula Rasa*, you had a four-year development cycle. What was launch day like?

Garriott: Launch day for an MMO was always scary because it's often the first time you've really put a lot of load into the servers, and each time you scale up the data flow or load by an order of magnitude, you inevitably unearth some new real problems. For *Tabula Rasa*, I'd actually say we had less problems than usual, just because we'd all done a handful of MMOs before, but it's still a day where you sit back, you start to throttle it up, you open it up to other people, and you wait for things to fail, and then everybody rushes off to go fix them.

It's a very exciting day, too, because you're switching modes from just being a financial drain to where there's finally going to be a return flow of money to support the project. So, it's kind of exciting and scary rolled into one.

Ramsay: What happens internally after a modern MMO is launched?

Garriott: Launching a MMO is a scary ordeal. It used to be that when you finished a game, you put it in a box, you shipped it, and that was the end of it. If there were any problems, there was nothing you could do. It was done and gone and out, and there wasn't even the Internet to send people patches or repairs. So, you immediately then moved on to your next game.

In a MMO, what you might call the finish line is releasing it to the public, but that's really where the work starts. If you thought you were working hard on debugging just prior to launch, it gets worse right after launch. Immediately after launch, if there's a problem that's bringing down the servers, you've now got people paying for it, so you better get those servers back up right away, or people could start demanding their money back. So, the days, weeks, and first months after the launch are in many ways terrifying. There's a lot to do.

On the flipside, you finally have people living in a virtual city you've spent so much time refining. And there's great joy in watching all the pieces move properly and come to life in the way they were supposed to. You've been running around in a largely empty city up to that point in time and now it's a living, breathing thing, so there's also great joy in it at the same time.

Ramsay: How were the initial tenants of *Tabula Rasa*?

Garriott: They just kind of ran the full gambit. I'm not sure if you've ever heard of Bartle's Four Player Types, but in RPGs, it commonly describes how some fraction of players are the Achievers who are just trying to get to the topmost level, some are the Explorers who are trying to really just go to see every nook and cranny of the game, some are the Socializers who like to hang out and role play in the towns and settle into the reality of the game, and then you have your Dissidents—the ones who are there just to muck with it, harass other players, and also try to bring down the service because that's how they get their fun.

And so you have all those people in the game on day one. Different people are finding different levels of joy with certain parts, and sometimes they're finding different struggles with parts of it. At this point, I couldn't tell you which of those paths were working the best and which of those paths had the hiccups. Inevitably, all have a few hiccups, but you fix one and let that group race on ahead for a while and then you fix another, and let a different group race on ahead. It's a balancing act to stay in front of everybody with updates and repairs.

Ramsay: Who are the loudest tenants?

Garriott: I don't think any one of them is any louder than any other. I think the most interesting group are the Dissidents. They are people who—if you don't give them an official way for them to act out—they will make up one of their own, which is usually worse for the game and worse for other players. And so you do things to help them channel their frustration. I don't know if you've ever seen a modern city, where sometimes they'll put up a concrete wall near a playground and tell anybody that might like to do graffiti, "Here's a free graffiti wall that we won't yell at you for. Please do you graffiti here." The real challenge for managing Dissidents is giving them an outlet, letting them feel sated without making them feel like they were cowed into something politically correct.

Ramsay: Was your Dissident problem a significant problem?

Garriott: No, our dissident population was no more and no less than the usual number in other MMOs. Dissidents represent only 5% of the total population; they are a vocal minority that you just need to manage carefully.

Ramsay: Despite their size, they have a sizable impact though.

Garriott: They can, like in *UO*. A lot of player killers started preying on newbies, and that damaged our game in that we had a hard time attracting new customers. New customers would have a really bad experience because more experienced customers are purposely giving them a bad experience. That's the kind of behavior you want to stop the most. We didn't really have a problem with that on *Tabula Rasa*, fortunately. It was worse, much worse in *UO*.

Ramsay: What kind of hijinks could they pull off in *Tabula Rasa*?

Garriott: That is a good question. You know, since we didn't have PvP, the hijinks were much less overt. So much less overt, I can't even find you a good example. Instead they were be pushed farther underground to try to do things like sniff packets and try to interfere with the function of the service.

Ramsay: I remember vaguely that when Tabula Rasa's reception was mixed.

Garriott: Yes, it's interesting that people know me so well as a fantasy RPG creator that people had more mixed expectations when I started to go off into sci-fi. When we did the sci-fi game, we felt that having to be a little bit more action-oriented is thematic with the setting. But because it was from me, the *Ultima* creator, a lot of people expected it to be more like a themed *Ultima*. And because it was me, we didn't get a purely *Wing Commander* audience, you might say. But because it was sci-fi we didn't get the purely *Ultima* audience, so we had a mix of audiences, and so we had a mix of responses.

Ramsay: Was your attachment to the game actually a detriment?

Garriott: Oh, no, I don't think so. I actually still look back at that game, and I think we did some really great innovative work on control points, how to handle multiplayer quests , and how to make creature AI more sophisticated than just standing in front of each other and trading blows like is true with most other MMOs and most RPGs for that matter. A lot of those lessons I'm taking further here into *Shroud of the Avatar*, so I still look at the things we did well very fondly. There were some great successes that we'll carry forward.

In my personal opinion, I honestly think *Tabula Rasa* could still be an extremely successful game. It's just that NCsoft was so accustomed to their instant mega hits for their one or two products they had done in Korea that their patience for getting it right was lower than I would have at least recommended.

Ramsay: Before we go there, can you describe some of those systems where you had innovations?

Garriott: Take control points. If you think about most RPGs, you either run into monsters out in the wild, or go into a dungeon and monsters are pre-set there or spawn randomly in that environment. If you leave and come back, you see the same monsters there again. If the instance closes, the monsters respawn, and it resets for the next player.

What we did in Tabula Rasa is we said, "Let's build some points on the map where if the players occupy them continually, then there will be NPCs, quest givers, shops, and maybe ships to take from place to place." There were all kinds of goods and services that were valuable to the players.

But if the players either completely abandon the location or if the location succumbs to the ever increasingly strong waves of bad guys, then the control point flips to where it is under enemy control. That means all of the valuable goods and services are no longer available, and the only way for those goods and services to come back and become available again is for enough players work together to retake the control point.

Ramsay: What about creature AI?

Garriott: Another example is creatures taking cover. For example, if you look at most RPGs, a monster walks up, stands in front of you, at its maximum weapon range, and then repeatedly starts using its abilities and its weapons to just throw things at you. Occasionally, they have enough AI to decide to target the wizard in the back first, or decide what opponent to face on your team, but largely, it's just trying to lay out the most damage over time and resist whatever damage you can lay out over time. So, you quit looking at the screen because the screen is largely standing there, animating whacking each other and now you're really managing the shortcut bar and playing a spreadsheet game. You're just managing your hit points, healing, and such.

That makes creatures fairly unintelligent in my mind. If you remember going back to Napoleonic warfare compared to the American Revolution, armies used to walk down the street in columns, the first row would shoot their guns at you, the second row would walk through them, shoot their guns at you, and the third would walk through them to shoot their guns at you. It would be kind of this constantly advancing line.

But then the Americans who were used to hunting in the woods said, "Screw that! Instead of standing there and getting shot, why don't we hide behind a tree? Then we'll just shoot from the side, and we'll run around back and shoot from behind. Why would we want to stand in a formation and take this thing head on?" That was true for players fighting each other and players fighting monsters. Our monsters were smart enough to take cover.

Ramsay: How do you successfully operate a live game post-launch?

Garriott: Once a game goes live, you're sort of in this race to make sure people know you're listening to them. I would say that's the first and most important part: people need to know they're being heard. If they think the game's got bugs, they need to know you've heard them. That's step one. It just takes time to reply to people in a way that they know you're listening.

Step two is addressing a lot of those bugs or concerns as quickly as you can. But, inevitably, there's more coming through the door than you can deal with in short order, so you have to begin to start building priority lists and communicating to people, "Hey, by the way, here are the ten things you've said, here's the three we're going to do immediately, here's the three that are going to wait a while, and here's the four we'll get to one day, hopefully."

Then the third step is you have to recognize that people are going to consume all of the content you've created fairly quickly. Those Achievers and Explorers, especially, will power through whatever it is you've created. They're going to see every monster, every quest, and they'll have been to every corner of the map long before you could ever create new monsters, new stories, and new maps. So, you can't just be supporting the game you've launched; you've got to add to it in a way that retains people who have chewed through your content.

Ramsay: During the operation of Tabula Rasa, you went somewhere where no game designer has gone before.

Garriott: Yes, that's true.

Ramsay: You have a family background in space, correct?

Garriott: True. My father is a NASA astronaut who flew twice: first on Skylab and then on the ninth launch of the shuttle. I'm actually the first second-generation astronaut, and I flew with the first second-generation cosmonaut.

Ramsay: I remember you sharing a story about when you, as a kid, would be sitting around the dinner table, and there'd be various people visiting with you who were astronauts. You lived in an astronaut neighborhood.

Garriott: All of my neighbors were astronauts. My left-hand neighbor was Hoot Gibson, another shuttle astronaut. My right-hand neighbor was Joe Engle, another shuttle astronaut and an X-15 pilot before that. Over my back fence were a few more astronauts, and I lived just two or three blocks from the front gates of NASA. So, when I went to college and met people who were butchers and bakers and firemen and policemen, it was culture shock. Suddenly, I met these Sesame Street people that I had thought were a fantasy before, and then I realized they were, in fact, normal, and I grew up living in the fantasy world.

Ramsay: You're saying that you saw the space program as mundane because you grew up with astronauts all around you?

Garriott: Yeah, absolutely.

Ramsay: Is that why you didn't pursue it?

Garriott: No, I didn't pursue it as a career for a variety of reasons. When I was young, one of the NASA doctors told me I was ineligible because I needed glasses, and the other reason was that although I was a great self-study student and a constant competitor and winner of things like science fairs, I was not a super studious grade-A student.

Ramsay: And, of course, you heard a lot of stories about real space, and so much so that space travel didn't catch your imagination as it did the rest of us?

Garriott: I did hear a lot of stories, although not as many as you might think. If you had to say what movie character is most like my dad that people would recognize, the answer is absolutely, unequivocally, and precisely Spock. He's not the storyteller. He's not the guy who sits down and says, "Come sit around the fireplace and let me tell you a story about how I went to space." My dad would never ever do that. And so when I had kids at school ask me, "Hey, your dad's an astronaut. That's cool. What did he say it's like being in space?" I'd have to say, "I don't think he's ever said. Let me go ask." And then I'd ask, he'd say, "Oh, it's a lot like the training; it's kind of like scuba diving." I'd go tell my student friends that, and then I'd be sad that they'd asked.

Ramsay: What attracted you to medieval history?

Garriott: I think it was things like *Lord of the Rings* and *Dungeons & Dragons*. I don't remember having much interest before. I was interested in haunted houses and things that were a little bit historic and scary, but nothing as explicit.

Ramsay: Was your trip to space a publicity stunt for your sci-fi game?

Garriott: No, no. If I'm going to space, we might as well use the publicity around it, but my desire to go to space had nothing to do with publicity. I just always wanted to go, and I've been investing the money I've made in computer games in building a space frontier since I was very young.

Ramsay: This was personal then?

Garriott: Absolutely.

Ramsay: How do you feel about being called a space tourist?

Garriott: I'm not a fan. I don't think what I did was tourism. First of all, I was one of the cofounders of the XPRIZE that brought private vehicles into existence. I'm the largest and first large shareholder of Space Adventures that has flown every private citizen into space. On my own flight, I did tons of experiments for profit for NASA and other commercial partners, as well as many for the businesses I was starting. I am a private astronaut, period.

Ramsay: You've said before that there was a year of training. Is that the same amount of time that a government astronaut goes through?

Garriott: Sort of, and here's the qualifier for that. The way a crew is put together for a space mission is there are three levels of training on any system. The first level of training is to be a user, meaning I'm qualified to use that device, like the radios without mucking it up. The highest level is to be an expert, and an expert on radios, as a case study, is somebody who could disassemble the radio, repair defective parts, put it back together, and make it work again.

In any one crew, every member of the crew has to be at a minimum user level on every system that they will ever possibly interface with, otherwise they're not allowed to use it and that, of course, would make sense, you would think, right? Similarly, any crew has to make sure that amongst the three or four or six or however many crew members there are, one person is an expert on each system. They don't want to get into space and say, "Oh, look the radio's failed," and no one in the crew is an expert on it.

Professional astronauts want to do enough training to become an expert in as many things as possible. That way, they can be assigned to almost any crew, so professional astronauts go through many more years of training. For people like me, however, who are not staying up for six months or not doing this professionally, and who are flying under the assumption that if their seat were to fly empty, the other two members already have the expertise to cover all the other systems, then it allows me to train only to the user level on all systems. But we do the exact same user-level training as any other astronaut or cosmonaut. One year is sufficient to become a user on all the equipment and International Space Station subsystems that you would need to interact with.

Ramsay: A year of training still doesn't actually sound like a whole lot.

Garriott: I don't know if you're a scuba diver, but I imagine that you believe if you're not, you could be. If you aren't, I know you probably have some friends who have gone through the scuba training courses that take you a few nights in classrooms and pools. At the end of scuba diving training, you learn about partial pressures of various gases, and why if you go really deep, certain things like oxygen become toxic, and why if you come up quickly you can get things like the bends, as nitrogen bubbles out of your bloodstream. Those are the same type of things that are true in space. If you can handle a scuba license, you can handle learning about the life support systems aboard a spacecraft.

Similarly, if you can handle getting a ham radio license, you can handle the communications gear on a spacecraft. And the list goes on to where there are a lot of systems to learn, but no one of them is rocket science, so to speak. The hardest part was actually learning the Russian language. I mean, half of my day every day was spent in language classes.

Ramsay: Before you arrived at the International Space Station, you went up, of course, on a spacecraft. In the spirit that your young school friends asked you about your father's experience, what was that like?

Garriott: What's interesting is launch and reentry, which you think of as the most exciting and dangerous parts, but they're a lot different than you would imagine based on, for example, TV. It's really like a beautiful ballet move, lifting you ever faster in the sky compared to say dropping a clutch on a sports car at a green light to take off in the sky. It's quiet, smooth, and the g-forces come on very gently. It was much more elegant than I would have anticipated, both for the launch vehicle side and the reentry side.

Ramsay: It's actually quiet?

Garriott: Yeah, on the outside, it's extraordinarily noisy, and the shuttle has solid rocket boosters that add a lot of vibration inside of the shuttle, but all of the liquid-fueled rockets are very, very smooth and very, very quiet inside.

Ramsay: So, you never thought the giant explosion beneath you?

Garriott: Oh, you think about it, of course, but you're pretty well resigned by the time you're sitting on top of it. If it was going to cause you any alarm, you were long over it by then.

Ramsay: How much of a view did you have on the way up?

Garriott: The capsule you're sitting in has a protective cowling over the entire orbital module during launch. So, my right shoulder was touching the window, but there was nothing to see out the window. It's not until you reach space that that cowling pops off, and that gives your first view out the window. At first, it's just space, which is black, but once the engine shuts off, it rolls over and you can see back toward the Earth in a much more beautiful scene, of course.

Ramsay: At what altitude does the cowling pop off?

Garriott: It pops off before you reach your apogee, but I couldn't tell you exactly what the altitude is, but your full apogee altitude is 250 miles above the surface of the Earth.

Ramsay: When you returned to live among us surface dwellers, why go back to video games, especially after seeing firsthand the insignificance of mankind?

Garriott: I needed more money for another spaceflight! Very simple!

Ramsay: I would have thought that going into space would have been a life-changing experience. Your life doesn't seem to have changed at all.

Garriott: I would differ. I still really love making games. It's a passion. I still have my feet in space, too. I'm a member of the Commercial Space Federation. I was on the NASA Advisory Council and met regularly with NASA. But I would actually say that there are parts of my life that changed dramatically.

I now no longer think that the world is very big. Since you said that humanity seems insignificant, I actually think the globe itself is tiny and insignificant. I no longer think hopping from country to country as being a very big deal, so I feel like a master of the Earth in a way that I didn't feel before.

The biggest change is that I do a lot more environmental work. I'm now devoted to living, championing, and showcasing an environmentally friendly lifestyle. I espoused those values in the past, but I just didn't live it. I'm now a much better shepherd of those sorts of things. But my passion for exploration, my passion for space, and my passion for games have not abated at all.

Ramsay: How long were you in orbit?

Garriott: Two weeks. The orbital altitude of the space station and other Low Earth Orbit activities are only 250 miles up from the surface of the Earth. That's only 10 or 20 times higher than airplanes fly. So, you get this very enormous grand vista out over the entire planet, but it's only one order of magnitude higher, so it still feels very intimate and the kinds of things you can see out the window of an airplane are very much like the things you can see out the window of the space station. You really get this incredibly intimate view of the Earth that goes by very quickly because you're traveling at 17,210 miles an hour, which means you orbit the earth every 90 minutes, and so you see a sunrise or a sunset every 45 minutes, and you cross continents like the US in 10 or 15 minutes. It's really stunningly rapid movement, being so close.

Ramsay: You docked with the ISS, right?

Garriott: Correct. A little more than 24 hours after insertion into orbit, and we free-flew in the Soyuz for about 24 hours as they kind of checked out a variety of systems aboard the Soyuz prior to docking.

Ramsay: During that 24 hours, what were you doing?

Garriott: We still had a lot of work to do. You're checking out all the systems aboard the Soyuz, and you're doing mundane things like stowing the gear that you went through the launch process in. You're doing mundane things like eating meals and shaving your face, and in no time at all, you spend one night and then you're onto docking.

Ramsay: Did you ever find time to sleep?

Garriott: Oh, yeah. Since there's no gravity, there's no bed either, so you just sort of relax, get into a fetal position, and drift off to La La Land if you can.

Ramsay: Could you?

Garriott: About half of the people who fly in space find it to be far more relaxing than being on Earth, and they fall asleep very quickly and easily. It's like the perfect bed with no pinch points. I found that I was just so excited to be there and I wasn't going to be there long that, for me, it was more difficult.

Ramsay: Docking with a space station at 17,210 miles per hour doesn't sound terribly easy.

Garriott: Well, you're correct, and in more ways than you might know or might be obvious to most people. Everything that's in orbit around the Earth orbits the precise center of the Earth. So, let's suppose you and I were in rockets, traveling parallel to each other. And we came up side by side and we were both going to go around the Earth with one of us slightly to the north around the equator and one of us slightly to the south around the equator. We're going to take a parallel path, or at least attempt to take a parallel path, around the Earth. We actually can't because we're both orbiting the center of the Earth, which means we'll actually collide with each other only one fourth of the way around the Earth.

Our centers of mass will be at the same spot as when we're switching sides, and since our centers of mass only take 20 minutes before they're in the middle of each other, it's really only about 10 minutes before you hit each other. You can't come close to something in space and then stop. You push on in and dock right away. As you're pushing in, due to orbital mechanics, you're usually going forward or up or you're drifting. You're changing your velocity, which is putting you at a higher or lower orbit, or a retarded or pushed forward orbital position.

So, it's actually very complicated to dock two crafts together in space, and that's why the Russians do it with computers more often than by hand. The US doesn't even do it at all. What the US does is they get close and then reach out with a robotic arm to pull them into docking.

Ramsay: Was docking a stressful experience?

Garriott: No, there was almost nothing about the whole trip that I would describe as stressful. The only exceptions would be that sea survival training is definitely a hardship that must be endured, and if you were at all claustrophobic, you would absolutely not like boarding the Soyuz; it's very, very cramped. But, otherwise, the launch, reentry, docking, floating around in space, and looking back at the earth never seemed particularly stressful or dangerous.

Ramsay: Once aboard the ISS, what was your first order of business?

Garriott: The first order of business after docking was to set up a wide variety of experiments. I immediately set to work, setting up a slow-scan TV device on the ham radio equipment that I brought up. I installed it so I could leave it on to transmit the view from space of the Earth back to ham radio aficionados around the globe to be able to pick up and decode.

Similarly, there was an experiment called protein crystal growth, which I've now flown a few times in space. In that experiment, we fly a couple thousand of these little tubes of protein and precipitant that we load on the Soyuz just before launch, frozen to minus 30 degrees Celsius or so. It's important we get them to the space station at its center of gravity where they don't get much vibration or movement, even if the station reorients, so they can thaw out, cross-diffuse, and crystalize.

And there are things you do right away from a safety standpoint as well. Upon arrival, you reconfigure everyone's seats to be in the emergency escape orientation. For example, I went up on the Soyuz TMA-13, but I came down on Soyuz TMA-12, so my seat was moved to the Soyuz TMA-12 immediately.

Ramsay: How many people were on the station?

Garriott: There were the three of us who went up on Soyuz TMA-13 and the two I would be returning to Earth with on the Soyuz TMA-12. There was one more for a total of six who had gone up by one shuttle and would be later retrieved by a different shuttle.

Ramsay: How big is the ISS internally?

Garriott: It's large. It's as a big as a 747 jumbo jet. In fact, you can kind of think of it as school buses parked nose to tail and also occasionally branching "T" shapes. There were more modules than people, so it was not uncommon after breakfast with the crew that you'd go off to a module to do your work and you wouldn't see any other people except at meal times, or while traveling back and forth through the stack.

Ramsay: Did you have any ideas for video games up there?

Garriott: Not a one. You know, it's funny because even before space, I've made trips to Antarctica or down to Titanic or hydrothermal vents and other things, and not one of those can I say, "Here is an idea that came from one of those travels that has shown up specifically in a game." That being said, I'm sure they all inspire a great deal of the detail that I put in my games.

A good example would be when I was in Antarctica, we came across this gigantic, long formation made by the wind that whistled across the top of a mountain, swirled around the base, and dug into the ice what appeared to be a tidal wave 100-feet-tall and a mile or two long. As we walked along at the base of what appeared to be a frozen tidal wave, you sort of half-expected to see frozen dinosaurs inside. It felt and looked completely otherworldly. And while I don't think we could actually build that in a game and have it be interesting necessarily, the sense of wonder and awe you get when you turn a corner and discover something like that is what I try to think about doing in a game.

A good example from space would be when you look out the window of the space station. Since there's no ground for light to bounce off, and there's no air for light to refract through, the sides of the space station that face the sun are very, very well-lit, while the sides of the space station that face away from the Sun are pitch, pitch, pitch black.

Ramsay: You said that nothing about your trip was stressful, even reentry. All of the Hollywood depictions of reentry paint a different story.

Garriott: Well, it really wasn't stressful, although we had reentry malfunctions. But what's interesting is part of your training is to go through the history of every malfunction that has ever either occurred or has been theorized to occur. When you actually see a malfunction, especially if it fits but even if it doesn't fit, 90% of the time you're going, "Oh, okay, I've seen that one. It's no big deal." And even if it's a new one, you kind of put it in a class of activity. You kind of go, "Oh okay, well, that one's sort of like this, so we'll deal with it sort of like that."

We had two malfunctions during my reentry. The first malfunction was when the heat shield dropped away at about 10,000 feet above the ground and the parachutes deployed. There is a valve that opens to equalize the air pressure from the outside of the vehicle to the inside of the vehicle. Right about at the moment we were going through the checklist for the sequence of events in our logbook, smoke started to pour into the cabin. It was coming in from underneath the control panel in front of me on my side. I took some pictures and video of the smoke coming in, and I pointed it out to the crew commander in the center seat, but we never figured out what it was.

A second malfunction occurred when right as those same parachutes deployed, it dislodged a large metal bottle that was supposed to be strapped above me on the ceiling. And when that metal bottle dislodged, it fell between my helmet and the window beside me and sort of got wedged in there.

The seat you're sitting in has an explosive charge that goes off to lift your seat into a landing position, so that when you hit the ground, it can compress and go back down. When my seat lifted, it wedged that bottle even tighter between my shoulder and a piece of instrumentation on the control panel. It hurt, but more importantly, it prevented my seat from lifting to the landing position. And so my seat was still in the down position, which meant that if I didn't get that thing dislodged and we hit the ground hard, I would get an extra hard wallop. So, I said, "Okay, I really need to get that bottle out of there."

I actually couldn't do it on my own, so I struggled and struggled with it, but I couldn't get it. I told the crew commander in the center seat who's obviously busy doing a lot of other stuff, but because I felt this was important, I got his attention. With him pulling on it at the same time as I was, we managed to dislodge the bottle, my seat raised to its upper position, I stowed that container between my legs and some place where it wouldn't bounce around too much when we did impact the Earth a few seconds later. And, bam, we hit hard.

Ramsay: I have this picture in my head that you're in a capsule and you're hurtling toward earth at an ungodly speed with no ability to control your descent past a certain point and you're going into the middle of the ocean.

Garriott: We were actually headed to land in the case of the Russian capsule. We landed, bam, like a car crash. So, once you undock with the space station, you're free floating at over 17,000 miles an hour. The first thing you do is burn the engines to slow down just a little bit. If you slow down much slower than 17,000 miles an hour, you will not stay in orbit and you will fall back to Earth. And so you do a controlled burn that you can barely feel, just a little bit of pressure, and you burn for two or three minutes. In that two or three minutes of running the main thruster that you have still some energy in, it slows you down enough to where now you will reenter Earth's atmosphere. It's fairly predictable, mathematically, where you will enter, not exactly but pretty close.

As soon as you impact the upper atmosphere, you begin to slow down; the atmosphere has some thickness. But you start very high in the atmosphere where there is almost no thickness, and still you're moving at 17,000 miles an hour, so the few molecules you run into you're ripping apart and creating a plasma hotter than the surface of the Sun and the vehicle begins to melt around you. So, just three inches away from my shoulder, it's hotter than the surface of the Sun and the heat shield's bleeding away.

As you get deeper into the atmosphere, you slow down faster and faster, and, even with no parachute, your terminal velocity drops to only a couple hundred miles an hour. However, you don't hit the ground at a couple hundred miles an hour; you want to hit the ground as close to zero miles an hour as you can. But before you deploy a parachute, you can actually steer.

Although you're in a teardrop-shaped thing with a heat shield on it, you can actually tilt it slightly left, slightly right, and by tilting it slightly left or slightly right, you can actually steer slightly left or slightly right. You can actually guide your descent, even if your mathematically predicted reentry is slightly wrong, you can actually steer right back on course.

We landed within 500 feet of the mathematically predicted place at the end of the orbit burn. When you get down to about 10,000 feet—that's at terminal velocity—that's when you deploy the parachute, which is the first time you actually feel a big whip crack; that's jolting. As you get very close to the ground, right before you touch the ground on the Russian Soyuz, there's what they call soft-landing thrusters, which are basically explosives that go off underneath the vehicle to make it where, instead of just banging on the ground directly, you get a softer kick from the thruster that slows you down before you hit the ground.

If you just hit the ground without the thrusters, you'd probably hit the ground with about 25 g of force, which is survivable but just harsh. And if, as usually happens, the soft-landing thrusters work properly, you hit the ground with only about 9 g worth of force, which is actually quite comfortable.

Ramsay: Where did you land?

Garriott: In Kazakhstan. There's farmland in remote parts of Kazakhstan where you land.

Ramsay: On someone's farm!

Garriott: Yeah, on somebody's farm, exactly. They got a show for the day. They were like, "Wait a minute. There's space men popping up in my yard."

Ramsay: And you were in quarantine after that?

Garriott: Correct. Your quarantine lasts really just a few days or a week. It takes you at least three days for your brain to readjust to gravity, so you need to relax for a good fraction of that time. The main reason you're in quarantine though is that most everybody's involved in medical experiments. If you get contaminated by somebody on the ground before the people who are studying your physiology get a chance to run whatever battery of tests they want to run on you, that spoils all the time and money that's been put into those tests. So, the real reason for quarantine is to finish your medical workups.

Ramsay: When did you learn that you lost your job?

Garriott: While I was in quarantine. I was bedridden. For three or four days, you really can't stand up without getting the spins. And I got a call from one of the principals at NCsoft in Korea, and they said, "Hey, Richard, we decided to part company." And that's their legal prerogative.

Ramsay: So, there you were in quarantine, your brain readjusting to gravity, and, suddenly, you're fired. What were you thinking?

Garriott: It wasn't that much of a surprise. The launch process of *Tabula Rasa* was fairly contentious, and it was obvious that NCsoft's heart wasn't really in it. Although, my immediate reaction was "can't this wait one week so I can get back to Texas and be with the team?" Their answer was "no, we want to make a public announcement about it right now, so we're just calling to tell you."

Ramsay: Given that face is so essential to Asian cultures, perhaps the fact that they couldn't wait a week was not that they couldn't wait a week, it was because they were saving you face?

Garriott: I think it was the other way around, I suspect. Again, I don't know. They had a shareholder meeting where it came up in that intervening week that if they didn't do this, they would have to explain something to shareholders or make up a different story. I think they felt like they had to make it public so that they could share it with investors on very specific timing.

Ramsay: You now sound very matter-of-fact about the whole thing, but you were engaged in a big lawsuit, right?

Garriott: Well, the lawsuit came up for very specific reasons, which in federal court and appeals court, my position was unanimously upheld, so therefore I can describe it in cold detail. It was clearly obvious to anyone I did not wake up on my quarantine bed and decide to quit long distance from quarantine in Russia.

NCsoft had acquired my company Destination Games for a combination of stock and options. I had sold my stock in order to pay for my trip to space, and I had held onto my options because you're going to want to hold options as long as you can towards their maturity from a financial perspective. But NCsoft noticed that if I quit, they could force me to exercise my options. This was at the end of 2008, right at the end of the stock market crash, so they tried to interpret my contract to say that I had quit, in which case I had to sell my options at the low end of the market.

What clearly happened was that I was fired and the courts upheld that. There were e-mails around NCsoft from executives to other executives saying, "Hey, it's time for us to get rid of Richard Garriott." The evidence was not just obvious from the outside. The trail is completely clear that if they had to let me exercise them at a much later date, they'd be much more valuable. In fact, they were much more valuable at any time other than Christmas 2008.

And so the lawsuit was about was how to deal with my options, and the federal courts agreed with me. NCsoft appealed, and the appeals court also unanimously agreed with me, so NCsoft paid me that difference in value.

Ramsay: So, was the lawsuit just about money to you?

Garriott: Yeah, I think it was mostly a money issue. It could be for NCsoft that they thought, "Look, if we're going to cut Richard loose, we have to make sure he doesn't have enough money to start competing with us immediately, and take all these things he helped us acquire and start sucking them back out into doing other things." They did their very best to kill off value they didn't control. While that's speculation, that would be a reasonable business strategy—without regard to whether I might personally find it to be offensive.

Ramsay: A few months later, *Tabula Rasa* was closed. You started Destination Games to make that MMO, and you had spent several years doing just that. Were you surprised that NCsoft so quickly shuttered that game?

Garriott: At that point, it wasn't much of a surprise; it was my presumption that that was their intention when they let me go. However, in NCsoft's defense, they are used to mega-mega-mega-hits. If you think back to Lineage again, it's pretty hard to think of a level of success that is relevant in contrast to Lineage. From an NCsoft perspective, they just said, "Look, we just don't have time, bandwidth, management bandwidth, or interest in playing the long game." They'd rather circle the wagons and focus on the things that are the strongest immediate hits for them as a company.

Ramsay: After the NCsoft incident, how long did you take a break?

Garriott: About a year.

Ramsay: Another year before starting your next company?

Garriott: Portalarium was started by my teammates in September 2009.

Ramsay: When did you get involved then?

Garriott: I was around when they started, but I was just busy doing my own thing. And then pretty quickly, they wanted access to the Lord British IP, even if I was still a little bit busy, but I agreed to provide that access. Then they needed some office space, so I let them operate out of my lake cabin in Austin prior to growing big enough to require office space.

I joined in a full-time capacity as things were getting going, so there really wasn't a moment when I was not some part of Portalarium. I've always been part of Portalarium, but the amount of time that I've put into it has grown and grown and grown. I was also an investor soon after it started.

Ramsay: You're listed as a cofounder. Who started the company, if not you?

Garriott: Dallas Snell and some of our other staff members, but, really, Dallas is the main cofounder. Dallas and I now describe ourselves as cofounders, although he really started it ahead of me. I was already around from the very beginning, and more importantly, they floated a few ideas before I formally joined, but once I formally joined, this was the path we were on together.

Ramsay: Portalarium was established to develop social games, right?

Garriott: One of the very first games we did to get the team together was a social game, but more importantly, we knew we wanted to leverage the Lord British history and do the next great ultimate RPG. We also knew that one of the key factors in doing that was being able to leverage the social graph that was emerging in this new era of games. I think that social graph actually helps games reach a much broader audience, and helps people find people they already know in the real world versus just strangers as you commonly find in most MMOs.

And then, thirdly, we were big fans of making sure that we can migrate to whatever platforms players are playing on these days. These days, that's mobile as much as it is PC, so even though I'm a huge PC fan and we're doing Shroud of the Avatar first for PC, we also think that mobile needs to be a part of any growth strategy. It's a little more complicated than just saying we're doing social games, but one of the first games was a social game.

Ramsay: What game was that?

Garriott: That was called Ultimate Collector. It was a game about collecting as you might imagine by the name. It was a small game where you would build a home, and in that home, you would not only have collections on display, but you would build sort of a garage sale out of the back of your house.

As you ran around and collected items at other people's sales or at stores, you would build things you could show off in your house, and you'd get scores based on those. You could also sell off stuff you no longer needed to other people to gain more money, and you'd get scores on the sales side for finding bargains and flipping them for profit. It was a buying, selling, and home decorating game.

Ramsay: Around that time, a lot of people who had worked on blockbuster games, both online and off, were all getting into social and mobile games.

Garriott: Yep, and there's a good reason for that. Look back one generation. Look at *Star Wars: The Old Republic*, any *Guild Wars* product, any *Lineage* product, or any competitor to *World of Warcraft*. As I said earlier, they are enormously costly in time and money.

Ramsay: Wasn't there another dimension to that sometimes temporary exodus? Sure, social and mobile represented a big opportunity, but the games and their development cycles were also very different.

Garriott: Yeah, in fact, the way I would even say it is that mobile and social do offer great opportunity, but what's interesting about the first successes in mobile and social is that most hardcore gamers scoffed at FarmVille, Peggle, and just pick a small game. That's fine, but they are only part of the market. When we first did *UO*, people had that same opinion. People who were looking at screenshots of *UO* were going, "Wow, this game looks like it's five or ten years old graphically; it's kind of clunky, it's kind of slow, it's full of bugs, or the user interface is just inelegantly designed. I just don't get it."

And yet *UO* quadrupled the sales of any previous game. I think experienced game designers look at that and they go, "The reason why mobile and social is so powerful is because mobile is obviously ubiquitously available to everyone, and at a price point of free, or an app is cheap enough where if someone sees something cool, they're willing to buy it.

Ramsay: The ubiquity of social and mobile games also means that there's a race to the bottom, and not just a race to any bottom, but to the bottom of an oversaturated market where the chance of a big success is very small.

Garriott: If you think mobile games are more saturated than non-mobile games, I would potentially argue that case because I think all games are saturated. There's no shortage of games coming out on any platform. However, I would argue that there's a shortage of good games on all platforms. So, if you actually make high-quality content, you can still do just fine on basically any platform. The issue is: can you really make a good game?

Ramsay: Do you think the costs of getting social and mobile games to market will rise to the astronomical levels we see now for AAA console and PC titles?

Garriott: Unquestionably. I think that any mature market is, by definition, a competition to not only create the best product, but to simultaneously make people aware of it. And as much as you know if you're the first app on an app store, you kind of get free mindshare by being the only one available in a particular category on the app store.

Those days are long past and the only way to now get that mindshare is to start putting advertising wherever the best advertising is—whether that's on TV, radio, movie theaters, or virtual reality brain implants. Whatever method of reaching the public mind that can be bought, people will have to spend money to do that. Anything that doesn't do that is temporary because any free way to do it will quickly get jammed up.

Ramsay: You've now mentioned *Shroud of the Avatar* a few times. How did that project get started?

Garriott: *Shroud of the Avatar* has had several different names. There was a time where we called it Akalabeth Online, as an example. Helping kick off this game was the whole idea behind me coming to Portalarium. The origin of the game actually goes way, way back though. I've always wanted to return to medieval fantasy, and during my absence post-Ultima, I've been publishing for a decade or more little treatises that I used to call "Lord British's Ultimate RPG" to talk a bit about what I would do, given the chance to get back into medieval fantasy. This direction and interest of mine has been something I have been working toward for quite some time.

Ramsay: When did you decide to run a Kickstarter campaign?

Garriott: That was another decision where we kind of sat down and said, "Okay, what are we going to do here with this game?" We hoped that *Ultimate Collector* would do well enough to fund *Shroud of the Avatar*, but it didn't. We then had to say, "We have a few options available to us. We can find investors to back it, we can try to work with another large publisher, or we can do something like Kickstarter." Going with Kickstarter was not the easy choice, or the obvious choice, because you never know if it's going to work until you do it. It wasn't something we looked at and said, "That's the right way to go."

Kickstarter was rather was one of those things where you're going like, "Well, it's one way we could go, but if it works, that'll be great. If it doesn't, boy, will that be not only embarrassing, but would the company come crashing down around us?" If it worked, it would mean we could used that as evidence to tell another company, "See, people do care. Give us some money." But if it didn't work, then we couldn't go to another company because we'd have just demonstrated that nobody was interested. So, once we decided to pursue Kickstarter, we though, "Well, this is either the beginning of a new way of operating a company, or it is the end of Portalarium."

Ramsay: One frequent criticism that I read of Kickstarter campaigns like yours centered on your apparent wealth, or the apparent wealth of other prominent developers like Peter Molyneux, Brian Fargo, and Tim Schafer. How do you respond to the suggestion that Kickstarter is being used, or coopted, by wealthy people who'd rather spend other people's money than their own?

Garriott: If we didn't need your money, why would we bother asking for it? Why would be bother going through the pain and struggle of not only of running a crowdfunding campaign, but all the difficulties of keeping everybody up to speed, managing relationships, and building websites and stuff? Why wouldn't we just go build it, finish it, and ship it? Of course, we need the money, and, of course, by the way, I am wealthy; I'm just not *that* wealthy. I've already put millions of dollars into Portalarium, so how many millions of dollars do I need to put into Portalarium before I go, "Hey, that's enough of my money. Why don't we find a publisher or somebody else to join us on this risk?"

Ramsay: I'm convinced. Is *Shroud of the Avatar* worth that risk?

Garriott: *Ultima I* was the very first ever tile graphic game, and *Ultima IV* not only introduced the term "avatar," but also was the first game where you really had to play according to a moral code and the beginning of deep storytelling with you as not just as the hero, but the person who was evaluated as a hero. *UO* was the first successful MMO. I really do think that *Shroud of the Avatar* is going to introduce a whole new type of gaming again.

One of the really unique aspects of *Shroud of the Avatar* is a feature we call "selective multiplayer." Normally, one of the first decisions you need to make as a player is "which shard am I going to play on?" If some of my friends are scattered among different shards, it's difficult to impossible for us to see each other in the game. *Shroud of the Avatar* is going to start with everyone in the world on basically one shard.

As you move around the world, the game is constantly re-sorting into instances the people who know each other, or have purpose in finding each other. Like a good social game, it will reinforce the existing relationships people have with others in the real world. While you won't see 10,000 people on the screen, and you'll only see 1,000 people on the screen, but those 1,000 will be all of your close friends, plus most of 1,000 people you still don't know. I think we've got a really great system that will be the new standard for multiplayer games going forward, or at least a piece of the new standard.

Ramsay: We've now spoken for nine hours about your early life, your career, your companies, your games, and your adventures in space and Antarctica. When you look back on everything you've done and accomplished, and the challenges you've overcome, what are your thoughts?

Garriott: There was a science fiction author, a guy named Bruce Sterling, who gave a talk at a game development conference about how writing the best book ever as he would love to do is different from writing the best game ever as a lot of game developers would love to do. He noted that, in the book industry, for him to write the very best book means he has to beat every book that has ever been written, and there have been some mighty good authors writing some mighty good books in the 2,000-year history of the written word.

But if he does write the very best book ever, it would probably stand for a long time. And he said, "You in the game industry have the opposite problem." He said, "First of all, games haven't been around forever; they've only been around for a couple of decades. And there haven't been that many people making them. So for you to write the very best game ever written compared to writing the very best book ever written is actually pretty easy."

"Even if you do, in a few short years, not only are there going to be better authors that come into existence and therefore they'll write better games, but the technology's going to be a lot better, so their ability to manifest a better game will go up. Worse yet, the machines you wrote those early games on will be long gone, and the ability to see those early works in their original form will be more and more remote. And so even if you write the very best game ever, it won't stand nearly as long as writing the very best book ever."

And, you know, that's really true. It was saddening to me to realize that at that time, I hadn't seen my own first game *Akalabeth* operated in probably a decade or more. So, I did two things at that point.

First, I went and got my Apple IIs in shipshape and bought enough spare parts to keep them running indefinitely. In fact, here right next to me in my office, I have an Apple II. At our Austin office, I have an Apple II, one of my originals. And they're all still running *Akalabeth*. I just wanted to maintain that connection back to the beginning as long as I could.

Second, I said, "I'm going to write a really good game, after a really good game, after a really good game to where even though any one of them may not be remembered enough or withstand long enough, I'm committed to writing a series of games that, in aggregate, will hopefully be seen as relevant in these early days of game development."

I think I've done not too badly. I enjoy looking back both to my successes and my failures. To me, there have been important moments when I think have really helped the industry move from its earliest days into the future.

Gaute Godager

Cofounder, Funcom

Gaute Godager cofounded Funcom in 1993 with four others: Erik Gloersen, Andre Backen, Ian Neil, and Olav Mørkrid. Funcom was never the most successful publisher of massively multiplayer online (MMO) games, but at 22 years old, Funcom is one of the oldest.

Funcom is now best known for MMOs, but the company once developed single-player games, such as: A Dinosaur's Tale, based on the 1993 animation directed by Steven Spielberg; Disney's Pocahontas, based on the 1995 box office hit; and The Longest Journey, the acclaimed 1999 point-and-click adventure.

The release of The Longest Journey commemorates the year that Funcom refocused almost exclusively on developing and publishing for the PC, after a tumultuous history with console games. In 2001, the company unveiled Anarchy Online, an early digitally distributed entrant in the MMO market, with Age of Conan following in 2008 and The Secret World in 2012.

After 15 years, Godager, the last Funcom founder standing, retired from the company and perhaps video games altogether. Currently, Godager works as a clinical psychologist, diagnosing and treating psychiatric illnesses at an inpatient clinic in Norway.

Ramsay: Today, you're a psychologist. How did you get interested in psychology?

Godager: That was kind of weird. I was just shopping around trying to find what I was meant to be in the world. I studied computing, but I wasn't too hot on the math. I studied law for two years, but that was insanely boring. And then I just landed on psychology. I read the introductory book, and I was hooked.

Ramsay: And video games?

Godager: Before I started university, I was developing a game by myself on the Amiga for several years. I thought the game was interesting and a really big challenge. I was arrogant, thinking I could make the game all by myself, which was possible back in the late 80s. When I completed my psychology studies, the Amiga as a platform died in front of me. I had spent several hundred hours for several years, making this game I thought was really cool. I went to my reseller and said, "You tricked me! You said the platform would last forever!" I was very naïve, of course. One tends to be at 20.

So, he said, "I'm sorry, but I know people who are actually making games; they might be interested in what you know." That's how I met the other four founders of Funcom: Erik Gloersen, Andre Backen, Ian Neil, and Olav Mørkrid. Of course, they were making games on Sega and Nintendo systems. They just used the Amiga as a development platform, but my skills were useful. We hooked up and started Funcom in 1993.

Ramsay: How exactly did you meet them?

Godager: The Commodore guy gave me Erik's address and phone number. Erik became the driving force. He was the one who had a love of money and a love of making huge companies. He was the visionary. I tagged along, like an opportunist, if you know what I mean. I didn't have his great faith in the others, but I tagged along, supported it, smiled, and said my speeches.

But we hit it off! I think we hit it off because Erik had such a great belief in the possibilities. He was older, knew the video game industry, and knew what it would take. Andre knew how to raise money and make a good presentation. Tyr was a comic artist, so he could do help with presentations and stuff. Olav was a brilliant programmer. And I could make tools.

Ramsay: What was Erik's vision for Funcom?

Godager: Erik wanted to make great games, and to put it very bluntly, he wanted to get rich. In 1993, publishers threw money at developers. Everyone was growing, everyone was making money, and publishers were eager to fund small startups. To make our first game, our publisher gave us $85,000, which was nothing to them. It's unbelievable that you could make a game with that kind of money, so Andre shelled out enough from his own savings for us to run a basement office in Oslo for four months.

We had four months to get going. We invited publishers over to wine and dine them, to show them we have a good setup. When the publishers arrived, we had our friends bring over their own computers and fill the offices. There were actually only five people working. Of course, we weren't paid either, but at least we had shares in the company. We had enough people to make it seem like the company was running.

When the publishers came over, they could probably see through our hoax. There was a low probability of us making a successful title, and they probably knew it was a long shot. But having us work on something was still so cheap for them, like $10,000 to fund the first milestone. So, what we did was we made a quick contract with the first publisher to start us off, and then other publishers bought in.

Funcom grew quite quickly, from five people to almost 100 in two years. Of course, since we needed the first game to be a hallmark of our capabilities, the game cost us four times as much to make as we got paid. We really didn't know what we were doing! The publishers knew that; they had similar arrangements with other developers all over the world. Some studios made it; some did not. They took a Darwinist approach to game development.

Ramsay: How were the shares split between the five of you?

Godager: You must understand that Olav and I were very naïve, in terms of how to make companies. The shares were very skewed. Olav and I got 5% each while Erik got ten times as much, and the investors got one third of the company. That shows you how some people go into a startup, prepared with an understanding of the mechanics, while others just want to make games and be part of something fun. I was on a waiting list at the university, so I just wanted something to do while I waited for my studies to continue.

Ramsay: There were no objections to the split?

Godager: No, and that shows you our lack of understanding. I was okay with the 5% though, so I stuck with the company for the longest time. I wasn't there to make a lot of money. I was there to learn, and to do a good job. I was very interested in making games and I had a good set of skills, which ended up as the most valuable set of skills, of the founders, to the company.

I worked at Funcom for 15 years. The first founder was massaged out after only nine months. The second went after two years. It's very common that some people are very good at starting companies while others are very good at running them. The ones who are really good at starting up are looking for their exits. When's the exit going to happen? How much money are we going to make? But Funcom wasn't making money. Funcom almost never makes money. The game industry is extremely hit-based, and we've never had a massive hit. We've had good sales though. We've survived.

But because Funcom almost never makes money, every time there's a shift in leadership or ownership, the investors want to know where we can cut costs. And where do we cut costs? "Here we have this guy who owns a huge chunk of the company, and the company could really use that equity in other ways, so let's find a way to get rid of him." That's normal. That's what I've been seeing in the game industry. It's a very harsh environment. You're only as valuable as your latest hit. If you don't have a hit, you're nothing.

That's why the other founders drifted off. The last one to leave stayed for seven years or more. I had chosen to leave because I was tired of that industry, and really tired of the long hours. 15 years was more than enough for me.

Ramsay: You had investors? Why would anyone invest in a company that never made money, that doesn't have any hits?

Godager: I don't know what the numbers are today, but back then, 1% of the games sold made 95% of the revenue. You had titles that everyone bought, and then there were people scrounging to barely survive. Everyone was waiting for the one hit that would put them in the major leagues where they'd make massive amounts of money. All investors are looking for that, too. They understand that if you make World of Warcraft, you will be insanely rich. Investors are looking for that potential when they invest.

But I think our first major investor wasn't a venture capitalist. We got venture capital later in our investment cycle, but in the beginning, our investors in Norway had massive amounts of money stacked away from shipping and oil. They were spending money on new freight ships, so who cares about spending $5 million on a small business? That was just fun for them.

Ramsay: Did you invest?

Godager: Very, very little. I was a student. I invested my computer equipment I had at home, my time, and eventually, I invested in some rounds. Initially, I worked for free for almost a year. We were very young and very poor.

Ramsay: What was the video game industry like in Norway?

Godager: One thing that makes it very hard to succeed is it's quite easy to find people who want to work in the game industry, but it's very hard to find people with experience who want to work in the game industry. To be brutally honest, I don't know of any game company in Norway founded in the last 15 to 20 years that hasn't had a large proportion of ex-Funcom employees. Without Funcom, there wouldn't have been a game industry in Norway.

Ramsay: There wasn't a game industry then?

Godager: There was nothing. Nothing. Funcom pioneered the whole thing. Other Scandinavian countries were in similar situations. Games were made in Germany, the U.S., and England. Japan was massive in the 1990s. Korea wasn't that big yet and quite different then. Sweden and Denmark are now quite good. We have a couple of large companies, but we're small countries. Norway can fit easily into a Los Angeles suburb. The only thing going for us is we have tons of oil, so we literally grease the economy with oil money.

Ramsay: Without an industry, how did Funcom go about developing games?

Godager: When you work in the game industry, you understand that it's all about making good games. That's why Blizzard has succeeded time and time again with massive hits. They work on their games for so unbelievably much longer than anyone else can afford. They've probably been working on Diablo III since they launched Diablo II. That's like ten years! Who else can do that? And that's the only way to make sure you have a hit.

So, what you do is you develop good development methods. EA has these lines of engines they produce, so they can just pump out the next game with only a little bit more added to them. They have an NBA engine, an NFL engine, a FIFA engine, and then The Sims. I don't know exactly how they do it, but when we started, we didn't have any of that. All we wanted to do was make good games, and there was nobody in Norway who could tell us how.

Ramsay: What was the first game to come out of Funcom?

Godager: There were two that came out close to each other. The first one was A Dinosaur's Tale in 1993 for the Sega Genesis, where you were playing a dinosaur. The second was Daze Before Christmas, which came out in 1994 on the Sega Mega Drive. I think that's one of the few Santa Claus games. These were really, really small games where we developed incredible amounts of interesting technology. We had the first 3D flying game on the Sega Genesis. In A Dinosaur's Tale, you could actually fly in 3D through the world.

The reason why you could do that was because, on that Amiga I told you about, we had worked for many years on the Motorola 68000 processor—the same one in the Sega Genesis. And, since 1986 in Norway, we had the demoscene. That was huge in Europe, where people could show off their programming skills. Hundreds of people would meet in huge factories and school gyms, and make small demos over the weekend. Those kids were who we recruited.

Half of them were delinquent hackers and half were just plain nerds, but they were really good programmers. With them, we were able to squeeze the last few cents out of the Motorola processor, and that's how we showed we did better technology than anyone else. That's how we got the ball rolling because people were like, "Oh, my God! That's huge! And then we'd do this for $85,000, so we weren't just good; we were cheap. We had no business sense though. We spent four times as much on making A Dinosaur's Tale as we should have, and the same with Daze Before Christmas.

Ramsay: Why did you guys choose to develop A Dinosaur's Tale and Daze Before Christmas first?

Godager: That was not the question. The question was: which game can we get some slightly stupid publisher to fund us to make? In the beginning, we were a developer for hire. The publisher came to us with the money, a one-line description of the target audience, the type of game they wanted, the core features that should be seen in the game, and the size of the game. We did development, and they controlled the merchandise.

Back then, you had to make cartridges that were amazingly expensive. The game sold for $39.99 or $49.99. The price was basically the same as today, but it was very, very expensive to sell cartridges, and the hardware manufacturers were the only ones that could make them. Platform companies like Nintendo and Sega made money off publishers who would preorder 100K cartridges at $15 a pop. They had to shell out $1.5 million, and if the game sold nothing, the publisher went down. We got paid upfront though.

The only people who always made money were the hardware manufacturers. To survive, the publisher squeezed the only people they could squeeze: the developers. Publishers would start up ten games, can half and write them off as bad investments, and then put the big money into the remaining five. That means that when the publishers had made their money, we would get a percentage of the sales, which was basically never. You could build a developer for hire, but you had to make sure that you made the game exactly to cost. That's the only way you could grow the company. That was impossible for us because we had no experience, so we just floundered along. Fortunately, we had extremely patient investors.

Ramsay: Why were they so patient?

Godager: I'll never know. Our very first investor was a friend of Erik's and he was an old money guy, Tom Dahl. His father made a lot of money and his father's father made a lot of money. He inherited everything and wanted to have some fun. Our second investor was the Yates family, who made their money in oil and natural gas. For them, investing in a game company was their idea of fun. They came on board three or four years into the cycle, in our second round of investments. The third round was venture capital, and then Funcom became the first Norwegian game company to list on the Oslo Stock Exchange in 2005.

Ramsay: The way you tell the story, wealthy investors were perfectly happy to throw their money away. Was Funcom really such a bad investment?

Godager: In the 15 years I was there, we never made any money; we always lost money. We sold about one million copies of Age of Conan, but we didn't make any money because the cost of making the game was $40–50 million. Making these massively multiplayer online games is insanely costly.

But when I said our investors were patient, I think that's the best way of describing it. First, to them, they weren't there to make a small profit; they were there to get the big bucks. They wanted something in their portfolio that was cool and fun. We made headlines not only in Norway but around the world. The New York Times wrote about us, and I remember being interviewed on CNN. Investing a game developer was cool! I don't know how they feel about it right now, but that's the way it was.

Second, they wanted to safeguard their investment. When you invest, let's say, $30 million dollars, investing another $1 million to launch the next game is a relatively small price to pay.

The third reason was that the amount of money they were investing was just pocket change, at least to one of our investors. He's still an investor, and we're a listed company, but he hasn't sold any shares. He could have sold a lot of shares many times, but he hasn't; it doesn't matter to him. He can spend ten times as much, and that'll still only be third of an oil rig or whatever.

Funcom is also, in some ways, a national pride to Norwegian people. We sold one million copies of Age of Conan. Name one other entertainment property created in Norway that has ever sold that many copies. It doesn't happen. It's a cool thing, and it's probably way overvalued, but again, it's something that many nerds in Norway would like to have a piece of. Like, "I know I'm losing money buying Funcom shares because they keep going down, but it's cool having those shares; I own a piece of magic!" But they are patient. Maybe they're naïve like we were? Maybe they're stupid? I'm very grateful. I always take the opportunity to thank them for their patience.

We were always very good at public relations and marketing at Funcom, too, or at least we used to be? I don't know anymore. I haven't worked there for years, but we used to be really good at being a company that people wrote about. We did different things, we did new things, and people were interested in what we were doing. We could still sell dreams of the next game. We could still offer people the possibility of not making money, or only making their money back, or becoming filthy rich down the line. Because we have that ability, people just kept giving us chances. So, we made some bad games, but we also made some good games.

We were among the very first, and we made industry changing games. I could sit down with you in World of Warcraft and just list the features they ripped off from Anarchy Online that we invented before them. I can say they did this, they stole that, they did this the way we did, but we were responding to what previous games did wrong and they were responding similarly.

The difference is that while they did what we did, they did what we did better, which is always what I say. They were more experienced. They were smarter than we were, but we were creative, and I think that's why we've stuck around for years and years and years.

Our list of near successes is quite long. Funcom is one of the few developers and publishers that has not gone bankrupt while at the same time remaining independent. We don't make enough money to be bought by EA, but we make enough money to be invested in again and again. We're like a floater—with potential.

Ramsay: When a company develops MMOs, that company tends to publish their own games. Funcom had publishers prior to entering the MMO business. Why the switch?

Godager: By 1998, we were fed up with the developer for hire model. We were really fed up with making console games where we saw the hardware manufacturers make all of the money. We made excellent games, but they could screw us at a whim. I have so many tales of that.

I remember in 1997 when we worked in the Irish office on a really cool title, a comic book driving game. We had married some cool comic characters we'd made with Sega Rally-type driving. It was not only fun to look at, but it played really well. We thought that game had huge potential, so we made the game for the Sony PlayStation.

Sony was super interested in the game; they were asking for new copies all of the time. And they had said that for the approval process to be really fast, we had to submit games to them and we did. Suddenly, when had a really nice contract with them. Everything was fine, they were smiling, and we were hugging. But when the game was ready, they started finding bugs we couldn't replicate. So, the game remained in limbo for several months. And one day, Sony's in-house team releases a game that was a clear competitor. I can't prove anything, of course, but isn't that a weird coincidence?

In 1998, we decided to shift to developing and publishing PC games. PC development was the place to be because we could control everything. Retail still had to get their cut, but at least we could sustain lower sales numbers and make our money back. But we had less risk; we didn't have no risk. And so we eventually moved more toward the subscription model, where sales weren't dependent on normal distribution channels. We could sell games directly online.

It's important for me to give credit where credit is due. Marius Kjeldahl, the vice president of technology, was the one who actually had the vision of moving the company into online games. I am not saying I was against it, but I wasn't very happy about it. It was just a new place where I didn't really understand the games. I wasn't visionary enough. I hadn't been online enough, basically.

Ramsay: Was Funcom technically prepared for online games?

Godager: The development infrastructure we had was ready, more or less, on the client side. We everything we needed to make PC games. On the server side, it was a much bigger struggle. What type of server do we need?

What do we need to know? We didn't know, so we hired people who understood servers and server programming.

And although Marius was a visionary, he didn't really get the backend, so we launched Anarchy Online without any methods of receiving payment. That was a disaster! The game had been in development for three or four years. It wasn't that hard to make, but so many things needed to be coordinated and weren't.

We also had no crowd control system. Let me explain it to you very briefly. Let's say that you want to make an online version of the summer Olympics in London. There is a set number of people that can be gathered in one place. We could carry the load when they were evenly distributed throughout that world, but real people don't have that way. The second everyone hears that Usain Bolt is running the 100-meter dash finale somewhere, everyone rushes there. In our MMO, our system broke down. We didn't understand why.

So, basically, we had a leaky ship—a ship that when we poured water on it in the dry dock, it seemed to hold up, but as soon as we dumped the ship into the ocean and filled it with passengers, the ship started to leak everywhere and sink. It was just something that was almost impossible for us to predict. We failed quite miserably at launch and lost a lot of customers. And we were notorious.

We were the first to fail in such an epic way, but other games had come after us and done the same. If you go to MMORPG.com and read about launches, you will see that eight out of ten launches fail in some way. There are so many ways for a world to fall apart.

Ramsay: What did you learn?

Godager: Launch day was a remarkably happy event. We were sitting around in our offices—taking pictures, popping a bottle of champagne, and saluting each other for doing a good job. Of course, we didn't have the tools to understand how badly the launch was actually going. It took some time for us to understand how much crashing we had. We were in the dark about almost everything. There were so many broken pieces of technology glued together with hope and fear. Some pieces were just missing.

Our many patient and nice investors actually had a critical role in the failure of Anarchy Online: they pushed so hard for an unfinished game to come out because they felt like we had spent enough time and money. They were right, but they tossed their investment out the window by pushing so hard. Before launch, I remember we, the non-management people, were saying, "The game isn't finished! The game isn't ready! We need to wait. We need to do more." But we had spent so much money, and we had been saying the same thing for so much time, that we didn't have any credibility anymore.

We didn't know when we started how little we knew, which is always a problem. We were breaking in a new technology, a new platform, and, for the first time, we were the publisher and we didn't have another publisher's quality assurance organization. We had to do everything ourselves and make massive leaps everywhere.

Everything fell apart over the weekend after launch. It was really bad. There were many bugs, and players were demanding we fix them. So, we were working around the clock on a huge patch, and when that patch went out, we actually broke everything. We had gone from crappy to completely disastrous.

The worst thing we saw that we had to fix was cheating. It was bad enough that we had to implement a crowd control system. Players were using speed hacks to move ten times as fast, so our coders worked really, really hard to implement fail safes to ensure that a player's character was always positioned correctly. The fail safes worked really well in our office on our servicers, but the crowd control system, and the anti-spoofing and anti-cheating systems, kicked in constantly for players around the world. People would log in and start moving but then they were suddenly yanked back. The client would display a message saying "take it easy."

It was like spitting in the face of our customers. Players grew really frustrated, and we lost a lot of customers that first weekend. And, of course, all the coders were so tired that they had gone on vacation. They took some time off because they just delivered this big patch.

The launch of Anarchy Online was a really stressful and terrible experience. We learned a lot, and there's a lot of code in The Secret World that is probably many hundreds of iteration better than what was in Anarchy Online. Going forward, we built on what we had done, fixed it, and made it better, so The Secret World had a flawless launch with almost no crashes or bugs.

Ramsay: Who were your competitors?

Godager: The two biggest MMOs at that time, at least in the West, were Ultima Online (UO) and EverQuest (EQ). UO was extremely focused on online player vs. player combat, and there were no levels. You came into the game as a new player. I remember that I had two gold pieces and very little equipment. It was hard for me to make money because the game was styled around the hardcore player. I wandered around for hours, trying to find some way to make money, and, gradually, I spent all of my money on food.

Being extremely weak, I stumbled out into the world where these player killers were just waiting for me and several hundred other hopeful newbies. They slayed us over and over and over, and we'd respawn where we died, so we were just killed over and over and over. We had to log out, wait several hours, and then log in again. UO wasn't flawed from a technology perspective; the game was just super hardcore. UO was made for the winner, for the player killer. That was the philosophy of the people who made UO.

And the same goes for EQ. That was a game balanced around high-level game-play—a game that you had to spend hours and hours and hours playing. I played a spell caster. Every time I cast a spell, I spent mana points, but there were absolutely no mana potions in the game. There was nothing you could buy to replenish your mana. The only way to regain mana was to sit down and read your spell book, which took up to five minutes to regain your full mana. You could kill one beast, but then you had to sit down and read your spell book. The spell book was a full screen page, so you saw nothing for five minutes except your spell icons while you waited for your mana to replenish. It was really hardcore and balanced around playing in a group because you were really poor and puny by yourself.

These were our competitors and they were successful. The only reason UO and EQ were successful, in my opinion, was that they were first and people just accepted what they were given. It wasn't until World of Warcraft where Blizzard plied their "games for everyone" knowhow. They made an extremely solo-friendly MMO. The other games were really hard to play by yourself. That's why they had 12 million subscribers instead of 500,000.

With Anarchy Online, we remedied many of the problems with UO and EQ. We tried to create the first MMO, and we tried to create the first player-friendly MMO. Unfortunately, really broken server technology didn't really help our case.

Ramsay: What did you take away from Anarchy Online that you used in the making of your later games?

Godager: One of our Anarchy Online expansion packs, Shadowlands, was the biggest expansion pack that Funcom had ever made. It was set completely in another world, a new game in its own right with a portal to the Shadowlands from the main world. That was our test bed for our ability to execute a successful launch and make a really huge world. I think we learned more from that.

Shadowlands was a massive expansion. In terms of real estate, we almost doubled the size of Anarchy Online. In terms of complexity, we added a lot of new systems. In terms of graphics, Shadowlands wasn't 2.0; it was more like 4.0. We didn't have that many customers, but Shadowlands was still successful and we made money. That was where we wanted to be as a company.

We saw with Shadowlands that we can execute a huge game, that we can make a good, huge world, and that we can make something really visually appealing. At the time, my boss and I worked really well together; he put a lot of faith in me and saw that the team that I built with Shadowlands could go on to make another title. We were shopping around and wondering what we were supposed to be doing, so we picked up the rights to Conan. I wanted to do something with that. It was a happy coincidence that the IP had just been bought by some Swedish people. Norway is like Canada to Sweden. We speak the same language and we have the same mentality, so it was easy to get in touch with them.

They really saw that we understood how to take care of someone else's intellectual property through our work with Disney on Pocahontas. We were able to convince them we could make their IP worth more if they let us build a huge MMO. They thought that was a fantastic thing, of course. There aren't many MMOs coming out, maybe one or two every other year. There are fewer and fewer coming out because breaking into that market is really hard. So, we took what we learned from Anarchy Online and made Shadowlands, and then we took what we learned from Shadowlands and made Age of Conan. We started making Age of Conan in 2003 and continued until the launch in 2008—five years in production!

Ramsay: Before we talk about why you left that year, since you were the creative director, did you spend any time on developing creative talent? I ask especially because Ragnar Tørnquist is effectively Norway's Sid Meier. Did you play any role in building that kind of creative leadership within the company?

Godager: I don't think I can take credit for building Ragnar. Ragnar and I were the two big stars depending on which game was coming out. Ragnar did The Longest Journey, and I did Anarchy Online, and then he did Dreamfall, and I did Age of Conan. Now, he's doing The Secret World. We were on different teams. I don't remember if I hired them, but I remember when he started working with us in 1994. I thought he was a brilliant, brilliant guy. When everyone asks me about the talent, I would always say that Ragnar is probably the most talented person we had in our company.

I'm much more of an organizational development guy. I build organizations, I build companies, and I build relationships. I had a very, very conscious role in building talent. I always thought my role was to help build an organization that could run itself, especially if I were to leave, or if I was hit by the tram or the subway.

I was always trying to find talent and spend a lot of time with them, giving them responsibilities and letting them run with the ball. I'd check in occasionally and review what they were doing, but I was never in complete control. Sometimes you need more control than I had, but sometimes it's also very costly to have too much control. When I left Funcom, I was very proud of the organization I left behind. I was very happy about that.

Ramsay: What were the events leading up to your departure?

Godager: To be very honest, I was depressed. I had done everything I could, and exhausted everything I knew, when I made Age of Conan. I had tried so hard to make something that could be my legacy. I had wanted to leave Funcom in 2003 after Shadowlands. I was tired of the game industry and I was tired of making games, but I was dissatisfied because I didn't have a hit.

Age of Conan sold like a hit, but we lost customers because it didn't have enough content. It was too empty. People consumed the content too quickly and the end game was not. Age of Conan was substandard compared to World of Warcraft, or any other game out there for some time. So, we didn't really make it.

When I left in 2008, I saw that too many players were leaving, and I was depressed by that. I had really put all my soul into it. My boss was very sad that I left. He felt we had done everything right, and he felt I was a good game developer, a good game designer, and a good creative director, and that the company lost a lot of knowledge when I left. I know this because he doesn't lie about stuff like that.

I wasn't asked to leave, but I wanted to leave because I was so sick and tired of failing. I was sick and tired of the game industry. I just wanted to do something completely different with my life. I realized later that I left too quickly. I should have stayed on, helping the company learn more from our past mistakes, but I had to put myself and my own feelings first. For the first time in 15 years, I did that, and that felt really good.

Ramsay: In 2008, what was the trigger that motivated you to go through with leaving Funcom?

Godager: Before then, every day, I was receiving an e-mail message, automatically generated from Funcom, about the number of subscribers; I was watching the number of subscribers just dwindle. When I went to Portugal with my wife and kids, my life without Funcom felt so good. That's when I realized I can no longer stay on, so I wrote my letter of resignation on the way home. I just needed some time away to really understand how stressed, tired, and fed up with the game industry I had become.

Ramsay: On the way home? Was your decision to leave that easy?

Godager: It was very hard, but not in the sense of having doubts. It was very hard because I felt like I was killing a large part of my identity. I was Funcom. I was the only founder left. My life had been Funcom every day, every morning, for 15 years. I chose Funcom because it was mine. After I left, I chose psychology because it was good for me to help people after all that time.

Ramsay: What do you think makes an entrepreneur successful? What do you think makes him, or her, fail?

Godager: When you're starting your own company, I think you need to be able to disregard naysayers who say "ah, I think that's been done before" or "this is really hard; you shouldn't do it." Fill in where you don't have knowledge with hope and aspiration, and then surround yourself with people who can tell you what you don't want to hear, so that you can prepare yourself for your own mistakes. You can't give them power over you, or your company, but you need critics and you need to be able to disregard them.

I also think that one of the biggest flaws I've seen in founders is that they become hooked on investor thinking. Instead of thinking about how to make a good product, something interesting, or something you can love to make, they ask, "When is my exit? When is the next round of financing? What's the price of my shares today?" The people who lasted the shortest of the Funcom founders were the people who were most interested in becoming rich or powerful.

You can become powerful and rich, but that's not why you should become a founder. You must believe you can do something that's cooler, different, better, nicer, faster, or cheaper. I've seen many startups fail, and nine out of ten times, they failed because the founders were more interested in riches than products. I'm not saying you should want to be poor though. I'm not saying that.

Ilkka Paananen

Cofounder, Supercell

Ilkka Paananen cofounded Sumea, an early developer and publisher of mobile games, in 2000 with Jarkko Salminen, Mikko Kodisoja, Sami Arola, and Mika Tammenkoski.

At 23, still in university, with no experience, and without a strong professional network, Paananen was somehow able to land distribution deals with every mid-tier and major carrier in Europe. In a short time, under his leadership, Sumea had become the leading European mobile game publisher.

Sumea was acquired by Digital Chocolate, the mobile game company established by EA founder Trip Hawkins in 2004, and for the next five years, Paananen worked with Hawkins to transform the company into a global power.

After years of keeping up with the prolific entrepreneur, Paananen decided to leave Digital Chocolate in pursuit of new opportunities, but Paananen was soon drawn back to the world of startups. With Kodisoja, Lassi Leppinen, Niko Derome, Visa Forsten, Petri Styrman, he created Supercell in 2010.

Supercell, based in Helsinki, Finland, has been trumpeted as the fastest-growing game company ever, a company that has raised billions of dollars from venture capital funds and the sale of a 51% majority stake to SoftBank. Supercell, where Paananen continues to serve as CEO, generates more than $1.7 billion per year across only three games: Hay Day, Clash of Clans, and Boom Beach.

Ramsay: How did you get into the video game industry?

Paananen: By coincidence, really. As a kid, I had been a very enthusiastic and passionate gamer. When I started at university, I had almost stopped playing games, but while I was there, I met this group who called themselves "Sumea." Those guys wanted to make games.

I got to know them, and at some point, they decided that they wanted to found a company. They needed somebody to look after the business. I had zero experience, but I was very passionate. I decided that I would help the guys out. By August 2000, somehow I had become the CEO.

Ramsay: Who were the guys?

Paananen: There were four other cofounders of Sumea: Jarkko Salminen, Mikko Kodisoja, Sami Arola, and Mika Tammenkoski. All had a lot of experience with developing games; they were way more experienced than I was then.

Ramsay: Why did they ask you to join?

Paananen: I don't know. They wanted to focus on game development, so they needed somebody to look after everything else. I guess they did not have many choices; they had no money. I knew one or two of them, and they just asked if I would like to join them. I told them it sounded like a great opportunity and, of course, it was a big one for me. I was very eager to learn. I thought to myself, "If nothing else, I'll learn a ton." I did. I'm so happy I made that move while most of my friends were going into investment banking and management consulting. I was definitely the odd one out doing something completely different.

Ramsay: Were you drawn more to starting a company, or starting a company that makes games?

Paananen: Both. Games had been a very, very big part of my life previously. I loved games and I still love games. It was really intriguing to get into a creative business and a consumer business, too. You could create something of your own. Even when you're not part of the creative team, it's just cool to watch that happen—to watch the developers build from scratch something that people can play. I had also studied entrepreneurship at the university. Being an entrepreneur, your own boss—that sounded like a cool idea, too.

Ramsay: You didn't have any experience at all?

Paananen: Absolutely zero experience. I was studying at the university then. The system here in Finland is a little bit different from in the United States. Here, at least when I was a student, most people go to the master's degree immediately. I had barely started my studies when I joined Sumea. I graduated many years later. Prior to Sumea, I had only had summer internships and summer jobs. That's how fresh I was.

Ramsay: What was your first order of business when they came to you and said they wanted to start a company?

Paananen: These guys had no money, so somehow we had to get at least some of the bills paid. We needed rent, money for food, and those sorts of things. We needed to get the cash flow coming in from somewhere. I think I started on two separate but parallel tracks.

On one track, I was trying to sell their expertise on a work-for-hire basis to whomever was willing to buy. On the other, I was looking for venture capital. We came really close to closing a round, but then suddenly the dot com bubble burst and raising money just became impossible. That happened at the worst time for us. It was tough to get anything done. The mood was quite depressing. We were extremely lucky that we didn't get any funding though; we were forced to learn the basics of business.

I finally found a few clients who were willing to buy games from us and pay us something. Some cash flow started to come in, and these guys used their free time during the night to start building our own games. We used our client business to keep the company alive and finance what we really wanted to do. Of course, it was slow.

But the dot-com bubble bursting also wiped out a lot of our future competition. Back then, we had a few well-financed mobile game companies in Europe. They went bankrupt in 2001. That was a good thing for us when we finished our first mobile game in 2002. At that time, you'd distribute mobile games through carriers. Since there wasn't much competition, I had an easier time selling our games to European carriers.

Ramsay: You were strapped for cash.

Paananen: Yeah, I guess you could call it that. To take care of your personal finances in Finland, you can get these loans from the government; you can subsidize your studies. If you study at the university, you can get an extremely cheap loan, so I took that loan while I was still at the university. I had a very cheap apartment back on campus. That enabled me to work at no salary for a year and a half.

Ramsay: Were you the only one who personally invested?

Paananen: Everybody had to make sacrifices. We paid salaries to the guys who needed it most, but I think everybody had to make sacrifices. If somebody needed to pay their rent, we paid that guy's salary. That's how it worked.

Ramsay: Where were you meeting initially?

Paananen: We rented out an apartment for three guys who were part of the group, so they all lived in the same apartment. But then we also used that apartment as our first office.

Ramsay: What was the game industry like in Finland in the early 2000s?

Paananen: Small. We had a couple of companies that still exist, but most of the developers were making games for PCs. We had companies like Remedy Entertainment, who later made *Max Payne*, which was a massive hit. They then made *Alan Wake* and so on. They're still around.

We had a company called Housemarque that just recently made a game for the PlayStation 4 called *RESOGUN*. It was very well-received. We had a few companies like that who were amazing, working with international publishers and doing games that way, but our industry was small.

Ramsay: Not only were investors not terribly interested in investing, they weren't terribly interested in investing in games?

Paananen: Yes, that's right.

Ramsay: How much did you raise to get the company going?

Paananen: We never raised any money for Sumea. In late 2002, when phones with color screens came into the market, we managed to build a distribution network with all of the major European carriers. Consumers started to buy these phones and they started to download these games. We had 50/50 revenue-sharing agreements, so all of a sudden, we had cash flow and started to grow really quickly. All of a sudden, we went from this place where we definitely needed money to a place where, oh my God, we're actually quite profitable now. We no longer had an urgent need for venture capital and we immediately hired more people.

Ramsay: Who were your first carriers?

Paananen: Our first carrier wasn't even in Europe. It was a carrier in Hong Kong called CSL. They had maybe two million subscribers. Our second carrier was another small carrier in Denmark called Sonofon. They had maybe one million subscribers. Our first big deal was with O2 in the UK; they had something like 10 million subscribers. Then we closed a deal with Vodaphone that was really massive for us. I think they must have had like 60 to 70 million subscribers in Continental Europe. So, all of a sudden, this very small company from Finland had become an amazingly credible player in the market, compared to our size and our position. After that came deals with T-Mobile, Orange, and a lot of smaller guys as well. By early 2003, we had every single mid-tier and major European carrier in our network.

Ramsay: Were you personally responsible for landing these deals?

Paananen: Yes, that was almost my whole job. I was able to buy these flying tickets for students and I was traveling like crazy around Europe, meeting with carriers and trying to close deals. I was 23 at the time.

Ramsay: At 23, how did you even make any of that happen?

Paananen: It's funny to think about it looking back. Believe it or not, I just went to conferences where I knew the guys who were managing the media portals were attending and I would just approach them and show them our games. I obviously had nothing to lose.

Nokia was, of course, a superpower here. Thankfully, Nokia arranged events where they invited developers and mobile carriers. I actually met a lot of the carriers via Nokia. And I and everyone in our team just did everything we could to land these deals.

As always in sales, once we had a few good references, the job got easier and easier. Our games were really good at the time, especially when compared to the competition. We were all about quality. We were always pushing the limits of the technology. That made my job easier. If we had crappy games, I wouldn't have been able to do it.

Ramsay: What were Sumea's first games?

Paananen: The first game, and the biggest one for us, was a game called Racing Fever. If you remember games like Outrun, these isometric racing games where you look at the racing car from the back, Racing Fever was that type of a game. Racing Fever was the first of its kind for these color feature phones. Of course, today, the game would look really terrible, but back then, it was novel for color screen feature phones. Nobody had anything like that. It was one of our biggest hits at Sumea and sold extremely well through almost every single carrier.

And then later on we built a game called Mafia Wars, which was inspired by an old classic called Syndicate, and that also became a big, big hit for us.

Ramsay: I had a mobile phone around the time Sumea started. I don't anymore. I remember the phone had a black-and-white screen and wasn't very powerful. It couldn't handle very much—usually just an address book.

Paananen: Yes, those were feature phones. Most of them were Nokia phones, like the 7650, which was the first camera-enabled Nokia phone with color display and support for downloadable Java applications, and then a few Sony Ericsson and Samsung phones.

Ramsay: I think the only game I played on a phone back then was Centipede. Were your games more sophisticated?

Paananen: That was our big advantage, actually. Not many people thought about mobile phones as devices for playing games. We wanted to try building real games on these phones. We thought of them as computers. So, we grew quite fast; you could almost say too fast. In 2001, we had six people. Everybody was a founder. There were no salaries, no employees. By the end of 2003, we had around 30. In June 2004, we finally decided to sell the company to Digital Chocolate; we had around 40 people then.

Ramsay: Who were you hiring?

Paananen: Mostly developers, but we started to build a management team. Somebody came in and ran the studio. Another guy came in and ran operations. We had to localize the games to more than ten languages, so somebody had to do that. We also had to port these games to run on tens to, later, hundreds and hundreds of different feature phones. The market was extremely fragmented. Now, people complain about the fragmentation of the Android market. It's nothing compared to what we had to deal with back then.

We hired a guy who had been helping us on the legal side. We hired a CFO. I guess you could say that, technically, he was a cofounder of Sumea but then he joined full-time as our CFO. At some point, we hired somebody to run sales. I was still personally doing a lot of that. But most of the people we hired were just game developers: engineers, artists, and designers.

Ramsay: How many games were in development simultaneously?

Paananen: The number grew over time. I think we started two to three games simultaneously and then moved on to five or six. These games were extremely small compared to the games of today. Our first games were only 64 kilobytes in size.

Ramsay: How many developers were on each project?

Paananen: We had super small teams of one programmer and one artist, and then we needed two programmers and two to three artists per game, and then maybe a producer to run the team. The producer would often be a designer as well. Eventually, we had a dedicated designer on every game. It was really dependent on what exactly we were building. All teams definitely had less than ten people, though.

Ramsay: You went from two to six games in development at once. How did you determine which games to develop?

Paananen: First, as you might guess, of course, it was extremely informal. The group would just get together and brainstorm ideas. We knew what was out there in the market and we looked at the sales charts to see what was doing well. We combined all of that information together and we just made a decision.

Later on, we developed more of a process, especially at Digital Chocolate, where we hired product managers, performed market research, prepared concepts that would compete against each other, and had a small group of people who decided what we'd build.

Ramsay: Did a carrier ever ask for a specific type of game?

Paananen: Sometimes, and actually quite often we showed these game concepts to the carriers to get some early feedback, which actually was a great thing to do, because they had no idea what those types of games would sell either; but they may have had some insights, and that was a way for us to get the carriers a bit more committed to those games. And if the people on the carrier's side felt they had some influence over what was getting produced, that would usually show quite favorably in how they would promote that game.

Ramsay: And since this was pre-iTunes, how did the games even get discovered?

Paananen: These phones had a thing called a WAP protocol, if you remember. All of these carriers had their own WAP portal. There was usually a button on the device that would queue the carrier's portal. Vodafone's was called Vodafone Live, for instance, with all kinds of content: weather services, news, games, ringtones, and logos. T-Mobile had something else. And then Orange had their own version, and everybody was running their own stores.

Ramsay: Yeah, I'm starting to remember that now. It's kind of like remembering rotary phones. Would you say that app discovery is easier today?

Paananen: Oh, yeah, about a billion times easier. I guarantee you that no developer today would trade what they have today for the world that we had in 2004.

Ramsay: Today, when someone creates a game or an app, all they do is put it up on iTunes and watch the money roll in.

Paananen: Yes, exactly, they don't even have to talk to Apple if they don't want to; they just upload it. Back then, at every single carrier, there was a heavy negotiation process to get the agreement in place and they would only do business with maybe 10 to 20 content developers. Initially, they had a lot more, but then they realized, "Oh my god, we don't have time for everybody," so then they started to cut down the number of suppliers quite quickly. By then, it became almost impossible to get it in if you were new.

Ramsay: Did you have to do more work in terms of discovery to get your products into consumer hands then?

Paananen: If you had a good relationship with a carrier, usually how it worked out was we designed some kind of a marketing campaign and commitment. Maybe we would run a print ad or two, or a sweepstakes, and then we would use that to get the carrier excited. And the only thing that really mattered in that world was how the carrier placed your product in what was known as the carrier deck or portal. And, of course, if you got a featured placement, that would be a really important thing.

In those days, because these carrier decks were so slow and so clumsy, nobody was actually browsing these stores and asking, "Are there any new games I want to buy?" Everybody just bought these games from the top of the store from featured placements.

I guess you could say that if you had a good relationship with a carrier, then actually, it was quite easy to get your game discovered, but if you didn't, then it was impossible—no matter what you did.

Ramsay: Did you have nearly as many metrics then as you do now?

Paananen: No, we had basically zero metrics because every game used the pay-for-download model. There were no microtransactions, nothing like that. The only metric we got was how many downloads, or purchases, there had been per month, and we got those reports on a monthly basis.

Ramsay: What was the pricing like?

Paananen: It depended on the country, but you could say that it was roughly from three to maybe eight euros per download, and usually we would get roughly 50% of that.

Ramsay: For 64-kilobyte games, that sounds good. Now, Sumea was developing games, but were you also publishing third-party games?

Paananen: We tried that model one or two times, but it was just too complicated for us. We were a lot more efficient doing our own stuff. And as we got more developers to work for us, it was just financially so much more efficient for us to do our own stuff.

Ramsay: What was inefficient about publishing third-party games?

Paananen: I think the biggest inefficiency was related to the fragmented device market. Already in 2004, you had to support more than 100 phones, and every single one was different in terms of screen size, runtime memory, sometimes even input. It just became a massive nightmare.

First, you would develop games to come out on three different reference profiles: small, medium, and what was called the high-end at the time. Then, we would take these reference profiles, and use them to port to different devices that would fall into each profile category.

One of the most clever things that we did at the time was to develop our own game development platform that automated a lot of this stuff, and it made porting games very, very efficient. One of our very big advantages was we were able to support more devices than anybody else, and when our game would come out, carriers just loved that. They could sell to their users, and they could advertise that game, because they would know that it works in every single device that they have, more or less.

That was a big advantage for us. Many of the smaller guys and third-party developers didn't have that technology, and they really couldn't use our technology because it would have taken a lot of training. So, it was actually quite inefficient for us to take games from them, and try to bring them to market.

Ramsay: King started in 2003. Did you compete with them?

Paananen: With King, no. Locally, our biggest competitor in 2003 was a Finnish company called Mr.Goodliving, which was later acquired by Real Networks. But then you had the biggest company in Europe for mobile games was Gameloft in France; they still exist and are a major player. They are closely related to Ubisoft. Later, there was a US-based company called Jamdat. Jamdat even did an IPO, and EA bought them. THQ was a big competitor, very active in Europe, and they had a big mobile games division. And then there was a UK company called Macrospace that morphed into Glu, which also did an IPO.

Ramsay: You were very familiar with the competition?

Paananen: Yes, extremely. That's always been one of my things. I always want to know everybody who works in the industry, and I don't really see competition as competition. That's the one thing I do love about games: 99% of the people in this business are extremely friendly to each other, and I've always enjoyed going to industry events and getting to know people. Yeah, I don't really think of them as competitors in the old-fashioned way. I guess I don't regard business life, or life in general, as a zero-sum game. Of course, people are competitive, but that doesn't mean you can't talk with other people. Especially in European and especially in the Finnish games development scene, people help each other out. We talked to each other a lot, and always when we would go to conferences, we would go for beers together and just exchange information. I think that was a benefit to everyone. I think the real competition was more against the bigger guys, like Gameloft, EA, and later, I guess, THQ.

Ramsay: And, of course, a player buying Gameloft games wouldn't preclude them from buying your games.

Paananen: That's right. I think what we really competed on was who got the best placement for their games on these portals. That's really how you made money at the end of the day. That was seriously competitive. Later on, when the market matured, the carriers would take the vast majority of the games you had on offer. It didn't really mean anything if they took the game. What really was important is whether they'd place the game on their portal.

Ramsay: You mentioned before that you were working at Digital Chocolate. Were you working at Digital Chocolate and Sumea at the same time before the acquisition?

Paananen: No. So, now we are in early 2004. At that time, we started to realize that this was getting very competitive, and that the carriers were telling us, "You guys will need to start investing in co-marketing campaigns with us if you want to keep direct relationships. And if you don't, we'll have to work with you via a publisher." That was the last thing we really wanted. If you have a publisher in between, you've lost the game—they will be the king of the hill and not you, and you will lose all control.

We thought, "Okay, we need to keep a direct relationship." And then we thought, "Okay, if we are ever going to be able to compete here, we actually need to raise money." We needed to raise some venture capital to afford those co-marketing campaigns.

We had calculated that we needed to raise ten million euros or more, and, additionally, the US market wasn't really going anywhere for us. We had a deal with Verizon, and we had a deal with T-Mobile. We even had an indirect distribution relationship through AT&T, but we were not a credible player from a US point of view. So, we thought, "Okay, we'll invest, hire more people in the US, and that will make us feel more like a local company in America."

Finland didn't have the kind of reputation we have today. These days ,it seems that if you are running a games company in Helsinki, that alone enables you to raise money from abroad, but back then, none of these tier one venture capitalists had invested in any Helsinki-based companies.

To cut a long story short, raising the type of money we wanted to raise looked really, really difficult. There were lots of people who wanted to invest smaller sums, like two to three million euros, but we just couldn't put a large enough investment round together.

That option was ruled out, and then we hired this one guy who we knew to look for other options. Was there somebody who would like to buy us? Somebody who would like to merge? And while we were doing that, I met with Trip Hawkins, the founder of EA and who had founded Digital Chocolate just a few months before that, and we started to talk about the possibility of merging with Digital Chocolate.

Eventually, they bought us, and it seemed like a match made in heaven; they had what we didn't and vice versa. They had great financing through Sequoia Capital and Kleiner Perkins; they had raised lots of money from them. Those were the two top VCs at that time, the two most famous ones in Silicon Valley.

Then they also had very credible management, mainly Trip. He was a legend in the games industry. And they had relations with the US carriers we didn't have.

And we had what they didn't have; they had zero distribution in Europe. They didn't really have any good quality products, and we had many. In June 2004, we signed the deal with them.

Trip made me the managing director for Europe, so I was doing basically what I had been doing all along, but I reported directly to him. And then two years later, he promoted me to president of studios of Digital Chocolate, so I was essentially running all of the studios globally. We had a studio, of course, in Helsinki, we had a smallish studio in San Mateo in California, and then a bit later on, we bought a studio in Spain called Microjocs.

Ramsay: As you were moving towards co-marketing in this way, were the cofounders of Sumea pragmatic about selling the company?

Paananen: Yes, I would say so. I think we were extremely close as a group, and we talked about everything very openly. Everybody was pragmatic. That's a really good word to use.

Ramsay: No one was disappointed that controlling its own destiny wasn't in the cards for Sumea?

Paananen: No, no. One thing that was attractive about Digital Chocolate is when they bought us, they were maybe 20 people and we were 40 people. In the deal we made, we got roughly one-third in cash and two-thirds in shares. We thought that there's a very big upside left in these shares, and, in addition, we would get to work with people who had a lot more experience than we had. There was a great opportunity for us to learn, and we could be a very, very big part of this company, and we were.

That's why actually all of the Sumea cofounders stayed for a very long time. I stayed for six years, and I think everybody stayed for more than five years. That's almost unheard of. Usually, founders leave in one or two years.

Ramsay: If you hadn't sold, what would you have done?

Paananen: I think we would have probably continued as we were. Of course, nobody can say what would have happened with the carriers. Would they still have done business with us, despite threatening not to?

Another factor for us was that our salaries were still small. None of us had made good money, so it was attractive to get some cash on the table.

Ramsay: You all were like, "Finally, we're getting paid!"

Paananen: Yeah, exactly. Exactly!

Ramsay: Can you tell me what you and Digital Chocolate discussed during negotiations about technology?

Paananen: Yes. At that time, we had developed this technology that we called internally the Sumea Toolkit. As I mentioned earlier, the purpose of that technology was to make it easier for the developers to address the issue of handset fragmentation. If I recall correctly, their studio in San Mateo took that technology into use almost immediately.

Ramsay: After you sold to Digital Chocolate, what was next for Sumea?

Paananen: We started to grow the studio and the office quite quickly. When I look back, that's one of the things I probably would have done differently. We grew the headcount four times to 160 people in two years. During that time, the company started to change a little bit.

So, to cope with that growth, we started to introduce more process and new layers of management. And it wasn't apparent at the time, but that's something that I would have done differently. That explains why we've been extremely careful here at Supercell about not growing too quickly. We want to keep the creative engine going; we have been careful to not introduce too much process or layers of management. That's one of the biggest lessons learned during my time at Digital Chocolate.

Ramsay: In Digital Chocolate's press release, they said that Sumea was the leading European mobile games company.

Paananen: That's true. When they bought us, there was us, a company called Macrospace, a company called Elkware, and Mr. Goodliving from Finland, and then Gameloft was a big player in the European market. We were at the top of the charts and competing against each other.

Ramsay: Right. Since Sumea was the leading European mobile games company, how come Digital Chocolate acquired Sumea and not vice versa?

Paananen: Good question. Even if we were one of the leading companies here, the market was still small. In terms of revenues, it still didn't mean much. We were doing a few million euros per year, so very small in terms of the size of the business, and Digital Chocolate had access to capital; they had already raised quite a lot at the time. Compared to us, they had way, way more cash.

Ramsay: In order for you to stay at the company, did you have to integrate Sumea with the Digital Chocolate system and way of doing things?

Paananen: Yeah, yeah. I would almost say that, for the most part, we integrated Digital Chocolate to our system. Of course, from a financial perspective, Sumea was integrated into Digital Chocolate, but I think Sumea became the main engine for product development.

The integration was amazingly smooth. Maybe it was because Digital Chocolate was so small at the time that they were very open to adopting a lot of the processes and stuff we already had. And, to Trip's credit, he really trusted me and my team; he gave us a lot of freedom. He was driving this thinking of "let's use what's already working at Sumea." That was a very, very good thing.

Ramsay: You were the managing director in Europe at Digital Chocolate between 2004 and 2006. I assume that was during the integration process?

Paananen: Yes.

Ramsay: That took two years?

Paananen: Not quite. I think we were pretty much done in a year, if I recall correctly. And, initially, Digital Chocolate's organization was based on geography or markets, and we were operating quite independently. For example, in Europe, we would have our own specific road map of products for Europe and in the US, they would have their own. I had my own sales organization for Europe that reported directly to me, and in the US, they had a sales organization that was responsible to Trip.

After two years, we figured that we should move into a more global structure. All studios started to report to me, and all sales started to report to a colleague in the US. We moved from a regional organization to a more global and functional organization. That explains the change in title.

Ramsay: Why were you made the president of studios?

Paananen: I think probably the biggest reason was the European organization was the prime engine of new products, and we were responsible for most of the revenue as well. At that time, I don't think the studio in San Mateo had put that many products out and they were doing less well. Trip wanted me to try to improve it.

Ramsay: From your vantage point as president of studios at Digital Chocolate, what did you learn about the games space at the time?

Paananen: We tried to build the organization almost like a factory. We tried to be extremely organized. We had a well-structured organization with layers of management and processes, and a very detailed process for how to greenlight the products for production.

Now, having more experience and having experienced how that worked out, I think in a creative business you want to organize yourselves in a completely different manner. Rather than being top down, I think you want to be bottom up, and you really want to give the power to the creative guys, to the developers, and you want to minimize the amount of process.

Ramsay: At what point during your tenure as president at Digital Chocolate, did you decide to go off and do something else?

Paananen: When I was approaching my ten-year anniversary, I was starting to think that I've now spent ten years here, and I've given this company everything that I had. I felt I was running out of energy. I even talked to Trip quite openly about it. And when the company had changed its strategy so many times, and at that time, it was headed in a new direction again. The new direction was all about a new, patented platform called NanoStars. I didn't see a big role for myself. I just couldn't see how I could add more value to it anymore. We were having the best quarter we had ever had for the company. It was profitable and growing, and we had just finished moving Digital Chocolate from being a cross-platform provider of casual games to the social games space—and we actually did move it. We started to do Facebook games and transitioned to being a Facebook games company. We completed that transition in 2010.

I was feeling quite tired and I didn't really know what else I could give to that company. I felt that if I wanted to make a bigger contribution, I couldn't do it from here in Helsinki. I should move to San Mateo to the headquarters and work really closely with Trip, and take on an even bigger role.

Trip was really supportive of all that, but at some point, I realized that I don't really want to move my family to San Mateo. But then I was stuck in the situation: I don't want to move my family to San Mateo, but unless I move to San Mateo, I can't take the next step, so I have to stay here. But if I stay here, I can't contribute as much as I would like. On the other hand, the company's doing great, and at some point, I realized that I should let other people try to get some fresh blood in, take some time off, and figure out I what I really want to do. If I don't leave now, when am I going to leave?

I talked to Trip, and he just said, "Hey, if you really feel that way, then you should just leave." Then things started to happen very quickly, so I think I left one or two weeks after that conversation. Trip flew to Helsinki, and he threw this really great party for me to celebrate everything that I had done for the company, and was extremely complimentary of what I had achieved. Then I flew to Barcelona with him, and we did the same with the Barcelona studio, which I had acquired, and it was also doing well.

It was May 2010, I think, and I took some time off with the family and traveled a little bit, and started to think, "What do I want to do next?"

Ramsay: Were you tired of the strategic changes?

Paananen: No, it was just really exhausting and almost impossible to run a San Mateo organization from Helsinki. All of my C-level peers were in San Mateo; they were ten hours away. Just to give you an idea, for the last two years, we had this weekly management call that would usually start at 7:00 PM my time, and quite often it finished at 1:00 AM my time. It was every week. And that was just one management call. There were other people reporting to me in San Mateo, so that was another weekly call again in my evening, plus everything else. I had been living in that world for almost six years.

Ramsay: What exactly was exhausting about that job?

Paananen: You're under a lot of pressure, which I've always been fine with. I think I am pretty good at operating under pressure. But you need to work 24/7 at very odd hours, and it's extremely hard to manage people being ten hours away. Just imagine a situation where you don't actually see the most important colleagues in your organization that often. You have to rely on e-mail, which is a very bad method of communication. You have to rely on phone, and not only do you have to rely on phone, you have to do it at really crazy hours. And that means that you don't see your family all that much.

I also remember in 2004 when we did the deal with Digital Chocolate, Trip actually was the first guy who I ever heard about talking about social games. In fact, he called mobile phones "the social computer." At that time, people were laughing at that, outside the company, and thinking he's crazy. To think about the irony right now, if we had stayed on that course and really believed in this vision of social games on mobile, Digital Chocolate would probably would be at a much better place than it ended up. I think one of the things we learned the hard way at Digital Chocolate was you should really stay true to your vision. We ended up with this company that was always a little bit late to the party.

We went to all kinds of platforms, from downloadable PC games to an XBLA title. We were one of the first to ship a title on Facebook, but then we forgot that somehow. And when companies like Playfish and Zynga started to make money on Facebook, we again decided to again go back to Facebook, and we were late again. We should have stayed true to the vision.

Ramsay: What did you want to do after leaving Digital Chocolate?

Paananen: I always need something to do. Doing nothing wouldn't be me. I actually did a bit of everything, initially. I did one or two really small angel investments in very early stage startups, and then I became a partner in this small, early stage investment fund called Lifeline Ventures. I helped them with some games, as well as their mobile and consumer Internet-related investments. I knew Mikko was putting together a new team, so I started to help him. I guess I just wanted to see what interested me most. It didn't take long to figure it out that I really get the most satisfaction from being an entrepreneur.

Ramsay: How did Supercell get started?

Paananen: There were two guys I had worked with for a long time who left Digital Chocolate before me. One of them was Mikko Kodisoja, who was the creative director at Sumea, and vice president and creative director at Digital Chocolate. I think he was the original designer or producer on almost all of our biggest games.

Mikko and I started to talk about this idea: what if you could put together a game development company like you would put together a professional sports team? The sole goal of management would be to hire absolutely the best people, create the best possible environment for them, give them the freedom and responsibility to do their own thing, and then stay out of their way.

I remember that a few years before, I had seen this presentation from Netflix that was about their culture which they called "Freedom & Responsibility." That was a very big influence on me. At that time, I thought, "The next time I set up a new company, this has to be part of the thinking."

Mikko and I started to brainstorm. Who are absolutely the best and nicest people we have ever worked with? We came up with a list of six people, including us, and then we just started the company.

A big part of our thinking at that time was that app distribution was going to become democratized a lot, meaning that the only thing that really matters is the quality of the game. That wasn't always the case at Digital Chocolate. While we may have been known for quality games, there were many other factors at play.

The only thing that mattered after the quality of the product was the kind of deck placement you would get from a carrier. But, in these app stores, it was so much easier for consumers to discover products. There was actually some real word-of-mouth going on.

And then we thought, "Okay, what is the main contributor to the quality of a game?" Of course! It's the quality of the team. For every single hit product we had shipped in our previous lives, there was one common uniting factor, and it was that it was shipped by a great team. We thought, "Let's set up a new type of a company that will be all about people." We'd just get the best people, and create the best possible environment, and everything else would be secondary. With enough time and luck, something good should come out of it.

Mikko and I both had not made much money, but we had some money from the sale to Digital Chocolate, so we invested a large part of that money in Supercell just to get the company started. We also raised some debt financing from the Finnish government. There's an agency here called the National Technology Fund, or TEKES. If you put your own money in, they'll top it off with government money. You can get a loan with quite reasonable terms.

We raised that loan and that gave us a couple of hundred thousand euros to get started, and then we rented out this very, very small room in an old office building, and we got started.

Ramsay: How large was that room?

Paananen: Around 30 square meters. I remember that we had, at its peak, 15 people in that room. There were two square meters per person, and I can tell you that it was pretty crowded. And I still have this really funny picture I should send to you. At some point, the room got so crowded there was no room for me anymore. I decided that because I'm not really involved in developing games myself, it's better that I move out. So, I had this cardboard box that used to be my table, and I was sitting outside the room in this hallway. I actually have a picture of that.

Ramsay: Why did you need so much capital? What were you planning?

Paananen: Our product vision was about cross-platform game services, meaning that you can log into these games via any device, be it a smart phone, tablet, or even web browser, and on Facebook. One of our dreams was to create games that people would play for years, that would have the kind of longevity of big games like World of Warcraft. And we saw games more as services rather than products.

So, what was the platform with the biggest reach in 2010? It's the web, and the desktop web, combined with Facebook. They had hundreds of millions of consumers who play games and played Flash games, so we thought, "Let's start from that platform because it has the widest possible reach, and later on, let's port those games to smart phones and then tablets later on."

We started to work on Gunshine, a real-time Flash-based MMORPG. The idea was to launch it first on Facebook, and then port it. So, we started to develop that game in June 2010, and we got the game to beta in February 2011, and in between, we had raised €750,000 in a seed round from Initial Capital, London Venture Partners and a local business angel, Jari Ovaskainen. When we got that game to beta, the metrics looked quite promising. We thought we were okay.

We were quite well-capitalized, too. For such a small company, we actually had a lot of capital on hand, so we weren't in a hurry to raise more. But then we started to talk with Accel Partners about the company, and they got quite excited about it. We met Kevin Comolli, the managing partner at Accel here in Europe, and there was clearly a good synergy with him. He understood our vision, and he believed in the team. We started to think that maybe it would be a good idea to raise a lot more capital, just to give us enough runway in case this game isn't a hit. And we have to develop more new games. It's good to be really capitalized in this industry. Being well-capitalized enables you to think long-term. In May 2011, we ended up raising eight million euros from Accel and €200,000 more from a German games entrepreneur, Klaas Kersting. It was actually a very big sum for a company that had no revenue yet.

Ramsay: By that time, how was Gunshine doing?

Paananen: In autumn, as we started to scale the game more aggressively and get more users, the metrics started to change. As we got more users, retention went down. The metrics didn't scale.

We had been successful in making a game that a relatively small group of players enjoyed playing and paying for. But it just didn't have mass-market appeal. And it did not look like people would play it for years, which was our original vision. The key people at Supercell, the founders, and some other key early employees went into a room, we looked at ourselves, and said, "Hey, guys, this isn't working out at all. We have to do something else."

Ramsay: So, you just nixed Gunshine?

Paananen: Well, we had this massive discussion about what to do. We decided that there are a few problems here. One is the Facebook games market; it's not doing as well as we thought it would do, and it really isn't an optimal platform for games. I'm talking about the desktop Facebook. Second, at that time, tablets were taking off in a big way, and we were really excited about the tablet platform as a game platform.

We thought that if that's the future of games, if games are definitely heading to tablets and mobile, those would be the biggest platforms for games. If we wanted to be the number one game company on tablets, we had to focus our attention there. This vision of cross-platform game services, not just Gunshine, just isn't working out. We were spreading ourselves too thin. And if we really believed in it, we had to go all in.

In October, we had this board meeting where we decided to throw everything we had been working in the toilet, and to start from scratch to do games primarily for tablets, and later on for smartphones, too. We came up with the phrase "tablet first" that we used to describe our strategy.

We started four or five products on mobile and tablet. The first one came out in January at beta. It didn't work out, so we killed that immediately. Another game got quite a bad reception internally in focus groups, so we killed that, too. The next game that came out in May 2012 was Hay Day, the first game Supercell got out where our metrics looked extremely good at beta. We launched that in June, and it started to do quite well.

And the next game we put out was Clash of Clans, which went to beta in June. And, again, the metrics looked good. We decided to launch that game in August 2012. I could almost say the rest is history.

So, those games started to do really well. We had a lot of capital left, so we started to advertise those games quite heavily, and luckily, they had very strong organic growth. People loved those games and they spread. That's how Supercell, as you know it today, was born.

I went through the history quite quickly, but I think you know Supercell as a company struggled the first 18 months. Most people don't know that, or they don't remember that about us. I know that outside looking in, it feels like all of our success came so quickly. But trust me, it was quite a battle.

Ramsay: Interestingly, the media gives us on the outside the impression that Clash of Clans was your first title, a breakout hit.

Paananen: Yeah, I don't think that the media really gets that we are actually quite good at being brutally honest to ourselves when something isn't working out. We are not the type to just keep on working on it, and then just wish it will turn for the better. We make really painful and difficult decisions like killing products; and that's really the essence of Supercell. I think that's one of those things that makes us quite unique.

Ramsay: In your sports team analogy, you said that one of your goals is to create the best possible environment for your team. Killing games so easily doesn't sound that great, creatively speaking. So, what exactly is the best possible environment for game developers?

Paananen: One where they have as much creative freedom as possible, and as few processes as possible with as little hierarchy as possible. An environment where they can express themselves and what they care about.

Ramsay: As a manager, how do you make that happen?

Paananen: There's one really critical thing and that is that you must be extremely comfortable about yourself and about this strategy. This strategy essentially means you're giving away a lot of control to the developers.

A lot of leaders and managers want control because control makes them feel better. Most people feel better when they are driving the car, as opposed to sitting in the passenger seat, because then you feel that you can somehow affect the result. This is probably the biggest revelation I've had. It took ten years to get here, but I now realize that if I have control, it isn't necessarily better for the company. Actually, it's probably quite the opposite. When other people feel that they have control, they're way more motivated.

And the chances are that these other people, these developers, know their games much better than I do. It's such a complex environment, but they know it better than I do, so why wouldn't I give control to them? It really requires a completely different type of thinking, and it's tough because you have to be very comfortable with this idea.

When we give control over to developers, that means they have the freedom to express themselves, and they are in control of the creative vision of their games. But with that freedom comes responsibility. There has to be extremely tough criteria about what makes a game successful, and if the game is not successful, then that game must be killed. We have what is actually quite a results-oriented culture, ultimately.

Ramsay: With regard to the National Technology Fund, you put up some of your own money and they topped it off with government money. Can you tell me more about that system?

Paananen: We have an extraordinary system here in Finland, which is one of the reasons we are having this startup boom now. It's relatively easy to raise capital money. The concept is quite simple.

Let's say you have a project and a budget for building and rolling out the project, in this case a game, that you have detailed as a million euros. And let's say you have €300,000 to invest in the product. In the best case, they can loan you the money to fund the rest, and that's what we got.

It's not free money though; it's a loan, but one that you don't need to personally guarantee. You won't end up on the street if everything goes wrong. Of course, if the company goes bankrupt, you've lost all of your own money that you put in, but at least it's not a complete disaster.

Ramsay: There's no way for the government to recover? That's quite a system.

Paananen: Yes, it's a really good system. The genius about that system is that people will still put a significant amount of money on the table from their personal savings, or from some other private source. If the government loans out €700,000 and the individuals lose €300,000, that's a huge amount of money for ordinary people, and that really hurts. Just to give you an example of how the government benefits, we paid taxes last year to the Finnish government totaling €260 million. It's been a pretty good investment for them.

Ramsay: When you pivoted from cross-platform game services to tablets and mobile, what did it actually take to make that shift?

Paananen: That was a big decision, and the defining moment of Supercell. It was October 2011 when we decided to pivot the company and focus solely on tablets and mobile, and threw everything else away. It was an extremely tough thing to do at that time, but that has made us who we are.

We essentially bet the whole company on tablets and smart phones. Now, it makes a lot of sense, and it's easy to look back and say that was the right call, but at the time, it was way less clear.

When you've been working very hard on something, it's always hard to let go and admit to yourself and to others that whatever you were working on is not going to work out. It's not so easy to be honest with yourself and really admit when something is not working out.

Once the core team got to the point where we thought we could have an honest discussion about it with the whole company, we got everybody into one large room and just talked openly about it. I think we had 35 in that room. And then we talked about it with the board, and we told them that, based on everything we know, we need to do this pivot. We were admitting that the whole cross-platform strategy wasn't working out for us. We had to admit that the game we had been working on, that they had invested in, didn't work out and that we were starting again from scratch.

Ramsay: Why wasn't that switch clear?

Paananen: Now, it's very clear that the mobile sector is growing the quickest, and companies like King and us are growing quickly and are extremely profitable. But if you rewind back to that moment, we had no examples in the Western world that this would work out. We were convinced this was the way to go, but it was a leap of faith.

To prove it to ourselves, we bought iPads for every employee. That was a relatively sizable investment, but we wanted to get them excited about the device, and that's exactly what happened. They fell in love with the platform, and they started to think about what kind of games we could design.

The one thing that became really apparent was that there weren't many games specifically designed for the iPad, that took advantage of the larger screen and the bigger swipe movements. The games that existed were modifications of existing games from the PC or console smart phones. And the more we spent time with the platform, the more we started to work on new games that solely focused on the tablet, and the more confident we became that we had made the right decision.

Eventually, there started to be more and more market information about the rise of the tablet. Six months from that moment, there was a research study that showed that tablets were the quickest growing platform ever, and that they would pass the PCs, laptops, and so on.

Ramsay: You called this pivot "a leap of faith" and "a risky decision." Many managers try to reduce risk at the expense of potentially significant opportunities, so why not try to do something less risky?

Paananen: A way easier choice for us would have been to continue to believe in the existing games we had, work on new features for Gunshine, and just hope that it somehow took off. We could have also launched and released the games we already had developed for Facebook. Those would have been the most convenient and easy decisions because there would have been no changes.

But I still remember this one slide I presented to the company in that meeting: "If we really are honest to ourselves and if we look at the Facebook market, we were not even in the top ten." If you looked at the amount of users we had on Facebook, and you compared us to the competitors, it was clear we would not be able to catch up with them. Another slide said that mobile is an open territory, that there was no single big player in that market. There was no one like Zynga who had been dominating the Facebook market. And then I had another slide that simply said, "Let's start to play the game we can actually win."

Ramsay: And you started to play that game. When did Clash of Clans come into the picture?

Paananen: Once we decided to go full steam with mobile, we did some brainstorming. And two big ideas came out of that. One was a real-time strategy, which later turned into Clash of Clans. The other idea came from looking at the huge success Zynga was having with FarmVille on Facebook. We really couldn't find a farming game that was built for mobile and which was social, so we thought: let's do that. That's how Hay Day was born.

Ramsay: Were you working on any other titles that didn't make it out?

Paananen: Yes, I think we had five teams working on different games. And two out of those five made it to global release. Of course, you never know what's going to work and what will not work.

One thing that created a lot of faith in those games was that in February 2012, we had the first playable milestones for those two games. Everybody in the company received and played a build of each game, first Hay Day and then two weeks later, Clash of Clan. When people started to play these games, they were more excited about these games than any other.

As part of our playables, we organized competitions with prizes. Typically, they would play during the week, and then on Monday, gifts were given. At that point, people would stop playing, but with Hay Day and Clash of Clans, they continued to play after the prizes had been given out. They just loved the games. I think that created a lot of positive energy.

Ramsay: What were the other games? How did you decide to cut them?

Paananen: In January, we launched one game called Pets vs. Orcs, and it was a mobile game. We launched a beta in Canada. We looked at the user metrics, like retention, how many people came back after the first day, and how many people came back at seven days of play. We looked at monetization, like the average revenue per user and those kinds of things. The metrics weren't that good, so we decided to kill it a month later.

After we released Hay Day in June and Clash of Clans in August, we did a beta of a game we had been working really hard on called Battle Buddies. We were internally very excited about it. It was an amazing-looking 3D game, something we didn't think that the market had seen before. Apple and other partners were quite excited as well.

Then we did a beta. The metrics weren't good. The company had turned cash flow positive; we were making money, so we had no pressure to kill that game, but we did. That's one thing I'm proud of. From that point, it became easier and easier for us to kill stuff and get more focused.

Ramsay: How does killing a game like Battle Buddies impact the company?

Paananen: Well, it makes people sad. There was a talented team working on Battle Buddies, and they had worked on that for around a year.

You work out on something you are very excited about, everybody else around you is excited, you have high hopes, you put it out to beta, and then it turns out that the players don't care as much. It's always disappointing.

On the other hand, we try to take the approach that we learned something valuable here. And we also understand that games is a hit-driven business. Apple said in 2013 that they received more than 200,000 new submissions to the app store, and none made it to the top ten that year. Zero apps out of 200,000 didn't make it; that's pretty crazy. It's just so competitive that we try to create a culture where failing and learning from failure is essential.

Ramsay: You're doing very well with Clash of Clans and Hay Day, of course, but how do you hope to continue to compete in a market where zero out of 200,000 games make the top ten?

Paananen: We've thought about this a lot. We need to make sure that Supercell remains the best possible environment for the best people to create games. We have to continue hiring the best talent around us. And we have to maintain today's culture to maximize our probability of success.

But it's the games industry, so you never know; you just have to accept that. If you want to maximize your chances of success, it all comes down to the people, culture, and taking care of that. And then you just trust the people.

Talking about Supercell, we had some instant advantages. Financially, we are in a very, very strong position, so that enables us to advertise our games and tell the world about our games in ways that many other people can't.

And we have this brand, so that when we put out something these days, many people just find out about it; they already know about us. That's an advantage that many of the newcomers in the industry don't have.

And, most importantly, we have Hay Day, Clash of Clans, and Boom Beach. Our dream is that people will play these games for years and years and years. So far, it really seems that is happening; a big portion of players who started two years ago still play them.

In the traditional model, especially mobile games, it used to be that a game would go up the chart and come down a month later. Our model is based on this belief that you should think about games as services—that people want to log on every single day and continue to do that for years. I know people who have played World of Warcraft for seven or eight years. We would love to do the same but on mobile. And if we are successful in doing that, we don't have to come up with a new hit game every single year. Of course, it is still very early for us, we and we have a ways to go before we get there, but that is our dream.

Ramsay: When you look at a company like Rovio, which has a billion versions of Angry Birds, they really have only that one property. Do you see yourself extending Hay Day, Clash of Clans, or Boom Beach similarly?

Paananen: Not to the extent that they've done. After we launched Hay Day and Clash of Clans, and they were doing well, everybody was asking, "When are the new games come out? What's on your roadmap?"

And we would always tell them, "There are no new games at this point." We are trying to focus solely on what we have now and just make those games better. We believe that our number one priority should be to make the existing games better for the existing users. Our goal is to have our current users play these very same games for the next five years. Back then, I think lots of people still thought we were crazy.

It's almost the same thing with Facebook, which is, of course, a service. Nobody asks Facebook, "When does the next Facebook come out? What's after Facebook?" But yet within the Facebook framework, and within that core service they have, I think it gets better every single week, they keep launching new features, they tweak the service, listen to the users, and they make it better. We are trying to do the same thing with our games. If you look at Clash of Clans, today it's a completely different game than it was when we launched it almost two years ago.

Ramsay: Can you describe how Clash of Clans has changed?

Paananen: Oh, yeah, absolutely. In the first version of Clash of Clans, you could build your own village and attack random people. Since then, we've added stuff like the leagues, so you can compare yourself to other people in a league. Then we made a massive update recently, called the Clan Wars, so now clans in Clash of Clans can declare war on each other. That has been massively popular. We've added new buildings, we've added new levels to the buildings, we've add new troops to the game, and so forth. You have to keep these games fresh for players. We are on a monthly update cycle, so there's something new players can discover every month.

Ramsay: How do you try to monetize your games?

Paananen: Both of these are games are completely free to play. There are no hard pay walls or anything like that in the game. If you never spend a dime, you can still access all of the games, but if you spend real money, you can accelerate your progress.

For example, in Clash of Clans, let's say you're building a new barracks. Building can take, say, one hour of calendar time. If you wait for that one hour, you'll have this finished building, and then you can do stuff with it. If you don't want to wait, you can finish the building immediately.

If you want to do that, you have to use virtual currency. In Clash of Clans, the currency is called gems, and buying gems costs real money. The whole idea is that we are offering users more ways to play.

Ramsay: What wouldn't you monetize?

Paananen: This model has existed for a long time. I think free to play was invented in either Japan or Korea more than ten years ago. Why change something that the users know, and even in the Western world have gotten used to? If you want to really innovate on certain things, we think it's better to innovate the actual games, not the business logic.

Ramsay What wouldn't you monetize? For example, a hedge fund manager who owns shares in Nintendo was quoted in The Wall Street Journal as saying, "Just think of paying 99 cents just to get Mario to jump a little higher." Is there anything you wouldn't put a price on in your games?

Paananen: I think the most important thing is that you must be able to never spend any money on the game. You must be able to access all areas of each game, and you have to be able to play the game entirely. Also, you should not be able to "win" in the game by just paying money.

Ramsay: So, you can pay for time, but you can't pay for things?

Paananen: Yeah, for example, while the top players in Clash of Clans have, of course, spent some money, the amount of money they've spent isn't an indicator of their success because even at the highest possible levels of Clash of Clans, it's still a skill-based game.

If you go to YouTube and search for Clash of Clans strategy videos, you'd be amazed by how much user-generated stuff there is; there are so many strategy guides that detail the optimal layout of a village, how you should attack, and so on. The most popular Clash of Clans YouTuber, a guy called Chief Pat, has more than 250 million views! If Clash of Clans was a pay-to-win game, none of that would exist; players would just say, "Hey, if you want to win this game, just spend as much money as possible." That would kill the game.

The secret to a successful free-to-play game is not what you do for the people who want to spend money; it's what you do for people who are not going to spend money, which is usually roughly 90% of your player base. You have to make the game as fun as possible especially for the people who are not going to spend anything during their lifetime.

Ramsay: How much does skill really factor into Clash of Clans?

Paananen: Massively. If you just look at the strategy videos on YouTube, you will get an idea.

Ramsay: In a lot of mobile, tablet, social, and Facebook games, you can take two different players, have them play the same game, give them the same amount of money, and they'll always be equal.

Paananen: Yeah, exactly. Hay Day and Clash of Clans are the opposite. That's why people like these games so much; they're real games.

Ramsay: In 2013, you sold a huge stake in Supercell to two different companies, but you've maintained that you're in a good financial position. Why would you sell 51% of the company to SoftBank?

Paananen: Since the company became financially successful, there has been a lot of interest from outside the company. I'm frequently asked about when we're going to do an IPO and take the company public, for example.

But the way we see things is that the company's still very young, has very few products, and is in its early days both from a market and a company perspective. We almost don't want to think about an IPO. At the same time, we have professional investors, and there has to be a way for those guys to make their money back at some point.

We didn't want to sell the company. We absolutely love what we do, and we see that we have a very unique chance of building something very, very special here. These opportunities, for most people, don't even come once in a lifetime. Most people never ever have this opportunity to build something like Supercell. We are just so incredibly lucky.

So, my dream is that in, say, 30 years, Supercell still really means something great, and our games are something people remember and, hopefully, still play. That's when I think we will have achieved something, but that takes time. The question becomes: how do we fulfill that dream while being a good citizen in terms of fulfilling our duties to our investors? By accident or coincidence, we met the people from SoftBank and their founder, Masayoshi Son.

The very first thing we told him was "just to make it clear, we are not looking to sell the company." And I think he said, "That's perfect because I'm not looking to buy companies as such. I just want to grow the SoftBank family and become lifetime partners with you guys."

Our interests were so aligned that we agreed to sell them a big stake in the company, so they be part of our financial success, but we were able to keep control of the company. They got 51% of the economic rights, but he told us that he really wants the founders and the existing leadership to run the company, and the last thing he wants to do is to change anything.

We were able to provide a lot of liquidity for everybody, but even more importantly for us, it guaranteed that we could continue to build this business for the long term. There's no pressure to do anything in the short term, and we are able to stay independent. We've been extremely, extremely happy with the deal from that perspective.

There is also the added bonus that the biggest growth opportunities are in markets like Japan and China, and SoftBank is a massive player in those markets with a lot of great relationships. Getting access to those resources helps us move quicker to that goal of being a truly global games company. Hopefully, one day, we'll be a big player in those markets, too.

Ramsay: Where do you want to take Supercell from here?

Paananen: As you know, we wanted to create a different type of company. We wanted to create a company that could stay relatively small in terms of headcount; as we speak, we have still only 150 people, so we're very, very small compared to our competitors in the mobile space.

King and Rovio have around 800 people. Zynga has around 3,000, and then, of course, there are giants like Activision, EA, and so forth. We are small, and we have fewer processes and as little bureaucracy as possible. At the same time, we want to be one of the leading game companies globally.

The dream is that 30 years from now, we would like people to still be playing our games, to remember and love the brands we've created. More than that, in 30 years, I want you to be able to ask anyone who has worked for us what was the best job in their life, and I want their answer to be Supercell.

Jason Kapalka

Cofounder, PopCap Games

Jason Kapalka left his journalism career behind when he joined the Total Entertainment Network as a producer in 1995. Only six years later, he had cofounded PopCap Games with John Vechey and Brian Fiete, and introduced the world to the *Bejeweled* phenomenon.

Acquired by EA in 2011 for $1.3 billion, PopCap Games is now the leading developer of casual games, such as *Zuma*, *Peggle*, and *Plants vs. Zombies*. The *Bejeweled* series alone boasts more than 75 million copies sold and more than 500 million downloads.

Today, Vechey, Fiete, and Kapalka—who served as chief game designer until 2014—are no longer with the company. Kapalka owns the Storm Crow Tavern in Vancouver, where he operates a family-friendly sports bar and restaurant for nerds.

Ramsay: What were you doing before PopCap Games?

Kapalka: I had been a freelance journalist. I was writing for Computer Gaming World, and the editor called me up one day and said he had gone off to join a dot com in San Francisco called TEN, the Total Entertainment Network. He invited me to come down.

I didn't really know much about the Internet then. In 1995, there wasn't much of an Internet. It was more common for people to use online services like AOL and CompuServe. But I went down there and joined up anyway.

TEN was an Internet game company; they started out developing hardcore games. The first game I worked on was Duke Nukem 3D. We were trying to get that game to work over mostly 2400 baud modems. That was pretty tricky and kind of clunky. Gradually, TEN changed its focus to more of a casual destination, and that's why they changed their named to Pogo. I went from working on games like Duke Nukem 3D to working on bingo and roulette.

By the time 2000 rolled around, I'd been in touch with John Vechey and Brian Fiete, who would become my cofounders at PopCap. One day, we were talking about how we were dissatisfied with our current jobs, and we thought that maybe we could start up our own little thing. We never had any grand ambitions. The plan was for just the three of us to make web games on our own, and then sell them back to larger companies like Pogo.

Ramsay: What were your responsibilities at Pogo?

Kapalka: I started off as a writer, editor, and over time, my role morphed into a sort of community manager, running tournaments and stuff like that. Once we started making original games, I became more of a producer. I'd work with external groups that were making original Internet games, and when Pogo started developing games internally, I also worked as a game designer.

Ramsay: Sounds like you moved quickly into positions that creative people want, so why were you so dissatisfied?

Kapalka: The five years up to 2000 was a pretty chaotic, boom-bust period in the whole dot com industry. Business plans were changing all over the place, and I had seen a lot of changes at Pogo, too. There was talk about selling to Excite@Home around that time, but that fell through. I didn't have as much freedom as I'd like at the company, and I was dissatisfied with a couple of my bosses. It just seemed like by going off on my own, I could have more latitude to work on the games I wanted to work on.

Ramsay: What games did you want to work on?

Kapalka: Generally, the same types of things we had been working at Pogo. I wanted to do casual games, which I guess wasn't really the name that was used back then. I wanted to make simple, mass-market, online puzzle games. Nothing too radically different. In the end, we thought we could do it more efficiently on our own instead of just part of a bigger bureaucracy.

Ramsay: How did you meet your cofounders?

Kapalka: In 1997, I was trying to find Internet games that TEN could publish, and I ran across a game called ARC. I thought the game was pretty neat and tracked it down. The developers turned out to be two guys in Indiana, Brian and John.

We flew them out to San Francisco. I was supposed to come out, chat with them, and get them to sign up with us. They were a bit unusual in that they were just high school kids. I think they dropped out of the first year at Purdue University. They were working out of a trailer somewhere in Indiana, so they were pretty goofy.

Our business guys had a hard time figuring out how to deal with them, so it was left to me to entertain them. They were obviously pretty young and a bit silly, but I thought they were really smart and had a good handle on games, so we got them to sign up.

I produced a game that went up on TEN, and that game was around for quite a long time. I think that game still exists in some weird form on the Internet, run by fans or something. After that game helped give them their start in the industry, a year or two later, they moved to Seattle to join Sierra, which had a similar online service. A year or two later, they were a bit unhappy with their situation. That was when we decided we could go off on our own.

Ramsay: When you were coming to that decision, what did the three of you talk about?

Kapalka: I think mostly we'd talk about our current jobs, how we were doing. We'd bitch and moan about our bosses, what we were doing, and how we thought we could do better if we were on our own and able to pick our own projects and so forth.

We were all in the same position and would occasionally get in trouble at our jobs for just wanting to make games, but occasionally the bureaucracy would make that more challenging than we thought was necessary. We'd all get in trouble once in awhile for doing something. I think Brian got in trouble at Sierra because they took a week off and wrote this game called Wordox. They got in trouble for doing that rather than whatever it was they were supposed to be doing, although the game turned out to be pretty successful.

And, similarly, I got in trouble at Pogo for various things I was trying to do. I was trying to get more games done. I got in trouble for not going through the right channels, for not going through engineers and designers, for the game specifications, and so forth. It was a little more bureaucratic than I preferred.

Ramsay: You were doing what an entrepreneur does.

Kapalka: Yeah, I think we were all kind of keen to get stuff done, and we were not super happy with too much structure or process.

Ramsay: There's a structure and process for starting a company! Did the three of you ever sit down and write up a plan?

Kapalka: We didn't have much of a grand design. We certainly had no knowledge of venture capital, and we didn't have a large-scale vision for growing the company. And we didn't have any money really. We just had enough money to live on for awhile. We were working out of our apartments and making games, and we didn't have any plans to hire people.

But we eventually started growing organically, like "I guess maybe we should hire an artist" and "maybe we should hire this programmer." As our team grew, we thought we should get an office, and then an accountant. Nothing was planned very well, so we certainly made a lot of mistakes. On the upside, we didn't have the pressure to deliver anything as we might have if we had investors.

In some ways, that was bad, but we started this company in 2000, which was not the ideal time to start an Internet company. Everything was collapsing. If we had done our research and wrote a plan, we might have been discouraged by what was happening.

Ramsay: Without much more money than what you could live on, do you think you should have stayed at Pogo to see if the Excite deal worked out?

Kapalka: People told me I was silly to leave when we're on the verge of this big deal. But I had heard of these deals many times before, and they'd never come to pass. When all was said and done, I didn't care much about stock options at the time. I think I ended up with $25,000 or $30,000 out of the whole thing, which is not bad, but for five years at a startup, it was not a jackpot either.

Ramsay: So, you had no business plan, no startup capital, and a lot of mistakes. What mistakes were those?

Kapalka: We made some decisions we might not have, if we'd been more professional, but that turned out to be for the best. For example, we held onto our IP, and we didn't sell out when we could have because we didn't quite feel comfortable with that. There were some missteps on the business side that just caused us headaches. We took awhile to get up to basic levels of competency in areas like accounting, business, and marketing.

We had a couple of years when our contracts were really poorly made. We never had too many disasters, but we had a few where some contract we thought was signed had never been signed, or some contract we thought was pretty good turned out to be actually terrible. And we had to buy people out.

None were critical disasters, but if things had gone a slightly different way, we'd have deeply regretted some of those things. We spent a couple of years going through the process of renegotiating and dealing with lawyers to repair some of those contracts.

Ramsay: When did you incorporate PopCap Games?

Kapalka: That was a bit messy. We incorporated before PopCap was officially PopCap. We made one product that isn't in our official corporate history. Before Brian came onboard, John and I made a strip poker game. It wasn't very pornographic, but we basically built a strip poker engine, and then sold it to people to raise money. We just thought we could do a much better actual game engine than what most of the sleazy porn sites were doing.

We originally incorporated under the name Sexy Action Cool and made this game called Foxy Poker. As a strip poker game, there wasn't an awful lot of stripping. It was just an illustrated cartoon girl, and she never became nude. It was like an Austin Powers thing where, by the time she stripped off enough clothing that it would be risqué, there would be objects interposed in front of her.

It was actually not a bad game, but we found that we didn't really have the stomach to deal with the actual porn sites. They were a fairly sleazy bunch. We learned there were people who will do something a little bit sleazy to get their real business off the ground, and that once they're done, they'll think everything will be fine and they'll never have to be sleazy again. But you can't just be half-sleazy. If you're going to be sleazy, you have to go full-bore sleazy. You have to embrace it, or forget about it and do something else. We chose to forget about it and do something else.

Ramsay: What did you learn from the incorporation process?

Kapalka: If you're going to start a company with some people, get at least a basic structure in place. These days, you can probably get something basic off the Internet, and a lot of people will just go ahead with that and start working. That's pretty common, but they should be aware that the longer they do that, the more they risk something going wrong without any way to handle it.

Facebook, for example, has gone through years of litigation from various people who claim they had some percentage of Facebook from way back when. It's pretty clear that, in the early days, Mark Zuckerberg was not exactly extremely cautious about how they dealt with all the legal stuff. That's understandable because he didn't have the time or money, but you can see what happens.

It's a good idea to put in a minimum amount of effort to cover your bases, but not so much effort that you end up wasting your time and money on lawyers when you should be building a company.

Ramsay: Was Bejeweled your first game as PopCap Games?

Kapalka: Diamond Mine, as Bejeweled was originally called, was our first real game. We put that together quickly. The game didn't do anything special for us at the beginning, so we certainly didn't have any idea it would become a big game. We just kept going, and so we were cranking out a web game every month or two. A few months later, Diamond Mine became pretty successful.

Ramsay: That's when you officially became a publisher?

Kapalka: We only became a bit of a publisher, a portal of our own, by accident. We didn't really intend that. It just happened to work out that way. What happened was we had talked to Pogo, MSN, and Yahoo because they were obvious places you would go if you wanted to play games on the Internet. We could still stick our games up on our website, but there was not much traffic going there. We had also worked with some of them in the past, so it was fairly easy to get in touch with them.

When Microsoft put Diamond Mine up on their portal in 2000, this was all fairly new at the time, so a lot of the requirements were fairly lax. The loading screen for the game had our logo and our URL. We started getting some spillover traffic from that. Presumably, people would go to Microsoft, play the game, see the loading screen, get curious, and go check it out.

In later years, of course, companies like Microsoft and other online game publishers started getting pretty uptight about that sort of thing. They wouldn't let you stick a link to your website on their website, but at the time, they didn't think it was a big deal.

That's how we got our start as a publisher. The traffic was significant enough that our website became a destination, so we started looking at it more seriously. The customers who came to our site were worth more to us. If they bought something, we didn't have to share that revenue with anyone else.

Ramsay: When did you start hiring people?

Kapalka: Well, generally, we started hiring when we needed to do stuff we couldn't do ourselves. When we did the first downloadable version of Bejeweled, I was no musician, but there was this musician in the mod scene, Peter Hajba, who's also known as Skaven in the demoscene. I got in touch with him by e-mail and asked if we could use some of his songs for this game we were doing. He was okay with that. Since then, we've contracted with him quite a bit in the last decade for all of the Bejeweled games and other stuff.

We also hired other people we knew from the Internet, some from earlier games, and some of them we met playing a game and found out they were artists or programmers and so forth. We stayed in touch with them and had them work on art, which would lead to them becoming full-time artists, or we'd contract programmers to do a game and then hire them full-time. It was fairly free-wheeling. We didn't really know where they were in most cases.

Ramsay: Were they all developers?

Kapalka: Mostly, but once we had a few people in there and we were starting to make a little bit of money, we figured that we had better get an actual book-keeper. Initially, John just hired his aunt to do our books, and then, gradually, it was all development, and then, once we decided to get an office, we figured we'd have to hire somebody who can actually run this place and so forth. That's when we had to add people who were not development staff.

Ramsay: Most game developers then were looking for publishing deals. Why were you instead looking to license your games?

Kapalka: It wasn't really by choice. We approached some publishers to sell them games outright, but they weren't interested. At one point, we offered to sell Bejeweled to somebody for $30,000 or something like that, but they didn't think it was worth that. Microsoft wasn't willing to spend that much money on it, but they were willing to spend $1,500 a month to rent it. In retrospect, that was not the best deal we could have made, but they were hesitant and didn't think it would be worth that much.

One other company looked at Bejeweled. I recall specifically one guy saying it's not even a game. That was true in a sense. In the original version, Diamond Mine, there were several skill levels. We had started with the idea that the game had to have a timer because, otherwise, the basic version would just end at a random point when you ran out of moves. That seemed like it could be a problem because there wasn't any skill involved. If you just kept playing, you'd end up with a configuration where you couldn't make any moves.

So, we'd have a timer just so there would be some difficulty, but we decided to make the first skill level untimed to act as a tutorial. I figured that people would play that level, to understand the rules, and then switch to the higher levels where the timer was involved. As it turned out, most people didn't. They stuck with the first version, which was untimed. That was poor user interface design on our end, but also good fortune, I suppose. It turned out that a lot of people playing back then were okay with the game not needing a lot of skill. They didn't mind that it would go on or end randomly. We realized that the kind of people the game appealed to were not classic arcade gamers.

Hardcore gamers these days can trace their favorite games' DNA back to arcade games. Arcade games were, of course, tests of skill: the better you were, the longer your game would go. But people like my mom who were playing Bejeweled didn't come from that background. The games they might play on the computer were games like Solitaire. And Solitaire is pretty much the same as the untimed Bejeweled, in that once you know the basic rules, whether you win or lose is more or less down to luck. You might make a decision here or there that has some small influence, but generally speaking, once you know the very simple rules of what cards to put down or which gems to swap, it is up to luck. And people have been pretty happy playing Solitaire for a long time. As it turned out, they were happy to play Bejeweled the same way.

Ramsay: When revenue started coming in, what was the feeling between the three of you?

Kapalka: The story we've told is that Brian put together a program that, whenever someone actually bought a copy of Bejeweled, it would play this ka-ching sound on his computer.

John was sitting in the living room. I think his mom was telling him he had to get a real job at some point because he wouldn't be able to make money just sitting on the couch, and then there were some ka-chings from the other room. And he said, "I just made money right now, sitting on the couch."

The ka-chings started coming in fairly frequently until we realized, "Yeah, okay, maybe this is actually a pretty good business plan." We were happy we were making some money. It took a year or two before we could persuade our partners, like Microsoft, Yahoo, and so on, that downloadable games was a much better idea than ad-supported games. That wasn't something anybody had thought would work too well. They had been worried that downloadable games would cut into their ad revenue. And why would anyone pay $20 for a game they could play online for free?

That was an interesting education. It actually took quite awhile to persuade them that regardless of whether downloadable games cut into their ad revenue, their ad revenue was so small compared to what they could make from somebody who was willing to pay $20 for a game. We proposed to Microsoft, "Look, we'll give you the web game for free, and we'll give you 50% of any sales of the downloadable game. Just put it up and advertise it like that." They finally agreed, and that did very well. Using web games to get people to try the downloadable version became the model for the downloadable game business for the next few years.

Ramsay: Why 50%?

Kapalka: Honestly, we just pulled that figure out of the air. We were trying to get them to agree to do anything. 50% was just an even, easy number to talk about.

Ramsay: When did you turn off the ka-ching program?

Kapalka: I don't recall exactly, but at some point, it was happening often enough that the noise became kind of annoying! And, at that point, we knew what we had was going to work.

Ramsay: How had Diamond Mine come together?

Kapalka: John had seen this game on the Internet called Colors. He sent us a link; it was really primitive. But we've tried to find Colors again using the Wayback Machine and other sites, but no one has ever been able to re-locate it. It's semi-imaginary, I guess, but it was real! Colors was a really, really crude JavaScript game whose mechanics were similar to Bejeweled, but it was really, really clunky. Colors had just colored squares in a 7x7 grid with no animation. You had to imagine things were falling down. I don't think there was even an end condition or any scoring.

So, John pointed to that and said, "That's kind of an interesting mechanism for a game. Maybe we could do something like that?" Brian went off and programmed a new engine for it, and we had animation and so forth. I went off and did some graphics that were not squares. That was where the Bejeweled gems came from.

We wanted to have seven different colors. It made sense that you'd want seven different shapes. It would be easier to pattern match. I tried to figure out what kinds of things come in families of seven that make sense together but which are different shapes, so you can recognize them quickly in seven primary colors or whatever.

Initially, I thought fruit. I tried fruit. It didn't work out too well. It's hard to find seven different colors of fruit. There are a lot of rounded shapes in fruits. There aren't that many square fruits. So, then I thought gems. The first gems I tried were not that good because they were sort of realistic gems. Most real gems are not in weird triangular shapes or anything like that. I thought that maybe I'll just do some geometrical shapes and pretend they're gems. I drew a bunch of squares and triangles, and then drew crude facets on them, as if they were gemstones. That was basically it. They're squares, circles, triangles, and whatever else, but users at least recognized they looked like gemstones. That worked pretty well. And that was the first version of Diamond Mine.

Ramsay: So, Diamond Mine wasn't a passion project that took years to foment. The game was just a design problem to solve?

Kapalka: By that point, we were used to making games quickly, and I had worked on dozens and dozens of these smaller games. The idea was that you did your best on one and moved on to the next. We developed Diamond Mine fairly quickly, and we thought it was good. I thought it was neat, but I didn't think that it was going to be a big thing or anything like that.

Ramsay: Since you were targeting short development cycles, how technically complex were your first games?

Kapalka: They were programmed in Java for browsers. That was tricky because there are a lot of limitations. At that time, Java was not a terrible programming language, but the implementation of Java in a lot of the browsers was pretty glitchy, in terms of how the code was executed. You had to work around that because the alternative was waiting for the browsers to get patched. It was closer, I suppose, to old school Atari 2600 programming, where you had to work around the very serious limitations of the platform.

The games also had to be really small because we were dealing with dial-up modems and stuff. Users had really short attention spans, so the initial version of Diamond Mine and most of our other games, we figured, would have to be in the range of less than 200 KB to keep their attention when they're trying to load the game. Trying to make stuff that worked in a browser in Java in less than 200 KB meant there were a lot of technical headaches to deal with.

It was not exactly cutting edge in terms of 3D graphics and stuff like that, but making everything fit and work was definitely a challenge. I think they look very primitive now, but compared to what other people were doing at the time in web-based games, the stuff we were doing was actually quite advanced and very slick-looking. By trying to make our games look more like real games with actual polish and attention to detail, they stood out.

Ramsay: How did you decide what games to build?

Kapalka: It was fluid. Somebody would play a game and get an idea from that. There were puzzle games, for example, where you had to line up five symbols in a row on a board and they'd disappear. It was interesting, but they weren't very much fun.

When you ran out of space to put objects, the game would penalize you for trying to put them in the wrong spot, and you'd lose the game. You'd lose the game because you tried to put something in an invalid location, which I thought was pretty lame.

I was trying to figure out a way to do a game of that nature but where you didn't lose just because you couldn't find a valid location. So, Alchemy ended up with a mechanic where when a piece couldn't be used, you could discard it, but you had a limited number of discards before your game would end.

Like books and movies, our games were inspired in some way by earlier games, but by the time we finished them, they had morphed quite heavily.

Ramsay: What do you mean by "inspired" exactly?

Kapalka: "Okay, let's start with this and experiment." You try different things and see what comes. When you're taking something that's unsatisfying and trying to improve upon it, I guess you're trying to fix it. When you're taking a mechanic that's interesting, there's not much point in copying the mechanic directly unless you'll be able to do something that improves or fixes it. With Peggle, we started with Pachinko. Originally, we didn't want to do a down-loadable version of Pachinko, but the experiments we tried proved that basic Pachinko as a video game wasn't very much fun. That led to us experimenting with ball-shooting games and gradually Peggle.

Ramsay: When I work on the design of a thing that'll be used by other people, especially when trying to find solutions as you did through experimentation, I like to know all about who I'm designing for. Did you try to learn more about your players?

Kapalka: At the time, there weren't a lot of sophisticated metrics, so we couldn't track people as closely as you can now. On the other hand, we'd get feedback really swiftly because our games would be live on Microsoft or on our site. Thousands of people would be playing all the time, and they'd write e-mails and stuff like that. We'd hear them, and we'd gradually recognize that everyone seemed to be playing, for example, the untimed version of Bejeweled.

That was an example where we, fortunately, miscalculated. We hadn't designed the interface very well. If we had done a better job, everyone would have been forced to play the timed game, and maybe Bejeweled wouldn't have done so well.

We also learned that people didn't seem to care very much about the mining aspect. So, later on, when we came out with the deluxe version of Bejeweled, we were like, "Do we really need to care about the mining stuff? Whatever." By the time Bejeweled 2 came around, we abandoned that entirely.

Ramsay: Sounds like early feedback from your players shaped how you developed future products. Is that correct?

Kapalka: We saw what happened, what worked, and what didn't work, but we reacted less to what players said and more to what they were doing. When we saw that Diamond Mine was doing really well, I realized that kind of game is clearly resonating with people, so that was a good direction for us to go in.

We had multiplayer games early on that we had a hard time doing much with. They're really hard to sell to other companies because it was a pain in the ass to maintain the servers. And they were difficult to run on our site because the servers had to be maintained all of the time, and you had to deal with policing the chat rooms and those sorts of things. But those were games we thought were good, fun ideas, but they just weren't that successful. We just couldn't find a way to make it feasible, so we left multiplayer out for awhile.

On the Internet though, you have to take feedback with a real grain of salt because the people who talk the most are a self-selecting group. The guys who are complaining the loudest, or most often, represent a section of people who are unhappy, but the people who are happy maybe don't say anything. You have to be careful how much you read into individual feedback.

And then people say one thing and do other things. We verified that when we started selling the deluxe games for $20. If we had asked people if they'd be willing to pay $20 for a downloadable copy of Bejeweled, no one would've said yes. When they had the option to do so, a significant portion of them did! You have to be careful about what people say, and look at what they're doing.

Ramsay: Where was your first office?

Kapalka: Initially, we had just a very small section of one floor in downtown Seattle, in the Belltown area on 4th and Battery. We're still in that same building, but we've taken over several floors now.

Ramsay: How was the location chosen?

Kapalka: I wasn't part of that so much, but, at that point, we hired an office manager. I think she just found a place that was affordable and relatively close to the employees living in Seattle.

Ramsay: What was the next step?

Kapalka: By the time we had the office, we were making games. We just kept making web games until, gradually, it became policy that we'd make a web game and then a downloadable version afterwards. That would be the way we'd make money off things. But as time went on, we put more emphasis on downloadable games.

Ramsay: Why did you focus more on downloadable games?

Kapalka: More sites like Real Arcade and Big Fish started to show up. They were really pushing downloadable games since that was where they actually made money. We started making the downloadable game first, and then the web version, but eventually, we didn't even bother with the web version. We evolved with the casual games market.

Ramsay: How were your games priced?

Kapalka: For Bejeweled Deluxe, we weren't sure what to price it at. We thought we'd price the game really low at $4.99. A guy we knew, Howard Tomlinson at Astraware in the UK, had done shareware in the past. He said that we should price the game as high as we thought we could possibly get away with. When you priced low, people thought the product was crap. He suggested we should price the game at $19.99. We thought that was crazy, but we also figured it would be easier to lower the price later than to raise it. It worked out pretty well.

The players who were buying these games were a different audience. If you weren't one of those players, you'd compare Bejeweled to a triple-A game and you'd say, "Well, geez, $20 for Bejeweled versus $50 for a new Star Wars game? I don't know." You'd think we were trying to rip you off with a game that cost less to make or whatever. But the people who were interested in games like Bejeweled weren't interested in triple-A games. For them, that comparison wasn't relevant. You know, $20 was a reasonable price to pay for a game they were going to spend hours with, so $19.99 ended up as the standard price point for downloadable games for quite awhile.

Ramsay: How fast was the company growing at this time?

Kapalka: We grew from the three of us to 40 people in the first three or four years, but we weren't trying to grow specifically. We were growing as we needed. But, obviously, 40 people was a big change from three. At that point, you can no longer go to lunch with everybody because there's just too many people around.

Ramsay: What was the culture like then?

Kapalka: It was a bit more rambunctious, I guess. A lot of the people were pretty young and just out of school. There was a little bit more partying, misbehavior, and whatnot. Yeah, there was a bit of that stuff, and over time as we got to be a bigger company, there were more people who were not at all like that. We'd have one or two cases where something would make you realize that when you have both 20-year-old guys and 48-year-old women in the same company, they're not going to like the same stuff, or appreciate the same kinds of jokes, or go to the same parties.

Ramsay: Can you tell me about the composition?

Kapalka: We were pretty heavy on the development front. We didn't really hire very many business people for quite awhile. We had a handful, like an accountant, an office manager, and one or two IT people. I remember thinking we were really trying to not hire very many business and marketing people because we didn't think they would add much value. When we were talking about hiring Dennis Ryan, I remember asking someone, "Why do we need another business guy? Don't we already have one?" In retrospect, that seems a bit naïve. It was a bit silly.

However, I don't think we missed out by not having marketing people in the earlier years. There was only so much you could do to really flog these kinds of games. People would try them and decide whether they wanted to buy them after they played them, so it's not like you could advertise it in any meaningful way.

Once in awhile, people say that PopCap had really good marketing, and I'm always a little bit surprised since we didn't really have any. I mean, we do now! We have a marketing team, but they're not very large by comparison, and they mostly work on boxes for retail versions of games and stuff like that.

Ramsay: How did you feel about growing from three to 40?

Kapalka: Well, I was generally pretty good with it. We had moments where we seemed like we'd have increasing levels of bureaucracy. You know, "I have to fill out an expense report? I can't just say I spent some money and get it out of the company bank account?" Or we'd have some sort of employee dispute where someone was unhappy because of something. We began to see the complexities grow, especially as we tried to maintain a workplace that was welcoming to everybody. It was a bit odd realizing that not everybody in the company is going to be a close personal friend.

Ramsay: How did your process for selecting games to develop change as your company grew?

Kapalka: Over time, we had more latitude for more people, and we were more ambitious with some games. Initially, we were doing a game every month or two, but with more flexibility, we started taking more time to develop games. That gave us a lot more freedom to experiment and prototype. That was really what made a lot of our other games possible, like Plants vs. Zombies, which took three or more years to complete, from beginning to end.

Ramsay: As a designer, was more time more liberating for you?

Kapalka: Yes and no. At the time, I thought it was certainly a good thing. In retrospect, I'm not entirely sure. Sometimes having too much time is a bad thing. Sometimes you want to have tighter deadlines. When you have too much time, you can start going in circles, or you can start second-guessing yourself. With a tight timeline, you might focus a bit more on what's critical.

We probably could have shaved a year off the development of Plants vs. Zombies. All of the minigames turned out to be nice, but they weren't really what people cared about in the game. Other games we did took a long time and probably could have been done a lot faster without affecting their success too much. Overall, I think having more time was good, but I increasingly feel like if you have an unlimited amount of time to work on something, that's dangerous.

Ramsay: Have you taken any steps to address that problem?

Kapalka: There has been a bit of a reversal, but dictated by the changing nature of the market. It was possible to take three years to make Plants vs. Zombies because we were making the game for PC, and PCs were pretty much the same three years after you started. Nowadays, you're making games for social networks or mobile devices, and the environment is changing so quickly, so you really can't plan ahead. If you decide to start a three-year mobile game development cycle, you'd be in big trouble. Whatever you have at the end might not even work on the new devices. The nature of the industry that we're in has forced us to change.

Ramsay: Entrepreneurs, as their organizations expand and contract, typically find that they're not just wearing multiple hats, they're wearing different ones. Did your roles change?

Kapalka: They didn't change too radically. I pretty much have always remained the head creative guy. I'm responsible for supervising the direction of the games and making sure we're happy with them. I can't be involved as personally with every one of them as I was at the beginning. I've designed and produced some of our games, but others I certainly wouldn't claim I designed or anything. Peggle and Plants vs. Zombies are in that category. I hired the people who worked on them, gave some feedback, approved the budget, and supported them, but I wasn't involved in the way that I was with Bejeweled, Bookworm, and Zuma.

In terms of Brian and John, Brian's pretty much remained the same over the years. He's a really talented engineer and programmer who's not very interested in management and business. He's happiest when he's off coding, so he's trying to remain so.

And John, well, was always kind of a jack-of-all-trades. He has bounced around from job to job in PopCap over the years. He took a couple of years off to make movies and then he came back. Yeah, I couldn't honestly tell you all of the different job titles or positions John has held over the years. There has been a lot, but he has less direct responsibility for the business.

Around the time he was away, we hired people who were more experienced with the business side, like Dave Roberts. We were getting in people who knew more than we did about running a big company, so they've been doing more of that in the last few years than any of us three. We've always been on the board, controlling the company—until we sold to EA, of course.

Ramsay: How large is PopCap now?

Kapalka: We have 500 people, give or take. It's a fair number, scattered around offices in Seattle, Dublin, Shanghai, Vancouver, San Francisco, and Tokyo. The Seattle office is still the main office.

Ramsay: I assume that some of those offices were different companies at some point. When did you start doing acquisitions?

Kapalka: I think the first acquisition was Sprout Games in 2005. That wasn't exactly an acquisition of the company though. We'd heard about Sprout Games. We knew a few of the people there. They were having a rough time. They had some okay games, but we were hiring the people more than we were buying their games. We did get some good games out of them like Feeding Frenzy though.

The Sprout Games guys are still very active. Ed Allard is our head of studios worldwide. That was our first significant acquisition, I guess. Then we acquired a Dublin studio, which was doing mobile games but was about to go out of business. We swooped in and picked up their salaries to get something going there. We also bought Loose Cannon in Seattle and then ZipZapPlay in San Francisco. Those are the most recent ones, I think.

Ramsay: You've picked up smaller companies, too. Gastronaut Studios, which created Small Arms, comes to mind.

Kapalka: Yeah. Typically, we buy companies that have people who we think are smart and if their studio is in some trouble. That makes it easy to acquire a whole team that already works well together. That's usually a better way than trying to hire people individually.

Ramsay: Prior to the sale of PopCap to EA, were there any great opportunities that you think the company missed?

Kapalka: We came close to acquiring Runic Games, the guys who did Torchlight. Yeah, I regret that one not working out. We just happened to be right at the peak of the recession when everything was crashing, and we just didn't think we were able to swing the deal. We had to back out, but obviously, Runic is a pretty cool company, and that was before Torchlight had actually come out.

Ramsay: Was Runic Games going to be another acqui-hire?

Kapalka: In that case, it was a little bit different because they were working on Torchlight, which was a Diablo-esque RPG. We would have been expanding into a slightly more hardcore action genre.

Ramsay: Why would a casual games company want to do that?

Kapalka: It was more opportunistic than anything else. We weren't saying we absolutely needed to do this, but we knew the developers, they were in Seattle, and we thought they were really good. If they hadn't been there, we wouldn't have tried to run out and find someone else to do the same thing. And that's the case with our other talent acquisitions. We weren't running around thinking we had to buy some company to fill a gap in our strategy. It was more if we happened to run into somebody or a company we thought was really going to be a good fit, we'd think about it.

Ramsay: Some founders stick with their companies throughout the entire life cycle, but most of the time, they don't. I know John left briefly and returned, but did the three of you ever think about how the company could keep going without any of the founders?

Kapalka: Yeah, to some extent, we did consider that. When John took two years to pursue filmmaking, we didn't really know if he was coming back. We considered the possibility that we could leave and not return, too. That was one reason we made the deal with EA. We didn't have any immediate plans to leave, but we can't necessarily stay with the company forever. We had to make sure there was a plan in place for the company to continue without us.

Ramsay: Have you ever wanted to take a step back from management?

Kapalka: If I was going to choose what I wanted to do, I'd prefer to work on only one or two games at a time while not having as much corporate stuff to do. On the other hand, it's necessary to keep the company going the way we want it to go. We realized fairly early on that we couldn't just hand over the reins to somebody else. If we wanted to make sure the overall direction continued the way we wanted, there's no shortcut. You have to take that responsibility.

There are some companies where the founders will hire somebody and back out of the day-to-day stuff, but in my case, at least, I didn't want to do that. Brian's a programmer; he just found himself a niche where he can do a lot of high-level programming. That worked out for him, but for me, I felt I had to remain involved, or else I couldn't complain when the company went in a direction I didn't like.

Ramsay: Other than succession, what sparked the sale to EA?

Kapalka: We had been toying with the idea of going public for awhile. We started down that road, looking into what we'd need to do. But we had talked to other companies about selling, too. We entertained offers a few times, we had negotiations, and there was a bit of back and forth, but it never worked out.

There were several different companies in these high-stakes negotiations. That was a little hair-raising. In the end, we thought that going with EA would get us the benefits of a bigger company. We'd hopefully be dealing less with the bureaucracy, headaches, and an awful lot of the troubles of running a larger, public company, and without necessarily changing our culture or creative direction.

Ramsay: Why did you want to go public in the first place?

Kapalka: It was a combination of things, but part of it was just the idea that's the direction most companies go at some point. It just seemed in some ways a natural evolution to go public or sell.

It was also just one of those things where PopCap had become bigger and better, and we felt like we had been doubling down at the roulette table for ten years. We felt like things were pretty good in the industry, and there was a lot of money being talked about for these sales. Did we want to be greedy and hold out for even more money? Or did we want to take the amount offered now and say, "Okay, we did pretty well"? There was the idea that maybe now was a good time to take some money off the table—maybe now was a very good time to sell a game company.

In a couple of years, things could be different and maybe we'd say, "Oh, we were foolish to sell back then. We should have waited a few more years and we could have sold for $20 billion!" We would have also felt very foolish, of course, if we had turned down a bunch of offers only to realize we should have taken one of them.

Ramsay: Why EA, specifically?

Kapalka: It wasn't that long ago that EA was considered the evil empire. There was some concern about how people would feel if we were bought by this company that then eviscerated PopCap. No matter what anyone says, you always have some degree of fear that whoever buys your company is going to do something different.

But the nature of the deal suggested they wanted our creative leadership, especially in social, mobile, and casual. For them to acquire us and immediately lay off everybody? Or tell us to start making sports games? Well, it's possible they could have done that, but that would have been a really poor move on their part.

EA had gone through a dark phase and they seemed to have come out of it. The studios we talked to over there, like BioWare and DICE, managed to maintain their identities, so we didn't feel like we were going to be absorbed into the Borg. And we felt like we had a great deal of faith in John Riccitiello's vision for EA.

EA had also been around for so long and had been through some bad times. Inevitably, for any company, things get bad at some point, so we had a sense that EA knew what to do when things got bad.

They'd make some cuts, lay off some people, and reorganize, but at the end, they'd come out of it. EA has made some generally good decisions. They've maintained a high standard of quality for several decades. When you're thinking about the long term, not just the next year or two, EA is a pretty good choice.

Ramsay: What goes into selling a company?

Kapalka: Well, there's a lot of stuff I didn't directly work on. A lot of people eventually became involved. On our side, there was the core group: me, John, and Brian; Dave Roberts, our CEO; Bob Chamberlain, our CFO; and Dennis Ryan, our vice president of business. This was the first time we had worked with an outside group of bankers, Qatalyst Partners. They're a group of Silicon Valley bankers who broker deals. They had just done the deal for selling Riot Games to Tencent, so they came highly recommended.

There was also certainly an awful lot of legal paperwork. There were hundreds and hundreds of pages of documents that enumerated everything PopCap owned, mostly in terms of intellectual property. Everything had to be documented very clearly to make sure that EA understood exactly what they were buying, and that we owned all of the properties. Were there any parts of games, like code, graphics, music, or sounds that were licensed from other people? Is there any open source software? And that's just on the software side.

There was a fair amount of negotiating about various things that would follow after the company merged. Who would get paid what? Where would stocks go? What would happen to healthcare plans? It was all just boring meat-and-potatoes corporate things, but, boy, there was a lot that had to get done in a really short time. Our business, legal, and accounting people definitely had to do a ton.

But I didn't have to do much of that. I was mostly coordinating on a high level with the big agreements, making sure the top people in the company, for example, knew the deal was coming up and that they were going to be okay with it. There was definitely some concern and trepidation about what might happen. We had a few tense negotiations here and there, but when all was said and done, we had only one or two people who left PopCap around the deal. They just decided they wanted to go to a smaller company and didn't want to be part of a big company or something like that. It was actually fairly smooth. There wasn't really a huge shakeup.

Ramsay: Who was directly negotiating? Did you let the lawyers take over?

Kapalka: The lawyers were involved, and they did do some of the negotiating, but they were in the position of being the bad guy. When you're negotiating, you can have the lawyers take a hard line, so you can remain the good guy.

Ramsay: How did the buyout change the company?

Kapalka: Not dramatically. There are some differences. We're still struggling a bit with being part of a public company, like suddenly, people are interested in stock prices because they own stock in EA. At the high level, there are now quarterly reports and earnings reporters. We didn't really have to worry about any of those things before. When you're a private company, nobody really cares whether you have a bad quarter. You still have to worry about whether you're making money, but there's not a date when you have to talk to Wall Street and say how much you made. That forces you to think about short-term profits over longer-term plans, but that also forces you to do more planning and have more discipline about the kinds of projects you're working on. And that's something PopCap has not necessarily always been the best at.

It's been interesting. We spend more time with other EA groups. We had some BioWare people come by and spend a week in the Seattle studio just last week actually, working on our experimental game projects for a week. And we talked to the guys at DICE about doing shooters. It's actually been kind of neat to connect with people in different parts of EA and see how different kinds of video game organizations work. We haven't quite figured out how to do a full collaboration or anything like that, but we're able to plug in to get some insight that we never had before.

Ramsay: To get PopCap up and running, you were really focused on shipping as many games as you can. Is that still the case today?

Kapalka: That's definitely changed quite a bit. In the first year, we were just trying to knock out a game every month because we didn't have a business plan and we didn't really have any money, so we had to produce stuff really quickly.

We now have some franchises, obviously, like Bejeweled and Plants vs. Zombies. We want to do more with those franchises, but we've not always been the best at doing that. We haven't exploited the heck out of Bejeweled or Plants vs. Zombies as extensively as we could have if we had just been doing that exclusively.

But if we focus on only those franchises, we'll never create something new. Our franchises came out of experimental projects; nobody knew if they were going to work. Plants vs. Zombies was not a surefire hit. It was considered pretty weird, actually, and there weren't high expectations for it commercially.

The challenge is to keep those franchises working for us, but at the same time, retain enough freedom to experiment. That's a little bit scary. We'll do three or four experiments, and hopefully, one of them will turn out to be something we can ship. Maybe they'll turn out to be hits? If they don't, well, that's okay.

John Romero

Cofounder, Id Software

For 36 years, **John Romero** has been one of the video game industry's most accomplished developers. Credited on more than 100 titles, Romero has built nine studios, such as Id Software, where with John Carmack, Adrian Carmack, and Tom Hall, he pioneered the first-person shooter across Wolfenstein 3D, Doom, Heretic, Hexen, and Quake.

By 1996, Romero had left Id Software to start Ion Storm with Hall, as well as Todd Porter and Jerry O'Flaherty. Although the Dallas office was best known for the bold advertising of Daikatana and the critically acclaimed Anachronox, the Austin branch fared better under Warren Spector with Deus Ex, Deus Ex: Invisible War, and Thief: Deadly Shadows.

Seeing the future of mobile games in 2001, Romero and Hall cofounded Monkeystone Games, producing 15 titles in four years across various mobile platforms. While closing up shop in 2005, the duo worked at Midway Games on Area 51, where Romero stayed on until production wrapped on Gauntlet. In 2005, he cofounded Gazillion Entertainment with Robert Hutter.

In 2009, Gazillion landed a ten-year deal with Marvel Comics, out of which came Marvel Heroes. For a time in 2010, Romero was also lead game designer at LOLapps, where he shipped Ravenwood Fair, which he calls "one of my most successful games ever." That year, he left Gazillion and cofounded Loot Drop with his future wife and veteran game designer, Brenda Brathwaite.

When this interview was conducted in 2013, John and Brenda Romero had become directors of the Master's Program in Games and Playable Media at UC Santa Cruz. Months later, Brenda was awarded a Fulbright Fellowship to advance video games in Ireland, and John had continued his work at Loot Drop, in addition to joining Brainquake as chief game designer.

Ramsay: Everyone who follows games knows your name and has probably played every game you've released, but you had a career before Id Software. What were you doing back then?

Romero: I had been programming Apple II games for ten years, and then, in 1981, I started my very first game company: Capitol Ideas Software. I was getting a lot of games published in magazines. Remember Nibble Magazine and InCider Magazine? People would type their game listings into the computer. I sold several games there, and I even got the covers three Decembers in a row. I published 15 games through my first company.

I got my first real job in the industry at Origin Systems in 1987. I was porting 2400 A.D. from the Apple II to the Commodore 64. I also worked on Space Rogue with Paul Neurath at Origin. I then left to start my second game company with my manager: Inside-Out Software. I did the conversion of Might & Magic II from the Apple II to the Commodore 64, as well as the conversion of Tower Toppler from the Commodore 64 to the Apple II at Inside Out.

I left that company because the market dropped out on 8-bit games. We were directly tied to Epyx. They were developing the first set of games for the Atari Lynx. When that happened, I said, "I've got to get off the Apple and onto the PC." After leaving that company, I started my third company with my friend Lane Roathe: Ideas from the Deep. We made three or four games and published them before going to Softdisk. I stayed with Softdisk for about a year and a half.

After Softdisk, I started my fourth game company, Id Software, in 1990. Well, officially, we started on February 1, 1991, but we laid the groundwork in 1990 with the Commander Keen series and other games we were making.

Ramsay: How old were you when you started programming?

Romero: I was 11 when I started learning how to code, but I didn't actually come up with the name of that company, Capitol Ideas Software, until I was 13. I finally got the Apple II at home, and that's when I really took off. I could spend every second that I wasn't in school on the computer.

And I really played so many of the games I was trying to emulate—you know these games were on the shelf and that meant to me they were successful. They're being sold, right? I wanted to emulate that success and because they were made by companies, I thought I should make a company. The games were all in these Ziploc bags with cardboard folders, so I started making those, too, and started making advertisements. I did a whole lot of drawing and writing and stuff for marketing for my early games, for my first company.

Ramsay: What started you on this path?

Romero: I was playing arcade games. That was back when arcades rose up in the late 70s and the early 80s. Games had turned from pinball parlors into electromechanical arcade games like Dune Buggy. I was really, really excited, and I started spending as much time as I possibly could in the arcades. I started learning how to code in 1979. Learning how to program was just unbelievable. I had never experienced anything like that before.

Ramsay: How did arcade games get you interested in programming?

Romero: The problem is with being a kid and having arcades all over the place is that it costs money, and if you don't have a job that's generating money, you can't play in the arcades. At that time, I actually had a job delivering news-papers in the morning, so I'd have to wake up at 3:00 in the morning, deliver papers, and then get ready for school. I made probably 250 bucks a month that I would then spend completely on arcade games.

I was so crazy about arcade games that, when I ran out of money and couldn't really play anymore, I'd go and just watch. One day, my friend rode quickly to my house and said, "Oh my god, they have games up at the college and they don't cost any money." And I'm like, "Oh my god, no money; I've got to do this." And so we rode back up to the college—Sierra College in Rocklin, California—and we went up there, got in the computer lab, and the computer lab was basically a bunch of HP terminals connected to an HP 9000 mainframe in another room, so it filled the whole room.

The games there were nothing like the arcade games; they were more thought-ful. They were Hunt the Wumpus, Poison Cookie, Colossal Cave Adventure, and primitive stuff like that. That experience expanded my brain as far as game design goes, and those terminals had keyboards, so I thought, "These were probably made on this machine here. I wonder if I can do that."

In that computer lab, students were programming, so obviously, I knew it could be done. I started asking the students there, "I'm 11. How do you make that come up on the screen?" And they would tell me, "Print." They would use the word "print" and put quotes around whatever you want, but you've got to put a line number before it because it was HP Basic.

I slowly learned how to program just by asking questions. I didn't have a book. And the only way I could save programs was by putting them on paper tape, or making punch cards. I did that until I lost all of my cards in a puddle one time. I was like, "Okay, I want something that's not going to be destroyed in a second." I waited for discs to appear before I actually went to save programs again.

Ramsay: When did you get your own computer?

Romero: 1982. That was when I got the Apple II+ with 48K memory. I was really lucky to get that computer. The keyboard was really nice.

Ramsay: Who bought that for you?

Romero: My parents. In 1981, the college opened up a whole room, filled it with Apple IIs, and I was like, "I only care about the Apple II now. I don't care about these ancient HP machines." I cared about the thing that has sound, graphics, and color." I started spending all of my time in that room. For two years, I was always going up to the college, coming back, and telling them all of the things I was learning. And he my stepdad started thinking, "Wow, he's really learning a lot of stuff. I have no idea what it is and I'm an electrical engineer. Maybe he's got something going with this computer thing. Let's get a computer for him." And I think my parents spent $6,000 on getting a computer.

Ramsay: Wow, computers were expensive then.

Romero: Yeah, they were, but he didn't just buy the computer. He bought a printer, a color monitor, a Microsoft SoftCard that had CP/M, in case I needed to use the computer like I did up at the college. You know, it's funny, because back then, Microsoft was making Apple II peripherals and software before they started making their own stuff.

Ramsay: What were your parents' backgrounds?

Romero: My stepdad was an electronics engineer, mostly in recordable media. He was working for the military. Specifically, he was working with the Air Force spy program on reconnaissance cameras for TR-1s and U-2s. He had a top secret clearance. He never talked to us about anything, so I didn't really know what he was up to for a long time. My mom is basically a homemaker.

On January 1, 1983, we moved to England. I got to take a BASIC programming course on the Apple II there. On the very first day, I showed the teacher a bunch of the games I had written and that I was learning assembly language. She was super blown away, so the next day, she had the class work on a project while she took me in her car across the base to the 527th Aggressor Squadron to meet with the captain there.

Eventually, I got a job programming for the military in a bank vault. They locked it, and you had to say code words to get it unlocked from the inside. I was converting a program from an older system over to a computer system using HP BASIC, and they were doing work with Russian flight paths for dog-fighting, like analyzing them. This was the height of the Cold War.

Ramsay: When did you get your first industry job?

Romero: It was awesome. In 1987, at the very beginning of the year, I had a girlfriend, and I was working at Burger King. By May, she was pregnant, and she had just graduated high school. I had been out of high school for two years. So, I was like, "Wow, I have to get a real job. I cannot screw around." I left Burger King, and I started working for Manpower, which was a temp agency.

At Burger King, I was making $3.50 an hour, but through Manpower, I immediately started making $9.00 an hour because I have total computer skills and that was much better. It wasn't my dream job, obviously, and because we were going to have a kid, I decided I had to get serious.

I went to Applefest in 1987, and I brought a box of my disks. I went there to the Moscone Center in San Francisco, and I went in the door and went to UpTime. UpTime was a disk monthly. It was like a magazine on a disk. Jay Wilbur was the editor-in-chief of the Apple II disk. I had already been talking to Jay for a year or more at that time. When I went up to the booth, everybody was playing my game. It was the latest one I had sold to them, and they're showing it off in the booth, so I was like, "Okay, these are some good prospects. I've got one of my games being played at Applefest. This is great!"

The owner of UpTime came over and talked to me. He was wondering if I'd be interested in joining the company as programmer. I was like, "Wow, okay, one job offer down. I didn't even have to try. This is great." So, I walked over to Softdisk, their competitor, and I told them, "I've been submitting to UpTime. They've been publishing my stuff every month for a while now." In fact, they had been publishing my stuff pretty frequently, so Softdisk was like, "Well, why don't you come work for us?" Job offer number two!

And then I'm thinking about what I really want to do. I want to work at Sirius Software, I want to work at Sierra, I want to work at a real game company like Origin that I really respect. I went over to the Origin Systems area. They had a huge corner, and big posters on the wall for Ultima 5: Warriors of Destiny, coming October 31. I was all excited; I love Ultima and Origin.

They had a computer there where they were showing off the re-writes in assembly language of Ultima 1 on an Apple II. I thought, "They probably don't care so much about this Apple demo as much as they do the Ultima 5 display, so I'll just pop one of my disks in here and show them my stuff." I popped Ultima 1 out of their demo machine, I stuck my disk in there, and I booted it. The marketing lady ran over really quickly, and she was like, "That's our display. You know we're showing our games here. What are you doing?"

I said, "Well, just check this out." I showed her one of my games, which was written in double res, and back then, that was really difficult to do. There were very few double resolution games, so she was like, "Wow, did you write that?"

"Yep, and I'm looking for a job working at Origin." And so she goes, "Okay, I need your information." I gave her my number, name, address, and all that stuff. She said, "We'll be in contact." I was like, "Well, can I have your card?" She gave me her card, and I'm thinking, "Awesome. Maybe I have a job there."

But when I got back, I had to call and pester her until she connected me to someone who was a project manager. They said that in a month there's going to be a position opening up for a Commodore 64 programmer in New Hampshire. I went, "I will take anything. I'm really interested. I really, really want to go." I just called every day—just pestered the hell out of them—to get this job.

Finally, they said, "Okay, the job is now open. We can now start the interview process for this job." I asked, "What do I have to do?" He said, "We're going to call you. There will be three programmers on the line, and we're going to ask you questions. We're going to be doing this with all the candidates, and then one of you we'll fly to New Hampshire for the big interview."

I said, "All right. Do it. Ask me anything." I had known this call would be taking place in a few days, so I bought the book, Mapping the Commodore 64 by Sheldon Leemon. I knew everything about the computer. I read the whole thing, and I had it with me, ready to look up anything. When the programmers called, I easily answered all of the questions, no problem. A couple of weeks later, I'm the one they chose to fly to New Hampshire for the big interview. They had called four other programmers across the US; they were all Commodore programmers. I was the only Apple programmer.

When I had the final interview, there were nine programmers there: Steve Meuse, Paul Neurath, Stuart Marks, Herman Miller, and just several other programmers at Origin. It was very easy. At that time, I knew everything that there was to know about the computer; there was nothing that they could ask me that I didn't know. I knew every byte in the machine. That's what happened. I did the interview, blazed right through, and they hired me.

Ramsay: But you had never programmed games for the Commodore 64?

Romero: Yeah, I hadn't actually programmed the Commodore 64 until I went to Origin. I just had a really good idea about how to code it. But when I started working on the port, I immediately ran into a wall. I said, "I need to move this code over to the Commodore. Where's the cable, guys?" They went, "What? There's no cable. We don't port stuff here; you're the first guy to port stuff."

I went to RadioShack and I got a telephone cable, which has four lines in it, and I got a 16-pin chip, like a little integrated circuit chip that you would plug into a motherboard. I soldered the wires from one end to the 16-pin chip, and then I soldered the other end of the four wires to a joystick plug, like the kind that plugged into the Commodore. I made a cable, and programmed it on both sides to transfer data one way from the Apple to the Commodore. The computer only took in data from a joystick; it never pushed data out to a joystick. They do now because of force feedback and all that stuff, but back then, joysticks only output data; they didn't ever get data from a computer.

When I started at Origin in 1987, my salary was $22,000 a year. Back then, programmers topped out at $30,000. But after I had built a transfer cable and programmed a system on both computers to transfer data between an Apple and the Commodore, they immediately bumped me up to $26,000.

Ramsay: You didn't have any trouble learning how to program for the C64?

Romero: No, in fact, the next job I did on the Commodore was porting Might & Magic 2 over. That's where I had to get really technical. I had to set up vertical blank interrupts and control the screen—which meant switching the screen mode so the screen is in mixed mode, but a certain line on the screen switches into high-res mode, and then it switches back at the top of the screen back into mixed mode. I could have two graphics modes on the screen at the same time: one for displaying super crisp, high-res fonts, and then the top being the most colorful resolution to make the graphics look as good as possible.

Ramsay: How long were you at Origin?

Romero: I was there for eight months. Origin was my dream company and I loved it; it was the best thing ever. But the guy who hired me at Origin said, "You're the best 6502 programmer I've ever met. Let's start a company together. I need to get out of here. We could make bigger money." And I thought, "Okay, I could start a company." It was a huge decision, and it was crazy, but as long as he could ensure that I'd make the same amount of money, then that sounded pretty amazing.

Isn't that nuts? I got that job at Origin in October 1987, but I didn't start there officially until November. In October, I got married, I got my first real job, I moved across the country to New Hampshire from California, and then we had a baby in February. So, from October to February, I went through the four biggest life-changing things that people go through other than buying a house or death, and I did that when I was 19. A few months later, I started a company.

Ramsay: Every entrepreneur I've talked to has said that starting a company takes a toll. Was that the case with Inside-Out Software??

Romero: My former boss and I were partners at Inside-Out Software, and that didn't take a toll on me because he was the one who wanted to handle the business stuff. He had to worry about the contracts, if we were going to have enough money, if we could hire people, and all that. I didn't care back then about what was in those contracts. I just signed them and got money.

My job was to focus on just making games, just porting stuff all day long as fast as possible. I didn't have any stress because I love programming. But I learned the value of networking and business relationships. He was older than I was, and I saw him stress over things, dealing with everything.

Ramsay: Did you invest anything in this company?

Romero: The only money we needed was to get the loan for the computer, and he used his contract with New World Computing to get that loan. I used my partner's Apple II GS computer until we bought some new ones. I used his to start and went to his apartment coding on that while he was next to me coding on the Compaq PC. As we got bigger, we added more projects, and more money came in; we never had to actually put in our own money.

Ramsay: You were bootstrapping from the beginning?

Romero: Yeah, almost all of my companies have been bootstrapped. The best part is you own the whole deal. If you bootstrap, you own it all, and you don't have to give it away for money or an interest. It's just the beginning that's the hard part. If you have great ideas, you've just got to sweat it out.

Ramsay: Who did you work with on Ideas from the Deep?

Romero: Lane Roathe was the guy I started that company with. He had a company called Blue Mountain Micro, but he didn't do games; he basically did disk utilities. He was really great at disk access and disk operating systems.

I met Lane at Applefest in 1987. Lane worked for Jay Wilbur at UpTime. He was his programmer, and Lane was an expert badass programmer in assembly language. Not only was Lane great on the Apple II, but he was great on the Apple II GS and the Macintosh.

When I met Lane, we hit it off, and from then on, we were friends. I actually hired Lane at Inside-Out from UpTime, so he came to New Hampshire from Rhode Island, and worked at my company. But the problem in the 1980s was the Apple vs. IBM culture. You were either on Apple's side, or you were on IBM's side. It wasn't even Microsoft; it was IBM.

I was an Apple guy, and Lane was a 100% Apple guy. He hated PCs, and my cofounder was an Apple guy, but he really believed in the PC, like as the future. He and Lane didn't get along ever at all, so Lane did not last long. He just quit because he had enough pestering from the cofounder. Lane left, super disgruntled, so he stole a contract away. It was totally legitimate because we didn't have an Apple II GS programmer. What Lane was working on at Inside-Out was an Apple II GS port of Dark Castle; it was a classic.

So, he called 360 Pacific and said, "Tom [Frisina], I was the guy working on the port; they don't have anyone to do the port. You can just assign the contract to me." And they said, "Hell, yeah, let's do that." My cofounder got even more pissed off.

When the game I was working on disappeared because Epyx cancelled everything industry wide, I decided to leave the company, too. I moved in with Lane, and I did the graphics for the Apple II GS version of Dark Castle while he did the programming. We started our little company, Ideas from the Deep, and we made some games. Then, I got both of us jobs at Softdisk, and we moved from New Hampshire down to Shreveport, Louisiana, together.

Ramsay: Why did Epyx cancel everything industry wide?

Romero: So, Epyx canceled all ports because they needed to conserve cash to dump into their first-party development of Atari Lynx games. My port was canceled for a game called Tower Toppler.

Following the Epyx cancelation, Inside-Out was having money trouble, so I left and moved in with Lane. Meanwhile, my wife was in California with her parents having our second kid; I was in the middle of a job change. We started writing some code, making games, while we were porting Dark Castle.

I had to get a job, so I asked Lane what Jay Wilbur was doing. He said, "I think he's interviewing at a company down in Louisiana called Softdisk." I said, "Why don't we just go work down there with him?" Lane's like, "Okay, that sounds cool." I got the number for Softdisk, called them up, and I said, "Can I speak to the president?" His name was Al Vekovius. I said, "My name is John Romero and I'm interested in working there." Al said, "Yeah, I've heard of you." I said, "Wow, really? You've heard of me? That's cool." He goes, "Yeah, Jay Wilbur's down here and Michael Amarello." Mike had been an editor-in-chief at UpTime.

I said, "Well, I'm interested in coming down for an interview." He replied, "I'll send a plane ticket immediately." Then, I said, "Oh, there's another really awesome programmer. His name's Lane. He worked at UpTime, too." And Al said, "I'll send two tickets."

So, we fly down and meet Al. He drove us around Shreveport, and we got this awful tour of downtown. There were prostitutes walking all over the place and stuff. But then he took us to this cool building, and I thought: "Holy crap, this is amazing!" It was filled with developers and programmers. They're just our kind of people, so we were excited to meet everyone. Later that night, we went to Al's house and had a big dinner. We came down in late February of 1989 from New Hampshire, where it was freezing, and we fly down to Shreveport, where it was warm with green grass. We were thinking, "We're coming here!"

Ramsay: Money had been an issue for you. What were you offered?

Romero: Al offered us jobs for a $1,000 more per year than what we were making, which was $27,000 total. We signed up and moved down. He was trying to get us to make some commercial products. He wanted to do what Origin did in forming a group called the Special Projects Division.

During the first month I started programming on the PC, I made a game called Magic Boxes that was a port of an Apple II game over to the PC in text mode. I wrote it in Pascal even. I ported the games I had made on the Apple II to the PC, some of them mixed Pascal and assembly language, and then full-on assembly. I was pumping out so much stuff that the PC department was falling behind, so they decided they needed me on PC and scrapped the Special Projects Division.

After a year working in that department, I really wasn't doing what I wanted to do, which was make big games. I went and had lunch with the president, and I said, "I need to make games, so I'm planning on putting my resume in at LucasArts." And he was like, "No, no, no. We need to keep you here. Okay, what can we do?" I said again, "Well, I want to make games."

He was like, "How about you make games on a new disk that's just games?" And I said, "Well, that would probably be cool, but I don't want to do it in one month." And he said, "Two months. How about two months?" And I'm like, "Well, yeah, two months is a lot better than one month. How about a team: an artist and another programmer?" He said, "Okay," and I told him, "Now that's cool. We can do way cooler stuff than what I was doing before."

It took months to get it together, and I needed somebody to be the other coder. I knew of a game called Tennis by John Carmack. I'd run that game and I saw how smoothly it operated. I could tell that was quality programming on the Apple II. And so I told the Apple II department, "Hey, I'm setting up this game division, and I want to talk to the guy who programmed that. That's some really good programming." They said, "Yeah, he's not going to come down here; we've already tried to hire him two times and he keeps on telling us, 'Forget it.'" And I said, "Let me talk to him. You guys are trying to hire him for non-game programming, but he will come here to code games."

And so we set up a meeting. They called him and he came down to interview with Lane, Jay, and Al, and we had a great meeting. He was excited; he felt that he had finally met two programmers who he could learn from, and so John said, "Yes, I want to work here." He drove his little MG all the way from Kansas City to Shreveport, and moved into an apartment complex.

I got the room we would move into, start coding, and make our games. It was a big deal to start this game division, so I got pretty much everything I wanted. I wanted three 386/33s with 4 megs of RAM, and they were like, "Okay, you got it." I said I needed an NES with Zelda, Super Mario 3, and Life Force, too. The place was turning into an arcade, and we kept the lights off, so it was a cool cave. We got secondary monitors for debugging using Turbo Debugger, and we got this giant refrigerator. We were playing heavy metal all day long, and we left the door open, otherwise it would get too hot in there. And I was looking for an artist, so I went next door to an office full of artists. Al told me I could pick any artist I wanted, so I picked an intern: Adrian Carmack.

The rest of the company thought we were spoiled brats. Al tried to calm them down by saying, "They're going to save the company. This is a big deal."

Ramsay: What was your first game?

Romero: So, we got started in August 1990. John was doing his game, and I was doing mine. In one month, we got both of those games done. I had ported a game from 1988 that I had made for UpTime called Dangerous Dave.

Little did I know that this game would live on for decades. Tons of people have since played Dangerous Dave all over the world, and one of the reasons for the game living so long is that, in parts of the world where computers are not as nice as they are here, this game is one of the few that runs at a crazy fast speed on old computers. The graphics routines were all written in assembly, and the game is only a 73 KB compressed executable.

But our first game together was Slordax, which was a clone of Xevious. When John, Adrian, and I started working together in September, we had never worked with another person to make one game. We had ten years of experience, but not in a team. And that team worked out extremely well. Oh my god, that was the best thing in the world.

On September 18, there was a lot of coding going on. Tom Hall was there late at night. Super Mario 3 was running on a Nintendo in there, and John had just got horizontal scrolling in. Tom saw it and he was like, "Oh, that's cool. What if we replicate the first level of Super Mario 3?"

And John was like, "Yeah, that would be awesome." And they said, "Yeah, we could surprise Romero with it." So, they stayed up until 5:00 AM in the morning. Tom was replicating, pixel by pixel, the blocks you see in the first level and using my level editor to put the world together. John was taking the graphics out of Dangerous Dave because it has animation cycles for a character jumping and everything, and put them in this little demo. And so, because they were using Dangerous Dave inside of Mario, Tom made a little title screen that said: "Dangerous Dave in Copyright Infringement." They put this little executable and everything on a disk, and stuck it on my keyboard when they were finished. I came in the next day, and I saw the disk on my keyboard and it said "run me."

I stuck the disk in the drive, and I ran it—and I see, holy crap, there's Mario—it's a level of Mario right there on the screen. And the character jumps up and it's a demo that's playing. And so as soon as the character runs across the screen and it smoothly pans, I was totally destroyed. It was the entire Mario game on a PC, right there, actually happening, and no one on a PC had ever seen that happen because no one had mastered the panning registers.

It was mind-blowing that you could make Mario for real on a PC. It was really huge because it meant so much for PC games. Until that point, PC games had a lot of static screens, and a lot of experiments in ways of making action happen, but at a really slow frame rate. This was the real thing.

So, John and Tom came into the office at 1:00 PM, and they go, "So, what'd you think?" And I went, "Absolutely unbelievable. We need to quit." Their reaction was, "What?" And I said, "This company can't do anything with this game. They can't actually market it; it will go into a black hole if they have this game. It will disappear. This needs to get out, we need to make something that gets out there with this technology. This is unbelievable; this is company-starting shit." And Jay Wilbur was there when I was saying this stuff, and I said to him, "I'm serious." So, Jay closed the door and I outlined the beginning of Id Software, how we're going to get out of here, and what we're going to do.

Ramsay: What was the plan?

Romero: The first plan was we were going to try to make a really good Mario demo with Mario, the turtles, and everything from the beginning of Super Mario 3. We got it together, and sent it to Nintendo. We heard that our demo went to NOA, and then to Nintendo Japan.

Hiroshi Yamauchi decided then that Nintendo games will be on only Nintendo consoles, not on the PC, which is great. That's the Apple strategy, right? "This is our stuff. This is our hardware. This is what our stuff goes on." And so they said no, and wrote a letter back that said, "Thank you very much. You've done a really great job, but we plan to stay on only our own consoles."

So, we thought, "Okay, well, we'll just make another game that's not with Mario in it." And the funny thing is that, at this exact same time, Scott Miller was trying to get in touch with me. He had published a bunch of stuff with Softdisk, and he saw my games coming out. Scott had a shareware software company, Apogee Software, and wanted me to make another version of my game.

He called me and said he wants to see my Pyramids of Egypt game. He wants that game, but with different levels to publish with his company, Apogee. This was just a few days before this Mario demo happened. I said, "Oh, you should see the stuff we're doing right now; it's way better than that thing that you're talking about." That was Slordax.

I sent him a disk with Slordax that's in the middle of progress. And he gets it and says, "Oh my god, we need you to make a game for us." Then, I said, "Speaking of the Mario demo, you won't believe this, but we blow away that thing I just sent you with this new tech." He asked me to send that, too. He got it, and he was like, "Oh god, please. Seriously, right now, let's do a deal."

I said, "Okay, we'll make a game for you," and he's like, "No, no, you need to make three games. This works only if you do three games; we'll give one away and sell two." I said, "Okay, well, we'll just use the same engine and put different data on it for the other episodes, so we'll do the three episodes for you. But you need to send us $2,000 upfront for us to start."

And Scott's like, "No problem. Done. What's the address?" Holy crap! Back then, $2,000 was a lot of cash. His last question was: "what is the game you are going to make?" I told him we would talk about it and get back to him.

So, I gathered Tom and John with me, told them the story, and asked what they thought we should make. John Carmack said, "I don't know. What about a game about a genius kid who saves the universe?" And we're like, "That sounds great," and Tom's like, "I love it. I'm going to write it up right now." Tom ran into the Apple II room and wrote it up on the Apple II in AppleWorks, printed it out, came back in, and he goes, "Okay, here it is." Tom read it in a radio announcer voice: "Commander Keen, defender of the galaxy…" We were laughing and clapping, so I go, "That's amazing. We're going to go run with that."

We printed it up on paper for Scott. We all signed it, and we sent it to him. I still have a scan of that paper we sent. Scott said, "That's it. We're in business. Let's go." So, we got started.

We would work all day, and when 6:00 PM rolled around, we changed directories in DOS to the Commander Keen directory. We'd work on Commander Keen until 2:00 AM in the morning, and we'd do that every day. On Friday nights, we'd take the computers out of there, put them in our cars, and take them out to the lake house where we would work on weekends. We'd work all weekend long nonstop, and we'd do that for three months. We made three games, and that was the first Commander Keen trilogy.

Ramsay: How was that first trilogy distributed through Apogee?

Romero: I mastered all the disks after a whole bunch of compression fun, and sent it to Scott. He uploaded it on December 14, 1990, to the Software Creations BBS for the PC back then. It had tons of games on it. We had a really great advertisement. As soon as you logged into the BBS, it would scroll Commander Keen. The guy who ran the BBS was mind-blown by how great the game was, so people downloaded the game like crazy. We just waited for our royalty check, which Scott said would be sent to us on January 15.

And we got a check on January 15 for $10,500. We were excited! We had, I think, a 45% deal with Apogee, so we got 45% and they got 55%. Combined, we were making not quite $100,000, so we thought, "Okay, we can live on this. Now, we need to quit, and tell Al what's going down."

Ramsay: Oh, you hadn't left yet?

Romero: Yeah, so when I told Al, he was so upset! He had set up this whole division for us. I explained our opportunity. After some time, he told me, "We need to figure out how you're going to leave. You can't just leave me high and dry here with subscribers expecting games and nobody here to make them."

I made a proposal I thought would be good for him and us. We hammered out an agreement where Id Software would make a whole year's worth of games for Softdisk. Every two months, there'd be a game, and we'd get $5,000 for each game. That's it. Meanwhile, Softdisk would have a whole year to get up to speed while they brought a team together to build games using our technology. They also agreed to not sue us; they obviously had an IP case because we coded all of Commander Keen on their machines. So, that was our agreement.

Ramsay: When did Id Software actually get started?

Romero: We incorporated Id Software on February 1, 1991. We counted on Commander Keen's income staying the same or getting better. It was a huge risk for all of us to leave, based on one check, especially at Christmas. But back then we just took risks all the time without thinking.

After our year of making games for Softdisk, we had $30,000 and we had made Hovertank 3D, one of the first 3D first-person shooters. We had also started prototyping our next Commander Keen series, but this time, we planned to take six months instead of three. We had a more complex engine, more art, and at the time, we were still make games for Softdisk by day. In 1991, we made 11 games in total. We were just cranking out these games, and then by 1992, we moved down to Dallas where Apogee was located.

Ramsay: Was that when Mark Rein became involved?

Romero: So, one day, we got a letter from a guy, in which he says, "Game's amazing. I'm blown away. These are the best games on the PC, but I found some bugs in all three of the games." He tells us where the bugs are, and I thought, "This guy is super sharp. Somehow he found bugs we haven't even found."

And so I contacted him and asked if he'd like to become a beta tester. He said, "Yeah, I'd love to be a beta tester, but do you have a biz guy in the company?" And I'm like, "Nope, we need a biz guy; we don't have one right now." He's like, "I'm a biz guy. I make $100,000 a year doing business. I live in Toronto."

And I'm like, "We're really small. There are only four of us, and adding one more person is a really big deal, especially if they're not making a game. You're going to have to sell yourself." So, he said, "This is what I'll do. I'll fly down, and I will present myself as your business development guy and tell you some of my ideas—and you guys decide whether you like me or not."

So, Mark Rein came down, we talked, and we decided that we needed to be careful. We didn't want to be giving away stock in the company or hiring people until we knew they could do something for us. We told him, "You can be the probationary president and present yourself as president to do deals. Can you do deals for Commander Keen? What kind of deals can you get us?"

Mark went out and found a company called FormGen in Toronto. He signed us up for a two-game deal: one to be released at Christmas, and the next to come out after that at no specific time.

Ramsay: What happened with the second Commander Keen trilogy?

Romero: We got Commander Keen 4 done in three months, Commander Keen 6 in two months, and Commander Keen 5 in one month. Commander Keen 6 had to be done before 5 because it had to go to retail; they had to get it out to stores quick. Commander Keen 4 and 5 would just be uploaded to the BBS. So, the games went out, and people loved Commander Keen, so it did okay. But it was nothing like the first one; it was broken into two pieces instead of three, and people didn't feel like they were getting their money's worth.

Ramsay: How did Wolfenstein 3D get going?

Romero: I could see that the 3D thing was going to be cool. And, one day in 1990, I'm talking with Paul Neurath, and he says, "We're working on this really neat technique called texture mapping, where you take a picture and you project it onto a surface that is displayed in 3D." I figured he was doing this with Ultima, since he couldn't tell me for confidentiality reasons. I thought, "Wow, that's awesome." I got off the phone and told John, "Hey, there's a thing called texture mapping," and he looks up in the air for a second, and he goes, "Yeah, I could do that."

The funny thing was that Origin worked on Ultima Underworld for two years, and we worked on Catacomb 3D for two months. Both 3D games ended up using the mapping technique. We released Catacomb 3D around Christmas and went on vacation. Well, John stayed home because he heard about a great new computer he was so excited about: the NeXT. It's $11,000; he had to have it.

When we came back, he had the NeXT computer all set up, and he was doing tests with vector quantization: taking 256-color VGA graphics, breaking down the RGB values, converting them to another color space, and figuring out if he could compress it better. And we're just like, "Okay, time for another game." This was January 1992. I said, "We need to redo Castle Wolfenstein in 3D."

I decided to send a copy of Commander Keen 1 through 6 to Roberta Williams at Sierra. In January, she had written back that she loved Commander Keen, that it was super exciting, and we should come out and talk to them.

We flew out there with Mark, our probationary president. We got the whole tour; we got to see Warren Schwader, who was an Apple II programmer from 1981, and Ken Williams, who had two Software Publishers Association (SPA) awards in his office. Ken brought up the idea of buying Id Software for $2.5 million. We talked further the next day and told them we were seriously thinking about it, that we'll make our decision when we get back.

We went back home, we talked about it, and said, "Yeah, let's do this. Let's have them sign a letter of intent and pay us $100,000 to keep us bound, and then go through the acquisition contract and get bought for $2.5 million." We called Ken and told him, but he's no longer interested.

So, we thought, "Well, we're still making Wolfenstein, and we're going to put it out. Too bad that deal didn't work out." We didn't sell Id Software to Sierra for $2.5 million because Ken didn't want to pay $100,000 for a letter of intent.

We continued developing Wolfenstein. At the very beginning, we were doing the game in 16-color EGA, and Scott Miller said, "You know what, ditch EGA. VGA is where this game's going to look really great. And more people have VGA now than they did when Keen was out, so just throw away EGA, forget it, and don't even support it." We were like, "Hell, yeah, that makes it way easier." EGA was a hard mode to program, especially with texture mapping.

Ramsay: Where was Mark during this time?

Romero: While we were looking for apartments in Dallas, I had a conversation with Scott. He asked, "You guys have Mark doing all the biz stuff? He told me I'm not supposed to talk to you about business."

And I said, "What? No. You can talk to us. We just don't want you talking to us all the time about biz stuff because we wanted to see how well he would do with it. It's a distraction when we're trying to code, design, and everything."

So, when I got back to the hotel, I called John Carmack and Adrian Carmack, told them the situation, and John fired him. Mark then went straight over to Epic Games. That was the beginning of 1992, and that was fine because we were hiring Jay. It's funny. Now, Jay and Mark work in the same office at Epic, but Jay did stay as our CEO at Id Software for years.

Ramsay: When did you finish Wolfenstein 3D?

Romero: We finished Wolfenstein in Dallas, and uploaded the game to the Software Creations BBS around 4:00 AM in the morning on May 5, 1992. It was really just the shareware version, and we didn't have any other episodes. The reason why we uploaded the shareware version was because Scott said, "Let's get this out fast; let's upload the first episode. You guys finish the other two episodes, and then we'll have all three ready to go."

We agreed. We thought we could get the other two episodes done pretty quickly, and that's what happened. We finished it out well; it wasn't like it was just blasted out. The engine was working really well, so the first episode came together great, and the second and third were just bam, bam, we're done.

And when we got done with the three episodes, Scott said, "Hey, so here's a crazy idea. You guys make another three episodes as an expansion pack. When the shareware goes out, the other two episodes will be $35. The expansion—which will give you double the levels—will be an additional $15. On top of that, how about you guys make a hint guide for all six episodes, and we'll sell that for $10? Everything together would be $60. What do you think about this?" So, in the summer, we finished the pamphlets for advertisements, we did the hint book, and we finished all those episodes.

Ramsay: What happened when Wolfenstein 3D was released?

Romero: When Wolfenstein came out, there was just a massive amount of downloads. Just huge. We found out that the first episode sold 4,000 copies, which was a lot back then. Nowadays, it's a joke, but back then, that was a ton of copies. That was a quarter million dollars in one month, which we had never seen before. For us, a quarter million bucks was like five months of income, and it was just, bam, instant. It was pretty amazing to see that in one month.

And then we got a call from a company in Japan that wanted us to port Wolfenstein to the Super Nintendo; they would give us a $100,000 down payment. We were like, "Let's all give ourselves raises." Everyone had been paid the same amount then. There was no difference in payment, no matter what our jobs were; we all had crazy amounts of experience. We were paying ourselves $27,000 a year. When Wolfenstein came out, we raised ourselves to $45,000 a year. After a few more months of Wolfenstein just really rocketing and going crazy, we raised our salaries to $60,000 a year.

Ramsay: Today, after major releases, game developers often take time off, when they aren't laid off, of course. Did you guys take a break?

Romero: Yeah, after Wolfenstein, we all decided to go to Disney World as a group vacation. We stayed in Disney World for a week. And while we were there, people were like, "Holy crap, you guys made Wolfenstein?" The word was out, which never happened with Commander Keen, so it was pretty cool to finally see some people recognizing a game that we made.

Ramsay: After you left Softdisk, you were working out of an apartment. It's strange to think that Wolfenstein 3D was made there. How long before you decided that you needed a real office?

Romero: Once we had real money, we had started looking around for real office space in October. By November 1, 1992, we had moved all of our stuff out of the apartment complex into the black building in Mesquite, Texas.

In the black building, we had only one quarter of the floor, and there was a dentist and a lawyer next to us on one side. Eventually, we took the whole floor, except for the dentist because we liked him, and changed our suite number to 666. But that took a couple of years.

We all got NeXTSTEP machines. We were thinking we could develop our next game on this rich platform, probably easier. DOS was super primitive. And we all got on the Internet, we all got email, and all that stuff at the end of the year.

Ramsay: How did Doom come together?

Romero: Before Doom, each of our games had been the brainchild of one person, often Tom, and we would build out that vision. This time was different. This was the first game where we decided to collaborate on the idea.

We thought about Dungeons & Dragons campaigns. There was so much happening in those campaigns that any one adventure would be epic. We thought, at the very end, that demons could overrun the whole place, and I asked, "What if you were fighting demons? What kind of weapons would you need?" We had been doing World War II, which was kind of limiting, so I was like, "What if we did space weapons and space marines? And what if the space marines were fighting demons? How about that?" Tom came up with the fiction, and we all agreed that would be really cool. What would the engine do though? We came up with a laundry list of what we wanted to accomplish, and then we realized that the game would take longer than Wolfenstein. We realized that this would be the biggest game we had ever made.

One idea that John had for Doom was portals that would allow the player to look into other areas, other maps maybe; the player would look in the doorway or something, and it would actually be a view into another section of the map or another map entirely. He started thinking about how his data structures would handle this, and then decided, "Okay, it's not the time right now, but I can see being able to do that later when there's more memory."

In January, we wrote up a press release to announce our plans. That was the first time we told the world what our next game would be. We put the press release out, and we hired Shawn Green, who worked at Apogee, to be tech support for the game. He would know the game while it was being developed, and when it came out, he would know everything about it and be able to answer tech support questions.

Ramsay: What were the rest of you doing?

Romero: At the very beginning, Tom Hall was in charge of making the levels, I was busy making the map editor, and John was writing the engine. For a couple of months, Tom was thrashing around; he couldn't get really inspired about what kind of levels he could make. And after two months, the engine was there to make stuff work. So, we spent another two months trying to figure out how we could come up with a really interesting level design.

One day, I just said, "Okay, I'm going to do it today. I'm going to solve this level problem." And that day, I came up with the abstract level design style, and I showed it to everybody. I'm like, "Here's some round stuff, and here it opens up into a huge room with really high walls, cool areas on top that are brightly lit, the room's kind of dim and dark, and it's got two paths out of it."

And the design looked way, way more interesting. The textures were cool and everybody liked it. "That's the direction that we need to go. It can't be realistic; it needs to be abstract. It needs to be fun, look cool, have a great design for puzzle solving, and have a great general flow for combat." Tom started working with that and we continued making the game.

We just kept on making progress, getting monsters in, and scanning stuff with a video camera. We added a Lazy Susan that had eight slots. You could rotate it, and it would stop at each slot; we had someone build that for us. Adrian was building models out of clay, so he built the main Doom marine and the Baron of Hell. He made only two of those guys. Clay turned out to be the worst thing because when you wanted to animate the characters, the clay would tear.

Ramsay: What did you use for the other characters?

Romero: After making a couple of those guys, we hired somebody, Greg Punchatz, to make actual latex models that fully articulate and are colored correctly instead of just clay color. We had a video camera hooked up to a NeXTSTEP that could take a video image. We'd aim that right at the Lazy Susan and whatever monster was on top, scan a frame, and save. We'd scan all eight frames for one type of animation, animate it, and do another set of eight frames. It was kind of tedious, but we got them all scanned in.

We had to clean up the images. There were extra dots all around each image that had nothing to do with the image. And we ran the images through something called "The Fuzzy Pumper Palette Shop." We created a palette for Doom, a 256-color VGA palette, and we applied that palette to those images, so that each image would conform to the Doom palette. An artist could then go through them, clean up the images, and color them correctly.

Ramsay: What about the weapons?

Romero: All the weapons we got were from Toys 'R' Us. There was a shotgun, a pistol, and some other kind of space weapon. We took the space weapon and we used it in multiple ways to get the BFG and the plasma gun. We had a toy gatling gun as well. And, suddenly, Tom just wasn't into it.

Tom really didn't like blood and violence and gore, and that's what the games were turning into, starting with Wolfenstein. Doom was even worse. And so Tom just wasn't very happy. In August, he took off and went to Apogee—and then we hired Sandy Peterson to take over as the full-time game designer. We also hired Dave Taylor to help with stuff like the menu system, the intermissions screens, the auto-map, and those things. He integrated the sound engine we had licensed, too. He came on for the last five months

Eventually, we started working on deathmatch, probably around September. Getting that in there just changed everything; it became the coolest game ever. But by the time we got to the end, when we were going to upload the game finally, we were like, "We don't even want to see this game again." We had been living with this game, playing it over and over a million times. That's the only way to make good games—play your game tons of times.

Ramsay: Doom was released on December 10, 1993. What was that day like?

Romero: That last day was 30 hours long! We stayed up getting DOOM tested and ready to upload, and then we uploaded the game to the Software Creations BBS and the University of Wisconsin's FTP site, and we went to sleep. We didn't want to see the game again, but we were going to.

Everybody knew Doom was coming out. In fact, some people got Dave Taylor's phone number at Id somehow, and they were calling up, asking when the game's coming out. In the University's FTP directory, people were creating bogus files with file names that were sentences like "when.will.it.come.out" and "oh.my.god.i.cant.wait." And when we tried to upload, we couldn't because we couldn't log in; the site was packed. We had to have the admin dump everybody so we could try and log in while everyone else was automatically logging back in. We finally uploaded the game, and then people slammed the site, crashing the servers two times in a row. It was pandemonium.

Doom did really well. The game went out like a rocket; everybody loved it. We fixed some problems. We also added support for a version or two for three monitors, where you'd have a middle main monitor and two side monitors that would show your view wrapped around. That was pretty neat. And we just kept responding to everybody going nuts over the game. At the same time, we started Doom II, which would be the retail version; Doom was shareware.

I started working with all kinds of people on the hint books, hint guides—you know, do this and do that. I even started up Heretic in January 1994. We took about eight months to get Doom II done and launched that on October 10.

Ramsay: I recall that you had a launch party, right?

Romero: Yeah, we had a launch event for Doom II in New York City at a club called The Limelight; the club was all gothy. We had a 15-person deathmatch station set up in back for the journalists, and we held the press event on a stage where we would all just sit on the sides and answer questions.

At that launch event, a couple of people came over, gave me a disk, and said, "Just run the thing on the disk. We're super excited about our thing; you can play Doom at any time, night or day, through this." That was very exciting, because the Internet was then in its early, clunky stages. Jay and I flew back home, installed it, ran it, and came in the next day and we were like, "Wow, did you run that thing last night? That thing is awesome." That was DWANGO.

And I told Jay, "I'm going to work with those guys. I'm going to get that thing done." It was extremely crude. So, I got in touch with the company owner and said, "I've got to work with your server guy. I'm going to do the client. He's going to do the server, and we're going to get this thing rewritten. It's going to be nice and professional, so I can put it on my master disks when I do a new version of Doom II, or when this new game Heretic comes out."

We raced to get it done. People could run "DWANGO.exe" and connect to a server. When you connect with DWANGO, you're inside of a lobby and you can see all the other people in there. You can connect together with other people, chat, and then you can start deathmatching. And this was at any time of the day, so there was no calling up your friend on a modem; it's like they were sitting there, waiting for you. To me, this was going to be the best thing ever, especially when you could play over the Internet anywhere.

So, anyway, that was pretty cool, and we wrapped and launched Heretic at around 11:30 PM on December 23, 1994. "DWANGO.exe" was on the disk.

Ramsay: Since you wanted to get Doom into retail stores, did you find a publisher for Doom II?

Romero: A company called GT Interactive approached us and asked if they could be the publisher for Doom II. We said, "Well, we don't even know who you are; you're brand new. You've got to prove you can actually move games." And so we said, "How about this? We'll give you Commander Keen 4 and 5, and if you can sell 30,000 copies, you'll get Doom II."

And so they did that. They sold 30,000 copies pretty quickly, came back, and said, "Boom, there it is. All right, let's sign you guys up." We signed up with GT Interactive and preorders went crazy after they announced they were the publisher. They were doing marketing, and the preorders were just insane—just tons of preorders. And when the game came out in the stores on October 10, Doom II was selling so fast that they didn't even put the game on the shelves. Stores would bring in a huge pallet of Doom II boxes and just drop the pallet right inside the doorway of CompUSA, for instance. People just went in, picked up a box, and went to the register—that's why they were coming in.

Ramsay: Although Doom was originally shareware for DOS, the game spread quickly to other platforms, including the Super Nintendo. How did that happen?

Romero: One day, we got a package in the mail from Sculptured Software. We opened it up and there was a Super Nintendo cartridge with "Doom" written on it. I thought, "I know Sculptured; they're one of the best SNES developers around." We put the cartridge in our SNES and it was Doom!

We didn't ask anybody to do that; they were just so crazy about the game that they decided to make it. I think they were thinking, "Okay, so we're the best Super Nintendo developers around, and if Id gives Doom to anybody else, we're not going to get it, so we need to just do it." So, that's what they did. They made Doom without our knowledge, and then sent it to us to see if we wanted to publish it. We were like, "Um, yes. Great." That's what happened with that.

Also, in 1994, there was a Cybermania award show in Hollywood that Robert Stack was MC'ing. We went to that show and we didn't get an award. It was ridiculous. Doom didn't get an award. And I remember when Doom came out, in Computer Gaming World; Doom was just in the back with a bunch of newly released software like it's no big deal. It was hilarious. This was before they were writing articles all over the planet in every magazine about Doom. I remember Matt Firme wrote in PC Gamer about how Doom had taken control of his life. It was everywhere then, but when it first came out, nothing.

Ramsay: When did Quake get going?

Romero: In December 1994, we were thinking about the next game: Quake. At the beginning of 1995, we started actually coding. John was spending time on architecture, and he was trying to get Michael Abrash to come join Id.

Because Doom II was now in stores, and Doom I had been out for a year as shareware, we decided to put the full registered version of Doom together with Doom II as a package, and add another episode to give it more value. And so we were working on that and Quake. I was building the level editor for Quake, and I was also working on Ultimate Doom, which is what we called the package.

I was also kicking off the Hexen game; Heretic had just launched and I really liked it. I wanted to do something new, so I got Raven, the company I worked with on Heretic, to sign up for another game. We took over pretty much the rest of the building, except for the dentist we liked, and built out new offices.

Finally, by the end of 1995, the engine was in a state that we could make Quake run at a rendering speed and frame rate that would help us deliver a great game. And we then knew how many polys we could have in a scene, so we could make our levels look really cool and not feel too slow.

So, we were at a time when we could really build an innovative game design, but the problem was that everybody was burned out from a year of nonstop work. We had a company meeting to decide what to do. Almost everyone said they were burned out, and they didn't want to even think about trying to innovate game design. Even Carmack was on the fence.

Some people were on my side to move forward and innovate game design. But most of the people had not been through a full hardcore dev cycle—they were kind of broken and just wanted to get the game over with. I was advocating, "No, we need to move forward with great game design and make cool new stuff that people haven't seen before. This technology is already something no one's seen; let's make a great game design."

But the consensus was "let's just slap Doom weapons in this stupid game and get it done, get it over with." I said, "Okay, I'll redesign it, and we'll just slap Doom weapons in and finish this game. Right then, I was done with the company. I thought, "I'm finishing this game and I'm leaving." In January, I contacted Tom Hall and said, "When I'm done with Quake, let's start another company." And he's like, "Sounds great to me." He was working on Prey.

For the next seven months, we were in just a crazy crunch mode on Quake to make the levels, all the models, all the weapons, tie them all together, make them work, test it, ship it, and we're done. Around February 22, we put out Qtest, which was our technology test with three levels and people got to check it out. We had seven people in the Doom community come to our offices to test the game, so we could watch them and get feedback immediately. We made some changes, finished it up, and shipped.

In March, we actually got an offer from GT Interactive to buy the company for $100 million and we decided to turn it down. We were just not in the state of mind that we could even make a decision about it. We were all mentally done with thinking about anything else but getting this damn game done. We could not make good decisions about anything, so we just told them to forget it.

We got the game together and I launched it by myself because the company was just destroyed. The game was finished, everyone was done, and so I came in on a Saturday to get the game packaged for online distribution. I was there for awhile, figuring out all the compression stuff and everything. It was the first Id game that had a subdirectory in it, so it was a little more complex. I called one of the Qtest guys over and said, "Hey, do you want to be here when I upload Quake?" And he's like, "Holy shit!" And I just spent hours trying to get this thing perfect; mastering something really takes a long time.

I uploaded Quake probably around 5:30 PM and then I was done. I was in the office by myself, but everyone was just done. It was the last game we were going to make together. In August, I finished mastering the retail disc version of Quake, and I was helping with the design of Quake II. One day, I decided to call GT Interactive. Talking with the president, I said, "I'm going to be leaving Id to start my own company. I was wondering if you guys wanted to talk about investing or publishing." He was very excited about that.

Well, the next day when I got into work, the guys call me into a room and ask me to resign. Evidently, GT Interactive talked to Id about me leaving. But, anyway, I just signed the resignation thing because I was done.

Ramsay: This was the start of Ion Storm?

Romero: Yes, I spent the rest of 1996 putting together the people in Ion Storm. Tom left Apogee, so he could work on planning with me for the last half of 1996. We were meeting with a lot of publishers, and finally, we whittled it down to Eidos Interactive as the company that would be around with a good amount of money. Eidos was doing well and they were kicking butt, so I chose those guys and we got funded in January 1997.

I started to design Daikatana, and Tom Hall was there and he was starting to design Anachronox. We licensed the Quake engine, and we hired a bunch of people for the team. By the middle of the year, we had probably 40 people.

In September 1997, I brought in Warren Spector to Ion Storm. I heard he was released from working with Looking Glass and he was making Thief: The Dark Project, and the second I heard that, I e-mailed him and said, "Dude, you've got to join Ion Storm. Let me come down and convince you." And I did. I convinced him to join, and he was really happy with how things turned out.

Anyway, I thought we'd be able to get the game done in a year. We already had finished technology, we had a lot of people, and we were off and running in January, but a lot of the people I hired were inexperienced. I gave a lot of modders their first job at Ion Storm, and they didn't have professional experience or a work ethic. Some had never had a job before. And so with all of that inexperience, it took much longer.

Ramsay: Why didn't you hire experienced professionals?

Romero: I thought they made cool stuff at home and they would continue to do really cool stuff, so I figured, well, they're doing what they love, why wouldn't they do a good job here? But there's a lot more to working than just that.

Ramsay: They had to do a lot of learning on the job?

Romero: Yeah. They had to learn how to go to work and be on time, how to work with other people on a team, and how their work fits within a game that's in development versus a game that's already made. And they had to learn how to work with programmers because, if they're level designers, they've never even known a programmer. There were a million things I didn't even think about. They had to learn everything; it was like a school.

Ramsay: What were you doing?

Romero: I was making my game constantly, and so was Tom Hall, and so was Warren Spector. We were working on our games 100%.

In May at E3, I saw Quake II and it looked unbelievable. The technology looked amazing with the colored lighting, and I realized there's no way we could do that for Daikatana with the current engine. We could not be competitive with Quake II. In the contract, I could get any successive engine upgrades—Quake II was the upgraded version of the engine—but I had to wait for that before I could continue developing our game.

Waiting for Quake II took more time. It was 1998 before we could really get down to developing. We worked hard to make the game work with this new engine, and we thought we'd be able to ship by that Christmas. But Mike Wilson, who had been my CEO and who I had to fire, was planning to take my team out of Ion. He started a little company, got a development deal, and contacted people on my team.

In November, eight people left my team, and two others went to Id and 3D Realms. I lost ten people in one day. I had to try and staff up as soon as I could, so I could finish the game. When I got the new team in and new programmers, I hired people who had experience. And they found there was a lot of data that had to be remade; there were lots of issues with what had been created already. They decided, "We need to recreate a bunch of levels and art." So, we had to work really hard to try and release the game sometime in 1999.

And during 1999, we had a nightmare situation with two cofounders, so we got rid of them, leaving just Tom Hall and me in charge.

Ramsay: Was the loss of those ten people more of a blessing in disguise?

Romero: I don't know if the game would have been better if they stayed on or not. I couldn't say. They were kind of poisonous; they were not happy and they could have spread more poison throughout the company if they had stayed, so losing them could have been a blessing. But I have no idea what would have actually happened if they had stayed.

Ramsay: Losing them gave you an opportunity to bring in experienced professionals though.

Romero: Yeah, that kind of helped. It would have been much better if I had hired them in the beginning rather than halfway through the project at which point they're going, "What in the hell is this? What happened here?" And it's like, "What happened here was a bunch of modders tried to make a game, and now we have to fix it."

Ramsay: What was the nightmare situation with the two other cofounders?

Romero: Just a crazy number of issues, and ridiculous things like, "Hey, let's start a comic book division and hire a bunch of comic book artists." Like, what does that have to do with the games we're making? Nothing. You know, so they hire a bunch of people and that defocuses the other people working right next to them, who are like, "What? What are we doing? Why are we making comic books now?" And then Eidos finds out and they say, "What? You're not doing that. Fire all of those people that just moved here."

That's what they did on top of buying a whole bunch of computers for those people that then went unused; they were completely specialized machines. They wouldn't be useful development machines, so that money was just thrown into the trash. There were stupid things like that constantly.

While I was at a show or something, they took over the game, went to the dev team, and had them start changing all this stuff in my game. Just one thing after another. It was just a nightmare. It was super stupid. It would have been better if I'd just decided after that first team quit, "That's it. I'm rebooting the whole game. Just everybody go. I'm going to rebuild this the right way." But that would have probably sent Eidos into a panic and I didn't want to do that.

Ramsay: What was the process for removing cofounders?

Romero: The chairman of Eidos told them he didn't invest money in this company because of them; he invested because of me, and he doesn't care at all for them and they need to leave. They then negotiated how to get out.

Our next challenge was to help Tom's team finish Anachronox, which took another year. It took him a little over four years to do Anachronox. His game got out during the summer of 2001 and it was a really great game. He did a really good job on it. But we left Ion Storm in July, and in August, we started our next company, Monkeystone Games.

Ramsay: What did you want to do at Monkeystone Games?

Romero: I could see that the future of games was going to be handheld mobile phone games. It was pretty obvious. The Pocket PC was out, which was basically a proto-iPhone. I saw the crazy processing power, the graphics, the multitasking functionality, and I was like, "Oh, man, this is what everyone's going to have in their hand. Let's get into it quick, and start making mobile games."

The first thing we did was make Hyperspace Delivery Boy! for the Pocket PC. We started on the game in August 2001 and we shipped on December 23, 2001. It was a pretty cool game, but it didn't get any marketing, advertising, or anything like that. We worked on PC, Linux, and Mac versions, too.

After that, we made Congo Cube on BREW and J2ME, and we worked on Cartoon Network: Block Party for Majesco Entertainment for awhile. We got that thing done, and then worked on several other little things that never got out. We worked on Red Faction for the N-Gage. Nokia wanted that game done. So, we made that one and that was my last game at Monkeystone.

Ramsay: For the four years that Monkeystone was around, you released around 15 games. Sounds like a lot of games to make in that short period.

Romero: We were cranking! We were working really hard. That was an amazing time. There were so many different platforms we put stuff out on.

Ramsay: Without much in the way of marketing and advertising, was Monkeystone not in a position to make any real money on mobile games?

Romero: Yeah, we didn't have any business people, so that was not helpful. We didn't do all of the stuff we should have done.

Ramsay: You were a business person, weren't you?

Romero: That wasn't really my focus though. The focus for me when we were starting Monkeystone was coding 100% of the time. I don't want to do business stuff. I just want to code. But it got to the point that it became clear we were going to have to do something. The company had not made really any money and we needed to pay back a huge loan.

I was working on Red Faction for the N-Gage, and probably five months after that, I decided I had enough of Texas. I just had been there for too long. I knew everybody. So, I finished Red Faction, and I told Tom I wanted to leave Texas and get back to California. I said, "I'm thinking about going over to Midway in San Diego because San Diego's a really great town." And Tom was like, "You aren't leaving without me." We left in October 2003.

We had one of our guys at Monkeystone, Lucas Davis, run the company while we went to California. We still had some projects they should work on. And, with Tom and me leaving, that freed us up to figure out how to make the money we needed to pay off our loan. And so we went to work at Midway.

Midway was working on Area 51 in Austin, and they needed to have their multiplayer deathmatch mode done. We said, "Hey, we have a whole team that can do multiplayer no problem, and they'll just move down there to Austin." And so Midway said, "Hell, yeah, let's do that. Bring them down." I had Monkeystone move down to Austin and start working at Midway Austin. We made lots of money and paid the loan off. The company then had no debt.

When we completed Area 51, we shut down Monkeystone. Tom went back to Austin to work at KingsIsle on an MMO. I left slightly later to Redwood City to found my MMO company. Each of us took half of Monkeystone with us, so everyone got jobs. It was a good closing down of the company.

Ramsay: I understand you needed to pay off your debts, but why go back to being a full-time employee of a company you didn't control?

Romero: I really wanted a break from running companies. You know, the only other times in my whole life that I worked for someone else since I started making games was at Origin and Softdisk. I didn't spend very many years at any of them. I was at Origin for nine months or something, Softdisk for two years, and Midway for about two years. That's less than five years, probably.

Ramsay: Of the places you could've worked at, why Midway? Midway hadn't reported profit since 1999, and every year, they'd readily admit in their annual report, "We may not become profitable again despite our efforts."

Romero: I went there because they promised whatever it took to get 80% or higher review scores. I thought, "That's great. They're dedicated to quality. I'm interested." When they saw that 80% cost too much money, they were like, "Okay, well, we're done with that. We care about fiscal quarters and your

game must come out in Q4. Whatever is in that box is going on the shelf."
It was all corporate politics coming from on high.

Ramsay: What did the two of you manage to do at Midway?

Romero: Tom worked as a third-party creative director and I worked as the project lead on Gauntlet. I hired Josh Sawyer to be my lead game designer and he came up with a great idea for a game called Seven Sorrows. It was turning out to be a really cool game, but it was going into overtime. We knew it wasn't going to ship for Christmas 2004, but we knew it could ship for Christmas 2005.

Around the middle of 2005, we knew Gauntlet was not going to make Christmas. Midway had planned for five games to release at Christmas, and four of them were delayed. Three were at studios they had acquired, but Gauntlet was made at their own studio, so they had direct control over the game. They decided the game was definitely going to come out no matter how bad it is. They would just hack it up, put it in a box, and sell it. They knew I wasn't going to like being around for that, so they told me and the studio head, "Thanks very much. We have to do this hack job on your game. Thanks for everything."

Ramsay: You mentioned you started an MMO company then?

Romero: I took about three months off and went to Redwood City to start an MMO company with Rob Hutter that we initially called Slipgate Ironworks. We later renamed that company Gazillion Entertainment.

Ramsay: Gazillion has a confusing history. I thought Slipgate was a separate company that was bought by Gazillion, and various sources indicate Rob Hutter as the sole founder. Is that not the case? Can you set the record straight?

Romero: Yeah, in November 2004, Rob filed papers to create a company called NR2B Research. He spent time at GDC and E3 in 2005, meeting people to find somebody who could deal with designing an idea he had for an educational MMO and running an MMO team. Around the middle of 2005, I saw on LinkedIn that he was looking for a lead game designer, so I contacted him. After we talked, Rob decided, "You need to be a cofounder of this company."

"NR2B Research" was the name of the company before I got there, but we kept that name hidden. I told him, "It's going to be really hard for me to hire any game talent into a company called NR2B Research. That's not a game company name. I need to use something more exciting." He filed a DBA, or Doing Business As statement, for NR2B Research. I suggested "Slipgate Ironworks." We finally settled on the name "Gazillion Entertainment," and officially changed the name in the corporate record. NR2B Research didn't exist anymore.

Ramsay: By March 2009, the Wall Street Journal reported that Marvel Comics had signed a ten-year deal with Gazillion. What games were you going to make?

Romero: We actually started two Marvel games at once. One of them was a kid's game called Super Hero Squad, and the other one was Marvel Universe, which got retitled to Marvel Heroes. We hired David Brevik to make that game.

Ramsay: Shortly after, you left Gazillion. The company had basically just started to get going. Why did you want to get out?

Romero: Well, my game hit a critical tech issue and we couldn't proceed, so we had to stop development in October 2009. The board wanted to lessen any kind of risk, and original IP is a risk versus existing IP that you can just license. I don't really like to work on any licensed IP, so I was trying to get the company interested in Facebook games. The board decided we needed to focus on MMOs, but Facebook games were taking off. I was more excited about that.

My wife Brenda—we married on October 27, 2012—was the creative director over at a company called Lolapps in San Francisco. They had a game she took control of to get it to launch. She needed someone to fix it, so I came in as a consultant and worked for almost three months on the game design using the existing code base. I came up with a game called Ravenwood Fair, redid the graphics, and designed it. We had a team of about 12, including Brenda, on the game, and shipped on October 19, 2010. By the end of the first month after shipping, the game had four million players; it was doing really, really well.

Because Ravenwood Fair was doing so well, we decided to start a social games company. Brenda and I created a company called Loot Drop. The plan was for me to start talking to publishers while she continued working at Lolapps, and at some point, she would leave Lolapps and join Loot Drop full-time. That point was at the end of February 2011.

I got a deal with a company called RockYou and we started Loot Drop on January 11, 2011. We worked on a game called Cloudforest Expedition, a game I designed. We worked on that for about nine months until we handed the whole game over to RockYou to launch it, but they had an implosion and shut down all game-related publishing activities.

During that time, we started doing deals with EA, Ubisoft, and other companies. We got Loot Drop up to four games in development simultaneously. But at the end of January 2013, we decided to put Loot Drop into hibernation mode.

Ramsay: Why?

Romero: Well, one big reason was that we saw that all of the major players were losing interest in social. EA and Ubi were going, "Forget it. This market's done. Zynga's already jacked it up." And so they started cancelling projects. They saw Zynga going down and decided the bubble's gone. Instead of thinking of Facebook as a long-term viable game platform, they were just thinking about the bubble and the bubble was popping.

We decided, "Let's not keep pursuing projects from these big publishers in this space. Let's just wind it down." We'd figure out what we were going to do with our last game that we had actually almost finished. But we just weren't interested in continuing because the money wasn't flowing.

We shut the company down at the end of January last year. Over the next several months, Brenda became the first game designer in residence at UC Santa Cruz in December 2012, and I started to lecture at UCSC in April 2013.

During the summer, I did a consulting gig. That turned into being president of the company. That led to starting a studio for that company out here in Santa Clara, right across the street from UCSC's Extension building. Brenda became program director of the new master's degree program in games and playable media, and I became the creative director of the program.

In the fall, a new company contacted us about doing a game for Facebook. They told us about the IP and we were very excited about it. We decided, "Well, why don't we do it? Why not just do that game?"

We spun up Loot Drop again, hired some people, and we're going to be back in full production in February 2014. We've finished that game we had on hold for a year, and we're publishing that within weeks. So, hopefully, we'll get something from the half million we invested in that game last year.

Ramsay: It was an actual hibernation then!

Romero: Yes, it was an actual hibernation. We have Greg Costikyan working as our lead game designer. We're working here in the same building as the New York company. I have Loot Drop in the other half of the building, so both companies are in the same space right across the street from UCSC.

Ramsay: Sounds like you're building your own incubator?

Romero: Yeah, we have a little trio of companies. I've got three jobs, but it's working out really well, and we'll be back in full production again.

Ray Muzyka & Greg Zeschuk

Cofounders, BioWare Corp.

When **Ray Muzyka**, **Greg Zeschuk**, and Augustine Yip formally incorporated BioWare in 1995, they were medical doctors, recently graduated from the University of Alberta in Canada. Although Yip left soon after, Muzyka and Zeschuk moved forward, recruiting a passionate, hard-working team to build a company that would become a living legend.

BioWare, acquired by EA in 2007, is today best known for cinematic role-playing games, such as the Dragon Age series, the Mass Effect series, and the narrative-driven MMO, Star Wars: The Old Republic.

In the beginning, however, the steadily growing studio had rapidly gained notoriety for Baldur's Gate in 1998, Neverwinter Nights in 2002, and Star Wars: Knights of the Old Republic in 2003—all now considered not merely classic games but master classes in role-playing game design.

When this interview was conducted in early 2012, the company had just launched its MMO. Later that year, the duo retired from video games. Currently, Muzyka is an angel investor and entrepreneurial mentor, focused on information technology, medical innovations in diagnostics and therapeutics, and social entrepreneurship at Threshold Impact, while Zeschuk has been exploring craft beer through the web series, The Beer Diaries, and building a brewery in his hometown of Edmonton.

Ramsay: How did you two meet?

Zeschuk: Ray and I both went to the University of Alberta, and we actually met a little bit before medical school. We didn't really hang out or get to know each other very well, but I think we were in a chemistry class together and a zoology class, so we kind of saw each other around. It was actually when we both went to the University of Alberta Medical School that we met each other. That was when we found we had these really common interests: video games were probably the biggest one, but, you know, movies, comics, the usual fun entertainment stuff. But, definitely, a passion for video games was a big driver for us. I think we both had grown up playing them and liked the same kinds of games. We got to know each other pretty well there.

Ramsay: Medical school? You became doctors?

Muzyka: We were both medical doctors. We graduated from the University of Alberta in 1992 and specialized in family medicine. I also did emergency medicine in small towns across northern Alberta, and Greg did geriatric medicine. We practiced as we did our residencies and afterwards in medicine for a couple of years before we started BioWare. We incorporated BioWare in 1995 and both of us continued to practice medicine part time. We just did less and less medicine, and more and more BioWare.

I would do what they call locum tenens. In Latin, that means "temporary replacement." You go around and you fill in for other docs in small towns where you're the only doc for 100 miles or so, and I worked in the emergency room several times a month, or on weekends. I did that until 2000, shortly after I went back and got an MBA. I think Greg stopped doing medicine a couple of years before me, but both of us worked for quite a while doing medicine, too. We didn't leave medicine because we didn't like it. We liked it quite a bit actually, but we loved BioWare.

Ramsay: Why medicine anyway?

Zeschuk: At that time, computer games weren't even really established as career paths. We were very avid hobbyists. I don't think we went to school yet then, so we're talking about the mid-1980s. We never conceived of the possibility that you could have a career in video games. You know, we're from Edmonton, Canada. There were no companies that did that. There were some in Vancouver, but I think they were just starting out, like the Distinctive Software guys who would join EA.

Academically, we were pretty strong and really wanted to be doctors. I grew up from a young age wanting to be one. I think Ray as well, but he can probably speak to that better than I can. And then we started making medical educational software while we were in school, and just played around, making games as hobbyists. When we saw what was being done in med school, we said, "Wait a minute! We can do as well as this and even better!" That's when we actually realized we could try the game thing. That was really what led to us pursuing it.

Muzyka: Oh, it's a similar answer for me. I always wanted to be a doctor growing up. I also enjoyed computer games quite a lot since I was maybe 9 or 10 years old when I first got an Apple II. That's when I started to learn how to program. I taught myself programming in BASIC and assembly, and later Pascal, Fortran, and other languages. I just really enjoyed that. I found it was a really fun hobby for me.

We transitioned into BioWare from medicine because our hobbies became our careers and our careers became our hobbies. Starting out, we didn't pay ourselves salaries for the first few years of BioWare. Medicine was how we made enough money to live on, and to get money we could invest back into the company as it was growing in the first four or five years. Video games were always our passion and they still are. You know, it's still one of my favorite activities even today.

Ramsay: When you decided to get into video games while you were doing medicine, was your decision: to start developing video games, or to start a company to develop video games?

Muzyka: The decision was to make video games, and the vehicle to do that was BioWare. We actually really enjoyed the business aspects as well. Right from the beginning, we didn't have anybody who had ever made a video game before on our team until after our first two products, Shattered Steel and Baldur's Gate, were released. Initially, we had no professional "managers," professional financial advisors, HR experts, or anything like that; we had no operational people. It was just Greg and me, and our teams making games. And Greg and I trying to figure it out as we went.

How do you build a company and scale it to 60 or 70 people? At that point, we hired a couple of great people who are still at BioWare. One was in finance, our director of finance at the time, and another one was a director of HR. They were at BioWare going on almost 20 years in different roles. They're awesome people, and we continued to hire great people around us.

But, yeah, the business of games was really exciting and engaging in its own right. We enjoyed the idea of creating systems, structures, and processes that would allow the teams to be successful, to communicate with them well, and incent them to deliver and feel like they were rewarded and actually part of the process. You know, I found that really engaging. I still do.

New business models, organizational structures, and thinking about marketing, PR, finance, and HR are all really interesting challenges. So, I think for us, it was probably a mix of both. We wanted to make games, and then we learned how fun it was to have a growing, vibrant company.

Ramsay: Any experience with startups before?

Zeschuk: No, neither of us. It was a lot of learning on the job. We spent a lot of time being students in a sense. We did a lot of reading and research, and we tried to learn as much as we could. We tried to meet other people who had video game startups and learn from them, but a lot of it was figuring it out ourselves. It was an interesting experience because up in Edmonton, there weren't a lot of other video game companies. There wasn't really anyone to ask or talk to about starting something. It was kind of interesting that way.

Ramsay: Did you think starting a company would be easy?

Muzyka: That's interesting. We didn't have an exit strategy, and we didn't have any expectations, per se, of what success looked like. We weren't seeking a specific outcome. We were just striving to do the best we could, hiring great people around us. Every day, you try and make every aspect of what you do better, and that's exemplified by our core values, which BioWare still follows today. There are three of them.

One is quality in our products for our customers. We try and make the best games we can, try and be humble about it, and try and improve them. When they're not perfect, we try and do the best we can to make them better so the next one is better than the last.

Quality in the workplace is another core value. That's for our employees. And that's about trying to make the workplace better every day, where you try and do something to make it better for our valued and passionate teams, and just everything you can do to make it feel like it's not just a job. It has to be a career, something they can invest in for decades and stay with us. We actually have a lot of people who have been with us for a long time. I just did a one-on-one with somebody who was one of our very first employees back at Edmonton. He's now down in Austin, leading the creative team there. We have a lot of people like that who continue to grow, flourish, and continue to advance and progress.

And the third core value is entrepreneurship for our investors, for shareholders, for partners, and so on. In the early days of BioWare, that was us and our employees. We gave a lot of stock to our staff, so they did well through our various company sales. Now, it's our EA parent company. We're shareholders in that company, and obviously, there are wide holdings of that as well.

We have to try and find a balance between all these core values and make sure that the needs of our investors, our employees, and our customers are always being met. Not one at the exclusion of the others, not two at the exclusion of the other, but all three together, trying to find a sustainable environment. That has always been our philosophy of how we approached it, and that helped us a lot to make decisions and just balance things every step of the way.

And that's been probably the most consistent thing during our journey over the last couple of decades. Everything else changes: the business, the products... they evolve, as do the people. Some stay, some go, we add new ones, you add new locations, but the things that are really the most enduring about BioWare and the things that'll last long after we're gone are our core values and what they mean to our brand.

Ramsay: Were those values articulated at the start?

Muzyka: They evolved, actually. The core value we started with was quality. That's what we want. We want quality. It's more than that though; it's about quality in the context of humility and integrity. Then we split quality into quality in our products, quality in our workplace, and we added quality in entrepreneurship to make the complete package.

We describe these as our core values, and we talk about that all the time with all of our teams at our eight locations. And they believe it because we try and act true to it, and when we're not, we try and fix it. We try to make sure it's more clear and specific. As our teams get bigger, everyone must understand what the core values mean.

Ramsay: Did you put together a business plan to deliver on that first value?

Muzyka: We had a business plan. I think we were seeking bank financing, grants, or things like that. We didn't get a lot. Actually, it's kind of funny. We were told by the bankers we dealt with that any loans we'd get would be based on the fact that we were medical doctors. They knew we would be personally good for it, if it ever came to that.

As a startup video game company in a primarily oil- and gas-rich province in Canada, video games weren't really understood by a lot of the banking people we dealt with. They were good folks, but they really dealt with more traditional industries. We were lucky to make great games that sold well, and we were lucky to get great publishing partners who helped us to get returns, and invest back into and grow the company.

Ramsay: Did the bankers think you wouldn't succeed?

Muzyka: I think they hoped we would. I think it was more they didn't understand the business we were in. This was 20 years ago in a province where there wasn't any software development, let alone video game development. It was more of a foreign concept to the locals.

Zeschuk: We also didn't come with any obvious expertise or skills in the area, so I think banks are not in the business of lending money to anything that risky without strong collateral. We were just two young punks in our early 20s, showing up to say, "Hey, we're going to make video games. Give us some money." It was a bit of a stretch.

Ramsay: Did you have any mentors?

Zeschuk: That was another funny thing because of where we were; there was no real opportunity. There was no one we could call on for advice. There was just no one around, so we were mentor-less. We had some good advisors: you know, a good accountant and lawyer. But we didn't have any real startup people.

Muzyka: Both of us went back and got MBAs from, I'd say, 1999 to 2001 for me, and a couple years after that for you, right, Greg?

Zeschuk: Yeah, 2004, I think.

Muzyka: At good schools in Canada. We did Executive MBAs. I went to Ivey, and Greg went to Queens. We're always going back and forth about which one is better. I won't comment on that, of course, but we learned a lot. That was for a growth opportunity. We were scaling quite a bit when I went back to get my MBA, and then we were scaling the company a different way when Greg went to get his. Both experiences really gave us a lot of direct insight into where we could take BioWare.

All of the students were professionals who usually had been working for more than seven years in a professional role somewhere. We were able to get their insights and feedback, and apply the systems and processes that the MBA brings to our everyday work at BioWare the next day. That was a really good experience.

Ramsay: In retrospect, was not having any formal mentors valuable?

Muzyka: It's interesting. I question it. I could see it being really valuable to have them, and I can also see it being valuable not to. We started out in a way that was kind of scary and new, but as a result, we were fearless.

In the first few years of BioWare, we took on risks that, in retrospect, were a little crazy at times. We paid attention to everything we could, and we hired good people. Everybody was willing to look at things with fresh eyes as well, so we asked dumb questions that sometimes led to good answers. Sometimes they just led to us learning things that other people knew for a long time before us, but either way, we grew.

Now, I think it would have been nice to have a blend of people who were really savvy and experienced, and people who were on a new startup, or a team coming in from a different industry, with fresh perspectives. Asking innocent questions can lead to powerful answers.

Ramsay: When exactly did you start BioWare?

Zeschuk: There was pre-BioWare stuff in the 1990 to 1992 timeframe, and we were definitely doing stuff in 1994. We officially incorporated in 1995, but there were a few years of exploration prior to that.

Ramsay: Was part of that exploration coming up with the name?

Zeschuk: Yeah, it definitely was. It's funny because naming these things is kind of interesting. People have had all kinds of thoughts about the name over the years. We called it BioWare for a variety of reasons. There's a bit of a play on the fact that we're doctors, and we had a concept of software for humans as the core of what we did.

Ramsay: What were some of the other names that you considered?

Muzyka: I can't even remember now.

Zeschuk: I think we had some sheets of paper with stuff written on them, but I don't know where those are.

Muzyka: The only one I know now is BioWare.

Zeschuk: Well, remember, at one point, we were going to call it Ascendant BioWare, but everyone said that's way too long and wordy.

Muzyka: Yeah, with the software for humans concept, our first logo actually had a computer hand and a human hand. If you do a search, you'll probably see that in some of our early logos.

Ramsay: When did you get your first office?

Muzyka: We worked out of Greg's basement for a year or two before we incorporated, and we stayed there until we got the first office in 1995.

Zeschuk: Oh, yeah. 1995 was the one with the really bad circuit breaker.

Muzyka: And we had only four circuit breakers! At the end, before we totally exceeded that space requirement, we had something like 50 people in there. We moved a year or two later to a new space that was bigger and nicer, but in that early first office, there were only four plugs in the wall. We had a power-up sequence for the computers in the office so that we didn't blow the circuit breaker for the whole building. Everybody would be like, "I'm on. I'm on. I'm on." We had found by trial and error that if you turned them on in a certain order, it wouldn't create a power overload. If you turned on the computers in the wrong order, for sure, it would just flip the switch and you had to run downstairs, get the key, and open up the electrical box. It was an interesting space. It was a fun time, but I'm glad we moved.

Ramsay: How did you choose the location?

Muzyka: It's what we could afford at the time, and it was a central location that was close to where we each lived. I lived a little bit on the north side of the river, and Greg lived on the south side. It was a quick drive. The office had some parking space behind the building, so we could accommodate the first ten people we hired.

And it was near the university, so it was good for new grads who happened to live in the area. They could walk there. It was just down the street from the big university at Edmonton, which has like 40,000 students. We hired a lot of good folks from there.

Ramsay: How much did you spend to get the company started?

Muzyka: I don't know. We maxed out. I think we took everything we personally owned and invested it in the company.

Zeschuk: It was definitely tens of thousands of dollars to small hundreds of thousands.

Muzyka: Probably several hundred thousand dollars each. That was basically everything we had, and we maxed out our debt and credit cards. We just kind of went for it. It was like, whatever it took, this is what we're doing. It never occurred to us there would be risk in that. It never really occurred to me. I think, Greg, you considered whether medicine would be something you'd go back to. For me, it was a fun hobby at that point.

Zeschuk: I thought of it as a safety net. If we blew it, I could go back.

Muzyka: I never thought of it that way. For me, it was BioWare was what we were doing, and, of course, it was going to be successful because we're going to work hard, hire great people, make great games, and that would lead to good results. Those results might take years, but we didn't care about that. It was about building something that was going to be awesome. It would entertain the world, and we really didn't worry about the risk that much. It was a little stressful. Sometimes we were like, "Hey I don't have any money. I guess I've got to go work as a doctor this weekend because I actually can't pay my rent." And there would be times where I'd be doing that and I think you as well.

Zeschuk: I was able to mooch off my wife, so I was lucky.

Muzyka: Yeah, I got married later.

Ramsay: Greg, you said you had a family?

Zeschuk: I had the beginning of a family when we started. My wife was also a doctor. Those were interesting times. We did a lot on the go, and certainly being a startup, it was very busy, but it was certainly a lot of fun.

Ramsay: What impact did starting up BioWare have on your family life?

Zeschuk: Oh, just less of it. The reality is that any startup is an enormous draw on your time and focus. That's a key thing: it's not just the time, but where your mind is. What you're thinking about all the time is a really, really big factor in that for sure.

Ramsay: Ray, you married later?

Muzyka: Just after I got my MBA.

Ramsay: Did either of you regret focusing on video games instead of practicing medicine, something you wanted to do as kids?

Muzyka: No, neither of us. I liked medicine a lot. I really liked it. I didn't leave it because I didn't like it. I've still got my license, actually. I don't practice anymore. I'm not going to go back to it, but I just keep renewing. I'm retired formally as a doctor, but for me, I went to school for a long time, ten years or so, and it's something I'm proud of. I'm glad I was able to help people's lives for the years that I did practice. I did a lot of emergency medicine in underserved areas in rural Alberta. It was really hard work, but really fun, really engaging, really exciting. For me, I realized early on that I loved BioWare. I love video games.

Ramsay: When you started BioWare, you didn't think there were risks, but in retrospect, how was starting this new company risky?

Muzyka: I wouldn't say we didn't think there were real risks. We actually were really worried about risks all the time quite actively. I think our medical training was helpful in that regard. As doctors, you learn early on that you can't be cavalier and not pay attention to the details. You really have to pay attention to all the details because the small things can come back to bite you in the ass.

If you want to take care of your patient, whether a human patient or a company, they're your customers and you have to make sure they're taken care of. It was more that we didn't worry about the risks, but we did try to deal with them. That was what I was trying to say, but go ahead, Greg.

Zeschuk: Yeah, I think the only real risk for us was failure, right? If you don't try anything, you don't accomplish anything. Failure isn't really something you should be thinking about. That's just the side effect of not succeeding.

Everything you do is risky. Actually, almost everything in life worth doing is risky. That's how I thought about it.

Ramsay: BioWare was two people. When did it become three?

Muzyka: No, it was three initially. There was a third founder who left the company after a year and a half. Augustine Yip, who is a medical doctor as well, was with us in our class. He went back to medicine full-time in Calgary a year or two after we incorporated. After we incorporated, we started hiring employees. In 1996, we really started to scale up in terms of employees, and we just kept growing at pretty much a steady rate from there. We had one team, two teams, three, three and a half, four teams, five, and then two locations, three, and so on. Over the last 20 years, we've had steady growth.

Ramsay: Why did your third cofounder join in the first place?

Muzyka: Well, I think he loved video games as well, and he was our cofounder, and he was passionate about the idea of making entertainment and video games. But he had a wife and kids, a growing family. I think he couldn't not have the income from medical work like we did. Greg and I didn't pay ourselves salaries for four or five years. It was hard at times. There were times where it was pretty tough for us personally. But when he decided to leave, we bought him out and it was all very amicable.

Ramsay: After securing office space, what did you do? What did you do with the hundreds of thousands of dollars you two invested?

Muzyka: We put the money in over time as we needed, but we had started a game, Shattered Steel, with some talented external contractors. We then hired the folks in, finished it up, and published it with Interplay, our first publishing partner. Then we started the second game and that was Baldur's Gate. It was going to be a return to the role-playing games that we grew up with and loved as kids. We published that with Interplay, too, and moved on from there to MDK2. We just kept on adding more teams, trying to reach new consumers, create innovative gameplay, build games with more online modes and more different forms of interactivity, and improve the interface.

At the same time, we were trying to improve our systems, processes, and structures. We were continually evolving, from a team-based structure to a loose matrix structure to a formalized matrix structure. When we went to MBA school, we learned more about the different kinds of operational structures, systems, and incentive systems to get people to stay with us long term. We tried to implement all those kinds of communication systems and processes.

BioWare evolved depending on where we were, who was with us, and how big we were. Meanwhile, the teams themselves were getting bigger the whole time, too. We started Shattered Steel with a team that was probably in the teens or so.

Zeschuk: Oh, 13, I think.

Muzyka: 13 peak. The peak team size for Baldur's Gate was 60 right before we launched. That was a pretty big team for that time in the industry. We had to improvise and find a lot of what at the time were fairly innovative practices in communication, project tracking, project management, and communication asset management. There weren't a lot of solutions available, so we had to create our own.

Later, we found there was good licensed software from enterprise companies that we could emulate, and we learned a lot from looking at Microsoft, Oracle, and other big software companies, what they did as best practices, and BioWare continued to grow from there.

Eventually, we had localized teams of a hundred people or bigger. Today, our teams consist of hundreds of people, but they're spread across the world in different locations. It creates even more interesting challenges for management and communication, such as to try to partner with outsourcers effectively and all those good things.

Ramsay: Did you see yourselves as an entertainment company or a game developer?

Muzyka: We were technically a developer, so really both of those, and then we added community, public relations, and marketing functions. Now we're a publisher as part of EA and we're still a developer at the same time, but we also have marketing, community, online and live team services, community management, customer relationship management, customer support, and all other functions of a fully integrated online company.

Basically, all of our products now have embedded online capabilities. But from the beginning, I guess I always thought of us as more of an entertainment company. Our competitive environment wasn't just games; it was also television, books, movies, and music. Today, BioWare's even developing social and mobile games.

Ramsay: What business model did you originally conceive for BioWare?

Zeschuk: I think, primarily, we ended up towards the development side, but we actually tended to add a lot of stuff that publishers would do, just because we felt it was stronger to do things like community locally. We tended to develop, too, and then do deals to get the games published.

We worked our first one with the Interplay guys way, way back in the day. We're still friends with a lot of those guys too. It was actually a really great relationship. Through Interplay, we had Shattered Steel, Baldur's Gate, Neverwinter Nights, and then Atari as well. We've done a lot of work with LucasArts. We kind of forget that we've actually been working on and off for well over a decade with them, too.

Ray said we differentiated ourselves by having a really strong community of our own, and our own public relations and marketing to supplement and to support our partners and also push the BioWare message directly as well. It's interesting that now that BioWare's a label within EA, that's the exact model we follow. Everything we used to do in parallel is now central to our overall business. We're not only a developer; we are effectively a publisher at the same time.

Ramsay: How did Shattered Steel come about? Why did you think that would be a good flagship title for BioWare?

Zeschuk: We liked big robots. Those were the days of MechWarrior and those kinds of games. It was actually a real popular genre, so that seemed like the thing to do at the time. One of the things we still do after all these years is find out what the team's passionate about, what they're interested in, what they like, and work with them to do that. So, we started with the framework, saying we want this to be a 3D multiplayer big robot combat game. And then we got the team together, and

Ramsay: Did you two come up with the concept?

Zeschuk: Typically, with all of our games, there's no one person who can say, "Hey, I did the whole thing." There's usually a large group of people involved. The producer, lead programmer, art director, lead designer, and the senior team would work on a concept together because we wanted everyone to collectively buy into it as a group. In this case, it was the whole team.

Ramsay: Did you develop Shattered Steel on spec?

Zeschuk: It was our design. Even when we did licensed titles, we would drive all of the elements, and then work with a publisher at various levels. Obviously, in the case of the Star Wars stuff, we worked very tightly in partnership with Lucas. However, we were never work-for-hire developers. We always had felt the need to drive the creative process.

Ramsay: Interplay and BioWare. Who approached whom?

Muzyka: When we pitched our first game, we had a list of the top ten publishers, and we divided the list into two. I called five of them, Greg called five of them, and we kept calling them until they took our calls. In the end, we got nine out of the 10 to make an offer, but initially, none wanted to talk to us because we were an unknown developer with no track record. And then we got most of them to make offers once they tried out the demo, and read the pitch, marketing plan, and the dev plan we sent them. We did something similar for Baldur's Gate. We only sent it to five publishers though, and we got offers from, I think, three out of the five pretty quickly. We went with Interplay again because we had a good relationship working with them.

Ramsay: How did you get the publishers to talk to you?

Muzyka: Sheer stubbornness and persistence. We just kept calling.

Zeschuk: And when they looked at the demos, they went, "Whoa!"

Muzyka: We made a point of sending a solid demo and some other materials. You know, here's our vision for how we're going to build the game, here's how we're going to use our resources, and here's what we anticipated people would want to see. We tried to imagine us in their seats. What would we want to see when people tried to pitch us an investment opportunity? In retrospect, it was kind of crude, but we did the best we could. I think they liked the quality of the demo, and they liked the fact that we were really stubborn. When we flew in and met them, they liked meeting us and obviously saw something they liked.

Ramsay: Who were your first hires?

Muzyka: First hires. Let's see. I think one of the very first hires was a really talented programmer who became our lead programmer for many, many years. He left a few years ago, but he was with us for over a decade. We hired a designer who's still with us. He became a lead designer, director of a design department, and then a creative director over a much larger product and team. Some artists have grown tremendously as well; one is the art lead in Montreal.

Ramsay: And given your location and the period during which you founded the company, how did you find your first recruits?

Muzyka: We initially hired a lot of really talented yet fairly inexperienced, in video games, people, and we used unconventional methods to do it. We hired a guy who became a really seasoned tech artist for us for many years. He had never turned on a computer before, but he knew how to paint; his primary occupation was carving wooden hunting decoys. We felt he would have good 3D spatial skills, and he could learn how to use a computer and all of the modeling programs to become a good animator and 3D modeler. And sure enough, he did. He was enthusiastic, motivated, and talented.

One of our most senior designers across our entire label within EA had never actually designed anything other than D&D modules. He ran a comic book store. He was the most popular Dungeon Master in this little town in northern Alberta called Grand Prairie. Everybody wanted to be in his adventures when he was dungeon mastering. They always talked about the great stories he would tell, and how they wanted to be part of that. There was actually a line of people in that town who wanted to get into it. He could only run a couple of these adventures at a time because they were time consuming. We thought that guy would be a really good designer. He creates worlds that people believe in and want to be a part of.

We interviewed another guy in a restaurant, and he brought some sketches on a napkin to us and they looked pretty good. He showed us some paintings he had done that were pretty promising. He didn't have a huge body of work, but he was sure enthusiastic and very talented. I hired him and now he's one of our most senior lead artists.

All these things happened more than ten years ago, and of course, now we have a very different hiring approach. We have the people who are going to work with the candidates do the interviews. But in the early days, Greg and I hired people based on their passion and enthusiasm, their ability to work hard, and whether they demonstrated related skills and capabilities; experience was a bonus.

Ramsay: How did you identify what games to develop?

Zeschuk: The early process was whatever tickled our fancy. I wasn't joking when I said we made Shattered Steel because "hey, we like big robots." Ray and I both had this driving passion to make a top-down RPG. We felt there was a really good market for that.

Muzyka: But I would also clarify that we tried to think about what the market would bear, too. Even in the early days, we tried to think about the potential for our customers to like it, too.

Zeschuk: I would say that, but we shouldn't put too much emphasis on that realm.

Muzyka: No, but it was a blend. It was a mix of passion and commercial reality. We didn't overrate the commercial reality. If anything, we overrated the passion, but we were always cognizant of both.

Zeschuk: I think passion was probably the primary driver. Certainly, from a creative perspective, I think that was the fundamental piece where we felt we really wanted to make stuff we would like, our friends would like, and later on, it got a lot more sophisticated.

I'm kind of counter referencing it to the way we do now, which is very different because we have this enormous amount of information at our fingertips and you can do lots of market analyses. Back then, none of that stuff was really there. It didn't really exist, so you were left with your gut, your impressions, whatever information you could glean, and what you think of the market, and it was very hard to analyze it.

Ramsay: You've said that BioWare is an eight-location studio group with more than 1,400 staff worldwide within EA. How large did BioWare become prior to the Pandemic relationship and joining EA?

Zeschuk: We were actually in the process of starting the Austin studio right around when we entered the Pandemic-Elevation relationship. We had one location and we were fairly large at that time. We still had a few products going. I think we were probably 400 people, somewhere in that zone. That's more or less about right, isn't that, Ray?

Muzyka: Yeah, probably something like that. We had 400 by the early days of the Elevation partnership. As we grew, we added another location after that. Montreal probably started about five years ago when we joined EA, Mythic joined in 2009, and then some of the other studios joined in the last year or so.

Ramsay: What were the unique challenges of growing and running business at a much larger size than a startup?

Muzyka: When we were in the matrix structure, we at that time had five products running and probably more at various stages of completion. They were different sizes, different types of products, and that was all within the one location. And then we were starting a new studio up, so that meant a second location, and we would have people working on different products at different times moving around.

We had to figure out a way to manage resources: allocating people to products, enabling each product to get their day in the sun, and allowing them to launch and be successful. We would have regular resource planning meetings every month, and we'd have regular product updates as well. We'd do those on video conference with Austin when the Austin studio started wrapping up, and we would do them in person for the other products. We had a number of processes that were put in place over the first ten years of BioWare that allowed us to manage different teams remotely, and to put in more production rigor, project management, and move from waterfall to agile development.

Ramsay: Was growing BioWare to 400 people easy?

Zeschuk: It was definitely not easy. There are probably two main areas that are challenging. One was just the fact that we were independently financed and ran independently; we weren't owned by anyone. It was a very big studio, to the point where if for some reason we weren't able to make payroll, there was nothing you can do to really make it at that size.

Two was that BioWare was not in a location where there's commonly a lot of folks making games, so most of the people end up being imports from elsewhere. That was, in a sense, a benefit unto itself in that when people joined BioWare, they really wanted to be at BioWare. But it was challenging to find people; it was a slow process. We couldn't grow really fast, which was an awful good thing in a way, but the people we did have were very dedicated and really into the products we made.

Ramsay: How did you feel about growing the company to that size?

Muzyka: Growing for the sake of growing wasn't really a goal per se, nor did either of us have an exit plan at any point. We always had the goal of enabling the company to get more valuable, and we had a lot of employee shareholders to whom we gave out shares—basically everybody prior to the Elevation deal. They all benefitted from that and the EA transaction. We had a long-term view.

We wanted to build value, and we also wanted to do interesting things. We felt we could take on new products, move into new genres, and new types of games that would still be high-quality and fit the BioWare brand fundamentals. But doing that carefully and growing along the way was a way to achieve that diversity, and ultimately, reducing risk because you're reaching different kinds of consumers with different publishing partners.

And if one product wasn't as big of a hit as the others, you had other ways to bring in revenue and cash flow. Growing was all part of risk diversification, the desire to do new things, and building enterprise value for ourselves and our shareholders, especially our employees.

Ramsay: Let's switch gears. Recently, BioWare launched a great big MMO in the Star Wars universe, but you've worked with LucasArts for a long time. In 2003, you released Star Wars: Knights of the Old Republic. How did you get that opportunity?

Muzyka: We got a call from Simon Jeffery, who was the president of LucasArts then, out of the blue one day. We had a product opening coming up, but we hadn't really considered a Star Wars game; we didn't know that was a possibility. When we got the call, both of us were like, "Hell yeah! We have to talk to our teams." We talked to our teams and asked if this was a product we should pursue. They said "hell yeah," too.

Zeschuk: It was the easiest product decision meeting ever. We had written on a board some big stuff, some big names, and then we put Stars Wars up last. Everyone was like "why are you joking with us?" And we said, "No, that's for real!" And so it was done.

Muzyka: "Gentlemen, I'm a big fan of your work. If you're interested, I'd love to work with you." That's basically what Simon said. We were like "holy crap." We were huge fans of Star Wars, and so were our teams. For us, it was a huge honor. First Star Wars RPG ever. It still is a great honor to work with LucasArts on the Star Wars franchise.

Ramsay: Why did they approach you of all the developers?

Muzyka: We had a good track record at that point. We had released Baldur's Gate, Neverwinter Nights, Baldur's Gate 2, MDK, and Shattered Steel. We had some good products behind us. I think Simon had played our games, and the other people there thought well of us. We had a good reputation for quality, and he wanted to partner with some developers who were seen as the main experts in different categories. We had signed up a few other partners around that time for what ended up being pretty good products as well, so it was fortunate that he wanted to reach out and find some new external partnerships then.

Ramsay: A couple of years later, in 2005, BioWare and Pandemic Studios merged. How did that happen?

Zeschuk: A guy name Greg Richardson, who was working with Elevation Partners, spoke to us at GDC in 2005. He said, "I'm working with this company, and they're making investments in the games business and putting games companies together." It was far from the first time we've been pitched. We had been pitched many times by many people, and we'd known Greg from his time as head of EA Partners back in the early 2000s. In a lot of those meetings, you come out going "oh, it's a crazy long shot." But we came out of that meeting with Greg going "wow, that actually seems like it could happen!"

Muzyka: We were looking for funding at that time, too. We wanted to build an MMO. That was right when we were starting up the Austin studio. We were seeking funding, and we had this invitation of funding from a group that seemed quite interesting. When we met John Riccitiello and the other partners at Elevation, that really persuaded us that these were really smart people we could learn from. For me, that was the most compelling part.

Zeschuk: Yeah, we learned from the people. We progressed personally in an educational kind of learning a business way. Absolutely.

Muzyka: They were really good partners at the fund. And then learning that we would partner with Pandemic? It was a group we respected, and it was great to have partners on the development side who were doing different kinds of games that complemented ours. We could visit their offices and brainstorm, and vice versa. It was a really good time.

It was a good two-and-a-half-year period where we worked closely with Elevation Partners. We were directors in a new company, and we got funding that allowed us to start off the MMO, as well as to pursue some creative new funding for our own development so we could become a quasi publisher ourselves. That was the idea.

Ramsay: And very soon BioWare Pandemic was acquired by EA. Under EA, do you have less control over BioWare than you had?

Muzyka: I think we have control over more things, and we have the ability to do more things more powerfully than we could before, but we also had to accept that we're part of a larger company. We're publicly traded and all the constraints that come with that; you have to adapt.

Ramsay: How would you respond to critics who claim that EA forces BioWare to do only things EA would do?

Muzyka: BioWare is a part of EA now, a business within EA, and each business within EA drives their respective business. They have targets to hit, goals, and objectives; and some of those are corporate objectives and others are local business objectives. But we're not separate from EA. We are EA, and we're BioWare, too.

Ramsay: That's a good way to look at it. I asked you about control, and usually entrepreneurs come out of acquisitions with less control, but I wonder now: does it matter? Are you still able to do what you set out to do? Is it possible to come out of an acquisition with more independence?

Zeschuk: I think yeah. Interestingly, neither of us had worked in a big company before. We joined EA, and that's definitely different than working as part of a group like Elevation Partners. It was interesting. It was very interesting for us in that EA gives you a lot of opportunity to control your destiny. I always joke that it gives you the rope you can use to hang yourself if you want. It's a lot of independence, a lot of responsibility put onto you. For example, marketing eventually got folded into our entire org, and now marketing is part of the BioWare label. We now have more control over marketing than before.

Creatively, we've always been in command. We make games how we want to make them. But in terms of just working at a big company, there's a certain amount of reporting you have to do, and rules and regulations you have to follow. Those don't take away your independence at all, but it's a practical thing that has to happen.

At the end of the day, we've been able to do things we otherwise wouldn't have been able to do independently. The only thing that I can't overemphasize enough is that we now have peers and other studios trying things out and learning from each other. If we have a challenging situation, we have lots of people we can talk to about it, who you can trust from a confidentiality perspective. Because you're in the same company, you're pulling the same direction. There are lots of benefits.

Ramsay: Ray said that part of the reason why BioWare did the deal with Elevation Partners, and was subsequently acquired by EA, was because you wanted to raise money for an MMO. Why did you need to go through all of that to build Star Wars: The Old Republic?

Zeschuk: MMOs are just huge Herculean undertakings. One of the analogies we give people is that it's very much like making one of the launch games for the Xbox and not only do you have to do that, you also have to create Xbox Live at the same time and all those things have to work flawlessly together on a certain day to get out. And not only that, the game has to be great and the platform has to be great.

In my personal experience, building an MMO has been one of the bigger challenges I've had the pleasure of dealing with. And, again, we had a fabulous team who made that possible. I think the number of things you have to juggle, the number of people you have to interface with, and the number of items you have to keep on top of is massive. You really do need a very big team to cover all those things.

Ramsay: Was there any new technical expertise that you had to introduce into BioWare?

Muzyka: Definitely. There's a whole range of different specializations. You're required to have online expertise around server architecture, infrastructure and network operations, platform, billing capabilities, security, and on and on. There's pretty much every aspect that you can imagine you'd need to have data flowing back and forth between computers in a secure, seamless, and stable manner. You pretty much have to stack up all those things. So, again, it's great being part of a larger company that has online infrastructure, that has those capabilities, that has people we can draw on, and that has the knowledge and skill sets to add to the success and likelihood of a good outcome.

Ramsay: Reflecting on those challenges, do you think you would have been able to do The Old Republic without having been acquired by EA?

Zeschuk: I think it would have been really difficult. We were able to utilize a lot of infrastructure and expertise within the company, and then there's the simple issue of capital. It's an expensive undertaking to make an MMO, so you need partners who are committed and backing it fully. I think we really had that. We really had a lot of support to make it possible. If we hadn't have done it with EA, it probably would have been a very different type of game or a different game altogether. It's hard to imagine. It's always difficult to look retrospectively at those things, given the number of variables in the equation, but being part of EA was definitely a key part of being able to deliver that product.

Ramsay: What do you think about your adventure, from plucky startup to major business unit of one of the largest game publishers in the world?

Zeschuk: It's been a fun ride for sure. When we look back and really consider that when we started everything, we had no vision of where we were going to end up. We just wanted to make great games. We wanted to be successful, but we didn't even really know what that meant.

It's kind of unbelievable now looking back at our careers. For both me and Ray, we've been doing this for about 20 years, which, in the games business, puts us into the serious veteran stage. Obviously, there are some dudes out there who have been doing it longer, but 20 years is still an awfully long time. I think the amount of change in the industry has been incredible. That's kept the industry really fresh and exciting for us. It's flabbergasting to look back now, for me at least.

Muzyka: I would just add that I agree with all of that. To see the industry develop from the inside over the last couple of decades, having grown up loving video games and then being able to make them, is such a privilege. And it has been such an honor to work with such great people, from the early years of BioWare as an independent developer to getting private equity investment with Elevation Partners to becoming part of EA and becoming a label within EA. Every stage has been just really fun, really fascinating, really memorable, and enjoyable. Hopefully, 20 years from now, BioWare and EA will still be vibrant and strong.

Ramsay: As industry veterans, if you two left EA right now and started a new company, how would you start that company differently?

Muzyka: For me, I don't think I'd start another video game company. I achieved so much more than I ever dreamed possible through BioWare. I couldn't imagine doing that again in a way that would be as satisfying or fulfilling. I'm really proud that we've been able to achieve the things we've done, and I think BioWare's best work is still ahead.

If we did form a new company, at least to give advice on how to form a new company, I'd say understand your core values early. Try and set a vision for your team, and measure your decisions against those values and the vision. Be ready to be flexible in your strategies, and adapt them to the environment around you. Try and hire people who are passionate and share your core values. And just try to do the best you can every day. Try to improve everything you do in one small way, if nothing else, and you'll improve every single day when you do that.

Ramsay: Greg, anything you want to add?

Zeschuk: Not really. Ray hit it on the head.

Raph Koster

Cofounder, Metaplace

Raphael "Raph" Koster is an award-winning game designer and creative director, whose work on Ultima Online for Electronic Arts and Star Wars Galaxies for Sony Online Entertainment has generated revenues exceeding more than a half-billion U.S. dollars.

A pioneer of massively multiplayer online games, Koster is regarded as one of the video game industry's foremost authorities on games. His book A Theory of Fun for Game Design, published in 2004, is now a classic text used in classrooms around the world.

In 2006, Koster left his position as chief creative officer at SOE to start Metaplace, a venture-backed developer of virtual world technologies, with product development executive John Donham. Four years later, Metaplace was acquired by Playdom, a leading social games company, which was subsequently acquired by Disney Interactive.

Ramsay: How did you get started in the video game industry?

Koster: A friend of mine, Rick Delashmit, applied for a job at a game company called Moraffware. They asked for a sample: a board game done as a video game. He then asked me if he could port over a board-game design of mine that I had playtested with him called "Nexus." He ended up getting the job, and I was paid a few hundred bucks for the digital rights to the game. In retrospect, the game was pretty terrible: the more we played it, the more we realized it was really susceptible to degenerate strategies! But, hey, it was my first real, professional game credit.

Moraffware was later approached to do contract work for Origin Systems. The way that story goes is that Rick and Starr Long got to talking about online multiplayer gaming. When Rick ended up working at Origin on prototypes for UO, he was asked to recommend a few designer candidates. Since Rick and his girlfriend, and my wife and I, all played the Worlds of Carnage MUD (Multi-User Dungeon) and worked together on LegendMUD, he suggested us. This did lead to oddities, like Richard Garriott logging into LegendMUD as "Lord British" and chatting with everyone there. No one believed it was really him!

Ramsay: When did you start working on UO?

Koster: We interviewed sometime in the spring of 1995, over our Spring Break, I think. We drove out to Austin from Alabama where we were going to grad school. We were offered jobs sometime before the semester ended, but they weren't ready to have designers yet. They asked us, "How about you work in QA over the summer and then move to design that fall?" We said no to that, figuring that if we started in QA, we might never make it out. We waited until the actual jobs came through in the fall and kept our regular jobs around campus. Our start date was September 1, 1995.

I didn't start out as lead anything on UO. When Kristen and I showed up at the Origin offices, we asked, "What's the game like?" We were told that a lot of the game was based on materials we submitted with our applications! I became "creative lead" later, after the original lead designer was let go.

Ramsay: What materials did you submit with your applications? What was the interview and onboarding process like?

Koster: A few weeks before we got to Origin, my wife and I were told "you absolutely do not want to work there; it's a sweatshop." We laughed nervously and went on anyway.

The whole interview process was kind of funny and a testament to how important personal connections are. We were recommended for the job. We had the in-person interview with Starr Long and Richard Garriott logged into LegendMUD to check it out.

Then we started to get sent interview questions remotely as they worked to figure out whether we were qualified. At the time, designers at Origin were often called "technical design assistants." There was scripting, there was dialogue writing, and so on. All the questions came from what was very much a single-player game slant. We were sent examples of code and asked if we could write code like that and find the bugs that had been intentionally inserted into the code. It was something like a misplaced closing brace.

But I also remember that we thought the architecture was wrong. We were used to running scripts on servers, so we were accustomed to event-driven architectures. These scripts actually ran inside the core loop of the single-player game. The scripts they sent us did things like have the light bulb check the switch every frame to see if it was on or off. We would have done that by having the switch send a message to the bulb when the state changed.

We were also sent sample conversation trees. As I recall, we thought dialogue trees were a very bad idea for a large-scale virtual world simply because of the sheer workload. UO ended up with a keyword recognition system instead.

Finally, we were asked for a sample quest. I sent them the entire code and text of my quest for the Beowulf zone in LegendMUD but then also said "but we wouldn't do quests this way at all now." Kristen and I had been working on a simulation system based on artificial life and economic theory. We basically sent in a description of our design work on that. It was a system that was supposed to simulate the behaviors of creatures and NPCs using a simplistic version of Maslow's hierarchy of needs with abstract properties behind everything.

When we got to the office on our first day, we found that our examples were the way the game was going to be. It freaked us out because we had assumed there was already a game design, I suppose.

Ramsay: What was your role on UO initially?

Koster: Kristen and I started out as just designers. Not the lowest level, one level up, I think. We each made a salary of $25,000. And when we started out, we did things like spec out background fiction, the AI system, object interactions, combat, how the skill system worked, etc. A lot of these were a meld of what we wanted to do based on MUDs and what the Ultima series had established.

We were the only two designers at first, except for our boss, Andrew Morris. Eventually, there were more, and eventually, Andrew was gone. And of course, all the core programming team had a lot of input on design too. It was a small and very tight-knit team, very skunkworks.

All of the programmers and designers except Andrew came from text muds. There was a big, big gap between them and the Origin vets, most of whom did not play online games. This absolutely led to piles of tension later on when the U9 team was pushed onto the project.

But before that, UO was run out of a couple of rooms on a different floor of the building. You had to walk through an ad agency lobby or something to get to it. The artists had to sit in the hallway because there was no room. And later, when the ad agency, or whatever it was, left, they did a build out; there was a period where the rooms where we worked were the only drywall standing on that floor. You had to walk across the bare concrete to get to the door labeled "Multima" with a color-printed sign tacked up with tape. You could literally walk off the building and fall to your death!

The prototype server sat under the thermostat, so it was always freezing. We used to bring fingerless gloves to work to be able to type. We rarely saw the rest of the company. When Warren Spector's entire group was dismantled, Richard came up to tell us, and said "as you have probably heard, we did huge layoffs today" and we all looked at each other in perplexity. We had not heard. We were skunkworks.

This was the period where we did things like launch our own marketing website, logo, and even a beta program that cost money, without letting marketing know.

This isolation continued after we moved downstairs back into the main LB production area. And that's where tensions got uncomfortable. I mean, our team loved things like the Lego or PlayDoh sculpting contests just as much as anyone else at Origin did. Or the prank wars—constant and hilarious. But there was a lot of tension there around questions of technical competence which cut both ways, I think; online vs. single player design; and a big dose of the F.O.R. factor.

F.O.R. meant "friend of Richard." It's hard to judge these things now with greater distance on it all. Richard and I get along well. I don't think any of this necessarily reflects on him. But there was always chatter in the halls about the degree to which the right friendships helped your career. I gather it was just as true for "Friends of Chris Roberts" and so on. There were fault lines in the company. They went between studios. There could be actual hostility if you went down the wrong hallways sometimes, but also within teams.

Ramsay: When you became creative lead, what were your responsibilities?

Koster: At that point, the alpha process where we asked players to send in money to get CDs had been launched. EA took notice and the Ultima IX (U9) project was put on hiatus and all those folks were merged into the UO team. And a lot of them just didn't want to be there. Andrew was burned out, unhappy, and was let go. I was named creative lead but I wasn't given managerial authority because, well, I was more junior than most everyone else. I wasn't a manager. My wife worked on the team. She couldn't report to me. But in practice, much of the game was built on the things that the original core team had done. Kristen and I were the two designers there. I suppose there wasn't anyone else to ask to own the creative aspect of the project.

Add in the tensions from a team that didn't want to be there. These things had big impacts on the UO product after the U9 merge. When Andrew was gone, we had Brian Martin and Joye McBurnett as managers of the design team. I was "creative lead" but I did not have the authority to tell anyone from the U9 team what to do. Well, I had no authority to tell anyone what to do, but the original UO folks would listen to me. Systems were redesigned; original designs were ignored, and so on. Sometimes this was for the good. Sometimes it was for the bad. The resource system, that original design for

AI and abstract properties we had sent in as part of our application materials, was one thing that fell victim during this period. Some of it was because it was not going to scale. But a lot of it was because the programmers on it didn't like it very much.

It was a very weird and awkward period. I had my own work to do, of course. I was still actively scripting things like artificial intelligence for the non-player characters, fruit trees, and object interactivity. I was doing all community management for our beta testers. I was the keeper of the patch notes and update cycle documentation. I worked with the programmers on system design—things like housing. I coded the original interface for that, actually. But I also had to try to herd the cats, and if something went off kilter, I had to persuade Brian to take action. I didn't have a lot of direct control.

Ramsay: Since UO was a far more massive project than the text-based games you had worked on, were you overwhelmed?

Koster: UO was exhausting. I think we worked six or seven 12-hour days per week for nine straight months. There were so many moving parts. Almost no one had a good picture of what all of them were.

The biggest lessons for me ended up being about scale. Many of the tactics we would use on MUDs just didn't work at a large scale. Players behaved differently. They were ruder to one another. They were far more powerful, collectively, when they took action. For example, exploiting a bug would cause catastrophic results within hours. We had very little time to respond in times of crisis and we didn't know that at first. We couldn't just talk to everyone and get a consensus going. There were too many people to talk to. Simulation systems that worked with a few players broke down with many. Simulation systems designed for truly large groups couldn't be tested without deploying them to the live audience.

These were issues we never had to think about for MUDs and their smaller player bases. It was overwhelming, sure, but also really exciting. We were moving at top speed and trying to stay on the track.

Ramsay: Although you worked on the creative side, what did you learn about building an online game business during your time at Origin?

Koster: I wasn't directly involved with the business. But I did get to see the very real and direct consequences of design choices affecting the business. The player-killer problem was probably the most visible of these, costing us tens of thousands of subscribers.

At the time, I held very closely to a philosophical ideal that this should be solved within the context of the sim, rather than with code banning all forms of aggression. I don't feel that way anymore. My position is a lot more nuanced now. But that original position powerfully shaped the initial experience of UO. I tried really hard to solve a problem in a particular way so that the game would meet artistic goals while also trying to make the business better. I failed at it, and after I was off the team, the game was changed to simply not allow player killing in half of the world.

That was a wake-up call for me: the limits on what we can get an audience to go along with, the extent to which a statement can or should be there, and how much it can affect the bottom line. A lot of people were emotionally hurt by the player killing.

On the flip side, UO taught me that the value of community, marketing, and, in general, building a strong relationship with customers and players just cannot be overstated. Almost twenty years have passed since I first interacted with some of those players; we're still in touch. That sort of long-term thinking is something that has been sorely lacking in games lately.

Ramsay: Why do you think UO has been able to continue operating for all these years? How long do MMOs typically last?

Koster: If it weren't for the emergent qualities and the freedoms UO provided, UO would have never lasted this long.

We don't know how long MMOs can last because we have never seen one be continually invested in over decades. UO is still running today, but it has not seen the sort of graphical overhauls that something like Runescape has received that keep the game fresh and available. If it had, it'd be a web-embedded client running in WebGL or Flash, it'd be available on iPad, and it'd look competitive with other isometric games in full 3D.

I think the longevity of UO speaks to the power of that immersive world, and the fact that it wasn't built out of consumable content but instead out of the notion of creating a living fantasy world.

Ramsay: How did you go from working at Origin on the Ultima franchise to working at SOE on the Star Wars license?

Koster: There came a point where I wasn't working on UO anymore. This happened before the Renaissance expansion, actually. I worked on a number of pitches for new titles, and eventually, one of them became a try at a MMO version of the Privateer license. This title was in development for awhile but was then cancelled. When that happened, almost all of our team quit as a unit and we joined SOE. After we went through a couple of pitches, we were asked to do SWG.

Ramsay: Your team voluntarily left? Why?

Koster: Well, the project had just been cancelled, obviously. And the cancellation was a bit of a political thing. We lost out in part because of another MMO being done elsewhere within EA. It had taken a lot of effort to even get started. I had done pitches for multiple other MMOs in the time since I moved on from UO, so it was, gosh, months without a project. I think we were all feeling like EA didn't know what to do with MMOs.

Ramsay: What did your team do first after joining Sony?

Koster: At first we worked out of J. Allen Brack's house—some of the other folks were his roommates—and we started developing pitches there in J's living room. J went onto great things at Blizzard eventually. There was a pirate one, as I recall, and some other stuff that has faded from memory. Then, SOE actually opened an Austin office for us. I would not call the team my team though. It was really Rich Vogel's team in most ways. He was the one who had the initiative to form a studio and it was he who cut the deal for us with SOE as well.

Ramsay: When did you start working on SWG?

Koster: I guess SOE wasn't entirely happy with where the SWG project was at that point. Rich and I were asked to go out to SOE in San Diego to look at the games there. They asked us to do a review of where it stood. It was kind of problematic already. There were a ton of great people on it, but the poor guy in charge was designing and producing two MMOs at once which was just impossible. There were a lot of technical questions that were tough open questions. So, we told John Smedley what we thought in a report. And before very long, we were asked to take it over and make SWG more like a "worldly" game like UO than like EverQuest. There was concern about cannibalizing the audience for EverQuest and having a diversified portfolio.

Another big factor was that we had several team members who were veterans of the Wing Commander team. The cancelled project at Origin had been a Privateer MMO, so we had been working on solving action space combat in a MMO setting already. In the end, we knew we couldn't get that done in time for the initial launch and decided fairly early on to push space combat to an expansion, later called Jump to Lightspeed. But we accounted for its eventual presence in the design of the ground game.

Ramsay: How much of SWG existed already?

Koster: There was a design doc there already, which was a few hundred pages long. A lot of that document was stuff like item lists and monster lists. The main game feature was real-time blaster combat using a "cone of fire" setup to cover up latency, which at the time was an unsolved problem. Planetside was a sister project happening at the same time, you see. The game was built around this feature, and we ended up making the call that, given the timeline, it was too risky to base the game on. Of course, we knew we had to solve this problem for the space portion, but it was a lot to take on for the initial launch.

The game design that was there was also basically about hunting monsters, in the EverQuest mold. That didn't feel right for the license. I know that some people feel that SWG wasn't Star Wars-y enough, but that first version was less so. That may be because it had been based on the design or tech of an earlier project called Exodus. Exodus had some really cool tech features in their prototype engine, particularly fractal terrain and freeform building stuff. That lined up really well with what we were thinking, which was also based on fractal terrain and players able to build. But SWG had moved away from the Exodus code base and was instead sharing technology with EverQuest 2, which was also pretty early in development.

There were two tech bases, a design doc, entanglements with two other projects that were at early stages, and a tighter deadline than either one. And we had to go through it all and figure out what was working out and what wasn't. This was in mid-to-late 2000. Ultimately, we had to switch codebases entirely and redo most all of the design.

This was, politically, very uncomfortable. Resentment was piling up on teams on both sides. The San Diego team felt like their game had been taken away. The EverQuest II guys felt snubbed, too, because we had stopped using their tech. It created a nasty rivalry between the programmers in Austin and San Diego. A bunch of the San Diego team quit over it.

I know from later conversations with people who were on the project before us then that we came off badly when we first showed up; like we were the saviors showing people "how it should be done." And then we had to build a new relationship with LucasArts, specifically with Haden Blackman, and get a whole bunch of stuff approved all over again.

Ramsay: How do you figure out what works and what doesn't in a game that isn't quite a game yet?

Koster: These days, my answer would be small prototypes. Take small parts and build them almost as standalone minigames and try them. Back then, that practice was not widespread. On big projects, it was still mostly all about excessive documentation. You had to try to anticipate everything you could in the design phase. Your chance to tweak the design once you had gameplay came after it was implemented.

On SWG, we did a very extensive alpha period with actual players. This was incredibly unusual at the time. We picked the best posters from the forums, tried to get a good representative spread of player types, and invited them in for testing very rough versions of the systems.

Ramsay: What is a "player type"? Why was a good spread important?

Koster: Different players all approach a game differently, but they do tend to cluster into certain behavior patterns. There are a bunch of different models for thinking about the ways players approach games, including Richard Bartle's player types, Nick Yee's research, and personality assessments such as OCEAN, for different market segments.

By having a diverse set of testers, you can better assess when you open the doors to the public and get all sorts of players suddenly showing up. We used mostly Bartle's model, which was widely used by everyone. Yee's wasn't done yet and I didn't know about OCEAN. We also created forums for various specialties and interests to draw on from a cross-section of players.

This testing was completely invaluable. We were able to do things like test the chat system, the combat system, some of the artificial intelligence, and other things that were completely in isolation from the rest of the game, like just standing in a desert on Tatooine.

Ramsay: How does stranding people in a desert help?

Koster: By putting them in a desert, we were isolating them from contact with anything else in the game that either wasn't ready for them to see or was not on the testing agenda for that day. It was a way to focus in, to concentrate on specific systems. If you'd put everything in the game in front of the tester, then each system wouldn't get as deep of a going-over.

Ramsay: What would you try to anticipate in the design phase on a big project, especially an online game?

Koster: Everything. Exploits. Fun factor. How hard or easy to implement it might be. The interface design. Player behavior. Interactions with other systems. With a big project, you don't get to iterate in the same way that you can on smaller projects. It takes so long to make things that you don't get to go over them and redo them multiple times. As a result, you have to do more planning in advance and you have to try to anticipate every contingency of every sort. Unforeseen interactions in systems, how players might behave, what the eventual interface might look like, what happens if there's a bug… all of those need to be planned for, so that when something does go wrong during the operation of the game—since it will—you have some idea of what to do to fix the problem.

Ramsay: Managers might call that scenario planning. How much documentation does this approach produce? How do you manage all that information?

Koster: I don't want to give the impression that this was about building scripts to run in the event of bad things happening. We did have run books like that, but they tended to be for operational things like servers going down. In a game design context, it was more about anticipating this stuff and then trying to design the systems so that these things wouldn't happen.

It can create a lot of docs, but more because you explain your logic than anything else. Ironically, despite our ending up with a design bible that was hundreds of lavishly illustrated pages long, that doc probably failed in that respect, because history shows that, by and large, teams running the game don't always understand why some things were the way they were. I think that is a common problem on large projects. Even if it were all documented, who's going to read that doc? It's too big to update and full of obsolete detail. I don't use giant docs like that anymore.

But you couldn't necessarily tell from the resultant doc what problem the spec was meant to avoid. A classic example was around the buffs system in SWG. The whole game had been designed around a cap on player statistical advancement, meaning that the power gap between a newbie and a veteran player was supposed to be no more than around 10%. This limited the possible advancement in the sense of raw firepower, damage per second, that sort of thing. Very much not the mainstream current of MMO design – usually you let players get crazy powerful as they level up. In SWG, we were trying to drive cooperation more, and so we said that a single player never became that much more powerful. Instead, for big targets, they needed to cooperate to take them down.

Some folks on the team didn't understand that or didn't like it, so they made the buffs system, a system for temporary enhancement of player power up to 400% capability. Nothing in the game was scaled to take that into account. Player progression through the combat game was ruined pretty fast. We had players who figured out how to take down the most powerful things in the game completely solo within a few months.

Ramsay: How often does reality surprise you by either never throwing you into certain planned-for scenarios or putting you in a position where you have no idea about what to do?

Koster: Daily. It's impossible to anticipate everything, and impossible to think that you can.

Ramsay: Since you can't anticipate everything, what can you do to spend your time and resources wisely on things that matter?

Koster: Your instincts. Some things are obvious, like possible exploits or player behavior around maximizing reward: "they'll sit here and do this over and over again for the credits or gold." Some things are weirder: "they'll hoard so much gold that they'll fill up our database to the point of causing slowdowns." Foreseeable, if you get deeply cynical about human nature, but this stuff is much more likely to catch you by surprise if you haven't dealt with it before. Some are downright nutty, like players intentionally creating "black holes" by dropping so many objects in one place that anyone coming close would lose their connection, thereby becoming another stuck object and making the black hole grow. That one happened to us on UO.

Ramsay: Public testing obviously helps you find exploits and the like, but you said that the SWG alpha was unusual. Why?

Koster: Alpha tests are common, but what was special about the SWG alpha test was the size and way it was conducted. It was much more like a focus group. We didn't just let people in to play freely, like the way we ran the UO alpha. Instead, we logged in with the players, walked them through features that were limited to just the ones in the test that day, watched them try them, and asked questions of them on the spot.

Ramsay: Why didn't more online game companies run tests like that?

Koster: Focus groups are far more common now, but I think there's always a reluctance to show work that is clearly unfinished or broken. Back then, we only did it because we were up against a deadline and had promised we would be in alpha, but we simply were not ready to run the traditional alpha test. Our alpha was an accommodation to reality that ended up being crazy valuable. You could really tell when the game shipped which systems had gone through that phase of tests and which hadn't.

Ramsay: After the game shipped, what wasn't working in early SWG? How did you plan to solve those problems?

Koster: Oh, God, all kinds of things. Not very long before launch we found out that the deployment servers didn't have as much CPU power as we had planned for. We had hardcoded combat ranges and limits. When the servers groaned under the weight of what we were demanding, we had to go in and manually cut the distances for combat in half, the AI update radius in half, and so on. The entire combat game fell to pieces, in my opinion. Our rifles were designed to be optimal in a combat range that suddenly didn't exist; it was outside the network update radius!

I am still not sure whether that was related to the issues we had with placement of structures on dynamic terrain, but something simple like "check if this space is empty" never seemed to quite work right. But we didn't have time to redesign game systems.

Ramsay: What were the biggest problems with early SWG that you, personally, had to solve? How did you solve them?

Koster: One of the biggest was the dupe bug. These days, it is common to have live updated dashboards that generate reports on aspects of your game: how much money is being spent by players, what they are fighting, how fast they are advancing, etc. Back then, we had to do manual database queries. I used to get a report from Chris Mayer with raw data every week. I would spend hours trying to piece together what the data was telling us.

This was how I was able to see that krayt dragons were being soloed far too often—the aforementioned buffs issue. It's also how we spotted that there was an inflow of money into the economy that was far faster than the amount of currency we were actually spawning. Because the sources of credits were tagged, we were able to identify the problem: players had found ways to duplicate currency, effectively counterfeiting it.

After fixing that bug, we still had the issue that there was a lot of cash sloshing around in the system. We did various things to drain it out, like providing luxury goods at high prices and plain ol' lowering the "income" level by reducing how much money everything in the game created. We actually ran the game economy at a net loss for awhile, in order to get the amount of cash in the system back into the range we wanted.

We posted up articles about this stuff at the time. They can be found via the Wayback Machine. Graphs, even.

Ramsay: One of the key original features of SWG was the era. Set in an era between A New Hope and The Empire Strikes Back, the Jedi were all but extinct. There would be only a handful of players who had unlocked that class. Some players believed this was changed because the number of subscribers was in decline soon after launch.

Koster: Actually, SWG did not have a steady decline in subscribers during the first few months. The subscriber base grew steadily month after month until the "Holocraze." I still believe that the Holocron debacle was what stopped the game's growth and started its reversal. Well, that plus the launch of World of Warcraft.

When we originally specced the Jedi system, it was supposed to unlock in a much more complex and nuanced way than what it eventually was. We had a huge list of all sorts of actions and activities within the game. Climbing the highest mountain, using a particular emote... all sorts of stuff. Every player had a different list; basically, it was a personality test.

We had grouped all of the actions in the game into the four Bartle types. We wanted Jedi to be those players who demonstrated the closest balance between all four or who moved through all four.

Then it turned out that we couldn't add all that tracking. We had to make a last-minute decision to track something much smaller. That turned out to be skills, as a reasonable proxy. But the issue there was that the means of becoming a Jedi was secret—even most of the team didn't know how it was done. By reducing the process to skills though, becoming a Jedi was something reducible to a trivial algorithm. As soon as some players noticed the pattern, it would be obvious to all, which is a perfect example of not extrapolating the consequences.

When the LucasArts marketing folks asked when we would see a Jedi, we ran the numbers and the answer was three years. They said, "Start dropping hints to speed it up." We implemented Holocrons, but dropping hints didn't just speed it up, Holocrons gave away the secret. This then hugely distorted the play of the game. Jedi were the big prize, you see. Until then, people played the way they liked. People who liked being musicians played as musicians. People who liked harvesting minerals harvested minerals. People who liked killing rancors killed rancors.

Then everyone saw how to become a Jedi and the path was clear: play all those skills that you didn't like, and that led to everyone botting the skills they hated, people grinding through professions they despised, and so on. Some players learned about stuff they wouldn't have thought about doing, I'm sure. Maybe that was good for them, but mostly, people gritted their teeth and played the game in ways they hated for the sake of a booby prize called Jedi. That was when the number of subscribers started dropping—not until that feature was in the wild.

Ramsay: Another key feature of SWG was the crafting system. That system was so successful that it hasn't been matched by any game to this day. Was crafting originally designed to have so much depth?

Koster: Crafting actually got deeper as it was designed. In UO, we had the concept of abstract resources that underlaid everything. We ran into issues when doing things like different types of metals. There wasn't a way to say "GOLD and STEEL are both METAL," so I had to hack that in on top of the system. In SWG, we wanted to address that. We started out with the notions of inheritance types: GOLD and IRON are both types of METAL; and the idea of stats, so that IRON could be tougher than GOLD. We also knew we wanted to have turnover in the resources to cause the game economy to have churn and obsolescence.

But the sheer volume of stats that went into it was a surprise to me. Reece Thornton was the designer who really pushed that forward. He added not just stats but a bunch of ways in which they mattered to the crafting system. He elaborated out the "gambling" aspect of the crafting minigame. We kept pushing him to hurry up. We thought that the crafting system was getting overcomplicated. In the end, I think we happened to land at a sweet spot.

Ramsay: What other takeaways from UO did you apply to the redesign and reengineering of SWG?

Koster: Tons and tons. They really were very different games in many ways though. UO had a pure use-based skill system: the more you did something, the better at it you got. In SWG, we changed that for an experience point system, but one where you earned points for a wide array of different activities. Basically, we added one layer of indirection into the mix. This let us have skill trees with some branching choices whereas UO had a linear path for every skill.

UO had also taught us a lot about the value of dynamic environments, the way players loved housing and building, the way they loved pets, and so on. All of those things in SWG were about capturing that and trying to make it even better.

Ramsay: What about content? I don't remember that UO had much of the linear, directed quests we see today.

Koster: SWG was supposed to have lots of content, but we ran out of time to implement even a decent quest system or even a library of reusable scripts for quests. The scripting in SWG was dramatically harder to use than in UO. I had expected scripters to build cool custom quests like the ones we had done back in the LegendMUD days. Instead, it was so hard; we barely got anything in at all. The industry then moved on to fill-in-the-blank Chinese Menu quests; we didn't even manage that. Basically, I think of content in that game as a big fail.

Ramsay: Earlier, you mentioned that you accounted for space combat in the design of the ground game. What do you mean you actually did?

Koster: In planning the skill trees, we designed it in such a way that it was easy to add crafting stuff related to ships and new professions. The systems for joining the Rebellion or the Empire were also set up to accommodate eventual piloting. We knew we wanted mouse-driven space combat, so that part was basically partitioned off. It was more about leaving the space for the space parts so that they would slot in naturally when the time came.

We could have used design elements that were better left to Jump to Lightspeed, for example, by putting spaceship engineering into the ground game and having it just generate cash. By holding off, we made it tie together better. We could have made the way you advanced in the Empire or the Rebellion not work well with the eventual addition of having ships. That sort of thing. But, really, one nice thing about the skill system in SWG was that it was easily expandable in those directions.

Ramsay: Speaking of the ground game, was there a reason for debuffs, or "state attacks," like Dizzy and Knockdown, which made the player unable to move for an extended period? I'm sure there are SWG veterans who would love to know who thought those were good ideas!

Koster: State attacks were directly inherited from classic DikuMUD gameplay, which included stun effects and the like. You would try to stun an opponent to be able to deal extra damage. Every state was supposed to have counters and defenses though. Frankly, the system was never well-balanced. In particular, these effects suffered a lot because the core Health-Action-Mind statistical system wasn't working right. It wasn't tuned to match what was originally intended, which was a much faster regeneration rate, so we don't even know whether it would have even worked out as designed.

Ramsay: Over the years, SWG changed radically, reportedly due to pressure from LucasArts—from the buffs system to the Holocraze and later to the Combat Upgrade and New Game Enhancements in 2005. Was there ever a singular, overriding vision? If not to provide that vision, what exactly was your role as creative director?

Koster: I don't think all of the changes were the result of pressure from LucasArts. I think—and this could be my memory playing tricks on me—that the Combat Upgrade happened because of internal team pressure to fix broken combat, which was in turn caused largely by the buffs problem and the broken Health-Action-Mind statistics implementation.

There certainly was a singular vision early on, but a singular vision doesn't mean a shared vision. You have to ride hard on it and people have to commit and recommit to it. I think that after awhile, the vision just sort of evolved. There were folks who bought in. There were folks who didn't. There were people who didn't even know what it was. Particularly in the face of live operations, it's often deeply impractical to privilege a vision over the day-to-day of keeping your players happy.

As far as what a creative director therefore does, the creative director tries to set and enforce a vision to maintain consistency across the game while serving a master—in this case, multiple masters, because we had a license holder in the mix. But I don't think of the role of creative director as a dictatorship, which I have been told is a failure of mine!

Ramsay: You've mentioned how SWG was influenced by DikuMUD and UO, but when we started talking, you said that the cancelled Privateer Online project at EA was a big reason why SOE brought the Austin team into the fold. How did your experience with Privateer Online shape SWG and Jump to Lightspeed?

Koster: Privateer Online was intended to be a procedurally created galaxy worth of planets with active trading between colonies on different worlds. For this, we were exploring a variety of procedural techniques, as well as thinking about means of doing economic structures in games. Both of these turned out to be very important directions for SWG, but both had to be completely reinvented because the games were so different.

For example, in SWG, we had only a few planets, not hundreds, so everything we had done around procedural planet generation was useless. Using procedural tools did unlock deformable terrain, player housing, vast planets, and a lot more. We had opened new doors by extrapolating from older thinking, although the new use case was completely different. The in-world economy was a similar situation. I'm not sure we would have arrived at such a dynamic economy in SWG without the thinking we had done on Privateer Online.

Ramsay: Can you tell me about the economy? What made the economy so dynamic and central to the game?

Koster: SWG generated new resource types on the fly, based on the master resource types. The master ones were set up in an inheritance tree, so we had IRON as a child of FERROUS METAL, which was a child of METAL, and so on. Each type had a range for its stats, so we could roll up variants. They could then get mined out and be gone, like really actually gone from the game. Eventually, we'd roll up new stuff, but it wasn't at all guaranteed to be direct replacements. It might be NON-FERROUS next time, for example.

When a player crafted something, they experimented with it, which was basically a little gambling and point allocation game. They could use any materials at hand. When they got a result they liked, they could "freeze" that result into a blueprint, which would then forever call for exactly the specific materials used in that run. Players could then mass produce that item, but when materials ran out, the blueprint became obsolete. The item couldn't be made anymore and maybe couldn't get major repairs anymore.

This resulted in constant turnover in the game economy. You couldn't just sit on your laurels. There was always a competitive crafting environment.

Ramsay: In the middle of your efforts to bring SWG to market, there was politically uncomfortable tension between the teams in Austin and San Diego. Did that tension ever subside?

Koster: Gradually. Split locations always meant communication problems. Those issues never went away, but I'd say that a year in, the worst of it had passed. Once people start working together on a daily basis and get to know each other, stuff like that just dissolves.

Ramsay: In retrospect, what could you have done to foster greater cooperation faster?

Koster: I honestly don't know what we could have done to make cooperation go faster. I think we probably laid groundwork for the challenges from the very outset by coming in with an attitude of "we need to get this going" rather than a very conciliatory attitude. We, meaning the Austin team, aggravated the early tensions by coming across as know-it-alls to a team that had just suffered a big disappointment. It took us a little while to realize that was what had happened. I think we did a lot to try to fix that, but we had gotten off on the wrong foot.

Ramsay: When did you leave the SWG team?

Koster: Close to the end of the development cycle for SWG, I was offered the chief creative officer role. I think I officially started just as SWG wrapped in June 2003. I worked out of the Austin office at first. Six months later, I was living in San Diego. In that job, I consulted on titles in development, trying to help them out. I did a lot of public relations work. I helped out on pitches and business meetings with potential partners. I also ran a small R&D group focused on speculative technology and gameplay.

Ramsay: What do you mean by "speculative technology and gameplay"?

Koster: I can't talk about most of what we did, but it was quite a mix of "stuff." The purpose of the group was to push at boundaries, basically. There was work involving social graphing that was way ahead of the curve, there was graphics technology, and there was a game project. From a technical point of view, the biggest thing that came out of that group was actually submitted as a patent. That's in the public record and you can find it by Googling me, so I suppose I can mention its existence. The work involved using the principles of cellular automata and artificial life to generate living landscapes and worlds. The goal was to make simulated virtual worlds that were way more interactive and responsive than what was around at the time.

Ramsay: Why did you break out on your own with a new company? It doesn't sound like you were designing games. Was that a factor?

Koster: My duties at Sony had me attending a lot of web conferences and meeting lots of folks from Silicon Valley. By going to events like Web2.0, Supernova, ETech, and so on, I was exposed to a lot of Web 2.0 thinking. A lot of it was radical and different thinking, coming as I did from the MMO role-playing game (RPG) market, which itself was a big shift from packaged-goods games. A lot of it also resonated very strongly because, of course, virtual worlds were on the cutting edge of the online community in a lot of ways.

Many of the practices we take for granted today in online social software—persistent profiles, reputation systems, badges, titles, and so on—were pioneered in virtual worlds. It took a long time for some of this stuff to make it to social networks, which didn't come along until a few decades after virtual worlds did.

I saw a convergence coming. I would return from these conferences and try to convey to folks back at the office the things I had heard about—ideas like the long tail, digital distribution, user-generated content, and the rise of browser applications. Sony was interested in these things, but it does take a long time to turn a ship that big. The very long development cycle of traditional MMORPGs—where thousands of people run around in the game, slaying monsters, gathering up treasure, and making their characters more powerful—meant that it would take quite awhile for some of these lessons to be absorbed. The traditional MMORPG model was largely taken from their predecessors which were text-based MUDs. There aren't many MMORPGs that aren't like this. There was a lot more diversity in the text-based days.

In parallel with this, there were some changes in my duties at the company. I had been working in a role where I wasn't making games directly and I missed it. As some organizational changes happened, it just seemed like the right time to go exploring this new territory. So, I set out to do something that was webby, independent, and centered on user-generated content. Luckily, all that time spent in the Valley meant that I had gotten to know a lot of well-connected folks from the venture-capital community.

Ramsay: What happened that caused you to leave?

Koster: Well, the core trigger was the disbanding of my R&D group. I had been spending an awful lot of time on meeting with people in Hollywood and those meetings never seemed to pan out. It just felt very unsatisfying, so I began to miss being involved with the hands-on creation of games. I had discussions with my bosses and got an R&D group started. We were working on some very cool speculative technologies for virtual worlds, many of which are still unmatched today in my opinion. But because of some high-priority projects that needed to ship, my team was gradually reassigned to work on game teams. Soon after, I was asked to head one of those game teams, too. The project was one that I didn't have passion for. On top of that, the things that I was interested in were pretty divergent from the product plan at SOE at the time—I wanted to chase after web technologies, social networks, the social web, user-generated content, and so on.

Ramsay: When did you begin talking to VCs? What was your experience with raising capital for Metaplace?

Koster: I didn't have any experience with raising capital at all. I had met many VCs and angels while I was attending these conferences. Among others, I had made contact with Reid Hoffman, who is incredibly well-connected in the Valley; we were both attending a conference in Switzerland for several days. It turned out that an old acquaintance from the days when I worked on multi-user dungeons (MUDs), the old text-based virtual worlds, had started working in venture capital—Susan Wu. I had met a variety of folks from the Valley at conferences, including Jason Hable and John Borchers of Crescendo Ventures, and had phone conversations with them about industry trends. So, there was a lot of informal stuff: just happening to meet people without any formal contacts or anything. At the time, I wasn't contemplating raising money; I was just doing the thing I usually do at conferences, which was meeting people and chatting.

I didn't start formally talking to VCs until after I was gone from Sony, of course. It turned out that several industry friends were starting initiatives of their own around the same time. Some of them were founding companies, like Jim Greer at Kongregate. We overlapped briefly way back at Origin. Some already had companies, but they were exploring projects in the Web 2.0 space, such as Daniel James at Three Rings, who was a friend also going back quite awhile. So, I had people to reach out to for advice.

Reid was probably the biggest single help early on, spending a long lunch with me and giving me introductions to a half-dozen possible sources of funding, to law firms, and so on. Our company lawyers, Stubbs Alderton, came out of that conversation, and really, from that point forward, Scott Alderton was my chief adviser during the funding process. None of the funding introductions Reid provided panned out in the end, but I got to meet a lot of great people. And I approached everyone in terms of asking for advice, not in terms of pitching something, at least not at first.

I do think that having a track record and a reputation was a huge help. It allowed entry into conversations, made it far easier to cold-call people, and made people more interested in what I had to say. But the biggest way to build that reputation is to share things yourself. By sharing ideas and information at conferences, I had made myself someone interesting to talk to, and someone perceived as, if not an authority, at least someone who was paying attention to the space.

The other thing that I suspect helped just as much is that I started building a prototype in our spare bedroom and was getting something working. I had agreed with my wife that we'd try to get something going for six months or so and see how far we could get. I wasn't going to wait for money to show up. I just started working the phones and the compiler on the day after my Sony contract expired.

Ramsay: Why were you meeting with VCs?

Koster: Well, at first, I didn't really quite know what I wanted to do. I assumed I needed to raise money and get a team to be able to do anything. But I started sitting down to code to try stuff out and stuff just sort of started to click. I had thought that I would just try sticking a graphical front end on a text MUD as a starting point. Keep in mind that my programming skills were pretty atrophied. I had been making puzzle games for fun on weekends but I hadn't done any coding for work while at SOE at all.

I started out getting a basic 2D engine going then slowly added isometric views and networking code and the like. It was a lot of fun because I basically had to relearn how to do everything. I had never written a user interface library before but I had to learn how to do this.

Meanwhile, I was meeting with a lot of VCs, at first just for advice. I started out with just "virtual worlds for everyone; let anyone make their own." The further I got into my prototype, the more it crystallized. I went and got a logo done. I put together mockups of the possible portal page for the user worlds. It looked a lot like a YouTube for virtual worlds, with featured worlds, categories, and all that.

One VC flew down in his private plane. He liked to fly, so I guess meeting me was a good excuse. For others, I flew up to San Francisco or Palo Alto. A lot of these meetings I got thanks to Reid Hoffman's introduction. I was new to the game. I didn't go in pitching. I went in saying "I'm thinking of doing this," and not at all like what I later saw in the Valley game of pitching up and down Sand Hill Road.

Crescendo Ventures showed interest pretty early on. And at one point, I told John Borchers, "I'm getting far enough along that I wonder if I shouldn't just launch this." That was apparently part of what pushed them over the edge into offering to invest.

Ramsay: Sounds like you were asking a lot of questions during this time. What didn't you know? What questions were you asking?

Koster: Who should I talk to? What should my pitch deck look like? How much should I be raising, and what valuation should I look for? What do venture capital deals look like? What sort of team do I need to maximize my chances of funding?

Ramsay: What did you expect to gain by asking these questions? What goals were you intending to achieve?

Koster: Well, the most basic answer is that I hoped to get funded! I figured that knowing more about the process—remember, I had never done anything like this before—would increase my chances of success. As it happens, the introductions and the advice that I received through this process netted me a lawyer, important contacts, and, in general, helped enormously. The advice of people who have done it before is worth a lot.

Ramsay: You designed the Metaplace platform to "enable anyone to create virtual worlds." How did you come up with that idea?

Koster: It's important to realize that user-created virtual worlds weren't a new idea at all. It was how the field had started, and the biggest reason the field had drifted away from it was because of the requirements that 3D graphics imposed. But Second Life was out already, the apartment idea was being executed very successfully by Habbo Hotel, and there were many other projects going with a "user-created virtual world" bent.

I had been tossing around the idea of user-created virtual worlds literally going back to the UO days. At one point, I proposed that we would allow players of UO to make their own parallel worlds, as a response to the "gray shard" phenomenon—users were creating their own servers that were compatible with the UO client. I figured that meant there was pent-up demand. But that idea didn't go anywhere. We, of course, did player housing.

For me, this was a natural evolution from the text MUDs—the text-based virtual worlds. They were based on the idea that there was a server codebase that was publicly available, and in many cases, the creativity and advancement of the medium came about because people took the existing servers and reworked, extended, or simply used them well to create whole new worlds and rule sets and experiences.

With SWG, we had done not only housing, but player cities. We really tried to allow players to affect the map in greater ways. And later, in talking about webby stuff with Sony, I had brought up the idea of creating something that allowed people to basically build their own apartments and connect them together and create objects to put in them. It was still a heavy 3D sort of environment in conception though and still in the mold of the MMORPGs so to speak, rather than what we ended up with. That project also didn't go anywhere; in fact, for a little while, it morphed into an action role-playing game!

Once I was off on my own and contemplating making something, the prevailing currents of Web 2.0 thought were very much about users contributing content and creativity. And I was driven in part by the fact that I saw the MMORPG industry hitting a wall because of the rapidly rising costs of developing these giant 3D extravaganzas. In approaching the very general notion of user-created virtual worlds, starting from the webby premises, I landed in a very different place. I wanted to "do Second Life right" in a sense by tackling what I saw as core architectural issues that limited both its accessibility and its scalability.

Ramsay: What issues were those?

Koster: Well, to my mind, Second Life had several big issues. First, Second Life had technical scalability problems. There were aspects of the system that were baked in early on that led to challenges later.

For example, individual objects in Second Life were very heavy. To get nice-looking objects, you had to compose them out of primitives, or "prims." Prims were mathematical solids that had a few parameters attached to them. This meant that making something with complex geometry required you to use a lot of prims, so then you started having things like prim budgets. Since the world was seamless, but chopped up into little regions called "sims," which is short for simulators, you had to worry about budgets per sim. The use of prims also meant that bringing in content from outside was challenging. It wasn't until much later that Second Life allowed users to import standard 3D object formats.

You also couldn't easily make something that truly felt like a different place—say, with different rules of physics—because you were sharing one world with everyone else. It wasn't a Web-friendly platform in other ways, too. You needed to run a pretty demanding 3D client at a time when lightweight experiences like Facebook and Twitter were gradually taking over our Internet lives. All of these things together, in my opinion, led to Second Life really limiting its eventual audience size.

Ramsay: You wanted to do something webby, independent, and focused on user-generated content. How far did you get with the prototype?

Koster: When I started out building the prototype, I was limited by what I could make in my spare bedroom. That meant I couldn't do advanced graphics for one. I also had to rely on extremely simple forms of network communication. I basically had to learn a whole bunch of programming I had never done, like networking and user-interface stuff. I built the prototype client in BlitzMax, which is a sort of object-oriented variant of BASIC, and for a little while, I used a MUD server just as something to hold stuff to send down to the client. The architecture was tag-driven, using plain-text tags, so I just put the tags in the room descriptions!

The prototype ended up able to load a map that was a 3D heightfield, display it in the client, move a simple little alien dinosaur thing around on the height-field, and load up terrain tiles and objects with images attached to them. It could save and load world data up to a remote site. I got pretty far with the terrain editor, too. I had also found a web plugin that enabled me to wrap this client into an ActiveX control, so you could use the client on a web page. I had conceptualized the notion of a tag language for the network protocol. And I had started putting together the high-level architecture design for how the technology would work, basing it on the LAMP stack that was driving so much innovation on the web.

The prototype evolved over time into a Metaplace client that we actually kept alive for another full year or more.

Ramsay: You had a big vision for the platform early on. Can you tell me about the role you saw Metaplace playing in the future?

Koster: Metaplace was explicitly designed to become a standard platform for virtual worlds on the Internet. Basically, it was designed to mimic the web stack because we saw that as the enabling force behind the explosion of web technologies and companies. It was architected to have components much like the LAMP stack: a generic browser, a text-based tag language, a generic server, a scripting layer equivalent to CGI, a name service layer for running a distributed network, and semantic tagging for search.

The plan was for there to be clients on multiple platforms, so that you could experience the same virtual-world content on any device. We never delivered on this promise to any end users in the user-generated content days. We pretty much focused on Flash as we pushed the "network of virtual worlds" product. Once we started deploying Facebook games, we made technology choices that locked us into Facebook and Flash more tightly, and that required work to undo. This made transitioning back to the multiple-client model harder, but not impossible.

In terms of a business model, we saw ourselves starting out with providing hosting for worlds, and evolving over time into running the network, owning search, and the like.

We were also chasing democratization. The Web 2.0 experience was one where users were empowered to contribute content. We were definitely interested in making the platform as open as possible for people, and putting worlds on the web as widgets, basically. The prevailing mode of virtual worlds was very much full-screen clients in heavy 3D with some thoughts that, a la Snow Crash, the worlds would swallow the Internet. We saw the reverse happening: the web swallowing up virtual worlds.

This turned out to happen, of course, only far more thoroughly than we thought. The "placeness" of worlds got lost in the process, and today, we have Facebook instead!

Ramsay: When you presented your vision to prospective investors, how did they react? Were there any concerns?

Koster: At the time, virtual worlds were a hot area for venture-capital investment and so were various sorts of web games. Generally speaking, there was a fair amount of receptivity to the pitch.

I went into the pitches, explicitly stating that I was not intending to be the chief executive of the company and that role was not what I preferred to do. I think that this allayed some of the concerns investors might have had about my experience, which was all in big companies rather than startups.

Some of the folks I talked to didn't know the space at all. I got the best rejections from those who were completely upfront about that and backed out, saying that they didn't really know what they would bring to the table.

Ramsay: Best rejections? How can a rejection be good?

Koster: When you are fundraising, one of the worst things is to be left dangling.

Ramsay: At what point did you start putting together a team? Who was your first recruit for the team?

Koster: In practice, the process of going from zero to having an office, having funding, having a cofounder, and being able to hire a team took six months. We didn't start hiring really until January 2007.

But the first team member was my cofounder, John Donham. We had worked together for years, starting with SWG, at SOE in Austin. Later, we moved to San Diego, although not at the same time. When he took over running the San Diego development studio, I took the chief creative officer role. I think he was the one who suggested to John Smedley that I might be a good fit for that job.

Ramsay: Tell me about your first office. How did you choose the location?

Koster: We looked at a number of neighborhoods around San Diego. We used a commercial real estate company to help us find the location. We were limiting ourselves to certain budget ranges—class-B office space and that sort of thing. We didn't need too large of a space either. There weren't many different locations that met those criteria, and in the end, we ended up in a building in Rancho Bernardo. We were quite close to where I lived, too. I could actually walk to work! We ended up remaining in that building for most of the company's life, but we moved offices within the building twice more as our employee count changed.

Ramsay: How did you determine your initial staffing requirements? What capabilities did you need?

Koster: There were a few roles that were tricky to fill, where we had to make tough choices, but the initial needs were pretty simple. We needed someone to work on the server, someone to work on the Web, someone to work on the client, an art director... you get the idea. We wanted to be highly community-driven, so having someone who was a community person early on was also important.

The first few roles on the team were pretty apparent early on. If I had to identify a need that we didn't really satisfy at the start, and should have, I'd say that business and marketing were underserved. We had someone doing business development and the day-to-day management needs were met by John, my cofounder. But we really could have put more effort into narrowing down our possible target markets. We just had too many of them.

Ramsay: Your technology was still in its infancy at that point, right? What was your next big challenge?

Koster: The immediate challenge was building the technology. Although, in retrospect, we spent more time working on the technology than we should have, and we spent less time working on marketing than we should have. We should have built the technology platform and developed one game: one game that the audience would want to play and build on. Having that one game would have unlocked the modding community, which would have possibly grown to the other aspects of the platform's potential.

In practice, most core elements of how the technology worked were established relatively early. The big questions ended up being about the purposes of the technology. In some ways, that was a challenge we never overcame. These days, that's called product-market fit on the entrepreneur blogs.

Ramsay: Why was building the Metaplace platform difficult?

Koster: Well, first, there was the infrastructure for the content. To make user-generated content for a virtual world, you need a virtual-world skeleton to start with! There's the world server, which runs the simulation, etc. Then you need a way for the server to talk to clients and a way for the user-provided assets to get to clients, which if anything could be moderately challenging. Then, of course, uploading just pictures and sounds isn't as compelling as creating behaviors for things in the world, so you then have to start working on a scripting system.

And after you have all that, people will ask for tools and capabilities. How about physics? How do I make my image anchor at the center rather than the top left? How do I display user interfaces? We ended up creating a whole user-interface markup system for that.

In the end, the core capabilities of the system came relatively swiftly—in months. The tools to actually use those capabilities took years, and we continued to work on them post-acquisition.

Ramsay: That's right, Metaplace was live. When did you launch? Did live, feedback-driven development challenge any of your assumptions?

Koster: We started letting in alpha users toward the end of 2007 after launching at the TechCrunch 40 conference. We let in a fairly limited number of alpha testers, as well as some potential business-partner developers who were trying out the system and considering using it for their own commercial projects.

We were immediately drowned in feedback. The tools were too complex! They were too simple! We needed to have dedicated support for professional developers. We needed to make everything self-explanatory for consumer-level customers. We needed a friendly web-based editor. We needed deep integration with Eclipse, a common professional-grade integrated development environment. We had not been selective enough about the types of customers that we wanted, and as a result, we got unclear direction back on how to alter the product.

The fundamental issue was that we had a system that solved many separate problems for separate audiences. And it was very hard to pick a specific audience once you had a Swiss army knife that did the trick for several markets because doing so meant giving up the users we had. Supporting multiple levels of user turned out to be our Achilles' heel. We were prevented from making the product awesome enough for any one of them.

Put that way, it sounds simple, but the architecture and business model depended on having an ecosystem of more- and less-advanced users. So, drawing the lines was very hard.

Ramsay: Was there ever a point at which you thought "we need to find a new business model because what we're trying to do just isn't working"?

Koster: We did this several times. One pivot was from a more tools-centric website that was focused on builders to an entertainment destination website with a central virtual world where users could explore everyone's worlds. Basically, one looked like YouTube and we pivoted over to a product that was more like Second Life in a web page. There were four or five different tries at a product there; none of which succeeded.

Ramsay: What were the other tries at a product? Why didn't they work out?

Koster: I don't want to overstate the word "product." We suffered from a lack of very specific product direction.

At one point, we were discussing being a tools company. The orientation then would have been toward doing middleware. We even had an external developer who was working on a commercial project using the tools at one point and hired someone just to support them. But this was a direction we did not pursue; although, Unity eventually proved this strategy very successfully. We did live with the legacy of supporting advanced developers from then on though, which meant that we never focused purely on casual consumers.

At another point, we were in the habit of referring to ourselves as a studio and talking about creating content internally. We had vision docs for two separate web-based MMOs that we were going to build with the technology. Neither one got anywhere because being a content company, as opposed to a platform company, was not the sort of thing that a VC-backed firm did then.

At yet another point, we had deals on the table—this happened more than once—to build web-based MMOs for other companies. We walked away from being a white-label studio for much the same reasons that we walked away from doing original properties. It's worth pointing out that at least one of the deals we walked away from was picked up by someone else and became extremely successful.

We tried being, essentially, an online virtual-apartment sort of builder. We were way too complex for that because of the scripting legacy, but we also simply never marketed. Other companies, such as MyMiniLife, were able to build giant audiences with relatively simplistic technology. They eventually became the technical backbone for much of Zynga's game portfolio.

We tried doing embedded worlds and games on websites, but we didn't sign any partners. And the fact that we weren't making content for them meant that they had to do all of the heavy lifting. We also talked a lot about being a distributed virtual-world network, but we didn't pursue the extremely important feature of allowing users to cash out.

And we launched on Facebook with a super simple, little chat space in early 2008 at a time when we likely had by far the best technology for Facebook games on Earth. But we backed away from Facebook and didn't try again until much, much later—and unsuccessfully even then. We never even considered launching casual games on Facebook, which was likely a massive mistake in hindsight.

I could go on, but the common thread is we lacked a deep commitment to a single direction. All of these were potential uses of what was, in the end, an extremely cool and powerful technology. With time, perhaps all of them could have come true. But we needed one profitable one early on and we needed to focus on that one way of using the technology.

Ramsay: Where did you finally end up?

Koster: The biggest pivot was moving away from user-generated content altogether, closing down the public virtual world, and switching to using the platform as an internal tool suite for the development of social games. This turned out to be successful, leading to two successful Facebook titles and then our acquisition by Playdom. It was an extremely painful pivot though.

Ramsay: Extremely painful. That's an interesting way to describe a change in strategy. Why was this pivot so?

Koster: Changing over was pretty traumatic. We had to shut down the live user-generated content service because, as part of the pivot, we could not afford to devote resources to it. There was a strong albeit small community there, but we were running up against huge financial pressures. We had to move really quickly. As a result, I fear that it felt pretty abrupt to a lot of folks. We tried to do everything we could to soften the blow, but it was still very painful. We held a party on the final night that the service was live. I played a live concert that we streamed out to users who showed up. It was a pretty emotional night.

At this point, as part of the pivot, I also wasn't running the company myself. I had asked John to take over as the chief executive since our focus was very much moving toward internal production.

Ramsay: Why did you ask John to take over your role as chief executive? Were you unhappy in that position?

Koster: It was an exhausting role, certainly, but the reasons were more complicated than that. It increased the chances of our landing the bridge funding that we needed to pivot to social games. John's background was specifically game production. Having someone running the company whose primary expertise was "shipping games" seemed like a smart move, given that we were engaging in a very specific strategy of shipping high-quality games at a rapid pace.

Ramsay: What changes did this pivot entail? For production? For the product?

Koster: We had a lot of process changes, and yes, design and technical changes, in order to better suit the platform for social-game production. Architecture choices had been made based on the idea that nontrusted users from anywhere in the world were going to be using the tools. There were compromises, too; security systems, fail safes, and much more had been put in place for that particular audience. The core of the technology remained intact, however.

Moving to an internal programming-savvy audience meant a very different set of demands. Ease of use, and robust yet simple tools, were still very much virtues, but there was plenty we had to change in a real hurry. We ended up making those changes largely due to the pressure of success. We made our first game, Island Life, in about a month, and launched it and got more users on the first day than we had ever gotten for Metaplace.

Trying to scale the game really quickly to the sort of audiences that exist on social networks led to many changes to the technology. We had to scramble on many fronts: the persistence system, the metrics system, greater support for Flash as an asset type in the engine, and even platform features that needed to be taken out or redone to improve performance.

We also had many cultural adaptations to make when we changed over to the heavily metrics-driven environment of social games. This was particularly challenging for me. I am a huge fan of metrics, but I also like digging for the why of things. Metrics, as practiced in the industry at that time, didn't much care about why.

Ramsay: Did you adapt to that "unscientific" metrics culture? Did you continue to ask "why?"

Koster: I wouldn't call it an unscientific culture! Rather the opposite. I've always been an advocate of better metrics in online games. I used to do quite a lot of metrics gathering and analysis on SWG and other titles. The culture clash though was very real because the emphasis on metrics penetrates everything and causes you to re-evaluate what your definition of "a better game" is. But the biggest hurdle for me was getting used to releasing things as tests first instead of as updates. There are some folks who make companies because they are excited by the process of making companies. And then there are some who are excited by making a specific company. There are some designers who are excited by the process of creating something that meets any need whatsoever and then some who are excited by making a specific product. I happen to be the latter sort. That means that testing to identify a product is something that just feels weird. Tests only seem to work for some types of products, some types of approaches, and they encourage having little loyalty to a given idea. Don't get me wrong: I am a huge fan and advocate of metrics and playtesting, but it definitely took a mental adjustment for me.

So, testing changes that were largish wasn't something that we had figured out early on and many possible updates to Island Life in particular were left on the cutting-room floor. Many of these were pretty frustrating for me because I believed that these changes would be for the better.

Sometimes we did things without testing, too. An example of that would be the way we handled land expansion in Island Life and later in My Vineyard. Rather than simply expanding the grid—the way that virtually all social games did—we let the player expand their space piecemeal, which added a bit of a sculpting element to the game. You could shape your island into particular shapes. Today, many games do expansion in a similar way, including the market leader. But at the time, we didn't test that one, and we got lucky. Early on, our hunches were only right around 10% of the time.

Ramsay: What were some of the hunches that were wrong?

Koster: Oh, we were wrong many times when tried to apply what we learned from MMO games to web-based games. The area where we were most often wrong was usability. We were wrong about the degree of tutorials needed. We were wrong about the impact a given feature would have. We just made things too complex. Just over and over and over again.

Another side to the metrics lesson was that metrics really don't tell you "why." You have to tease that out, and for that, classic design training is enormously helpful.

Ramsay: How does your classic design training help you tease out the why from the metrics?

Koster: If you operate with just metrics in a vacuum, you can see when A versus B has differing results. Anyone can form a hypothesis, but having a broader background in design helps you to faster reach an accurate one. Sometimes, of course, that same background can prevent you from acknowledging the truth, too.

But when the time comes to forming a new idea about how to push the metric dramatically higher, that's where design comes in handy. Metrics are best suited to tuning and iteration, not to quantum leaps pushing you forward to new heights. Metrics optimize the peak you are on, but they don't find new mountains for you.

Ramsay: Let's switch gears. You have a family. What impact did the startup have on you and your family?

Koster: Well, it was hard at times. I missed all of the family vacations for nearly four years. I barely took any time off for those years, too. And the years that I missed were the last years before my kids became teenagers and began to pull away. Work was all-consuming. If my wife hadn't been supportive, I don't think I could have done it.

At first, I worked out of our spare bedroom and there the challenge was teaching the kids I was working, and not just at home to play with. But during that period, I was pretty accessible to the family.

For the middle phase of the company, our offices were quite close to where I lived—a three-minute commute that was walkable, if I wanted. It was then possible for me to stay home later in the morning, or to go home for lunch, or to go home for dinner and come back after. Although, honestly, I usually just got home very late.

When we pivoted to doing social games, we moved offices, as part of effecting cultural change at the office and getting a clean slate. I suddenly had a 20- to 30-minute commute. And that change, along with the shifts in responsibilities and changes in what we were trying to accomplish with the company, led to a lot of personal re-evaluation.

I very much regret having missed those years; although, I don't regret trying to chase the dream that I did. But I also promised myself that I wouldn't compromise home life for something I didn't believe in passionately, and now I maintain a more rigid line about bringing work home.

I'm about to turn 40. I don't want to sugarcoat it: I gained over 30 lbs. I developed high blood pressure. Entrepreneurship was a very stressful process. While I loved doing it, I also love other things about my life, such as my family. I did not know the toll when I started. I probably would have been a bit more invincible when I was younger!

Ramsay: How did the acquisition by Playdom come about?

Koster: Once we had pivoted to social games, we had basically pivoted into a pretty frothy market where many companies were making acquisitions for growth and strategic reasons. With our first couple of games, we got enough traction to attract the attention of several of them.

A big part of what people noticed was the pace at which we were able to release the games that we had made, which was attributable in large part to the technology base we had. Some of those conversations grew more serious, and one of those conversations was with Playdom. We ended up deciding to work with them because of their amazing reach in, and knowledge of, the social-games space.

Ramsay: Who was involved in the discussion about selling to Playdom? What did you talk about?

Koster: The executive team: me, John Donham, and Jason Hable. Playdom was only one of a few candidates who were speaking with us. The decision came down to factors like whether we were confident in the future of the acquirer, what their plans were in the video game space, the length of the lockup period in our contracts, what roles they wanted us to take, and the size of the deal. All of those issues played a part in our decision.

Ramsay: How did you personally feel about giving up independence? Was owning your destiny ever part of Metaplace's identity?

Koster: It was hard. Owning our destiny was a big part of the original Metaplace story. And here we were putting ourselves not only back into a big company but into Disney, one of the largest ones out there. For me, personally, I was excited about the potential for Facebook games within a large company. I had correctly forecasted that smaller players would be forced out of the market, but I also knew that there would be a lot of hoops to jump through to get anything greenlit.

Ramsay: Disney bought Playdom soon after Metaplace joined Playdom. What was that like?

Koster: From where we sat, that all happened simultaneously. A deal as large as Disney's acquisition takes a long time, so that deal was being made in parallel with our own. In a lot of ways, I ended up doing more work with Disney than many of the Playdom folks.

Ramsay: How did you end up doing more work with Disney?

Koster: I don't know how much I can say. Basically, because of the technology that Metaplace brought to Disney, I ended up having conversations with a lot of folks in the larger Disney organization from pretty early on. There were a lot of folks who I knew within Disney from earlier work, too. I knew Lane Merrifield from the days when Club Penguin was a startup on the conference circuit. I knew Starr Long from UO, of course.

Ramsay: You seemed to be drifting farther from Metaplace under the Disney banner. Were you?

Koster: I wasn't in charge of the Metaplace technology anymore. Early on, I was involved with executive-level stuff at Playdom, but after awhile, as the union with Disney progressed, there was less and less of that. I was doing "internal consultant" sorts of things for a bunch of titles while I was there. Several shipped; a few didn't. None of the ones that shipped set the world on fire. A lot of those were very "light touch," so to speak. I was not very involved.

Through accidents of history, the teams I worked with weren't the one in San Diego. I was traveling a lot. When I was in San Diego, I was kind of lonely even when I was surrounded by my former team. I did a lot of game pitches but none of them were ever kicked off. I was pitching without a team, too. I was sort of at loose ends a lot, feeling underutilized. It was very stressful. I was grinding my teeth in my sleep so much I shattered a molar in my jaw. I had a heart scare and ended up hospitalized for a weekend and put on blood pressure medication.

Eventually, I ended up working directly on just one game in Austin, which meant flying back and forth a lot. It was tough and bad timing in terms of family stuff—kids dealing with the stress of being teenagers in junior high, you know. When that game was cancelled, there were layoffs.

We tried to find somewhere else in Playdom or Disney that made sense but there wasn't anything. There were some opportunities on the Disney side, but nothing that felt creatively satisfying. My contract had been over for awhile anyway. So, I just let myself be laid off in a sense. I was exhausted. I didn't particularly try to keep my job.

Ramsay: Was your departure a good decision on Disney's part? Was leaving good for you regardless?

Koster: Playdom and I were ships that passed in the night. We ended up not a great match for each other, I guess. We never found a way for me to work there and both feel like it was a success. I am sure they were disappointed with me in some ways. In that sense, my departure was a mutually beneficial situation. There's no sense in prolonging a relationship if the two parties aren't happy with one another.

For me, it turned out to be a very good thing. All in all, I see the Metaplace-to-Playdom journey as one long, stressful series of events—a real rollercoaster. It was most fun near the beginning when we were chasing impossible dreams, when we had a small team, and when we were being creative and pushing at what was possible. That's when I was having the most fun and also when I was most productive.

Looking back at my career as a whole, the best times in terms of personal satisfaction and productivity were those times. It was the skunkworks team when UO was born, having to invent everything. It was the small team at the start of SWG, developing the cool fractal terrain technology. It was the brief period with my R&D group at SOE, where we developed some really groundbreaking stuff. I just had a patent for one of those things come through. It was the first couple of years of Metaplace, when we once again reinvented everything. Small teams, common vision, and crazy big obstacles—there's where I feel I was at my best.

In that sense, leaving was good for me in a lot of ways. I have taken time to try to get healthier. It took a couple of months of not doing anything at all before I felt relaxed. I haven't been tackling crazy big obstacles, just small games and more like what I used to make for fun on weekends. That's what I've been doing but it feels good. I am sure I will gather up a small team and find a new windmill to tilt at sometime soon but right now feels like a time to recharge.

Ramsay: What happened after you left? Do you know?

Koster: The old Metaplace office is still there. The game team has made successful games for Facebook and mobile, and the technology is still in use. So, it is fulfilling its promise.

Ramsay: Where Metaplace ended up was not exactly your vision at the beginning. Would you say that you failed?

Koster: True. It definitely has not yet done what it was designed to do. There's still time though! I can count Metaplace a failure in that sense though. I can also count Metaplace a success from the point of view that we came close to building what we set out to and that it touched people. Of course, financially, it worked out well, and in that business sense, Metaplace was not a failure, although it sure came damn close.

Ramsay: How might you have turned things around? Was your impossible dream even possible?

Koster: The dream was possible. We've already seen elements of that dream come true: kids running Minecraft servers in their houses and an explosion of indie development. Of course, the technology did actually do most of what we were trying to do and the rest was within reach.

I think that we built the wrong product though. We tried to get into too many markets and didn't focus down the way we should have. Furthermore, we didn't provide enough of a core for the market easiest for us to reach. I bet that had we simply made a fun MMORPG and then allowed players to extend the world, we would have had quite a lot more people interested.

Ramsay: What are you doing now?

Koster: I'm developing new concepts, working out of my house. I've got a tabletop card game going, a few puzzle games, and an art game. I'm having fun getting to be creative and do small projects. Now is an interesting time in games where experiments are actually being welcomed by the audience. I am sure that sometime soon I will end up getting pulled back into online development in some way. But I don't want to give up the sense of creative contentment that I have now. It will have to be the right project.

Reynir Harðarson

Cofounder, CCP Games

Reynir Harðarson cofounded CCP Games in 1997 with Þórólfur Beck and Ívar Kristjánsson to create EVE Online, a vast galactic battleground that boasts more than 500,000 spaceship captains of dubious repute.

Launched in 2003, EVE Online is one of the oldest and continuously growing massively multiplayer online games, and one of the harshest persistent worlds. Trust and betrayal are prominent features of the EVE universe. Players regularly lose thousands of U.S. dollars worth of virtual goods, as a consequence of corporate espionage, deception, sabotage, piracy, and all-out war.

After nearly 17 years as creative director, and some time after our interview, Harðarson left CCP Games in 2014. Along with principal game designer Kjartan Emilsson and business development executive Thor Gunnarsson, Harðarson established Sólfar Studios, a virtual reality game company.

Ramsay: When did you become interested in developing video games?

Harðarson: Like most young boys, I always dreamed of making computer games. I gravitated very early on to computers. My first machine was the Commodore 64, and I was playing games like Elite, which opened my eyes totally to computer games.

I pursued computer graphics. I did some programming, but I realized that wasn't my forte. In my first job, I started working as a graphic designer at an advertising agency called OZ. I didn't study anywhere. At the time, computer graphics were so new, it was only possible to do it professionally.

When the opportunity arose to work at OZ, that was a major break for me. They had Silicon Graphics workstations and Alias Wavefront. Shortly after, the dot com wave heated up, and OZ began transitioning themselves toward multimedia and the Internet. The product we started working on was called OZ Virtual, one of the first 3D chat clients. Because of our strong background in 3D graphics and graphic design, we managed to make the client look pretty amazing for the technology then.

So, we had real-time 3D over the Internet in a time when the world was running on modems still. The business didn't really pan out, so the company transitioned to doing mobile apps; and I had no real interest in that. I wanted to turn the company into a computer game company. But that vision did not pan out at OZ, so I seized the opportunity to found CCP.

In collaboration with a friend of mine, Þórólfur Beck, we decided to leave our employers. I left OZ, and he left his business; he was doing multimedia software training. And we decided to found CCP. A problem was that we didn't really have any money, and this was before financing through venture capital became very fashionable. So, we just created a family board game, Hættuspil, which we published in Iceland. We sold 10 thousand copies, an Icelandic record! The proceeds went to the first prototype for EVE.

Ramsay: What motivated you to start CCP?

Harðarson: It was really the dream to make EVE. It had been some years as an idea before we founded the company. It was something we really had to make. It was highly inspired by Elite, which we played as children on the Commodore 64. The first MMOs were coming out. Ultima

Online was just released, and EverQuest was in development. We saw this revolution comings and games would be changed forever. We thought then would be a perfect opportunity to get the talent together. It just had to be done.

Ramsay: What did you give up to go off on this adventure?

Harðarson: I quit OZ without any guarantees. It was a very interesting time. I just had the baby, just bought the house, and left my employer with no guarantees. My wife was not very happy with that decision.

Ramsay: Did you have any prior experience with starting businesses?

Harðarson: No, not really. I had once run a pizza business when I was 18. It went bankrupt, so yeah. Knowing this, we founded the company a little bit strangely for a small startup. The first people we hired were the CEO and the CFO. That's before we hired the programmers and artists. We wanted to set up the company correctly because, like I said, I'm a creative guy, and usually we're not very good at handling money.

Ramsay: Although you weren't handling the business side, did you at least have a role in putting together the business plan?

Harðarson: Yeah, our business plan was more conservative than how things actually turned out. In the original business plan, the best case scenario was we'd have 50,000 subscribers paying ten dollars per month. We didn't expect the game to last long, and now EVE is turning ten years old in May. We made a lot of assumptions that turned out to be wrong, and as we learned how wrong we were, the more our belief in what we were doing was reinforced.

Ramsay: What was the plan?

Harðarson: Right, the plan was to build a new breed of game company. Before 1997, game companies were traditionally built by self-taught talent who had been working from their parents' basements, building computer games. We were seeing how the industry was changing. Things were getting more professional. There were more programmers, artists, and so on with actual degrees coming into the field. That was one of our strengths. After starting the company, we brought in artists with real graphic design backgrounds and trained software engineers; our levels of education and experience were really high compared to what was happening around us.

That part of our plan really panned out. In the last 15 years, the industry has changed quite dramatically. Making games is much harder now. The technology is much more complex, and the artistic and technical requirements for triple-A titles are today on par with what you need to create top-of-the-line special effects for movies.

So, our plan was to build this amazingly talented company with the vision of creating virtual realities. The goal was always to create MMOs. We really had no interest in creating single-player games. We felt that the time of the linear narrative was over, and plus, that's not really our forte.

From a financial standpoint, starting CCP was never about becoming rich. We wanted to build a very interesting company working on the cutting edge. We always wanted to be independent, too, but we realized at the beginning that might be difficult; the only way to sell games then was through retail channels. We thought that would change, so after we bought back the license from our partners who had the publishing rights to EVE, we went fully online. We've stayed independent since then.

Ramsay: Who had the publishing rights?

Harðarson: Simon & Schuster Interactive, which was a small division of the book publisher, and they were going into games. Simon & Schuster was owned by Viacom at the time, so the concept was to utilize their network, like Paramount Pictures and MTV Networks. That never really took off, and EVE was the biggest project they had then.

Ramsay: Online game companies usually make online games as products. Funcom has several, but for CCP, EVE is your business model.

Harðarson: Naturally, but the business model was really the subscription business. That's also a major difference from traditional game developers. Unlike single-player games, the subscription business is not something that grows and just fades; it's a much more stable business proposal. That is what got investors excited about our company.

Ramsay: The initial capital for EVE came from your board game, right? Can you tell me more about that?

Harðarson: When we made Hættuspil, or "Dangerous Game," we knew computer games would be pretty difficult to finance because we had no money. We didn't come from any families with money, and we didn't know anyone who had money. But my partner had a grandmother, and she owned a house, so we mortgaged her house to pay for the printing of the board game. That was a huge, huge risk. I would never do that today, but being young and a little bit naïve, that was something we did.

We didn't pay ourselves salaries for months—years even. We just paid ourselves minimum wages, which got us into financial trouble. But if you don't take these risks, you're never going to do it. You have nothing to lose. That was our motto. In the worst case scenario, we'd be able to work our way out. That's how we looked at it.

Ramsay: How did Hættuspil come about? What does that mean?

Harðarson: The Icelandic word is Hættuspil, which means "life is a dangerous game." It was about teen angst, being a teenager, going through school, and avoiding the hazards of life, like not doing drugs. It became a huge hit among teenagers and tweens in Iceland, and it was hardcore player vs. player.

Ramsay: I think this explains EVE.

Harðarson: Yeah, it does! Actually, that's quite funny. Hættuspil was a game for teenagers, but you could do anything with anyone. The game allowed you to change the dice rolls of your friends, forcing them to be good to someone, steal things, and do stuff like that. This created an incredible cult following. People loved to play it because of its incredibly aggressive nature. Many board games, especially family board games like Monopoly, did not have that component.

It was a mechanism we took from harder strategy games, like Risk or Axis and Allies. It was a lot of fun to play, and that's really why it was so popular. We even contemplated, because of the success, to translate the game into all languages and try to sell it abroad. We decided against that because we wanted to focus on creating EVE, which we thought was a much more interesting, and much better opportunity than going into the board game business.

Ramsay: Was the board game self-published?

Harðarson: Yeah, we designed, manufactured, and printed it. We created the TV advertisements, and we drove around the island to sell it at supermarkets ourselves. It was a lot of work, but also a great experience.

Ramsay: How many people were involved at the beginning?

Harðarson: For the first year, we were three: me, Þórólfur Beck, and Ívar Kristjánsson. We started hiring in 1999, and we did preproduction for a year. When we started production, we had around 25 people.

Ramsay: Did you have any other sources of capital?

Harðarson: I had no money. Zero. I was working as a graphic designer on the side while we were waiting for revenue from the board game. Throughout 1999 and into early 2000, we were also working on projects to fund the development of the prototype for EVE. The largest one was Lazy Town, a children's show in the U.S. We did a lot of production and product design. We ran the company like an advertising agency for the first year.

Ramsay: When did you start raising money?

Harðarson: At the end of 1999, we got angel investors who brought in around $200,000, and then in May 2000, we had an initial round of share offerings and raised $3 million. That secured the funding for EVE. This money came mostly from Iceland Telecom, but there were other Icelandic investors.

Ramsay: Were you involved in that effort?

Harðarson: Oh, yeah. All the way! We always planned on raising venture capital to fund EVE. In 2000, the environment was very favorable to startups, especially because of the dot com bubble. Everybody seemed to be making money off these wild startups, so we got one of the biggest investment banks in Iceland to lead the investment round of $3 million for 25% of the company.

We had a very strong prototype in our hands, and we were already showing the potential of our graphics engine, which was ahead of its time, so people were really excited. Interestingly, the dot com bubble burst the same week as the offering, and by the next week, NASDAQ had fallen, so we were really lucky!

Ramsay: Your wife wasn't happy with your decision to quit your job and start this company, especially after having a baby. How was your family life impacted?

Harðarson: It was a very risky business, especially when you have no income. It was very stressful and really tough on the family. We would be working every waking hour, so there was no time for family. That was really difficult for my wife and my newborn son.

Ramsay: Was your wife working at the time?

Harðarson: Yeah.

Ramsay: But you weren't bringing home any money?

Harðarson: Yes, exactly.

Ramsay: Were you working from home?

Harðarson: No. We had office space. We had very small offices in very strange places; it was quite exciting. But we would sometimes sit down in our weird little offices full of pizza boxes and ask ourselves, "Are we crazy? Why are we doing this?" There was no chance that we'd succeed, but we had already jumped into the pool, and there was no turning back.

Ramsay: What hours were you keeping?

Harðarson: We would work every waking hour and all weekend. We would just work endlessly; it was as simple as that. And that even got worse when we went into full production on EVE. We were, practically, living at the office. In the last year of development, we were sleeping at the office more often than we were sleeping in our own beds. It was very crazy and a lot of work.

Ramsay: Would starting CCP have been easier without a family?

Harðarson: If I was single, it would have much less risky. Also, in Iceland, we tend to have children quite young, so it's not uncommon for 23-year-olds to have kids. A lot of our peers had children, and not knowing when we could pay them was really worrisome. It's not just you and your friends at that point. Families are depending on you. That added a lot of stress to the equation.

Ramsay: Can you tell me more about your cofounders? I can't pronounce their names. How did you know them?

Harðarson: Þórólfur Beck, yes, just call him Toti, Toti Beck, or Mr. Beck. We had been friends since we were five. He's incredibly good, very motivated, driven, and generally very creative. Toti is a lot of fun to work with, so I thought he'd be the perfect partner for this. Ívar Kristjánsson is also an old friend of mine. He had just finished studying finance in university, so he was the perfect guy to handle the financial part of the operation.

Ramsay: How did you convince them to join up with you?

Harðarson: Toti and I talked about it a lot. We were super excited about the idea, talked each other into going forward, and just decided to jump in. It was a moment of insanity, and, I guess, we were drinking whiskey at the time. CCP was the hardest thing I've ever done, and I'd do it all over again.

Ramsay: What about your first hires?

Harðarson: We initially had a problem with recruiting because some people thought joining such a new company was too risky, and the proceeds from the board game was only $260,000, so we could only grow to a certain size with that limited amount of cash. But were able to hire a graphic designer, our lead programmer, and so on. We focused on art and programming, but more on art. Later, we brought on our CTO, Hilmar Pétursson.

Ramsay: How did you identify your staffing needs?

Harðarson: We worked on real-time 3D engines, and server and database technology, at OZ, so we had some years of experience. We had a running start, but we didn't have a code base. There was no middleware. We wrote our own 3D engine, our own server, and almost everything was developed in-house. But the scalability part was unknown. We were planning for a universe of 50,000 simultaneous players, and that had never been attempted before.

With game design, we were very much in theoretical waters because nothing like this had been tried before. We looked to sandbox games like Ultima Online and less to the theme park games like EverQuest. But our game wasn't really a game. It was more of a simulation, relying on the emerging behaviors of the players, which made EVE almost impossible to test without players.

Ramsay: What do you mean by "simulation"?

Harðarson: We would build this universe across regions. In the central regions, there would be some controlled security, and in the outer regions, we would have land up for grabs. Our theory was that players would gravitate to where the risk was higher because the rewards were potentially greater, and they would claim those regions as their own and fight over territory.

The game engine was designed to around perpetual, endless warfare. There was no real story. There was no quest line. We built an economy system, where everything in the game would be built by players. The systems would be claimed by players. They'd organize themselves, write their own stories, and go on their own adventures—all consequences of the interaction between them. There was nothing we could actually test or play, so that was a huge risk. Will the simulation actually work? We didn't know.

Ramsay: What was your process for designing the game then?

Harðarson: We'd theorize a lot. We'd talk about thought experiments. We'd make paper prototypes for user interface elements, or how you play the game. We made small gameplay prototypes, like how the fighting system might work. Should we use these kinds of weapons? What are the combat strategies? We were actually able to test some of that out at a small scale, but we invented pretty much everything as we went along. It was our first game.

But our team was a huge melting pot; everybody was involved in the process. There was a lot of pride in that. We empowered people to be part of the creation process and have input, so we weren't just giving orders. Everybody had a say. Everybody could talk. We all had a very strong sense of ownership, and we all believed that what we were doing was something groundbreaking and radical. It was almost like a religious cult. We had faith.

Ramsay: Do you remember the technical requirements of your simulation?

Harðarson: I don't really remember. I know we designed the game to be incredibly tolerant of latency and bandwidth. We knew that to create a simulation of this scale, the game would have to blow up fairly quickly. Fortunately, space simulations allow you to do a lot of trickery to minimize client-server communication and make the client very latency resistant.

Ramsay: How did you expect to support 50,000 simultaneous players?

Harðarson: We had EVE split up into multiple regions, multiple solar systems, to distribute players around the universe. This didn't pan out as we expected. Some stations became more popular than others, and players would form trade hubs, where a lot of players would congregate. At launch, this caused a problem immediately because there was more and more and more load. Now, for these incredibly contested spots, we run them on super-fast machines with the fastest hardware available to accommodate thousands of players. We can now scale the server cluster for when more players come in.

But what we did not anticipate—because it had never happened before in games—was the formation of massive corporations and, on top of that, huge alliances of tons of massive corporations. We had predicted that these social structures would fail at 150 people; that did not turn out to be the case. A corporation could have hundreds of players, and an alliance could have multiple thousands while still behaving almost like a single entity.

So, we would early on see incredibly massive battles between thousands of ships, crashing our servers because they just couldn't handle it. We had to up our game. We've been constantly optimizing. We've been doing this now for ten years. Now, we have the largest battles in any game; a single battle in EVE is like a whole shard in World of Warcraft. The scale is just so massive.

We thought these would be nice problems to have, and we'd deal with them when they happened. They were incredibly fun challenges to deal with, and we danced with them; having these problems meant our game was a success.

Ramsay: Early on, Simon & Schuster Interactive was your publisher. Had you always planned for EVE to be published by a third party?

Harðarson: Yes, that was the original plan. Internally, we had no expertise in marketing, customer support, or distribution, and, at the time, distribution was king. You needed a publishing deal to get your boxed product into stores. In 2003, the idea of buying software or games online had not yet really taken off, or for that matter, buying anything on the Internet. People were still very paranoid about using their credit cards online; it was a very different world back then. So, working with a publisher was absolutely necessary for us.

Ramsay: How long did your relationship with Simon & Schuster last?

Harðarson: We entered that relationship in 2002, and Simon & Schuster closed their game publishing division in the summer of 2003. EVE was launched in May 2003 after a six-month delay. By summer, it was very difficult for us to get EVE into any stores, so we bought back the rights and started selling the game online ourselves. That was a great, great decision.

But that also meant we had to build up our own customer support, which we did, in cooperation with our largest shareholder, Iceland Telecom. They had lots of experience with billing and support. We were only 25 people making a game; we couldn't operate like a publisher, but later, we took that over.

Ramsay: How did you buy back the rights?

Harðarson: We sent our chairman to negotiate that deal. I do not know what he did, but he bought it back for a very fair price. The rights were just lying in a drawer; they weren't going to do anything with them. It wasn't their business anymore. Just getting some money was a winning scenario for them. That was fantastic for us! If they had not sold us the rights, we'd have been dead.

Ramsay: Since EVE was a very large project and you needed a very large number of players for this game to be fun, why did you choose to develop this game, instead of a smaller, possibly more practical title?

Harðarson: That is a great question. We wanted to push the boundaries of technology. The reason we went for a single shard and this epic size was we wanted to push the boundaries, to do something impossible. We weren't making computer games as a business; we made them as a passion. It's not about the money. It's about creating something beautiful. It's about creating something new and revolutionary. We wanted to create his massive world where everyone would be playing together in a virtual reality. That we did that is something that has constantly amazed us. It's something incredible. And, frankly, when we look at theme park games, we just don't understand why some even bother. I mean, what is this? Where's the insanity and the beauty in what they're making? EVE is harder to explain. EVE doesn't really make sense because the experience is just such an emotional thing.

We tried to push the boundaries, of graphics technology, of server technology, and of game design, and because of that, we attracted the best people. It was a self-fulfilling prophecy. You cannot make these games without the best talent, and the best talent want to make beautiful things. And that's why people jumped with us into this opportunity, this madness, this dream we had. But as soon as people start thinking like accountants, that's not a business I want to be in.

Ramsay: You never thought "if our game fails, we'll go under"?

Harðarson: Oh, sure. We almost went under numerous times. The money we got to develop the game was not enough. The money we got from Simon & Schuster was still not enough. We had to raise more, and sometimes we had no idea if that was possible, especially when the dot com bubble burst and there was no venture capital anywhere in the world. They saw us as an Internet business, so we almost went bankrupt multiple times. And then there was 2003 before we bought back the rights, the game had sold only 30,000 units in the summer, and it wasn't possible to buy the game anymore. We weren't financially viable as a business, but so what? We were on an incredible adventure.

Ramsay: As the creative director, what are your responsibilities?

Harðarson: I did a lot of game design, but I was also the head of the art department. I was also heavily involved in the development of the graphics technology and 3D engine, although I was not on the programming side. I was also very heavily involved with designing the user interface. With a company this small, you have to wear many hats, and that's what we all did.

Ramsay: How did your creative role interface with the operation of CCP Games as a business?

Harðarson: I have never been involved in the operational part. I've never been managing people. I've never been doing any finance. Other people are just much better at it than I am. There are skills I have that they don't possess, and there are skills they have that I don't, so I let other people manage people. I think it's important to know your strengths and weaknesses.

It's often a trap that small companies fall into: they take their best people, and make them managers. It happens all the time because why wouldn't the lead programmer also be the manager? The problem is that when you make him a manager, he can no longer program. But we try to not do that. Let's have our best programmers do programming and have our best artists do art.

And everybody's happiest that way. Our experience is that once you promote someone to a manager position, he's not going to be happy in that position. He's just going to be a rather mediocre or bad manager, and his talent is just going to be wasted because he's not doing the thing he's really good at.

Ramsay: Tell me about launch day for EVE Online.

Harðarson: EVE launched on May 6, 2003, and we had been working for the past six months straight leading to launch. We practically lived in the office. We were sleeping under our tables. We had been having incredibly bad server and client stability issues, and we were still running a beta test, but not a very large one. We were incredibly stressed out, but for some miraculous reason, we managed to iron out most of the terrible issues. When we launched, it was tranquil.

We sat down in our office, logged in, and saw the first player fly around. It was an incredible experience because this just became real. EVE was no longer theoretical, no longer just a piece of software running on some hardware. Now, EVE was a real world with a real person, who we did not know, flying around. It was quite a beautiful moment. We even went to the local game store, and there was a queue outside; people were waiting to buy EVE. That was quite exciting.

We were incredibly tired though, and the problem is that once you launch, you can't just go on vacation because that's when the real work starts. We were crunching for months after launch, fixing issues, and all kinds of things. We had very limited quality assurance capability. We couldn't test the game on every combination of hardware, so we had a lot of compatibility issues.

But everything actually worked out great. Launch day went much better than we expected. We didn't crash the servers, and there wasn't a catastrophe. That was a huge relief! And people were really excited. Of those who bought EVE that first year, 20% of those who bought the game in the first week are still playing ten years later. Our players either loved the game or hated it.

Ramsay: When did you hit 50,000 simultaneous players?

Harðarson: A year after launch, I think. But the business had also changed by then. Then, $9.95 was no longer the standard for subscriptions. We were charging $15 per month for subscriptions because all of the other games had raised their subscription fees. That made a huge difference in our revenue, so we were profitable by early 2004. We still owed money though.

Ramsay: How long did it take to earn back your investment?

Harðarson: Well, the thing is we've never paid out dividends. We have always used the proceeds from EVE to fund the company, build the company, and fund our other game projects. Currently, we have EVE and two other games in development: one in Shanghai, Dust 514; and the other here in Atlanta, World of Darkness. The total cost of making EVE ended up at $10 million, which is roughly a month and a half of revenue now. So, whether we earned back our investment depends on how you look at it.

Ramsay: You launched EVE, the game was up and running, and the universe was alive. Is maintaining a live game is different from building one?

Harðarson: Yes, yes, absolutely! There are so many things that can go wrong because you're going to keep that game going for years. That's difficult for some people to understand, especially developers who are done when they release a single-player game. They can move and do the next thing, but we had a lot left to do to make EVE perfect. We were making expansions, planning to fix this and do that, and we were building momentum around that.

In the first week and months after launching EVE, it was a very tough time because we were so exhausted and still had to service it. We were only working on things that were not really fun, like fixing bugs and just trying to make sure the servers didn't catch fire. We were just very much in the trenches; it was very exhausting. We turned that around by early 2004, and we got into the new and exciting rhythm that we've been in ever since.

Some companies take a very different approach to what they call a live operation. Many companies build a game, and then have a small, live team supporting it. From what we had seen, I'd call that abandonment. If you look at Ultima Online, especially just before the turn of the century, it was just finished and then left in the hands of maybe ten or 15 people. They had no grand plans; they just wanted to make new games. With EverQuest, there were new expansions and content updates, but their big focus was EverQuest II.

We didn't want to go down that road, so we've been continuously growing the development team. We had 30 people working on the game at launch, and now we have 250 people working on the game. In the ten years since launching, we've totally rewritten everything in the game. We're constantly making changes, most of the time for the better. That is the nature of the game. EVE was never a product we'd sell once and then we'd been done with it. There's no reason why EVE couldn't go on for decades. After all, EVE has been growing every year for the past ten years.

Ramsay: Would you say that the launch was successful?

Harðarson: I would say it was not really successful. We sold about 50,000 units, but we were hoping to sell about 100,000. It was not terrible, but it was not good enough.

Ramsay: What impact did that have?

Harðarson: We had to let few people go quite shortly after launch. It wasn't a lot. I think we let go around six people, but that was 15% of the company.

Ramsay: Had you overspent on the technology?

Harðarson: The whole project cost a lot more than we initially planned. We were planning to do this for $5 million, but ended up at almost $10 million. By modern standards, that's low for a massively multiplayer game.

Ramsay: What did you expect for the game from that point?

Harðarson: We expected EVE to peak in the first two years and then dwindle down. Remember we planned for EVE to last between three and five years. That had been a very common pattern in other MMOs. I didn't really expect us to be any different. Other games would come out, and maybe a better space game.

We were going to start building a second product after two years, but what surprised us was that the game just continued growing. We felt that our best option was to continue developing the game. And what really surprised us was that within the company, there wasn't a great interest in doing anything new. Everyone wanted to continue working on EVE. Two years later, we started hiring people from the community who knew the game, loved the game, wanted to build this game, and they came from all over the world to join CCP.

Ramsay: How is EVE doing today?

Harðarson: At this moment, we have exactly 411,759 subscribers in the West. In China, we have almost 200,000. In total, we have more than a half-million subscribers, ten times greater than what we planned. EVE is doing great; it has never been better. We expect EVE to grow at least 10% this year, but EVE has been growing between 20% and 25% every year. On the development side, we have 250 people working on EVE, and every year, we're spending more on EVE than we did to create it. We're at almost ten times the manpower just working on EVE than we did at launch.

Ramsay: How has the world of EVE changed in that time?

Harðarson: It's a lot more populated. Everything is happening on a much larger scale. We have alliances of tens of thousands of people battling it out. Nothing even close to this has ever happened in video game history. The EVE universe is a lot richer than it once was, too. There was practically nothing in the universe when we launched, but every six months, we add something new into the game.

With EVE, the median age of our subscribers is higher than most games. We have a median age of 26 years old. We see people of all ages playing the game, of course, but the point is that the market is growing every year and a whole new generation is coming in and not dropping out.

Ramsay: How has CCP evolved with the game?

Harðarson: Well, we built up all of the infrastructure to be a publisher except retail; we just don't believe that much in retail. We sometimes distribute EVE in stores, but retail is dead; it's not the future, so we have no focus on that. We also have our own marketing teams. We do all of the public relations.

But until now, we've had these functions for only EVE. That's why we felt it was a logical step to create three games, so we could fully utilize this organization that we built for publishing and virtual world operations. We've gone from a 30-person garage operation to a fully fledged publisher with three game teams.

EVE also built for us quite a reputation in the industry. We've been able to hire an incredible amount of fantastic talent from all over the world, willing to move to a strange location like Reykjavík because of the love for the product. They have a love for the company too; we're doing something different.

CCP is a lot more international now. The company used to be almost purely Icelandic when we had just 30 people. Now, Icelanders make up maybe 25% of the company, and we have offices in Shanghai, Atlanta, and Newcastle.

Ramsay: When did you decide to really develop more games after EVE?

Harðarson: In 2006, we started talking about our next product, and we started talking with White Wolf Publishing, one of the biggest tabletop role-playing publishers in the world. White Wolf is actually number two after Wizards of the Coast. They have a series of games in the World of Darkness universe, starting with Vampire: The Masquerade.

We've always been fans of White Wolf. We played their games when we were teenagers. But when we talked to them, we didn't intend to do a game with them. At the time, we wanted to expand the EVE brand to more products, so we were making a collectible card game based on the EVE universe. We went to White Wolf to better understand that business, and then we found out they wanted to capitalize on their IP with a massively multiplayer online game.

Although we weren't interested in a licensing deal with White Wolf, we decided to exchange information. We started cooperating, and for some reason, the conversation came up: "why don't we just merge our companies?" Neither of us wanted to do a licensed product; we wanted to do our own things. In late 2006, CCP Games and White Wolf Publishing merged, and we started preparing to develop the game I'm working on now: World of Darkness. Two years later, I moved out here to Atlanta, and we built our US offices on top of White Wolf.

Ramsay: White Wolf had created other properties, like Trinity, Exalted, and Pendragon. Dark Age of Camelot was out, so I suppose a Pendragon MMO wouldn't be innovative, but Trinity was sci-fi, your wheelhouse. So, why choose to develop World of Darkness into an MMO?

Harðarson: World of Darkness has a much wider appeal. It's dark, it's about vampires, and it's about people. One problem we have with EVE is that the game is all about spaceships, and our demographic is like 97% male. Girls aren't really as interested in spaceships as guys. I don't know why, but it's just a fact.

And we know from experience with the World of Darkness tabletop and live-action roleplaying (LARP) games that there is a lot of female interest in the vampire thing. That actually surprised White Wolf when they published Vampire: The Masquerade because tabletop role-playing games had been dominated by guys, stereotyped as geeks in high school and college. There had been very little female participation. Let's say 10% of the players were women, and then suddenly, that became almost 50%, especially in LARPs, where people would meet together, play their parts like actors, and dress up. World of Darkness resonated strongly with both genders.

Ramsay: You mentioned three games. There was EVE, and then there was World of Darkness. What's the third?

Harðarson: Yes, we also decided to build an expansion for EVE called Dust 514, and we decided to do this in Shanghai. Originally, Dust 514 was supposed to be a small, interesting product, but it blew out of proportion and became this fully fledged triple-A shooter on the PlayStation 3. It's coming out very soon. But the key is that all of this has been funded through the success of EVE. We would not be able to do any of this without EVE growing and growing. Currently, we have around 550 people in three major studios.

Ramsay: Have there been any setbacks?

Harðarson: I think our biggest mistake was underestimating the challenge of building three studios at the same time. We totally underestimated the difficulty. Social dynamics change when you hire a lot of people. It causes confusion and chaos, so development has been taking much longer than we expected. And that, of course, means we're spending more money than we originally planned. But everything is quite happy in CCP land; we're in a good spot.

I would say that 2011 was our worst year. We totally overestimated the growth of EVE, and we made mistakes in three expansions. We were introducing features to the game that players didn't really like, and in the summer of 2011, we had this revolt in the player community, and there was incredibly negative feedback all over the Internet. We saw our subscriptions drop significantly for the first time—well, significantly by our standards. Instead of gaining 15% more subscribers, we lost about 10%, and all of our plans were then up in the air.

It is amazing how much cash you can burn in a very short time when your plans fail. We had to make very hard decisions, and we laid off around 100 people. We should have been more cautious because that was incredibly hard.

We now try to grow within our means, always making sure we have enough cash in the bank to weather catastrophes like that. We've never had to do that in our history. We've always been incredibly accurate with our predictions, but now we know that things can go wrong quite quickly.

Ramsay: Before we talk more about Dust 514, I'd like to know what exactly inspired you to create a sci-fi, spaceship-driven MMO.

Harðarson: EVE was obviously very much influenced by Elite. I played that game a lot back in the day on the Commodore 64, as well as Master of Orion, Free Space, and Wing Commander. I was also very much influenced by the science fiction and space settings of movies like Star Wars and Blade Runner. But the game design and philosophy were not only influenced by space games; we also drew from Civilization, Magic: The Gathering, and Ultima Online. EVE's influences came from many directions.

Ramsay: Prior to EVE, MMOs were focused on player vs. environment gameplay. By 2000, Ultima Online had even lightened its own player vs. player experience. Why did you focus on player vs. player?

Harðarson: So, we thought player vs. player was a much more interesting and rewarding experience. The theory is that when you play chess against a computer, it's marginally interesting, but when you play it against a friend, there's a meta-game happening around you. You bring your history you're your friend to the board, and winning against your friend is much more satisfying. Counter-Strike, Quake, and StarCraft are good examples of where we would see competitive play as super interesting and very exciting.

We also felt that a computer-generated narrative is difficult to deal with at a very high quality for a very long time. It's like trying to solve the impossible problem, and we've seen many MMOs fail here. And MMOs have to last for an extremely long time. If had written content for EVE, we'd need ten years of content; that's a lot of stories and a lot of dialog. We thought the way to do an MMO then was to build a universe with endless emergence, constantly refreshing itself by the actions of players.

And space operas are about combat, empires fighting empires. That's essentially the heart of the player vs. player concept. If you tried to make a player vs. environment game in space, that's just going to be weird; it's not going to feel real. We didn't want to do that; we wanted to make a real world, a place you could believe in. One of our game design principles is verisimilitude: we try to maintain believability. Once you start straying away from believability, you very easily go down, clinging to abstract solutions, and in the end, the game is full of strange and abstract things that don't really make any sense.

Ramsay: How does Dust 514 fit into your vision for EVE?

Harðarson: Dust 514 is an extension, an evolution, of EVE. With Dust 514, we are building on EVE, providing more things for players to do, and fleshing out this space opera. With EVE, you build star bases and claim sovereignty over star systems, but we also always wanted to have troops on the ground.

In 2006, we started that project. We wanted Dust 514 on a different platform because we wanted to make a new first-person shooter experience. We didn't want to make something where you'd have EVE on one screen and Dust 514 on another. We wanted to have EVE on PC, and then you'd go to a console to play as a mercenary on the ground. It was a more sentimental decision, more fitting. EVE is the machinery for operating space ships and empires, and then you'd use another technology to deploy your mercenaries.

Ramsay: You didn't know what was fun about EVE until launch day. Did Dust 514 have the same problem?

Harðarson: It's not as difficult because Dust 514 has session-based mercenary contracts, which is very similar to many other shooters. The exceptions are that there are space battles, vehicles, and an in-game economy. If you lose that expensive vehicle, that's it. You have to spend resources in the game.

Dust 514 is fairly easy to test because you need only 32 players for a session, but the bigger, untested waters are how territorial warfare and contract mechanics will play out within EVE. That's more of a thing we can't test, and we're very excited to see how that goes—and a little bit scared.

Ramsay: For a time, EVE was your only source of income, so when there are interruptions in service, how does that impact the business?

Harðarson: Every hour of downtime is lost revenue, and would reflect very badly on the company if we couldn't maintain full service. When LulzSec attacked us, we were down for two days—that's two whole days of lost revenue. That's a lot of money. This is very serious stuff.

Ramsay: When service interruptions are caused by intrusions, usually to steal credit card information, downtime in those cases is a double hit, right?

Harðarson: Especially back in the days when there was a lot of resistance to using credit cards online. People were very, rightfully wary of giving credit card information to companies that were security risks. We understood that from the beginning, so credit card information was never stored in our databases, but instead went to a third party. We understood that if somebody hacked into our databases and stole credit card information, that might mean the death of our business. It would be a single point of failure where we would just lose everything. So, we've never stored credit card information, and still don't.

Ramsay: What happens internally during that downtime?

Harðarson: We're constantly working. The security teams go into overdrive. In the case of LulzSec, we were afraid they would use this attack as smoke and mirrors to do something more serious behind the scenes. That's why we shut down the servers ourselves. Fortunately, that turned out to not be the case; they would have to be quite sophisticated to be able to do that. Their denial of service attacks were fairly low tech, mostly just bombarding us with lots of data. They were taking down websites, like CIA.gov and stuff like that, so they were never a serious threat. But we cannot take any chances.

Of course, it's a little bit scary when suddenly your product isn't working, it's your only source of revenue, and you don't really know how long it's going to last. So, we juggled the hardware and rerouted Internet traffic all over the world to withstand future distributed denial of service attacks much better.

Ramsay: EVE is frequently in the press as players continue to lose thousands of dollars worth of virtual items. As a designer, how do you feel about that?

Harðarson: That is what the game is really about! It's about trust and betrayal. It's about people working together or working against each other. Just like in the real world, sometimes you can't trust everyone, but in some cases, there are honest mistakes, like a Titan pilot jumping into the wrong system and losing the ship, which is worth roughly $5,000. But that's also what makes EVE interesting and exciting for players. Mommy's not holding your hand all the time. There's an adrenaline rush. Every choice has more meaning and weight.

There was another case there was this guy had set up a banking operation inside EVE, and banking is not regulated at all. In reality, it was a Ponzi scheme. He ran out, sold his ISK—which is our in-game currency—and paid for his college tuition. We had a lot of angry people, and this hit the press. But this is the reality of the game, and what makes EVE so interesting.

We can't interfere with those activities. Who are we to judge? He wasn't breaking any rules of the game. This was just totally emergent behavior. Almost every time this happens, it gets very wide publicity and we don't lose players. In fact, we start gaining more subscribers because people are very intrigued. "How can a thing like this happen in a game? What is this game? I want to see what it is because these stories don't really happen in other games!"

Ramsay: Speaking of trust, you said that not everyone can be trusted. I understand that you have an internal affairs division.

Harðarson: Yes, we've had incidents within the company; in one particular case, we had an employee using his power as a programmer to directly alter the data on the game database to help his character. That was a major breach of our trust when that got out, so we started the internal affairs division to monitor us. They also handle some of the more difficult cases, like using in-game currency to engage in money laundering and other illegal real-world activities.

We take internal security very seriously. When something like this happens, we've breached the trust of our players. We should have fired him on the spot, but we didn't fire him until three days later because our CEO was not in the country. It was mishandled internally, and the players got the impression we were okay with this behavior. They were massively outraged. It was not good.

Ramsay: Now, of course, you have a very good relationship with the players, in large part thanks to the Council of Stellar Management?

Harðarson: When we were developing the game back in the 2000s, we started to get a lot of useful feedback from the forum, and we weren't really expecting the feedback to be so good. We wanted to keep a dialog with the players open, to understand the game and what was happening inside the game.

We've felt that way since we had the first EVE Fanfest in 2004. We met some players face-to-face for the first time, and we had a lot of conversations. We realized that player feedback was an incredibly valuable resource for us to move forward, especially with a universe of this epic scale.

So, we created the Council of Stellar Management (CSM), a democratically elected council of players who we'd fly to Iceland a few times each year. They'd meet with the development team, and talk about the issues in the game, what was important to them, and what was not.

We no longer have a relationship where it's us vs. them, us just marketing to them. We're working together, and we have a common goal. The CSM just turned out to be fantastic, even mind-blowing. I'd highly recommend everyone start their own player councils if they want good community relations.

Ramsay: When you look back at all you've accomplished, the road you've traveled, and the challenges you've overcome, what are you thinking?

Harðarson: It's been an amazing adventure. It's been the greatest adventure of our lives. It has been very much a work of passion and love and incredibly rewarding, but also incredibly hard at times. We are very lucky to have been able to start this company and actually get the ship sailing. We are very lucky to have been able to recruit incredibly talented people over the years. I think a lot of our luck comes from our mindset. We're not in this to aspire to mediocrity; we're in this to do something that really matters. It's an incredible privilege.

Riccardo Zacconi

Cofounder, King

Riccardo Zacconi cofounded King in 2003 with Toby Rowland, Sebastian Knutsson, Lars Markgren, Thomas Hartwig, and Patrik Stymne. King is best known for the *Candy Crush Saga* series, whose massive success propelled the publisher toward an IPO in March 2014. But unlike certain other IPOs in the same category, King had been a successful video game publisher for more than a decade.

Prior to King, Zacconi was a marketing and finance executive, working predominantly in the European online dating business at Spray Network and uDate, which was acquired by Match.com. Zacconi had also spent time as a consultant with the legendary Boston Consulting Group, and as an entrepreneur in residence with Benchmark Capital.

When this interview was conducted, King had not gone public and was just entering mobile games. The company has since accumulated more than 1.5 billion average game plays per day, 149 million daily active users, and 533 million monthly active users as of Q4 2014, making King one of the leading mobile games publishers.

Ramsay: Tell me about your background. What were you doing before King. com, now King Digital Entertainment?

Zacconi: I grew up in Italy and studied economics at university. After my studies, I went to Germany where I worked as a consultant for ten years. For seven of those years, I worked for the Boston Consulting Group. In 1999, I joined a startup in a Sweden. It was a very small company then called Spray Network, and then we grew from a team of 30 to 800 people in less than a year. Spray was basically a portal, like Yahoo! and AOL, with a focus on content. We had a search engine, communities, and one of the first free dating sites in Europe. We also did games.

By March 2000, we wanted to do an IPO, but we missed the window. We acquired Caramail, the largest e-mail provider in France, and we wanted to include the company in our prospectus. But in April, the NASDAQ crashed, so we had to postpone. We ended up selling Spray in September 2000 to Lycos Europe for more than $700 million in stock. But the stock went from $10.50 to $0.30 in less than a year! So, at the end of the day, it was not a great deal, but we learned a lot.

After the Spray experience, I received an offer from Benchmark Capital to join them as an entrepreneur in residence. I'd be responsible for finding new businesses for them to sponsor. At first, I refused; it seemed too good to be true. I'd get a salary and an office without any financial obligations? I had never heard of that before. When they told me I'd really have no obligation to be financed by Benchmark, I said, "It actually is too good to be true, so, of course, I will join!" I moved to London, started at Benchmark in September 2001, and I came into the office with 50 ideas. One of those ideas was to launch online dating in Europe.

Online dating was already popular in the United States. Match.com was growing very well. There weren't any paid dating sites in continental Europe though. I looked into several options. One was to start from scratch. We had developed the one of the first free dating sites which was growing really fast. The second option was to buy a few free dating sites and then change their models. The third option was to invest in an existing paid dating site that had no business in continental Europe and build the company from there.

Ramsay: Which option did you go with?

Zacconi: We made an offer to a company called uDate, an English company listed on AIM, a growth capital market of the London Stock Exchange, which had a strong U.S. presence. They refused the offer because we made our offer at a lower valuation. We argued we would bring value to the company. They counter offered and said, "Riccardo, we don't need the money, but we would like you to be on the board to build the business in continental Europe." After discussing the situation with Benchmark, I left to join uDate in August 2002. We sold the company at five times the price in December to IAC/InterActiveCorp and merged with Match.com.

Ramsay: Like many entrepreneurs, you were motivated by opportunism. What was the next big opportunity you pursued?

Zacconi: I had remained in contact with my former colleagues from Spray in France. In early 2003, we talked about what was next for us. We saw an opportunity in the European games market. Portals were paying for content to make their offerings more sticky, and games were sticky content that they were paying for to make their sites more attractive.

The prevailing models were games you could play for free on a site and games you had to download. We said, "Okay, let's launch a new model where games would be offered online and you could play them with others in tournaments." I approached old colleagues in continental Europe who had left Lycos to work at the large portals in key European countries. I told them, "Look, I have a new model. I don't know how well this model will monetize, but you won't have to pay for content; it's going to be sticky content. We're also going to share these revenues, so let's work together."

Ramsay: They agreed, and you started down the road of building a video game company. What were video games to you?

Zacconi: I was coming from online, so I had quite a bit of experience with online B2C. But rather than coming from games, I came to games with a very fresh mind. I was playing casual games myself, but I was not a hardcore gamer. Our team had quite a bit of experience on the product side, especially with communities, games, and mobile. After the sale to Lycos, Spray was developing the games channel, mobile games, and all of the communities for Lycos Europe. But I was very much coming from online B2C though with little experience in games. I was more focused on building the portal, all types of content, and strong communities. I couldn't have designed games myself; that is not my area.

Ramsay: Did you expect that the business of games would be different than your previous experience with online B2C?

Zacconi: Well, not really. We had experience with games, but they were one of many categories we had within Spray. In B2C, there are a few fundamentals, like making sure you make your application user-friendly; you have to see that it's easy to understand. I'm a pretty good tester because the games we offer are casual games. And our definition of casual is easy to learn but difficult to master. If I don't understand a game, it's probably too difficult also for the average casual gamer to play.

From that perspective and back to your question, I thought we would have very good reason to be successful. The model was new, we had a small team of very knowledgeable people who had actually done games before and who had also had experience with communities, and we were organizing games to be played with other players. And I had contacts at all of the distributors, and experience with marketing and building reach. Those reasons are why we decided we needed to start the company.

Ramsay: How did King.com get started?

Zacconi: We started King.com initially—we were called Midasplayer originally—with quite small offices in London and Stockholm. I was in London, and Toby Rowland, a colleague and friend who I had met at uDate, was also in London. The development team was in Stockholm. They were people I knew very well. We worked in parallel. I had 100% trust in them.

Ramsay: Who were the other cofounders? Were they in Sweden?

Zacconi: The other founders were in Sweden. There was Sebastian Knutsson, who was the chief product developer; Lars Markgren, who was our CTO at Spray; and Thomas Hartwig and Patrik Stymne. Thomas and Patrik worked on the development side. Thomas is our CTO at King now. They're fantastic people. We were founders who brought in many different talents. I was responsible for marketing and finance.

Ramsay: Did you have capital for this new company? What was your stake?

Zacconi: We looked for financing, but it was a very tough time for the B2C model, which had fallen out of fashion in 2003. I invested with Toby and we financed the company. We had some money from part of the deal with Lycos. Around eight tech guys in Sweden also worked at a lower cost than usual in exchange for stock. We later closed capital deals with a number of distribution partners, including Key Online and FreeNet in Germany and Lycos Europe.

Ramsay: You and Toby made the initial financial commitment. Did the others invest any money?

Zacconi: The other four did. Sebastian put up money in the second round of internal funding. We did two rounds of funding internally: one at the very beginning, which was only Toby and myself; and then Sebastian also joined with some money in the second round.

Ramsay: Most entrepreneurs I talk to never wrote business plans, but you know quite a bit about finance. Can I assume you did?

Zacconi: Yes. I put together the business plan. We actually managed to do much more than what it said.

Ramsay: Were you solely involved with business planning?

Zacconi: We were contributors. When we started, we separated our jobs in the following ways. The guys in Sweden would develop the product, and we would focus mainly on closing distribution partnerships. I was traveling around Europe, meeting with the large portals and convincing them they should close deals with us. I was telling them, "Look, I don't know how well we'll monetize, but we can share the revenues together."

That's how we started. We set up a system to understand the key metrics for converting new registrations to cohorts, then after looking at each cohort and how each cohort was monetizing, we understood that we could also give guarantees. So, we changed our deals from pure revenue sharing to distribution deals. We would give guarantees in exchange for traffic guarantees, then an additional guarantee for exclusivity. The next stage would be to become the exclusive provider of games for a specific area or specific model, and then give an additional guarantee for media deals, where part of the media was online or TV, which was more complicated.

Ramsay: What was your standard of living after you invested in King?

Zacconi: To put some color on the start, since I put in all of the money I made from uDate, the most important thing to me was to reduce my costs to zero. I gave up everything I had. I gave up my flat in London. I gave up my car. And I had a very good friend who allowed me to stay in his guest room. I put everything else I hadn't sold in storage. I lived like that for a year and a half, and then Toby and I rented a flat in Stockholm together. I lived there in Stockholm for more than a year, traveling between London and Stockholm. All of my costs were basically zero, and all of my money went into the company. This was both a very fun time and a not so easy time, especially when I'd go out in London and most of my friends I'd see would be in banking and they'd ask me, "What do you do?" At that time, it wasn't cool to be an entrepreneur in London.

Ramsay: How large was your office in London?

Zacconi: In London, we needed to have a small office. It was maybe five meters by four, more or less, so it was really tiny. There was really not much more space than three desks, one in front of the other.

Ramsay: Did the distributed nature of your business present challenges?

Zacconi: No, because I knew Sebastian and the guys in Sweden very well. I trusted them completely to focus on developing the product.

Ramsay: Why didn't you move the London office to Stockholm?

Zacconi: It could have been an option. I think that I was always on the road, so I was spending, I would say, an average of four days every week, traveling mainly in Germany and closing distribution deals. From a finance point of view, there was nothing in Stockholm; everything was happening in London, so that's where we were looking first. We could have moved over to Stockholm, but Toby had family here, so it was fine.

Ramsay: When did you launch? Were you in good shape?

Zacconi: We launched immediately in four countries and languages: the United Kingdom, Sweden, Germany, and Spain. In December 2003, we expanded to other languages. This was with our team of eight people. While my money was running out, we were in discussions with several potential investors, but those discussions always took longer to materialize.

Finally, we had two angels interested in investing. One was Mel Morris, who was the founder of uDate and my former boss. The other angel was Klaus Hommels, a German living in Zurich, Switzerland. He called me one day and said, "Look, I have the same idea, but we would prefer to invest in you instead of launching ourselves." I said, "Okay, that sounds good." But these discussions were still just discussions. We had not received any money.

By December 2003, we were almost out of money. The day before Christmas—I remember that day very well—Toby and I were busy on the ground in our office in London. We were waiting for a contract to be faxed over, so we had not signed a deal yet. We were both sitting on the ground, looking at each other and feeling pretty bad about losing all of this money. We would have to shut down the company if we didn't receive the fax.

We had enough money to pay our debts though, but only just enough. And then we finally received a call from Mel who said we could proceed because he was faxing the offer through. But then the fax machine jammed! This was one moment during the building of a company I will never forget. The fax machine wasn't working, so we had to change the fax machine very fast. The fax finally went through and I could go to the airport happy because everything turned out fine. We then received money in early 2004.

Ramsay: Did either Morris or Hommels have experience with games? Is whether investors have experience, or at least a familiarity, with your business at all important?

Zacconi: No, and you should not count on investors to manage your business. You have to manage your business and do what is right. Sometimes investors can be helpful, or even save you, in this case. Over the years, our investors have been very helpful; we had fantastic investors. But that was more to get their experience to pass some of stages in the development of the company that I believe every company goes through.

Ramsay: In your experience, do investors try to be hands-off with regard to running the business?

Zacconi: In our case, yes. I think, often, that's not the case though, but our investors gave us trust at all times, which was very good!

Ramsay: Why do you think that was?

Zacconi: We would discuss things very openly. We had nothing to hide. We were open about what worked and what didn't. When things didn't work, we said, "Okay, here's what didn't work. We know why, or we don't know why, but here's what we're going to do now." And they could brainstorm with us about whether our plan made sense. Sometimes they'd come up with other things we should do, or should not do. But we've always had very constructive discussions because we're in the same boat.

Ramsay: After the money came in from Mel, you were home free. What did you do next?

Zacconi: We signed partnerships first in Germany, then in the UK, and later in Sweden. We became profitable pretty fast and were growing very well by January 2005. We signed an exclusive partnership for competitive games with Yahoo! Europe. The partnership worked so well, and we were monetizing so well, that we became one of the largest of Yahoo's partners and they offered to move us over to the United States. And so we signed an agreement to work with Yahoo in the U.S. In September, we signed a few more investors, namely Index Ventures and Apax who between them invested €34 million, part of which went to us as the secondary and part of which went to the company.

Ramsay: When did you launch in the US?

Zacconi: In January 2006, we launched on Yahoo! U.S. and experienced amazing growth. We became their largest games partner in the United States and Europe, so we were very prominent on the games start page. We had the main central placement above the fold and were riding a lot of traffic. We closed more partnerships and large distribution portals in Europe. And we worked with NBC, TBS, and Endemol. With Endemol, we developed a game using the Deal or No Deal branding, for example.

Ramsay: Sounds like despite a rough patch, you had a lot of early success. How fast were you growing? ?

Zacconi: We grew from eight people to more than 100 people over the next three years. We had around 110 people in 2009. And then something happened: we stopped growing. Our growth flattened; in fact, our rate of growth went down, but our revenues continued to go up.

We really didn't understand what was going on. We thought we had a technical problem. We thought there was a bug. We also knew that Facebook had a new platform. Some companies were doing really well. We didn't realize that 2009 was a year where the growth of Facebook had suddenly inclined to a 45-degree curve. From our perspective, traffic from our key partners was just suddenly going away. That's the worst thing: when you don't understand what's really happening to your company.

The next year was a very difficult phase because we had to manage a high-growth company during a period of no growth. We had to restructure. Our marketing operations were in Germany and were mainly focused on partner management. We had to shut down our marketing team and build an entirely new marketing team in London that was focused on direct customer acquisition. We built a very strong team with strong knowledge of Facebook and launched several models for bringing our games to Facebook.

In April 2011, one of these models succeeded. We wrapped one of our competitive games in an envelope called a "saga." You'd play the same game you'd play competitively on King.com, but you'd play in a non-time-based fashion. Bubble Witch Saga suddenly took off. We had launched it many years before on King.com and it had been doing well, and now you'd play the game on a landscape where you'd see your friends, and you'd progress from level to level by completing the same game.

Retention was very high, the variety was very high, and we started rising rapidly on Facebook from nowhere. We became one of the largest Facebook game developers after a few months. A year later, we were number two on Facebook in daily active users. This changed the outlook for the company entirely.

We found out—this was actually a game changer—that our games, which had done well with a niche model where players competed against others, were very appealing to very engaged players. In terms of the overall retention rate from visitors to players, the retention rate was much higher and had opened a very big opportunity. King.com started in 2003 and we had developed a portfolio of more than 150 games in 11 languages. Not all of our games have been super hits, but we had a large trunk of very strong games. We also had games licensed from third parties, such as PopCap Games and Mumbo Jumbo. Our games were performing well, but we had needed branded games to attract users to King.com. The cost of marketing these games was much lower, too. But we had built our own big games and we realized we didn't actually need those branded games anymore.

So, we began executing on a strategy where we started rolling out more and more games from our King.com portfolio to Facebook. Mobile is also an important part of our strategy and we now have a number of games on mobile. We also want these games to play seamlessly on mobile and Facebook, so you can play these games anywhere, seamlessly.

Ramsay: What do you mean by "seamlessly"?

Zacconi: What that means is I can start playing a game on my computer and I can stop playing the game at level 50. Then, I can step away and continue from where I left off on my iPhone, iPad, or Android device. I can even switch which device is in the game and check my achievements from anywhere on any device. I believe the degree of seamless integration we have implemented in the first game is the highest degree of seamless integration which has been done so far.

Ramsay: How do you find the right hires?

Zacconi: Before, I used to find them through my personal network. Now, my personal network is not enough anymore, so we find people through a number of other ways. Our existing employees often refer people in their networks they know and we have a fantastic internal recruitment team. We have a process for recruiting that every person goes through. Each person is interviewed by six different people within King, and the interviews go across the different areas, so it's not all people from the same department doing the interview. I approve every person who receives an offer, but I don't interview every person; and if one person disagrees or is not convinced, then we don't hire them. We have very high standards for recruiting.

Ramsay: Are you involved with recruiting at levels of the company?

Zacconi: It is true. I approve every person at all levels in the company. And of course, I interview everyone who reports to me and the level below.

Ramsay: Wow. I wouldn't have imagined that the CEO of a large company like yours would be that involved with recruiting.

Zacconi: Yeah, but it's very important.

Ramsay: How do you measure your personal success as an entrepreneur? What do you find gratifying about building a business?

Zacconi: I check the numbers every day. We have a strategy and we're all executing on that strategy. Our games have proved popular around the world, which has been incredibly rewarding to see. Some time ago, I was in Hong Kong, where we have millions of people playing our games. At the time, one in three who had a phone play our games. I didn't believe it!

I thought we had a mistake in the numbers, but you see people in public places or in the Underground, playing our games and asking each other what levels they're on. People are talking to people they don't know, asking to connect so they can continue playing. It's an incredible feeling, and very rewarding and very motivating to see what you've done.

But we're not big in just one country; we are big on a global scale. We've grown very, very fast. 70% of time spent on a tablet is spent playing games, and 40% spent on smart phones is spent playing games. Playing games is the number one activity of mobile users when they have time, so we are in a crucial position in a space that's incredibly important now to everyday life. That opens up, of course, future opportunities, and you always look ahead and you say, "Wow, there is so much more we can do."

Ramsay: For many successful entrepreneurs, success means living under the constant threat of failure. Given the success you've found with King, do you struggle with a fear of what's around the next corner?

Zacconi: Of course! I have a healthy level of paranoia about what could actually go wrong. And so I continue to think of all the things which could not go in the right direction in order to make sure we're always innovating — continuously. Yeah, it never stops.

Ramsay: How do you think that orientation affects your ability to lead?

Zacconi: I ask questions. What I say to everyone is you have to think two steps ahead. You can think of what can happen on the negative side, of course, but on the positive side, you have to think of the opportunities.

I also say to everyone that there is no bad news; news is information. If something goes wrong, we need to share it. Things are bound to go wrong; it's impossible for everything to go right. When things go wrong, we have to know about it immediately, and we have to share it so that others, other teams, and other parts of the company can learn from what didn't work.

If someone disagrees, they have to speak up. If I hear someone say, "Okay, I agree with you," then I usually ask, "Why?" I want independent thinkers. That's more or less what I do. I think we have excellent people. And I think, in the long term, the company that has the best people—and a culture which allows the best people to make decisions, to have responsibility, and to fail—is better off. At the same time, that culture needs to be one where, if you fail, you can talk about it; you're encouraged to share what happened immediately so that, as a company, we can go forward.

It's not always easy to understand what decisions might be right or wrong. But I think the most important thing is to have trust. You can't always be right, and I think that's fine. You have to accept that sometimes you are not right, and just test and try. But we do try to do things right the first time.

Ramsay: How important is developing new leaders within King?

Zacconi: I think that's super important, and second after recruiting. And we now have very professional HR people who understand that this is absolutely fundamental.

Ramsay: Have you found HR valuable?

Zacconi: HR is extremely valuable on several points. Number one, of course: from a recruiting point of view, because now that we're growing so fast, it would be impossible without recruiters who are professional and focused on finding the best. Secondly, the bigger the company becomes, you absolutely need a structure that takes into consideration levels, progression, and fairness in terms of payment and recognition. Of course, the third aspect is continuous development.

But the fourth point is the whole process of welcoming people in the company. First, they need to meet and know all our leaders, and then they need to go through every area in the company and understand what we do—an orientation process. Without people who are focused on managing that process, it's impossible to do this right and well at our size.

Ramsay: Are you busier than ever?

Zacconi: I'm busier than ever. I was actually very busy when growth flattened in 2009 and 2010. I was very busy because we restructured the company, and we were reviewing everything internally. And now I'm very busy because we're executing on our long term strategy. We have studios in 10 different places, and we have additional offices also in the US, and in Japan, Korea and China. I'm also very often in the Bay Area, where we have three of our largest partners: Facebook, Apple, and Google. I travel quite a lot.

Ramsay: Some business leaders would say that the burden of command can be quite heavy. Have you ever wanted to take a step back?

Zacconi: No, I think it's actually fun, but it has not always been easy. There were times when the company did not grow; it was not very easy. But King isn't a one-person company; it's a company where we have a team that manages the company. When decisions need to be made, we generally make decisions as a team, which also leads to better decisions. I hope. There are a few rules for how we communicate. The most important rule is we always tell the truth; there is no politics and no bullshit.

Ramsay: Like many entrepreneurs, you're fully immersed in your work with seemingly little time to yourself. Is that the case?

Zacconi: When I'm in London, usually I tend to go home around 7:00 PM. We have a young son, and I want to see him. I tend to keep the weekends free, too. But every second week I'm traveling, and sometimes my schedule is even more intense than that. And when I travel, I'm gone for three or four days out of that week.

Ramsay: Do you wish you had more free time?

Zacconi: I wish I had a 48-hour day sometimes, but I think that, overall, I have a balanced life. I've been doing this for more than ten years at King. I think it's important that you also do sports, and that you have time for your family. If you don't take time out for yourself, you risk burning out.

Ramsay: When we started talking, you said that your marketing operations were in Germany and focused on partner management.

Zacconi: It was more business development, meaning they were managing partners like Yahoo, NBC, CBS, and so on. They would negotiate distribution partnerships where we would integrate our games into the game or entertainment sections of portals and online media properties.

Ramsay: And you shut down that marketing team and built a new one focused on direct customer acquisition. Speaking as a marketing generalist, marketing is typically a discipline that covers a broad range of activities, so my question to you is this: why did you have to build a new team?

Zacconi: Because we had a very strong business development team in Germany, and the set of competencies we needed included the ability to buy advertising on Facebook. We were going through agencies at the time, but we needed to have those competencies in-house.

Ramsay: There was no time or room for training?

Zacconi: We tried. We tried. We had a six-month window.

Ramsay: How large was the original team?

Zacconi: I think the original team was between 18 and 20 employees.

Ramsay: And how large was the new team?

Zacconi: We decided to go with a smaller team, first starting with five people. Of course, today that team is much, much bigger.

Ramsay: As one of the largest Facebook game developers, what's your relationship with Facebook like?

Zacconi: It's very good. It's very constructive. We are treated exactly in the same way as every other developer. We don't have any special deals. When we work on the product, we work together, providing feedback to Facebook from our perspective on how to we can deliver the best possible user experience.

Ramsay: How closely does Facebook work with developers like King, Zynga, and other social game companies?

Zacconi: I think they want a games ecosystem, so they want to work with all developers. They do not want to work with only some developers. But, of course, larger developers can provide Facebook helpful insights. We are pretty good on stats and metrics, so we try to give Facebook feedback on what works and what doesn't along with the numbers, which at the end are used not only for us but for all developers.

Ramsay: You've accomplished quite a lot in the past ten years. When you look back, what do you think?

Zacconi: It hasn't been boring. We have a huge opportunity, and we're still getting started. For me, personally, the time has passed so fast that I can't believe ten years have already gone. But I'm very happy that we've made it this far. One of the fun things is to work with people who are extremely bright. It's fun to come to work every day, and discuss and think through things with the team.

Ramsay: What would you tell entrepreneurs who want to get into your business?

Zacconi: Focus on innovation. If you try to do the same thing, it's more difficult and you end up trying to catch up. If you start a new company or a new business, launch and create something new. This is what we do, or what we need to do, and everyone needs to do. We have to continuously focus on innovation, testing and pushing the boundaries.

Ramsay: Innovation in game design, or business process?

Zacconi: Fundamentally, innovation is about the user experience. How can we create the best possible user experience? You can create a new game, a new model, or a new way of playing games, but when innovation is only saving you money, it's less defensible in the long term.

Neil Young

Cofounder, Ngmoco:)

 **Neil Young** cofounded Ngmoco in 2008, alongside Bob Stevenson, Alan Yu, and Joe Keene, to pursue a burgeoning opportunity in mobile games. Within two years, Ngmoco was acquired by DeNA for US$400 million.

Prior to Ngmoco, Young started his career as a programmer in 1988, but by the early 1990s, Young had established himself as a producer at Probe Software, where alongside David Perry, he shipped The Terminator, among other games. In the four years he spent at Virgin Interactive, Young became vice president of product development before leaving for Electronic Arts (EA) in 1997.

At EA, Young was appointed the general manager at Origin Systems, where he oversaw the Ultima, Wing Commander, and Jane's businesses, as well as the company's relationship with Firaxis Games. In 1999, he left Origin and moved to EA's Redwood City Headquarters, where he would create Majestic, the pioneering ARG and then serve as the executive in charge of production for The Lord of the Rings series of games. After four years, EA made Young the general manager of both the Maxis and EA Los Angeles studios, and eventually the group general manager at EA Blueprint, where he was responsible for Maxis, Will Wright's Spore, and a partnership with Steven Spielberg.

After discovering the Apple iPhone, Young was inspired to build a mobile game business outside of the EA ecosystem. With the support of Kleiner Perkins' Bing Gordon, who had then recently been chief creative officer at EA, Young and his team raised more than $40 million in venture capital. Ngmoco went on to publish several bestselling games for the iPhone platform, such as We Rule, Eliminate, GodFinger & Rolando. In 2010, Ngmoco joined the DeNA family of companies, where the company remains today under the new name DeNA San Francisco.

Ramsay: You're known as a publishing executive, general manager, and entrepreneur, but you were a programmer once, weren't you?

Young: Yeah. I grew up in the United Kingdom and started as a programmer. I taught myself to code when I was about 12. When I was about 14, I started working on my first game for English Software, a game called Seven Treasures for the 8-bit Atari. I eventually graduated from 6502 8-bit machines to STs.

When I finished sixth form, instead of going on to university, I decided to work for a development company. I was first a programmer at Imagitec Design in 1988. The first game I worked on there was a port of Ferrari Formula 1 for Electronic Arts. Despite my efforts, I very quickly realized there were much more gifted engineers, and I found myself moving into producing. And that's what I've done since I was 18.

Ramsay: Can you tell me about the UK video game industry at that time?

Young: Oh, amazing! There are a lot of people in the games industry that come from the UK. I think it's because the weather is so bad that you don't have a lot to do, so you either go into a band or teach yourself to program.

Ramsay: How many companies were there? Were there a lot at the time?

Young: Yeah, there were, but the most successful company was probably a company called Ultimate, which went on to become Rare and which has since been acquired by Microsoft. There was Ocean, Gremlin, and others with vibrant, rich and thriving businesses. You could make good money as a young person. It was very exciting, very entrepreneurial, and also very creative. Building games, expressing yourself through computers, was really rewarding. And the fact that you could do it and make money was just wonderful.

Ramsay: How did you wind up at Virgin?

Young: I was at Imagitec for two years and left to join Probe Software, which was the largest independent developer in Europe. Our model was kind of like a management production company, so we had just producers on staff and we would work with independent developers—you know, a programmer in Oxford, and then an artist in Edinburgh, and a musician in Brighton.

We would organize and manage the creation of games for client companies, which were companies like EA, Sega, and Virgin, who were one of my clients there, and I worked on a range of games with them: a lot arcade machines and conversions, like Golden Axe to the Commodore 64 and the ST. Virgin was expanding their operation in the UK and they approached me to see if I would be interested in joining them.

Ramsay: Were you interested?

Young: I had really no interest in working for Virgin in the UK, and turned them down. In 1992 at the Summer CES in Chicago, I was hanging out with them and chatting, and they made the pitch again, but this time from their US office. It turns out they had just started the unit and a guy from the US team said, "If you're not interested in joining us in London, would you be interested in coming out to the US?"

I had been the producer for David Perry who's obviously pretty well-known in the business now, and I worked really closely with Dave. Dave had just made the transition to go move out to the US and work for Virgin in their internal studio, so I already felt like I knew people who were working there. They were having a great time, so I said, "Yeah, I'd be interested." The next week, I flew to California and met with people there for a few days, and two weeks after that, I got my visa and moved out to the US to work for Virgin.

Ramsay: You worked with David Perry?

Young: I was Dave's producer at Probe. Dave was one of those independent developers who Probe would finance, manage and organize. When we came over to the US, he was working on a game called Global Gladiators, and I wasn't on that title. I worked on the publishing side of Virgin's business, managing third-party development—essentially, the things we were doing outside of our studio.

But when we got the Aladdin project, I was made executive producer of that game for Virgin, and Dave was the lead. We worked together for a while before he left and started Shiny Entertainment.

Ramsay: I know your cofounder Bob Stevenson worked with David at Shiny Entertainment. Did you know Bob then?

Young: Yes. Yes, actually, Bob was an independent artist and he lived in Edinburgh. And we worked together on an arcade conversion together at Probe. Dave was the programmer, Bob was the artist, and I was the producer. When I came out to the US, Virgin needed an art director for one of the titles we were working on, and I called up Bob because he's a wonderful artist. He came out, loved it, and that's when we really got to know each other really well.

Ramsay: When did you transition to management?

Young: Well, I'm really a producer, and producing is managing and leading teams. The producer term has different meanings and different contexts in different companies, but to me, the producer is the one who either has the vision or can hold a vision for a game, from the very first word that's ever written about it until the last time it's put away by someone. That encapsulates everything from the game: the design, the vision, assembling the team, public relations, the marketing plan, and the marketing program.

My view has always been that, in order to be a successful producer, you have to be involved in all of those things, so then by default, you end up being in management. But just being in management and being disconnected from the things you're making is not something I'm capable of doing, or particularly enjoy doing, or, for that matter, think leads to success. Managers disconnected from products tend to be just dead weight, in my opinion.

I never thought I was transitioning to management. I just thought I was producing bigger and bigger things, and maybe producing more and more things. Even as a general manager at EA, I was really focused on the products.

I learned pretty early on that there are lots of things you need to do to get games and the businesses around them working and I'm not good at many of those things, so I need to hire people who really are. They need to be good at managing schedules and production details, so I can focus on the things that I think, at the end of the day, make the products what they are. I try to find great people to work on them and who can work together. I also try to be really clear about the two to three things that will end up defining whether the game is successful, commercially and critically. If we can do achieve both of those things at the same time, then we're good.

Ramsay: You were the general manager at EA, but you were also the general manager at Origin.

Young: Yes. That was when it was most clear to me that I love making things and being close to the process. When I left Virgin to join EA, the role I took at EA was to be the general manager of Origin. It was a pretty interesting time. From the perspective of EA management, Origin was moving sideways, so they wanted to put new leadership in place. So, Chris Yates, who was my technical operating partner at Virgin, and I moved out to Austin, Texas. I became the general manager and Chris became the chief technology officer.

We focused first on Ultima Online, which felt less like something that had tremendous opportunity and was really not well-understood inside EA. At that time, Origin had four units: the first was the Ultima Online unit team; the second was the Wing Commander team, which included Privateer and everything to do with Wing Commander; the third was the Jane's Combat Simulations group run by Andy Hollis; and the fourth group was a joint venture out in Baltimore with Firaxis. That was Sid Meier and Brian Reynolds' company; they were working on Gettysburg and Alpha Centauri.

The Jane's business just ran itself. Andy was just such a tremendous producer; he was just on top of everything. His products always shipped on time. The attention to detail was spectacular. They always beat their numbers. You just didn't want to mess with it.

Wing Commander without Chris Roberts was always challenged, and Chris' brother Erin did Privateer and the year before I joined, those guys had left to form Digital Anvil, and so Wing Commander was a little lost as a product.

Richard Garriott, Starr Long, and Raph Koster were focused on Ultima Online. Ultima Online was being beta tested across about 30 PCs to build an infrastructure we could scale, so delivering was quite an undertaking. So, Chris Yates and I focused on that. Chris became sort of the engineering leader and the infrastructure leader for the product. And then we focused on getting that out, and, you know, it surpassed everybody's expectations.

We learned a lot. We had tons of challenges. EA's sales force had predicted that the total sales for Ultima Online would be 38,000 units and we sold 38,000 units on the first day. We ran out of inventory, and that actually turned out to be a blessing. We needed those couple of weeks just to get the infrastructure to function again because it was getting crushed under the load. But Ultima Online went on to be a pretty amazing business and pretty much the first of its kind.

That was an amazing time! I had thought that success was about climbing the corporate ladder, but I reached a point when Origin was doing really well, and I was farther away from product than I had ever been before. It was like climbing a mountain, getting to the top, standing up and looking around, and realizing you've climbed the wrong mountain. The mountain you actually wanted to climb is over there, closer to making things and having an impact.

Ramsay: What were your actual responsibilities? What was your day like?

Young: I was responsible for the business unit. At that time at EA, the general manager was not a driver or a leader of products; the general manager was a driver and leader of the business and the manager of a team. The general manager was not someone who would make creative or product market decisions around titles, but I had full responsibility for the business unit.

My day was like a day in the life of any business. You sit down, you meet with people on the teams, and you try to understand what the challenges are and try to help people solve them. I would get into the office at 8:00 AM, and from 8:00 AM to 9:30 AM, I would catch up on things that had happened overnight.

And then I would pretty much have back-to-back meetings with the executive producers, the producers, and the people running different aspects of the business. Some of those were standing regular meetings where we would talk about milestones, production plans, and product statuses in general. Others would be unscheduled meetings, or phone calls. And then the day would end at 8:00 PM or 9:00 PM, and I'd go home, rinse, and repeat.

Ramsay: Can you give me an inside look at one of these meetings?

Young: My time spent with Chris Yates is a good example. When we got to Origin, Chris was immediately deployed onto Ultima Online. We said, "Go get this product shipped." Chris spent much of his focus on just trying to make that happen. That meant trading off features with technology choices and decisions every minute of the day. Chris and I would spend a lot of time talking about how we would scale for infrastructure to bring a product to market. What features would or would not be shipped with the software?

I think the role of a general manager at EA at that time was probably wrong. Although the general manager had ultimate responsibility for the business, they did not have ultimate responsibility for the products. It was difficult to run a product-centric business when you weren't responsible for everything.

In the following years, that definition changed inside EA. When I went on to GM at Maxis and at EA Los Angeles, I had full responsibility for everything. When you have full responsibility for everything, you make a lot of tradeoffs, but you can make the decisions you need to make.

Steve Jobs was an exceptional leader because he knew what the inflections were in his business, no matter how big or how small. Jobs could say, "Look, we're going to do one thing really well, and in the process we're going to kill a whole bunch of product lines." That's a very broad, sweeping decision that affects a lot of jobs, the whole makeup of the business, the sales team, and everything else. But he could also obsess about how many pixels to shave off the edge of an icon because he knew that that was important to the product. And so great leaders of companies that create things, I think, have to be capable of touching everything everywhere along that continuum.

Ramsay: Was Ultima Online the first time you were exposed to the challenges of connected games?

Young: No, Chris and I made a massively multiplayer space game at Virgin with Rod Humble, who later became CEO at Linden Labs. At that time, companies like Catapult had been telling us that without their modem, we wouldn't be able make successful games on the Internet. We just didn't buy it; specifically, Chris didn't buy it. Rod had this idea for a game called SubSpace and so we decided to prove that we could do it without their hardware.

SubSpace was a low-latency space shooter, and it worked really well. After we launched the game, we had about 100,000 users. That was the first time I had ever built anything connected. Ultima Online was the second, Majestic was the third, and now everything's connected.

Ramsay: Do you remember how many concurrent players there were?

Young: You know what? I don't even know. I don't remember. I think there were between 8,000 and 12,000. Something like that. This was in 1996.

Ramsay: When you were at Origin, did you get to know Garriott and Koster?

Young: Oh, really well. They're really super great guys. Richard was very welcoming, incredibly talented, and wonderfully creative. He was always committed and passionate about the thing he was making, although he didn't have to be. He was wonderfully wealthy and had a great lifestyle, but he would be in early in the morning, leave late at night, and work on the weekends when everyone else was working on the weekends. He had a tremendous work ethic and was very passionate and very committed.

Raph was prolific. He wrote a lot, which—if you're impatient like I am, and I especially was then—sometimes made it difficult to actually understand what he was saying. You were required to read everything he had written. But he was prolific in terms of his output, too.

And then probably the least known member of that team who had the biggest impact was Starr Long; he was the producer on the title. Ultima Online would not have been made if not for Starr. He understood Ultima inside and out. He was a great team leader and a wonderful guy.

Ramsay: Raph's a friend. What can you tell me about young Raph?

Young: He wrote a lot! He would be on the message boards where he'd get into debates with the players. He would spend a lot of time doing that. If the customer had a point of view that was different than his, they'd feel the wrath of Raph; he would write a huge diatribe on the forum. He was invariably right. He's great.

Ramsay: And now he's an expert on community relations!

Young: Exactly. Oh, the irony.

Ramsay: After Origin, you went on to work on The Lord of the Rings series.

Young: Well, when I reached the realization that I was managing this company and not really that happy doing it, I needed to get closer to the products. I called up my boss, Don Mattrick, who was the president of worldwide studios at EA. He was a really amazing producer.

And I said, "Hey, I don't know how to tell you this, but I'm really not happy. I really want to get back to making games. I've been thinking about building a product for the Internet. Instead of just using the Internet as a communication protocol, I want to use the Internet as a canvas to paint a picture on."

That product ended up being a game called Majestic. I moved from Austin in Texas to Redwood City, assembled a team and built Majestic, and worked on that from 1999 to 2001. I worked on that for 18 to 24 months. Majestic was one of the industry's first alternate reality games, and was certainly critically acclaimed, but not commercially successful.

When I was done with that, I was looking around for things to do at EA and I sat down with Larry Probst, who was CEO then. I said, "What do you think I should do?" He said, "Well, I'm going on these analyst tours and meetings," he said, "And, you know, no one's asking me about game A we're making or game B we're making. Everyone's asking me about two things." He said, "One is Harry Potter, and the Harry Potter license we've got; and the other is the license we've got to The Lord of the Rings." He said, "No one inside the company ever talks to me about The Lord of the Rings though, which makes me think it might be messed up. Could you take a look at The Lord of the Rings and see if there's anything that can be done there?" That's how I was introduced to running The Lord of the Rings.

So, first, some background: when EA acquired a license at that time, they'd take the license around to the internal studios, try to find someone to do it, and if no one wanted it, they'll give the license to a part of EA called EA Distribution, or EAD. That group ran external development, so they would find an external producer, get it made, and bring it to market. The Lord of the Rings had gone there because the internal studios had turned it down.

And so my development director, Arcadia Kim, and I went to Stormfront Studios, which was the developer working on The Lord of the Rings title. The movie, The Fellowship of the Ring, had just come out, and it was clear that they were going to miss releasing the title with the first movie.

What we found was a game that had an okay core mechanic, but which was sort of all over the place. And so we set about turning the game around and trying to focus on building something that would come out in time or ahead of the second movie, so that we could ride that wave of marketing.

The Fellowship of the Ring movie turned out to be a huge hit, and so there was a lot of pressure on us to deliver The Two Towers game for it to be successful. We did that, it did very well, and then we went on to make The Return of the King, which did tremendously well, too. We were also overseeing a lot of other things inside The Lord of the Rings universe.

Ramsay: Did that licensing relationship start with the movies?

Young: Yes. It began with the movies. We unified the rights sets after Vivendi basically totally screwed up the book rights, so EA had the rights to the movies because the Tolkien estate had licensed the books to Sierra, which became Vivendi. And so Vivendi was producing basically a competitive product and trying to release products at the same time in the same window against the movie, but backed with the fiction.

Our games were initially limited to using only the things that were in the movies, but obviously had the benefit of leveraging the imagery and official assets from the movie. And so because we essentially sort of won that battle, Vivendi stopped making those games, and we took the opportunity to unify the rights.

Ramsay: Sierra was developing a MMO around The Lord of the Rings. Was there any discussion at EA about building an MMO with the license, too?

Young: No, because while we were making The Lord of the Rings, EA.com was not doing well, and it got radically rescaled. The company—to the great detriment of EA, by the way—started to have an allergic reaction to MMOs. EA had invested a lot of money, but hadn't yet been successful with anything other than Ultima Online, so the company stopped investing in MMOs.

And the problem there was that a lot of the talent EA had acquired and maintained in Origin, Redwood City, and Canada left the company. They ended up at our competitors and helped bring out some very successful games.

Ramsay: I understand that the margins are exceedingly high for MMOs.

Young: Well, they can be. It all depends on how much it costs to make and operate. Some designs cost a lot to build, and some cost a lot to operate. The great MMO companies really understand how to build software that doesn't require an infrastructure that costs 30% of your revenue.

Ramsay: You spent a while at EA managing studios. What led to Ngmoco?

Young: After The Lord of the Rings, I actually thought about leaving EA. I actually resigned, but Larry Probst called me up again and he said, "Don't resign. Why don't you GM Maxis?" And I said, "I don't like being a GM. I was a GM at Origin, and I just didn't like it." And he said, "You can be whatever type of GM you want. Just hire other people to fill in the gaps for you." And I thought, "That's a really obvious and good point. Why don't I do that?" So, I GM'd Maxis and got The Sims 2 launched and got that business sort of in order.

We're skipping over a lot here, but after we shipped The Sims 2, I was one of two general managers at EA in Redwood Shores, including Nick Earl, who is now the studio head at Kabam. Our boss at the time, Bruce McMillan, sat down with us and said, "Hey, our LA studio needs help. I would like one of you guys to give the other one your current business, and the other one will go down to Los Angeles and take it over." Nick Earl couldn't do that for family reasons, but my now ex-wife, who was from southern California, wanted to be back there, and I liked turnaround challenges, so I decided to take that job.

I went down to LA, and we eventually turned the studio around; we had a good run. We re-launched the Command & Conquer franchise, and we got the Middle-earth games, two new Medal of Honors, and some other shooters out. We also had a partnership with Steven Spielberg, so things were going pretty well there.

Ramsay: Why did they need you to take over the LA studio?

Young: Basically, we had three teams inside that studio. We had the DreamWorks team, the Virgin team—we had acquired Westwood and Virgin in Irvine—and a new LA team. There were a lot of transplants, new hires, and movie people. There hadn't been a really good integration done, expectations were high, and getting that studio to a place where it could be really successful had taken longer than people had hoped.

A lot of the products were faltering, both creatively and from a delivery date standpoint, and there were some real cultural problems, from the merger of Westwood Studios and EA Pacific. There were no common goals and no common vision, so it was initially quite a divisive culture. If you can't build a really good culture, it's really difficult to build really good products. Culture eats strategy for lunch. So, we had to rescale the organization, focus on trying to rebuild the purpose of the company and the culture, and get the organization into shape. A lot of amazing people helped with that, like Mike Verdu.

Ramsay: You had tried to leave EA, but when did you get the idea to get out and start a new company of your own?

Young: After two years of being down in LA, I was going through a divorce. It turned out that my wife didn't actually come back down to Orange County, or to LA. My children were living in San Francisco, and I was commuting between San Francisco and LA at least once a week and sometimes multiple times a week. I decided I was going to come back to the Bay Area, and I would run the LA studio remotely and take on some other responsibilities.

And I did that, but while I was in LA on one of my trips down there to manage the studio, my trip coincided with the launch of the Apple iPhone. I found myself waiting in line in Santa Monica for an iPhone, and I eventually got it and I took it home. Within a couple of hours, I realized that the iPhone was changing my behavior. It had this unique blend of usability and capability, which drove me to use it much more than any other phone I'd ever had and in different ways. It struck me that that change in behavior could have a huge impact on mobile games if you could target the iPhone.

Games are entertainment and entertainment is a trade for the time. Anything that comes out that changes how much time you spend with a device is an opportunity to change entertainment. But the device couldn't be targeted yet. The mobile ecosystem was shitty. It was really hard to make money because the carriers controlled the deck, and even though you were paying for the development of the game, you were getting a small license fee. It just wasn't a very exciting industry.

And so time passed, I had moved back to the Bay Area, loved my iPhone still, and then in March 2008, I was watching the live stream of an Apple conference where they would be introducing an app store that would cut out the carrier, allowing people to distribute software directly to customers. I picked up the phone and I called Bob, who had become my closest friend. He's my daughter's godfather. I told him, "We really need to do something. This feels like the opportunity to do something together. Have you watched the video stream?" He said, "It's really, really amazing."

Both of us had commitments. Bob was the CEO at Planet Moon Studios, and I was a group general manager at EA with four studio groups, but we were so excited about the opportunity. We spoke the next day and agreed, "We should go do something. This is it. We have a tremendous opportunity to build a game company centered on these devices." On April 20, I told EA that I was going to leave. I told them that I thought it was just such a huge, new opportunity. EA tried to convince me it wasn't a really good idea.

That weekend, I went away on this annual guys' trip to Vegas with some of my oldest friends, including Bob. I'm there, and my phone rings. It's Bing Gordon. He's calling me, on Saturday night, and he said, "Hey, listen, I just want to let you know that we've worked together for a long time, but on Monday, I'm going to announce my retirement from EA. I'm joining Kleiner Perkins as a partner to focus on consumer internet and mobile."

I said, "Well, that's really funny. I just resigned. I'm building a consumer Internet mobile company." That call kick-started the conversation about financing Ngmoco. On June 26, I left EA. On June 27, we announced Ngmoco. On July 31, we closed a round of financing that was led by Kleiner Perkins, and Bing joined the board. On October 18, we released our first two titles.

Ramsay: When you went to EA and told them you were leaving to start this mobile game company, why didn't they try to convince you to stick around and develop mobile games for them?

Young: That's what their suggestion was. They said, "Look, we've got a mobile division: JAMDAT." We still called it that, even though it was EA Mobile. "You could do this here; you don't have to start a company to do it." And, really, the way that EA was configured, you had some studio groups that had product development, and some that didn't. I was in the group that was by far the largest in the company, and which did all of the internal, and much of the external, product development. The mobile team was housed inside Kathy Vrabeck's group. Kathy ran casual, mobile, and web, which was a completely different group, almost like a different company.

Given what I knew about the structure of EA, for me to be able to do that, I would have had to work across boundaries inside the company and it would have slowed me down. The one thing I knew about this opportunity was it had to happen immediately. There was a moment and we had to go really, really fast to capture it. I couldn't afford to be slowed down by the corporate apparatus. EA's a wonderful company. I loved and really enjoyed my time at EA, but just like any large company, EA has some great strengths paired with some limitations, and pursuing this opportunity within EA would have had me going headlong into those limitations. That was the primary reason that I didn't stay.

The secondary reason was just that the internal equity structure of EA meant that if I had created something really valuable—something valued in the millions, hundreds of millions, or billions of dollars—I wouldn't have had the opportunity to participate in that upside. I didn't know if we could create a successful company, but I knew it was exactly the right time and that timing was an important factor. If we could create a successful company, we would be able to yield a much better return for ourselves and the other members of the team.

And then, lastly, I just wanted to work with Bob. You know, it's such an amazing privilege to get to work with someone you really care about, who you understand, and who you have great muscle memory with. At EA, I wouldn't have been able to do that.

Ramsay: The Pulitzer Prize-winning writer James Michener once said, "Any person who has been divorced is a monument to failure." And yet while writing the book that won him that prize, he was going through a divorce. During the lead up to Ngmoco, you were going through a divorce. While you attributed your inspiration to the iPhone, would you say that your divorce had any influence on your drive to find success with something new and different?

Young: Yeah, good question. I don't think so. I think James Michener's statement is valid for anyone who has gone through the process of divorce because you really do feel like a failure. You're forced to reflect on a lot about yourself, and why, at the end of the day, people go on journeys with you. If they stopped caring about you or you stopped caring about them, something has changed, and if you once cared about them, it's difficult to look at yourself as anything other than a failure.

But that motivated me to be a better father, to understand the difference between your life's work and your purpose, and it was a huge learning experience for me, personally. My divorce didn't change how or why I felt that Ngmoco was an important thing to do, but I probably wouldn't have had the appropriate perspective that enabled me to keep the relationships I had stable and in place while I was building the company.

Ramsay: How was Bob doing?

Young: He was doing good. I mean, he went through divorce during the process of us building Ngmoco. I had separated from my wife in 2005 and Bob separated from his wife in 2009. There was a gap there, but I think those things are connected. In order to do anything really well, you have to commit yourself completely. If you're in a relationship that doesn't allow you to, it becomes difficult for you to be happy, and that becomes a downward spiral.

Ramsay: Speaking of happiness, you didn't like being a general manager. Were you that disappointed that you had to be a general manager at EA?

Young: I didn't have to always be a general manager at EA. You know, I could have always chosen to produce. I feel like I was disappointed in the GM that I chose to be when I was running Origin. When I became the GM at Maxis and then EA LA, it was a lot easier for me to define general manager the way I wanted, instead of some imagined expectation of the company.

I'm always wrestling with the need to be a manager of people and with focusing on what, at the end of the day, I think impacts the product. And I've come to understand that the two are inextricably linked, but I still daydream about products more than I daydream about the development of people or the management of people. In that regard, I don't really like the title "manager" that because implies something other than doer. I love the title "producer" because although that sometimes has a bad reputation, it really says what you do.

Ramsay: You were propelled from a company that held your interest for more than a decade not because of disappointment then, but because you were truly looking for something new?

Young: Yeah, the catalyst to leave EA and start Ngmoco was a desire to do something new and big, coupled with the opportunity that I saw with the iPhone. And when I was at EA, the mobile group and mobile games were not the pinnacle of the business. They were sort of an afterthought or an adjunct that was necessary to keep the company prominent in the eyes of the customer, and helped underwrite the large investments that were going into big games.

You'd make a big product, and it would cost a lot of money on the Xbox, the PlayStation, and the PC. You would then do whatever you could with licensing, secondary formats, or catalog formats for the mobile business to offset the cost of actually building those products in the event that they didn't perform up to expectations. So, they were more about insurance.

For mobile games—from what you could do on the devices, coupled with the device fragmentation, coupled with the stranglehold that carriers had on distribution—that meant that to build a viable business, you had to build lowest common denominator games for lowest common denominator devices that were ported into every language and onto every handset in the world.

And so you built a business that looked like a factory, providing a low quality widget and just stamping it in different variants in the lowest cost places around the world. That was a necessity because of the way the market was structured. I was never interested in mobile games until the iPhone.

The iPhone struck me as something that would be a very powerful game system—easily as powerful as the Nintendo DS and maybe as powerful as the Sony PlayStation Portable, but it also had all this other stuff, right? It had accelerometers, network connectivity, a camera, location awareness that was always on, and it fit it in your pocket. The iPhone felt like it could be a really good machine for playing games, if you could target it.

I also noticed that—and this is actually maybe even more important—I started using the iPhone differently than a telephone. I was rarely using it to make calls. I was frequently using it to browse the web, or to check stocks, or look at YouTube, or for other utility or functionality, or do e-mail. This device was changing my usage habits; it had this unique blend of usability and capability.

Ramsay: Had you ever thought about starting a company before?

Young: Yes. I dreamed about it a lot. But I know it's hard and you need to not just do it because you want to start a company; you need to do it because you see an opportunity. I hadn't seen the opportunity up until that point. I mean, I could have started a game development company, but I just didn't think that was a really great thing to do. The risk vs. reward wasn't right. Here, I was like, "Wow, what a great moment, a huge inflection in the business. I can get in early, I can build a company with my best friend who shares the same skills as I do, we can build something no one else is building, and we can move really quickly."

Ramsay: Did you have any idea about what would be involved?

Young: Not really. I knew we would need to raise money, but I had no idea how much money we would or should raise. I had never raised money before, so I had no idea about what a cap table was or what it should look like or who the investors should be. I just thought the VC community would be willing to invest in this company—not a game or a product, but a company that would try to be the definitive developer and publisher on these new devices.

Ramsay: Was your objective, in seizing that opportunity, to sell the company?

Young: No. We didn't really think about that when we started. Intellectually, we understood that someone could buy us or we could take the company public, but the focus was on "what does it take to build a great company?" If you start out to build a company to sell, I'm not sure you'd be willing to make the sacrifices necessary to build something anyone would be interested in buying.

Ramsay: Where were your expectations for Ngmoco?

Young: Well, a breakthrough moment for me was when I took over Maxis. I realized that you can look at a business and map it to the thing you know well. I knew how to build games, so I thought, "You know what? It's a lot like a game, right?" There is a core set of underlying systems or features—the people, the culture, and the organizational structure of the company—and then you've got all this content that sits on top or that spins off that. In a game, those would be levels or stages, but in a business, they're individual lines of business, like The Sims.

And once I had made that cognitive connection, it allowed me to draw on what I knew about making games to actually manage a larger business. It's like knowing the genre you're in and the type of game you want to build. In setting out to build a franchise, you know the first things you release have some success associated with them. And I started the company thinking of the business as a game development project, asking myself, "What's the analog to a game design? Who's the core team going to be? What are the features that are going to determine whether this is successful?" I actually used that cognitive connection I had learned while managing Maxis to start, run, and build ngmoco.

But I really had no expectations, other than to try to succeed going in to Ngmoco. While I had a dearth of expectations, we did have a myriad of questions that led us to our first learnings about raising money.

"We understand what the opportunity is here, so how much money do we really need to get it going?" We started asking ourselves, "Wow, can we get it going for like $500,000? Could we get some products to the market and start testing them?" We realized that if we do that, we've really only got one or two shots.

Through this process, you also realize is it's actually more difficult to raise a small amount of money than it is to raise a relatively large amount of money. In the venture capital community, people want to put capital to work.

They're dealing with funds in the hundreds of millions, or even in the billions of dollars. Although somewhat counterintuitive, you want to ask for a larger sum of money than a smaller sum of money. We realized when we started talking to people that not only would raising a small amount be too risky, you actually can't easily raise small amounts of money from the venture community; to do that, you have to go to the angel community. And when we started going down that path, we found out those investments top out at like $2 million, and what we wanted to accomplish wouldn't be possible for that amount. We immediately had to cross the chasm to the $5 million side of things, which is what we raised. We raised $5.6 million, predominantly from Kleiner Perkins.

The process of raising money was exciting and terrifying at the same time. We basically took our pitch out and we started meeting with people who had been recommended to us. Larry Probst introduced us to Allen Morgan, who worked at Mayfield Fund, and Rusty Rueff, who was the HR leader at EA, introduced us to a VC company called Morgenthaler, and we would just ask those people who they felt they competed with and we'd go meet with them. Eventually, we got a good picture of what the reception to the investment would be.

Ramsay: Was the VC community as receptive as you thought they'd be?

Young: In Silicon Valley, the iPhone was already perceived to be successful, and looked like the next great software platform with the launch of the app store. There was enough noise around the iPhone that everywhere we went, we found people who were receptive to the idea.

Our pitch strategy revolved around three things. Point one: we wanted to feel like a first party for the iPhone. We knew that Nintendo and Sony wouldn't build products for the iPhone, we knew that Apple wouldn't, and we knew that Google wouldn't for its Android system. We thought there was an opportunity to create a company that felt like a first party for these devices but, at the same, would become the voice of the industry—that would really understand how to make them work and what customers want from their experience.

Point two of the strategy was that we wanted to build a network that connected our games together, allowing us to move customers from game one to game two and cross-promote inside the network. I think we said something like we'd be "Xbox Live for the iPhone."

And then third thing that we wanted to do was we wanted to open that network up and bring in as many other companies. We believed that we could create a network on these devices that would scale and be really valuable to both customers and the business.

That's the strategy we tried to execute. Now, along the way, there were speed bumps and hurdles, but as we presented that idea to the venture capitalists, I think that what people were seeing was not a pitch to fund this app or fund this game, but to build a business on top of this ecosystem that had within it people who knew how to build this type of business. That felt valuable.

Ultimately, we settled on Kleiner Perkins really because of Bing. Starting a company is like going on an adventure and you want people you can trust. I knew Bing, I had worked with him for 11 years, I understood the value that he brought, and the way that he thought. He understood who I was, and we felt that it would just be more fun to tackle challenges together—to know that the person around the table with us cared about us and cared about us being successful more than they necessarily cared just about the money that they had invested. And that turned out to be true.

Ramsay: Was raising money the first step after deciding to start the company?

Young: Yeah, we basically just tried to raise money pretty quickly. I officially left EA on June 26 and we closed the financing around July 31, which was fast. And then we just hit the ground running. We started building a lot of stuff for it at the same time. We started MazeFinger and Topple, and Alan Yu had found and signed Simon Oliver who was working on this prototype called Rolando. We reached out to people in the community to see if there were partnerships we could do, and we slowly started building products with external partners.

Our view was that we wanted to provide a publishing infrastructure, the technology, and a common code repository, so that if you built products with us, the code from the last and next products would be available. We tried to find as many talented people to collaborate with as we possibly could.

We released our first games, MazeFinger and Topple, on October 18, and we decided on the pricing the day before we released them. We sat down with Bing, and we talked about the pros and cons of different pricing, and decided the most important thing we could do right then was learn about the market. At that time, it wasn't really about making money; it was really about understanding the ratio between paid and free, and the market size.

And so from the outset, we had this idea that we would measure everything we did, so we would try to get as much data as possible. If we had great game makers and great data, we felt like we would increase the chance at hit products. We decided to release Topple as a $0.99 cent app, and MazeFinger for free, and we would release them at exactly the same time on exactly the same day, so we could get a sense of the differences in the charts.

Ramsay: And did you?

Young: Both games went to the very top of the charts. MazeFinger went to number one in free and Topple went to number two in paid. Along the way, we were capturing data about what people were doing, how they were interacting with the software, how many sessions per day, and how many minutes per session. It was a really, really amazing learning experience. We then followed those up a few weeks later with Dropship and Dr. Awesome. They were both similar, but they were both $0.99 cents when we released them. We felt like we understood the delta between free and paid, and we had no method to monetize free then, so we thought, "Okay, we'll just release them as paid." One made the Top 10, and the other was number 15 on the charts.

And then we released Rolando on December 15, and Rolando became the number two highest-grossing game on the app store that holiday season, beaten only by Need for Speed. At that moment we felt, "Okay, we've just made more money than we've spent so far, we've tested the market, and we think that we really now understand the market. It's now time to go to the next level of the business, to raise more money and start stage two of our plan." Stage two was to start building more games and a network that would connect these games together, to take advantage of the data and put it to work.

In February, we raised another round of financing, just over $10 million. Stage one of the business had been validating, and we were moving onto stage two. As the financing was closing, we started looking at the market from not just our product's perspective, but from a perspective where we were intersecting the data about our products and the market as a whole.

We had acquired a small company in Texas, two people who built a web app that would hit the iTunes backend every hour in every territory and scrape it, so we knew what games were being released, when they were being released, how they were moving up the charts, and what the trend lines looked like for them. And because we knew how many downloads you could get and thus how much revenue you could make at each chart position, we began to build the first model of the market we could use for forecasting. And as that data started coming in, it became really, really clear to us that two things were happening: one was the number of apps that were being released each week was accelerating, and two was the average price per app was falling.

Ramsay: That doesn't sound good. Did you see the problem?

Young: Yeah, if you're building a business that's predicated on selling $9.99 games, and if the average price is falling from $7.99 to $6.99 to $4.99 to $2.79, you know that creates drag on the business opportunity for you. We realized then that the app supply exceeded the demand, and so price was falling to the lowest control level. We began to think that the premium game strategy we were implementing would not lead us to build a company of consequence.

In fact, at the time we did the study after the closing the financing, we realized that in order to build a company that generated $10 million a year, you would need at least one game in the Top 5 highest grossing for a whole year, and that basically meant creating super-hit products. To create a company that generated $20 million a year, we'd need three games in the Top 10 for a whole year. That just didn't feel like a great proposition to us.

Ramsay: What did you do?

Young: At the first board meeting following our Series B investment, we sat down with our investors and we said, "Well, we have two things to talk about: we've completed the financing, but we don't think we can build a company of consequence on the paid app store." We were half expecting the room to go, "We're doomed." To our surprise, our investors, and one in particular, Mike Maples, said, "This is great news. Before anyone else has figured this out, you've got this information. What are you going to do? You have an advantage that could be measured certainly in weeks and maybe in months. How are you going to capitalize on that?"

And we said, "We don't think we can build a company of consequence on the paid app store, but we have data that says our players are using our titles an average of 22 minutes a day. We think there's a way to monetize usage versus downloads." When you build a business on paid premium downloads, because of the way the discovery mechanisms worked inside the app store and the charts at that time, you actually only really made money when you were in the Top 25, and then revenue falls off really, really quickly. But people keep playing and enjoying games after that, so we thought there should be a way to monetize that usage. If we made games free, we would get way more users, and thus way more overall usage, and then we could create a more sustainable and scaled model.

Ramsay: What was a more sustainable model? Advertising?

Young: Actually, we knew we couldn't do it with advertising; the advertising industry hadn't then—and still, frankly, hasn't yet—reached a point of maturity in the mobile market. We instead thought we could emulate free-to-play games with virtual currency. There were games in the app store, basically clones of Mafia Wars, trying this already. You would download the free master app, and then there were apps at different price points on the paid app store. When you needed to buy currency, you would be directed to run the paid app, which would deposit currency in your account.

And because that currency was valuable, users could be motivated to do things in return for currency. If you had two versions of your software, you could tell users of version one to download version two, and the act of them downloading version two drove it up the charts, which got other people to see the software, which then brought in more organic users, and the total users in your ecosystem increased. It was a nightmare to manage, but it worked.

Our strategy then was to kill everything in our portfolio except two games, and use some of the capital we've raised to acquire one of the companies building these Mafia Wars clones. That company was Miraphonic, which built a game called Epic Pet Wars. We were going to quietly and silently run and operate that and learn everything about it. We were going to look for other products we could build from the ground up as free-to-play games. And we were going to lobby Apple to make in-app purchasing available to free games. The investors and the board thought that was exactly the right strategy, and we did that.

In October 2009, we released Eliminate, which was a first-person shooter, and in November, we released Touch Pets: Dogs, which was the game we had been doing with Andrew Stern. Both games were retooled to be free-to-play, and both went to the top of the charts. Eliminate was number one and Touch Pets was number two on the same day. Eliminate went on to be the number one grossing game on the app store, and the first free game to be the top grossing. We, along with other companies, had lobbied Apple hard enough that they made in-app purchasing available to free apps, and the business took off. Our revenue went from not very much to quite a lot really quickly. At that time, we were doing over $1 million a month in revenue, which was a pretty good start.

Ramsay: When you started raising capital, you were new to the process, but finance can be quite technical. How did you overcome that hurdle?

Young: There were two things we did to shortcut that. First, we invited a friend, Joe Keene, to join us as a cofounder. Originally, we hired him as a consultant, and then eventually, we brought him on as a full-time member after we closed the financing. Joe had gone through the process before. Joe had founded Perpetual Entertainment, a massively multiplayer online game company that was working on Star Trek and Gods & Heroes. They had raised a lot of money, so his insight and expertise were really, really valuable.

And second, we were introduced to Mike Maples, who runs a fund called Floodgate; he's one of the classic Silicon Valley super-angels who invested in Twitter, Digg, and a whole bunch of other successful companies. Mike talked us through the process and acted as a guide.

Ramsay: Did Joe or Mike help you articulate the plan for the business?

Young: No, that was all Bob and me. I put together the deck. And then Bob, Alan, Joe, and I would sit around my dining room table with a projector on the wall, and we would shoot the shit about the plan and iterate and evolve it, and then we would work through the night—and then take it out to investors.

Ramsay: Did you invest any of your own money?

Young: No, I didn't. I didn't have any money. I was going through a divorce.

Ramsay: Some founders believe you should really have skin in the game, and others don't. Where do you stand?

Young: I don't think it's necessary. I don't think I worked any less hard because I didn't have my own money tied up. I had my career and my reputation tied up in the company, and that was more important to me than money, frankly.

Ramsay: Did you consider options other than venture capital?

Young: No, not really. An important thing to note here is the dynamics of Bob and I. Bob and I were equal partners in Ngmoco, we're equal partners in our current company N3TWORK, and so my first loyalty is to Bob. One concern Bob had was whether Ngmoco would feel like EA, "You've got Neil and Bing who know each other really well, and they have EA backgrounds. What's my role?" It took a while for Bob to get comfortable with Bing. There were other super qualified investors who, when we started off the process, Bob felt more comfortable with. Bob had to have breakfast, lunch, and dinner with Bing for three days before he finally said, "I've made up my mind. Let's go with Bing."

Ramsay: You were also new to startups. Did you ever feel unprepared?

Young: Yes. Yeah, I did, but one of the great things about having a team of people founding a company instead of just one person is if you pick that team right, you get a lot of complementary skills. There was no one better in the industry than Alan Yu to try finding developers. Joe had raised money. Between Bob and I, we could pre-visualize, mock up, describe, pitch, and sell anything. The biggest missing piece for us was we didn't have a technical cofounder, so getting engineers into the building as quickly as possible to explore these ideas, especially around the network and R&D, was really hard.

Ramsay: You had a technology background though.

Young: I did, but I wasn't programming. Both Bob and I have a technical background, so we understand our way around pretty much all software, and we know what can be done and what can't be done. We also have generally pretty good ideas about how to do stuff, but we're not going to sit down and code. To be a great coder, you have to be focused on it, and it was impossible for us, given all of the other things we were doing.

Ramsay: And did you get a technical cofounder?

Young: We didn't. We never did. Our first in-house engineer was a guy called Tim Omernick; he called us out of the blue and said, "I think I have skills that you might need. I wrote the Stocks app and the YouTube app. I've been at Apple for a while. I really love games. And I think what you're trying to do is really cool. I would love to come and talk to you." And so we hired Tim, and he's just a really talented engineer. Once we had him, we were able to attract a few other people like Dave Grijalva, who went on to cofound a great company called FitStar, and Steve Detwiler, who is now our technical cofounder at N3TWORK, and ultimately ran technology for Ngmoco and DeNA in the West.

Ramsay: You had cofounders other than Bob at Ngmoco, didn't you?

Young: Yes. Bob and I were the founders, and then we invited Alan Yu to be a cofounder and later invited Joe Keene.

I first met Alan when he was the director of the Game Developers Conference, and quickly became a friend of his. Around the time I was taking over Maxis, I felt like EA needed to change its view of development talent. We needed to build different relationships with the community that were more about collaborating with the best and brightest versus just hiring people internally.

Alan had, by far, the best rolodex in the games business by virtue of his position. He built relationships over a long period of time, and those tend to be the relationships that endure. If you have a relationship with someone who has been there for a long period of time, when something happens in your life that might change the direction of your career, you're more likely to listen to it. And so I convinced Alan to join me at EA as director of A&R, or artists and repertoire. Alan's skills were a natural fit for a startup. So, at Ngmoco, he essentially went out and started finding developers we could partner with and started building relationships with developers that could turn into great things.

Then we asked Joe to help us originally as a consultant. I had worked with Joe at EA as well. He had been the chief operating officer of EA.com, and he was the chief operating officer of Maxis right after EA bought Maxis. And then Joe left and cofounded Perpetual Entertainment. We needed as many advisors and guides as we could possibly get in the world of venture funding, and Joe helped with the business planning and managing and overseeing the process of closing fundraising and financing. Bob and I did the fundraising, and Joe would handle the mechanics of it, which was quite a gnarly task.

Ramsay: Had you always conceived of Ngmoco as a publisher?

Young: Yes, from the very outset. The original pitch for Ngmoco was to build a next-generation mobile game company.

If we wanted to make one game, it was conceivable to hire a team of spectacular people to make that one game, we wanted to build a really big business and have lots of games. It's just not realistic, or credible for that matter, to make ten games and have every single team be world class.

We felt like we could have a few world-class teams internally, but we'd have to partner with developers outside of the company. We'd have to be more of a production, management, financing, and technology framework company, that's what we thought a next-generation publisher would look like.

Ramsay: When you approached Alan and Joe, did they express any doubts about the venture?

Young: We approached Alan first; he had no doubts at all. We have a very close personal relationship and he was just like, "Yeah, let's do it." And as the business became more real, Joe saw a great opportunity in joining us. So, there were never any doubts. Along the way though, we all had plenty of doubts about whether we had made the right choices and were on the right path.

Ramsay: The iPhone was your inspiration, so I know the app store was very important to you. But was Apple the only distributor that interested you?

Young: Yeah, initially. As we discussed, Apple was the venue. When we started the company, one of the people I called to tell them I was leaving EA was David Gardner. David was a very early employee of EA, and he went on to become the managing director of EA in Europe. He's a really, really, really wonderful guy. I called him up and I said, "Hey, I'm trying to do this," and he said, "That's really exciting. Good luck. You should meet my friend Erik Lammerding."

He said, "Erik is at Apple and has been at Apple for five or six years. He's really, really close to the inner workings of the company, and he's the guy that picks software to get up on stage. He's really integral to the Apple community." And so he made the introduction, and as we were starting the company, Bob and I went down to Apple and had lunch with Erik. And that's how our really great relationship with Apple originally began.

Apple were great supporters of ours, I think, because we were one of the few people out there delivering the message that Apple, the app store, and these devices were going to completely disrupt the handheld games market. We were very aggressive with the press we did on that message, and the position that we took. And I would constantly be chided by Nintendo or Sony publicly for those positions and those statements.

Ramsay: Why would a publisher want to start talking to distributors before they have any products to distribute?

Young: Businesses are rarely just about products; they're more often about people. You want to build relationships that transcend product A or product B, and you want to just really explain your business before you talk about your products.

Ramsay: Did you find any developers through Apple?

Young: No, we didn't. Our first product was MazeFinger. That was Mike Mika's idea. Mike was an early producer we hired; he had worked on Xbox Live titles and was a friend of Bob's. He's a super arcade and classic games fanatic, so Mike asked us, "Have you seen Flamin' Finger in the arcade?" We hadn't, so we went and checked it out in the arcade. It's this Namco game. He said, "I think the mechanic behind touching the screen and having limited time in a maze could be quite powerful."

Topple was Bob's design. He said, "I think a stacking game that fights against the accelerometer would be a really good idea." Alan found Simon Oliver who had put out little videos for Rolando, so Alan interacted with him.

And I knew Andrew Stern. I had met Andrew a long, long time ago shortly after he had made Dogz: Your Computer Pet. I had stayed in touch with him, so we commissioned Andrew to do Touch Pets.

Dr. Awesome was basically Mike again saying, "Could you do something like Qix?" And then Dropship was a design I came up with. I just loved those old vector games, but I thought you could do something different. We also wanted to begin exploring what dual analog might feel like when you're touching a screen, and how to pioneer the type of controls you need to do really great FPS games while respecting touch. We did that game internally.

Ramsay: Did you have games developed externally?

Young: Yeah, MazeFinger and Topple were done by third-party external dev shops. MazeFinger was built by Ryan Evans. Mike worked with him in the past. For Topple, we worked with an independent engineer, Chris DeLeon. There are lots of little independent contractors you can hire on a work-for-hire basis.

Ramsay: Just how many games did you have in development?

Young: We had 12 titles going at any point in time. When we started, we had eight games going simultaneously, and then we killed some.

Ramsay: How many people were employed during those eight?

Young: Probably 15. We grew pretty quickly to 15 people, and then the next plateau was 25, and then 55, and then we started getting really big.

Ramsay: What's involved with managing those teams on the publisher side?

Young: You must have producers and a development framework. We had a wonderful director of operations, Kristine Coco; she worked with Bob and me to build what we called the GDF, the Game Development Framework. That was a term we brought with us from EA. It was a method of having a common vocabulary inside the company to talk about our products, so we could say, "Oh, this product is at this stage," and everyone knew what that was. We had a review process, too, to move things from stage one to stage two and so on, and we had different points of integration along the way. When you start scaling a business, when you're a small team, process is the enemy; process slows you down. But when you're a big company or scaling, and you have lots of things going on, smart process becomes your friend. Smart process allows you to do more than you could do than by just keeping everything in your head.

Ramsay: For your first games, you had data, but were there any other reasons why you chose them as your flagship titles? Your best bets?

Young: We knew Rolando was special. As a basic guideline, we tried to do something that showcased the hardware—something you couldn't do on other devices. You couldn't do the controls for MazeFinger or Dropship without touch. I'm not sure we thought they were our best bets, but we thought they were smart bets and would, at the very least, tell us something. And because we had raised the money we had raised, we didn't feel any particular pressure to make money right away. We really wanted to understand the market.

Ramsay: Seems to me that many companies that raise venture capital don't have an urgent need to make money. Why do you think that is?

Young: Well, it's not that you don't feel the need to do it; it's just you don't feel like that necessarily is the most important thing. It's like why people go to college. Why do you choose college versus going and working in the grocery store? Because in the grocery store, you're going to make money right away. But if you go to college, maybe you learn something and it gives you the opportunity to ultimately have a much higher earning potential. If done right, venture capital gives you the opportunity to really understand your market, so that you can build a business that's worth something.

Ramsay: Your investors then weren't investing in the products or the company; they were investing in a higher earning potential?

Young: Oh, yeah, they were investing in the macro, which is like the market as a whole. If you're an investor, you go, "Do we believe there's a big business here?" And the answer is either yes or no. If yes, then, "Do we believe the entrepreneurs we're investing in are going to be able to find a big business here?" That's either yes or no. And then then lastly, "Do we believe that there's some inflection happening or on the horizon that can make their job easier?" The reasons why investors invest is very rarely because of the actual business. I don't think they even expect that the business model you pitch will be the one that ultimately succeed. It still has to make sense though because whether that model makes sense signals whether the entrepreneurs are any good. At the end of the day, I think they invest much more in the macro.

Ramsay: A little more than a year after starting up, Ngmoco started acquiring companies, like Apptism and Miraphonic. How many companies did you buy?

Young: Apptism was our first, then Miraphonic, Stumptown Game Machine, Freeverse, Rough Cookie, and then we acquired Atakama Labs in Chile while at DeNA. And that was it.

Ramsay: Were these acquisitions what people call "acquihires"?

Young: Acquihires? No, no. Apptism was bought because they had a technology that hit the app store every hour in every territory, and we could combine the data they had with the data we had, and it was a very easy system to maintain.

We acquired Miraphonic because Drew Lustro and Amit Matani were building Mafia Wars meets Pokémon on mobile, and we had made the decision that free-to-play was the path we were going to take the company. We wanted to learn as much as we possibly could, and we loved Drew and Amit—they were just really great guys—and we thought there was a lot to learn there.

Freeverse we acquired because we knew Ian and Colin were just a great team. Skee-Ball was a great franchise, and they were early to the app stores, where we felt like we could combine what we knew about free-to-play games with what they knew about building competent software for the app store.

We bought Stumptown because we loved Andrew Stern and the team of people he had assembled in Oregon. When they completed Touch Pets with us, we wanted to continue that relationship.

Rough Cookie we acquired because we wanted a development beach head in Europe. Super talented guys. We built Star Defense together and then we focused on trying to get them into the free-to-play space.

And we acquired Atakama because they were a development resource we were using to move games and products onto our technology; they were exceptionally competent, too, and it was also the much lower cost of development in Chile. So, they were both very talented and very cost-effective.

Ramsay: If you weren't VC funded, you probably wouldn't have bought so many companies. Did having that money influence, or encourage, you to make those acquisitions instead of just doing all those things yourselves?

Young: Absolutely. Part of the reason why we raised money was to acquire companies. Developing on your own takes time, and money can be a shortcut to time. The average time it takes to hire an engineer in the Bay Area is 90 days. If I want to grow a team of ten people from scratch, carefully integrating each person, it's going to take me years. And if I was able to hire all ten of them simultaneously, it would take me at least 90 days and they'd have to figure out how to work together, if they have the right chemistry.

Ramsay: Were all of these acquisitions the right decisions?

Young: Yeah, we weren't as successful as we hoped we would be at imparting what we had learned to them. I think we underestimated, across the board, how difficult it would be to transfer our knowledge to teams of wonderfully competent people with great cultures and great operating histories.

Ramsay: What were the difficulties? Can you share?

Young: Well, when you talk to people about free-to-play games, they have to embrace the concept of free-to-play for it to be anything more than feeling like a money-making scheme. You have to get over that first hurdle and they have to realize that this is not about making money; it's actually a different way of building software. You can't just tack on free-to-play monetization at the end; you have to design from the very outset to build a game that's going to be free-to-play. If you do that right, you can build a great business and great user experiences at the same time. Being able to impart that to teams who are not necessarily predisposed to thinking that way is hard to do.

Ramsay: When you were put in charge of EA Los Angeles, you were sent there to fix a problem with integration. A previous merger had gone wrong. Did you have similar problems with the companies you bought?

Young: Los Angeles was different in that those studios had been acquired and were then put in the same building. It wasn't practical, or possible, for us to relocate all of them to San Francisco. They stayed in New York, or Chile, or Oregon, or wherever they were. And our view was the integration was going to be as minimal as possible. We bought these companies because the people were talented, they had a culture we admired and we didn't want to mess that up, and we wanted to give them the benefit of all the things we had learned, all our systems, and access to the traffic we had. We were much less focused on merging the companies than on preserving the integrity of their organizations.

Ramsay: Was communicating and working across long distances challenging?

Young: Yeah, there was a lot of travel, a lot of video conferencing, and a lot of telephone calls. The plus side was that those companies tended to be very happy. The downside was the rate at which they were able to adopt the learning systems and technologies we had was slow. There's a push and a pull when you want to retain the integrity of an organization. We could have been more aggressive about how we managed those groups and they may have been more successful sooner, but we did not feel that would've been true to the social contract we had. And, frankly, we were learning as we were going.

Ramsay: You've started companies and bought them. You've since had experience with raising venture capital and how valuation works. I can't say I know that area too well, so when I read about venture capitalists, I get the impression that they're very focused on exit multipliers.

Young: Yeah, I think it's really easy to think VCs are focused on only money. I actually haven't found that to be true. What I found to be true about the really good VCs—and maybe there are VCs who are focused on only money—but the really good VCs recognize the path to a great outcome for them has everything to do with the team running the company and the decisions they're making. So they tend to engage there, and try to give advice or guidance and feedback. Sometimes it's critical; sometimes it's complimentary. They give you feedback on the decisions you're making to try to get the very best outcome possible.

For VCs, they have a very long road, so it's easy to imagine that a VC, when the company's very small, would force that company to make decisions that would get that company acquired. But if the company's worth $10 million and the VC tries to make the company look like it's worth $20 million, that would be a shortsighted and reputation-endangering strategy for a venture capital company that has $6 billion under management. So what VCs are really looking for are exceptional companies led by exceptional teams who can 10x their investment, but that tends to not happen when you try to manufacture that outcome.

Ramsay: Your VCs really weren't focused on an exit strategy? Strange.

Young: Not at all. Well, obviously, they were at the point when we were making decisions about whether to sell the company, and who to sell the company to because we had multiple offers. They gave us great advice there.

Ramsay: How do you then maintain a healthy, cooperative relationship with your VCs when they give you advice and you don't take their advice?

Young: Constant communication and transparency. At the end of the day, we run the company; we're the professional stewards of their investment and all of our incentives are aligned. We want to create something that's very, very valuable to our customers, our investors, and our employees; and everyone shares that goal. It's not as hard as it sounds. There are horror stories, but I've just never experienced them personally. I've found our investors to be first and foremost supporters of myself and Bob, investing in the belief that we and the market opportunity we've articulated will lead to something really valuable.

Ramsay: You mentioned that you received a few offers to acquire Ngmoco. How many did you receive?

Young: We were processing four different opportunities. We were processing the offer to acquire the company from DeNA, the offer to acquire the company from two other groups, and an independent path which had us raising a large round of financing. Up to that point, we had had discussions on and off with companies about merging or being acquired that are probably not difficult to guess, but I'm not able to tell you who they are.

Ramsay: Why didn't you decide to stay on that independent path?

Young: Two reasons. First, it was important for us to succeed as a company, and if we remained independent, although we certainly could have succeeded, the resources necessary to compete at scale with the companies that were either building up steam like Zynga or intending to deploy themselves in the market, like DeNA, really far outstripped what we could raise. We needed the resources to be able to be successful.

Second, well, the second was more of a calculation around optimal value. So what happens early in a market when things start taking off, it's difficult to predict the ceiling. Valuations for leading companies tend to be much higher. As the market goes from early stages, there's a high rate of adoption to slightly more mature later stages of adoption, and then you can start to see the peak of the market. And the market changes and evolves over time in waves.

In terms of smartphone mobile games and social mobile games, we assessed that the valuations were about as high as they were going to get for a while. If we remained independent while we could raise money at pretty high valuation and we could raise quite a lot of money at a higher valuation, the likelihood we would be able to dramatically increase the value of the company in the short term seemed less likely to us.

That was sort of a peak valuation moment, and our sense was we could sell the company at that moment. The next opportunity for us to deliver that type of value to our employees and our shareholders was probably going to be four or five years in the future, and I think that has borne out to be true.

Ramsay: Why were you oriented toward the short term?

Young: Our orientation was actually never to sell the company; the orientation was always to try to build something valuable. If you create something valuable, good things will come. That was always the motivation, but when opportunities present themselves, you have a responsibility to take a look. We never thought it would fail. For Ngmoco, we never approached anyone saying, "We would like to sell our company. Are you interested in buying it?" But we got this a lot: "How much would you be willing to sell the company for?"

Ramsay: Well, why didn't you stick it out regardless of the value?

Young: We did stick it out. I mean, we didn't see the sale of the company as an end. I think that was borne out by the fact that we stayed with DeNA for two years after the acquisition. Our intention was not to sell the company and bail; our intention was to join forces and try to get the company to the next level, and to try to build a leading company in the space.

I feel good about that set of choices. We were able to deliver a lot of value to the people who had helped us create the company: the employees and the shareholders. We helped DeNA with its objectives globally. And we were able to learn a lot about not just social mobile games, but the science and psychology behind the next level of engagement.

For us, teaming up with DeNA gave a five-year head start on our competition. What happened in Japan in the mid-2000s were that devices with their own unique blend of capability and usability on top of a pretty good national 3G network and the relatively low cost of fixed price data plans spawned media companies like DeNA. Our sense was that, in 2010, the US was in the same place that Japan had been in. So teaming up with DeNA was such a head start.

Ramsay: At the time that you were getting the offers, how far from your vision for the company were you?

Young: A long way. The original logo for Ngmoco had, underneath, Japanese writing. This was long before any thought of selling the company to DeNA. The Japanese writing translated to "future entertainment company." That was the underlying secret vision for Ngmoco. Only two years into the company's life, we had the opportunity to partner with a company that had a similar vision. Since that time, my definition of what media are up for grabs has broadened, but that vision, I think, ultimately only gets accomplished if our new company succeeds.

Ramsay: When you were raising money to buy companies, you were buying companies to save time. Were you trying to save time by selling to DeNA?

Young: Yeah, we were trying to be in a position where we were ahead of the competition and where we could get to a scaled network of value faster than anyone else. At the time, the competition looked pretty dire. We had lots of independent companies that were trying to repeat or replicate what Ngmoco had done. We had larger companies that had been successful in the web space trying to move into mobile, like Zynga, Playdom, and CrowdStar. And then we had overseas companies that had a lot of expertise in building free-to-play games like Nexon from Korea and DeNA from Japan.

In order to beat out that competition, I think it would have been a pretty tough fight. Now, in hindsight, it probably wouldn't have been as tough as we imagined. A lot of companies folded. There's a lesson for us in that, but it's always good to be aware of the competition, respect it, and factor it into your thoughts.

Ramsay: Can you tell me a bit about the actual acquisition process?

Young: We were heading down the path of raising a new round of financing that would put somewhere between $30 and $50 million into the company, and we had secured about $25 million from various people. We were sitting down with investors talking about the potential for our business. We described the opportunity as creating a business that was not dissimilar to DeNA.

One of our investors said, "Look, it's true that those guys are probably going to find it very difficult to make the culture transition here to the West without a partner. But it's also true that there's a really big market in Japan that your products aren't tackling. Is there an opportunity for a strategic investment from one of those companies, so you can offer developers an outlet into Japan?"

And so I e-mailed Tomoko Namba, the CEO at DeNA, who I had met previously about a year before the sale. We had the Plus+ Network growing in scale and our free-to-play games business was starting to take off, and Tomoko had approached us and was interested in acquiring just the Plus+ Network, or doing a joint venture that involved spinning the Plus+ Network off into a separate entity. At the time, we had no interest in doing that; we saw it as a really important strategic asset that created this defensible position for our business.

But I had met Tomoko then and got to know her a little bit, so I e-mailed her and said, "Hey, we're going through a fundraising round right now. I would love to see if DeNA is interested in becoming a strategic investor."

And she said, "Hey, I'm coming out in a week, so maybe we could sit down when I'm out there. In the meantime, if I could send my team who are already based in the US to come out, meet with you ahead of time, and do a little Q&A, that would be great."

In the week between sending that e-mail and Tomoko coming out, we met with, among others, Dai Watanabe, who was the president of DeNA in the US and an amazing, wonderful guy. One of the questions they asked us was "if you were to sell the company, what valuation would you ascribe to it right now?"

We said, "We're not interested in selling the company, but if someone was to offer us ten times what we think our revenue run rate at the end of this year will be, we would be interested in looking at that." That multiple was at the very, very high end of what we thought was the peak of the peak. At the end of December, we had forecast our revenue run rate would be somewhere between $40 and $50 million, so if someone offered us between $400 and $500 million dollars, we would certainly have to consider that offer.

Tomoko came out and sat down with me and Joe Keene, who ran business affairs for us, and we started presenting to Tomoko the vision for the company. We got halfway through the deck when she said, "Your vision and our vision are exactly the same; we share the same vision. You don't need to continue with the presentation because my people have already gotten the presentation. I think I understand exactly where you guys are coming from."

"You might not know this, but we've tried to be successful in the West two times and failed. And the fact that you don't know about it is a measure of how unsuccessful we've been." She went on, "But expanding our company beyond the borders of Japan is an absolute strategic imperative to us. So, I understand that you would be willing to sell the company for $400 million."

We said, "Well, we would certainly consider that." And she goes, "I would like to offer you $400 million." So, we said, "What?" And she said, "Yes, I would like you to think about it." And we went, "Well, yes, we would have to talk to some people and try to figure stuff out."

She said, "Okay, I'm going to go to Starbucks across the street and I'll wait there for an hour. When I come back in an hour, you tell me if it's something that you would like to pursue." And she went off to Starbucks, I got the rest of the founders together, and called a couple of our investors; there seemed like there was no harm in entertaining a conversation. She came back and I said, "You know, we would be interested in entertaining discussions."

She said, "Okay, I'm going to be here for a week, so let's negotiate a term sheet over the course of the week." And we basically negotiated the term sheet over the course of that week and just a little over a week later, we reached an agreement. And, of course, we were at the same time communicating with the other companies that had made us offers or had expressed interests in the company, as well as talking to potential investors to remain independent, and we had a board meeting and it went on for a very long time. We talked about the pros and the cons of everything, and we had people calling into the board meeting from other companies, basically changing their offers on the fly.

The board finally said, "Look, at the end of the day, Neil, whatever you decide we're going to support." And so Bob and I dismissed the board, and Bob and I went into one of the corner offices. We thought about the offers we had on the table, and the choices we had to make; and we made the decision to sell the company. I called Tomoko and I said, "We're signing the term sheet and we accept the offer. Let's go the whole way."

Ramsay: When did you sign the term sheet?

Young: The signing of the term sheet happened in August. The deal didn't close until November. There were really two things that most notably happened along the way. The first was we worked on the final paperwork. The term sheet just outlined the general terms, but the devil's really in the details of the contract, so we worked through our attorneys and DeNA's attorneys, and our banker and their banker. We would negotiate back and forth, we would reach impasses, and then Tomoko and I would try to manage through the impasses.

I got married on September 18, 2010, so that was a Saturday. And just before the rehearsal dinner, which was on Thursday, September 16, we reached what we thought was the final agreement. We hadn't signed it, but we had negotiated through everything. Everyone felt really good. And I got married.

But because we were in the process of finalizing the sale, I didn't take a honeymoon. I did a mini-moon with my wife where we got married in southern California, and we would drive up the coast, stop at a few places, and then we came back to San Francisco where I would see my family and so on. That was a three- or four-day trip. On the first day of my honeymoon, Tomoko called me and she said, "You know, I have a really big problem."

And I said, "Well, what's the problem?" She said, "I don't think that we can do the deal at the valuation we agreed." And I said, "Well, why's that?" She said, "I'm trying to get support from all of the other people on my side, and the board has asked me to come back and try to renegotiate the valuation."

That made for a very, very stressful honeymoon, and over the course of the next two to three days, we jiggered the structure of the deal a bit so that Tomoko got agreement from her board and management team. But we still felt like we were getting the value that we wanted.

We signed the final paperwork, but because DeNA is a Japanese company and we were a foreign entity, it had to get approved by a Japanese governing body that has to approve all these types of mergers. We already had approval from the State of California and from the United States for the sale, and now they had to get their approval, which was a month-long process where we knew nothing. The deal could have fallen apart at any point in time. That was probably the most stressful period of my life; there was a lot riding on that deal. But on November 9, we got approval, the deal closed, and it was done!

Ramsay: You said that you signed the term sheet, but the deal didn't close until later. Tell me about term sheets. What's the difference?

Young: A term sheet is just a statement of intent. The money doesn't change hands until the deal closes. So, between the term sheet and closing the deal, there is a full contract that has to be written up, a whole set of things that have to be negotiated through, deals that need to be put in place to retain key people, employment contracts, and then certainly federal or state regulations that require compliance before the sale goes through. And then once the deal closes and everything's approved, the funds or shares or whatever it is that's being exchanged are distributed by an escrow company.

Ramsay: Prior to the sale, you were personally insolvent.

Young: Well, yeah, pretty much. I personally had $60,000 dollars in the bank, which might sound like a lot, but I had to pay for my wedding and I just got an American Express bill that came in at $55,000. You know, if you've got a company that has value, you always do have options. Someone might want to buy some of your personal shares, so my situation was not quite as dire, although it was very, very stressful because I certainly didn't want to do that.

Ramsay: When the deal eventually closed, how'd you feel?

Young: I felt good. I felt like a chapter had closed and we were onto the next chapter. I didn't feel like I wasn't in control anymore because I was still running that unit. I mean, I definitely wasn't in control anymore—the company was then owned by someone else—but I didn't feel remorse. I felt excited about the future. It was life-changing for me and for my family, and life-changing for my partners and for a lot of our employees.

Ramsay: According to the breakdown I saw, the investors took half? Do you think their share was fair compensation for their contributions?

Young: Totally. Absolutely. I think, actually, the investors took about 60% of the proceeds, the employees took 18% or 20%, and the founders took 20%.

Ramsay: Do you think the founding team deserved more?

Young: No, I was really happy with the outcome.

Ramsay: Did everyone on the team feel the same way?

Young: Yeah, I think so. I think it was a very happy day and people had worked really hard. I remember sitting down with people shortly before the deal closed, and I explained to some of the key people in the company one-on-one what we would like to offer them as an incentive to stay with the company, and what they were going to make from the sale of the company. Every single one was just blown away. They had just never thought that they would get that type of money, so that was really exciting.

Ramsay: Key people?

Young: There were about 17 people in the company we considered critical to the business going forward, so before the sale closed, we sat down with each one of them and said, "Okay, here's what this deal means to you. We want you to commit to the company for a period of time, so here's what we'd like to put in front of you as well."

Ramsay: How did the regular employees benefit?

Young: Yeah, the employees' portion of the deal, excluding the founders, was $65 million over the life of the deal payout. At the time of the sale, we had about 180 people in the company. Some people had been there for a long time and some people had just recently joined, so that money wasn't evenly distributed, it was paid out over a period of time, and there were performance requirements—some of which were met, some of which were not. But there was a lot of money that was distributed to employees.

Ramsay: What happened after DeNA acquired Ngmoco?

Young: There were three months of just trying to understand how to inter-act, and then there was a period where we realized the gap in our knowledge of monetization was bigger than we thought. DeNA had said, "You know we think you can 10x the monetization here," and we were like, "Well, we're not so sure about that." We came to the conclusion that we had a lot to learn.

That year, 2011, was a very hard year; it was hard because we had to learn a lot of things and make a lot of mistakes; we tried a whole bunch of different things. Some worked, and some didn't. We retooled our entire product development line, we retooled the platform, and it was very important for DeNA that we had a strong position on Android, so we switched a lot of development to Android. We tried to get into a position where we launch titles on top of Mobage, which we started doing about 12 months after the acquisition.

And it really wasn't until April of the following year that we started to see the fruits of that labor. The revenue really started to pick up again, and we started to find ourselves in a place where we had multiple titles in the top grossing charts on Android and then iOS.

Ramsay: After the sale, what was the first thing that you, individually, did?

Young: I was still responsible for the West, seeing as Ngmoco didn't have much of a business in Japan or China; it was really business as usual for me, other than the fact that we had to map our course to the greater good of the business. I spent a bunch of time in Japan and a lot of time on late night video conferences, trying to understand exactly what needed to happen in order for us to be successful, and then we started trying to execute against that.

Ramsay: Did you end up reporting to anyone?

Young: Initially, I reported to Tomoko, and then Tomoko took a leave of absence because her husband got sick, and she appointed Isao Moriyasu to be the interim CEO and I reported to him.

Ramsay: This all happened in the span of a few years since starting the company, but was going back to reporting to someone a bit of a switch?

Young: Yes, it was. That was, personally, a difficult transition. When you report to a board, the board are a group of advisors, and you make you make the decisions. When you report to an individual, you can make recommendations, but at the end of the day, the individual has the ability to make the call. So, you lose some element of ultimate control.

Ramsay: But you joined the DeNA board of directors, didn't you?

Young: I did, but I had to be voted in, so it couldn't happen immediately. It was the next summer that I was nominated to the board of that public company.

Ramsay: The vast majority of people in business, if not the world, has never been involved with corporate governance, especially at the level you were. Was being a member of a board a new experience for you?

Young: It was, and the board was a uniquely Japanese board. The board was a check and balance for the management team, but most of the decisions were made by management and then ratified by the board. As I was on the board and the management team, I got to see both sides.

During that time, DeNA acquired the BayStars, a professional baseball team in Japan. We had a lot of different businesses, including a payments company, travel company, auction company, e-commerce company, storage company, and so on. A lot of different parts of the business were very interesting.

Ramsay: Was the language barrier a real challenge?

Young: Yeah, I would say there was three challenges: first, the language; second, national cultural differences; and third, company cultural differences. Those three things meant that you would invest a lot of time and effort and energy into just really trying to understand what's said or intended through translators. I spent a whole lot of time on late night video conferences with translators, just trying to follow quite complex conversations about where the business was going and how and why it was succeeding.

Ramsay: What were your responsibilities?

Young: Well, for Japanese companies, the board has important check-and-balance and fiduciary responsibilities to validate, debate, or discuss the decisions that the management team makes. It's a little different than the way a board of directors works in the West. It's a very formal post. Most of the day-to-day management decisions are made by management and the management committee, which I was also on. I was responsible for DeNA's business outside of Japan and China, and expansion into the US and Europe, predominantly.

Ramsay: What are the differences between a board in the West versus Japan?

Young: For a board in the West, the founder and CEO are typically the only members of the management team who sit on the board. In Japan, it's much more common for every key leader of the management team to also be a board member. In addition, there are independent directors, auditors, and senior board members, so there's a lot more crossover between the management and the board in a Japanese setting. That's one difference.

The second difference is a Western board, or at least in my experience, has a much more collaborative relationship with management. What you're really trying to do is to solve problems together. In Japan, it's not adversarial by any means, but the job of the board is to debate and vet management decisions that may have been already made, and then authorize or validate those decisions.

I would say, in a nutshell, a Japanese board is much more formal, and has much less impact over the actual direction of the business, while a Western board is much less formal, and much more collaborative with the executive team.

Ramsay: What do you mean by "validating" decisions?

Young: If the management team is taking a course of action, they would report that course of action to the board, and then if the board had any questions or objections, a discussion would then evolve from there. For really big decisions, like the buyout of the DeNA BayStars, there was a lot of discussion at the board level before that deal consummated.

Ramsay: Did you enjoy that aspect of your role?

Young: It was educational. It was interesting. Each month, it exposed me to a lot of different areas of the business that I might not necessarily have been exposed to. DeNA's a really interesting company, and I enjoyed personally all of the board members and found everyone to be great.

Ramsay: How well do you think you fit in with the mostly all Japanese board?

Young: Yeah, although that wasn't a requirement to be on the board, Namba san, Tomoko, thought it was really important that DeNA internationalized. She thought DeNA should figure out how to grow beyond the boundaries of Japan, and knew everyone had to appreciate the markets beyond Japan.

So, I think I fit in fine. DeNA's quite a unique company with a very unique culture; it's unlike any other Japanese company that I've interacted with. The management team is pretty young, very entrepreneurial, energetic, very open to debate and dialogue, and there's not a whole bunch of decoding that has to be done to try to understand the specific customs. With the people at DeNA, what you see is what you get; they're just very forthright and upfront.

Ramsay: What did you learn from the Japanese approach to business?

Young: Well, I don't know a lot about the Japanese approach, but I learned a lot about DeNA's approach. They might be the same thing, but it's very difficult for me to delineate between what was DeNA and what was Japanese.

In terms of general management practice, somebody once said this to me. A team of American managers and a team of Japanese managers are standing at the edge of a field where there was a river. They couldn't quite see how wide it was or how fast the water was running, but on the other side of the river, there was a castle that had to be taken. The American managers would start running immediately towards the river, thinking that speed was the most important thing. They would trust that when they got to the river, it would be either narrow enough to jump over or the current soft enough that they could swim, or they would be able to jump on a rock in the middle, very quickly build a raft, or do something to get to the other side. Then, many times, the Americans would get to the other side before the Japanese.

The Japanese approach would be to walk to the edge of the river, analyze it, and then nine out of ten times build a bridge and get 100% of their managers across that river. That meant they might not get there first, but it would ensure they got there in force. And so even if the castle had been taken by one American who made it across, the hundred Japanese could take over that castle.

That's the difference in business ethos between how American companies think and how Japanese companies think. DeNA was at the very entrepreneurial end of that Japanese spectrum, but it was a definitely a company that thought about things, planned, and then acted, and then iterated very quickly.

The other thing I learned was that you build your case differently in Japan than you do in the West. In the West, if you're presenting, you make a statement about what you want to accomplish, and then you back up that statement with supporting material. So, you basically state a vision, support that vision with a strategy, support that strategy with an execution plan, and then support that execution plan with data.

A Japanese presentation is the complete opposite. You build a case over the course of a presentation to reach a conclusion, and each piece of data supports the conclusion that you've reached. And if you don't know that, presenting can become tricky and difficult in that setting.

Ramsay: You stayed on with DeNA for two years after the acquisition. Was that a requirement stated in the terms of the acquisition?

Young: No, actually. I could have left immediately after, but there were certain incentives that motivated me to stay around, beyond wanting to see the business succeed. But there was no contractual commitment that I had to work with DeNA for a particular period of time.

Ramsay: What did they want you to achieve post-acquisition?

Young: It was really important for DeNA to shift their mix of revenue from 100% Japan to a 50/50 split between Japan and the rest of the world. So, the fundamental belief we had at DeNA was that the growth of social games in Japan, from a monetization standpoint, was not an anomaly.

It was actually just a function of the Japanese market having at least a three or five years head start over the Western market, in terms of knowledge, insight, and understanding with regard to free-to-play social mobile games, and how to generate revenue and income from them. We believed it was just a matter of time before the usability and capability of the devices proliferating in the West would drive the same type of usage patterns that had been seen in Japan. And on the back of those patterns, we could build a really big business.

Ramsay: When you're an entrepreneur, you tend to be more hands-on with everything. As the CEO at a subsidiary of a large enterprise, did you ever feel that you were becoming disconnected from the day-to-day?

Young: Yeah, I would say so. When you sell a company, that's a pretty life-changing event, so there are a few months you're just dealing with what that means. On a purely personal level, it knocks you sideways a little bit. We closed the sale in November, it wasn't until February that I really felt like my head was back in the game and in the right place.

Ramsay: What does that mean exactly? Was that downtime?

Young: It wasn't really downtime; it was just having to re-orient to a very different situation. I had gone from not having very much money in the bank, and, essentially, living paycheck to paycheck on my venture-backed yet unprofitable startup to working for a large company after selling the company I started for $400 million. That just changes your outlook a little bit, and it just takes time, I think, for any human to adjust to that.

Ramsay: I think most people would think that coming out as far ahead as you did would think all your problems were solved.

Young: Yeah, well, money doesn't solve all your problems. That's for sure, but it can certainly help.

Ramsay: Would you say that your fear of failure was tempered?

Young: I still fear failure. I fear failure at a macro level, but I don't fear failure at an everyday level. I think it's essential to fail in order to succeed. I didn't want this company to fail. I wanted this company to succeed because I really would like to make an impact on the life of the people who both use and make the stuff that we build. I didn't want to let those people down. So, if I feared anything, it would be just that.

Ramsay: What were the consequences of not having your head in the game?

Young: Oh, I think it slowed our development a little bit. I think we could have been faster by a few months, if I had been as close to the company as I was when it was independent. When we sold the company, we essentially said, "Okay, we're stopping our current development path, we're going to roll that back, and we're going to start deploying Mobage on Android."

That basically meant the revenue ramp of the company started to slow, and we started to go into essentially deficit spending, investment spending, as we started to build products and learn new skills and turn Ngmoco from a game company with an affiliate network to a platform company that had first-party and third-party products and technologies. That was a huge transition; it took 14 months to get to a place where revenue started to inflect up again, and you could start seeing the trajectory of the company. It was pretty exciting though.

Ramsay: What do you want for Ngmoco's future under DeNA?

Young: I wanted DeNA to be successful, globally, at building this social mobile game platform company and everything that could become. I think there's a tremendous opportunity still. The market is still up for grabs. Everyone is one hit away from being able to take the crown. And DeNA had the expertise, network, and the capital to seize on those opportunities and turn them into an accelerant for the company.

Ramsay: When companies are acquired, they often lose their identity, becoming less cohesive, and eventually, just fade away into the larger corporate body. Were you concerned about that happening?

Index

Young: I think that's necessary and inevitable. Fighting it is stupid; it doesn't serve any purpose. The right approach is to, as fast and effectively as you can, integrate the companies for a successful outcome. That's how everyone wins. Creating a moat around the culture, or business, is keeps it from growing in the short term and doesn't serve anyone's long-term objectives.

Ramsay: You eventually left Ngmoco. Why did you leave?

Young: It was just time. You know, the company was on a pretty clear path to the type of success we imagined. The revenue ramp up was significant. Whether it ultimately succeeds is out of my hands, but when we were sure we had put it on the right trajectory, it was clear to us that it was time to do something else and go on to the next adventure.

Ramsay: It was just time? The life cycle of Ngmoco was very short as an independent company. Do you wish you had created a company that lasted a bit longer as an independent company?

Young: I think it's really good to try to build an enduring company, and I definitely wish we could have built Ngmoco into an enduring company that could have been successful and independent at the scale we imagined. But this was the fastest and best way for Ngmoco to achieve the objectives we originally set out for it. It was a really, really great experience. I don't regret any of the decisions we made over the life of Ngmoco. Starting a new company, I would definitely like to build a great and enduring company that is ultimately very successful. And so that's certainly a motivation.

Ramsay: Why was it important to get there fast? More than 90% of businesses in the US are small businesses and they're not really racing.

Young: It's a race, especially in technology. You want to get to the audience faster than your competitors. There's a big difference between a lifestyle business and wanting to build an impact consumer business that touches a lot of people and takes advantage of an inflection, a disruption, in technology. I don't think you can afford to be slow. Speed is a really important weapon. The faster you go, the more iterations you get; the more iterations you get, the more you learn; and the more you learn, the more likely you are to succeed.

Ramsay: Do you think you can replicate the success of Ngmoco again?

Young: I think that we can. It's not without its challenges. We're in a different space, although utilizing a lot from our experiences. We're trying to build something that has the potential to be much bigger than Ngmoco or even DeNA was, so there's a lot more reward and a lot more risk. The competition is at a different order of magnitude.

Ramsay: Is there a formula?

Young: Work hard, hire great people, and have high personal standards. That's the formula.

Get the eBook for only $5!

Why limit yourself?

Now you can take the weightless companion with you wherever you go and access your content on your PC, phone, tablet, or reader.

Since you've purchased this print book, we're happy to offer you the eBook in all 3 formats for just $5.

Convenient and fully searchable, the PDF version enables you to easily find and copy code—or perform examples by quickly toggling between instructions and applications. The MOBI format is ideal for your Kindle, while the ePUB can be utilized on a variety of mobile devices.

To learn more, go to www.apress.com/companion or contact support@apress.com.

Other Apress Titles You Will Find Useful

Gamers at Work
Ramsay
978-1-4302-3351-0

Lawyers at Work
Cosslett
978-1-4302-4503-2

Lobbyists at Work
Leech
978-1-4302-4560-5

Inventors at Work
Stern
978-1-4302-4506-3

CIOs at Work
Yourdon
978-1-4302-3554-5

Advertisers at Work
Tuten
978-1-4302-3828-7

Venture Capitalists at Work
Shah/Shah
978-1-4302-3837-9

CTOs at Work
Donaldson/Siegel/Donaldson
978-1-4302-3593-4

European Founders at Work
Santos
978-1-4302-3906-2

Available at www.apress.com

GPSR Compliance
The European Union's (EU) General Product Safety Regulation (GPSR) is a set
of rules that requires consumer products to be safe and our obligations to
ensure this.

If you have any concerns about our products, you can contact us on

ProductSafety@springernature.com

In case Publisher is established outside the EU, the EU authorized
representative is:

Springer Nature Customer Service Center GmbH
Europaplatz 3
69115 Heidelberg, Germany

www.ingramcontent.com/pod-product-compliance
Lightning Source LLC
Chambersburg PA
CBHW071358050326
40689CB00010B/1686